Healthcare Delivery in the Information Age

For further volumes:
http://www.springer.com/series/8783

Rajeev K. Bali • Indrit Troshani
Steve Goldberg • Nilmini Wickramasinghe
Editors

Pervasive Health Knowledge Management

Springer

Editors
Rajeev K. Bali
Biomedical Computing and Engineering
Technologies (BIOCORE) Applied
Research Group
Coventry University
COVENTRYWest Midlands
United Kingdom

Indrit Troshani
The University of Adelaide
Business School
Adelaide, South Australia
Australia

Steve Goldberg
Thornhill, Ontario
Canada

Nilmini Wickramasinghe
School of Business Information Technology
RMIT University
Melbourne, Victoria
Australia

ISBN 978-1-4614-4513-5 ISBN 978-1-4614-4514-2 (eBook)
DOI 10.1007/978-1-4614-4514-2
Springer New York Heidelberg Dordrecht London

Library of Congress Control Number: 2012948189

Printed on acid-free paper

Springer is part of Springer Science+Business Media (www.springer.com)

This series is dedicated to Leo Cussen:
learned scholar, colleague extraordinare
and good friend.

Foreword

The challenges of medical practice have been the same for decades; to provide the best possible medical care and advice to each and every patient. To be well versed in the most up to date evidence based medicine and to be the best doctor one can be.

There has been a change with a steadily increasing pressure for our healthcare system to maintain optimum care. Our population is steadily increasing due to births and immigration without an equal increase in the number of healthcare providers or healthcare funding. People are fortunately living longer and as such there are more patients suffering from a multiple of chronic diseases. To say that the average life expectancy is increasing is a very good thing and something the medical community is proud of. As a result, we are being forced to find new innovative ways to help us be more efficient in caring for our patients so that we can maintain the gold standard of care expected.

Offices like mine are overwhelmed. We cannot always service our patients in a timely fashion. Obtaining appointments with specialists is ridiculously difficult—upsetting for the office and disappointing for the patient.

So, what can we do? Healthcare delivery is becoming less hospital centric with satellite health units reaching out to patients and providing community care. This is expensive. Offices coming together as family health units, where family doctors and specialists are under one roof may improve communication and the processing of patients. Looking to technology, many of us are incorporating electronic medical records' (EMR) as a way to streamline the following of laboratory parameters, booking our patients and facilitating the communication between primary care providers. Our provincial government is developing a Diabetic Registry which will enable the physicians to easily track their diabetic patients with regards to office visits, eye care assessments, and various other parameters that are important to diabetic care. The Ontario Ministry of Health is optimistic that this close tracking of diabetic patients will result in less morbidity and mortality and thus reduced healthcare costs.

There is something missing; an essential piece of the equation for us to be successful in using our new developing technology. In my opinion, patient involvement in self-care is the key to our hope for success. Patients must be active in their own care and must be part of the healthcare team. Our new technology must be used to bring the patient into the loop—so that they can easily communicate and receive support from their various primary care providers in an efficient, low-cost manner. A lot of excellent care can now be done remotely, especially when dealing with chronic diseases such as diabetes, hypertension, and chronic obstructive lung disease.

Mobile technology, the use of cell phones, may in fact be what we are looking for. It can be used as the key method of transitioning from centralized care to decentralized community care. We would be following chronic diseases in an efficient and inexpensive manner that directly connects the patients with their healthcare providers.

This book edited by Bali, Troshani, Goldberg, and Wickramasinghe serves to highlight not only the benefits of mobile and more especially pervasive technologies to facilitate superior healthcare delivery, but also and more importantly maps out how to proceed in order to move from idea to realization successfully. This book has far-reaching relevance and appeal to practitioners, patients, medical professionals, scholars, and the community at large; i.e., all of us who are impacted by inferior healthcare delivery and wish for things to be better and want to know how a brighter future can be attained.

I hope you enjoy reading this most invaluable work.

October, 2011 Dr. Sheldon Silver

Preface

The healthcare delivery system in the United States is in crisis as noted by several scholars and practitioners. Runaway expenditures and problems with access and affordability of care are plaguing the industry. Several chronic diseases such as diabetes and hypertension consume a disproportionate slice of healthcare services. By some estimates, chronic diseases account for more than 70–75 % of direct healthcare costs. These figures are consistent with global trends which indicate that chronic disease management should be a key consideration for any healthcare system throughout the world.

Diabetes is one of the five major chronic diseases. It afflicts more than 20 million people in the United States and accounts for almost US$ 100 billion in medical costs. The prevalence of diabetes in the United States and worldwide is increasing exponentially. This has led the WHO to now refer to diabetes as the silent epidemic.

It has long been established that technology may play a role in contributing to a more efficient delivery of care that may also assist in controlling costs. Given the exponentially increasing number of incidents predicted for chronic disease in general, and diabetes in particular, coupled with the fact that there exists no cure for patients once they contract a chronic disease, and that if the chronic disease is not well managed then it lead to complex and unpleasant secondary healthcare problems, it would appear prudent indeed to examine the benefits of a pervasive healthcare technology solution to facilitate superior chronic disease management.

Pervasive healthcare is an emerging research discipline focusing on the development and application of pervasive and ubiquitous computing technology for healthcare and wellness. Pervasive healthcare seeks to respond to a variety of pressures on healthcare systems including the increased incidence of lifestyle related and chronic diseases, emerging consumerism in healthcare, need for empowering patients and relatives for self-care and management of their health, and need to provide seamless access for healthcare services independent of time and place.

Pervasive healthcare may be defined from two perspectives. First, it is the development and application of pervasive computing (or ubiquitous computing, ambient intelligence) technologies for healthcare, health, and wellness management. Second, it seeks to make healthcare available to anyone, anytime, and anywhere by removing locational, time, and other restraints while increasing both the coverage and quality of healthcare.

This book attempts to address the emerging area of pervasive health in a unique fashion. Not only is the field of pervasive health defined but the key management principles, most especially knowledge management, its tools, techniques, and technologies are introduced in order to show how superior pervasive healthcare delivery can be achieved. In addition, this book takes a sociotechnical, patient-centric approach which serves to emphasize the importance of a key triumvirate in healthcare management namely, the focus on people, process and technology. Last but not least, this book discusses in detail a specific example of pervasive health, namely the potential use of a wireless technology solution in the monitoring of diabetic patients. Specifically, it describes the journey from idea to realization and how such a solution contributes to superior chronic disease management.

Given the crisis currently US healthcare system is facing as well as the major dilemmas faced by numerous other healthcare systems throughout the world, the need for a book that proposes to demystify the new frontier of pervasive health and simultaneously offer a solution to facilitate superior chronic disease management could not be greater. We are confident that this book will play a pivotal role in designing and fostering research and understanding of pervasive health, its advancements, and the adoption and diffusion of superior chronic disease management. Moreover, we are confident that scholars, practitioners, those in the community who suffer from chronic disease as well as anyone interested to understand critical issues pertaining to better management of diabetes will find this book invaluable, informative, and enjoyable.

The Editors

Rajeev K. Bali, Indrit Troshani,
Steve Goldberg, Nilmini Wickramasinghe

References

Geisler, E., & Wickramasinghe N. (2009). The role and use of wireless technology in the management and monitoring of chronic diseases. IBM Center for the Business of Government, Washington, DC.

Sharma, S., Wickramasinghe, N., Xu, B., & Ahmed, N. (2006). Electronic healthcare: Issues and challenges. *International Journal of Electronic Healthcare, 2*(1), 50–65.

Von Lubitz, D., & Wickramasinghe, N. (2006). Network centric healthcare: Applying the tools, techniques and strategies of knowledge management to create superior healthcare operations. *International Journal of Electronic Healthcare, 4,* 415–428.

Wickramasinghe, N. (2008). Building a learning healthcare organisation by fostering organisational learning through a process centric view of knowledge management. *International Journal of Innovation and Learning, 5*(2), 201–216.

Wickramasinghe, N., & Lichtenstein, S. (2006). Supporting knowledge creation with e-mail. *International Journal of Innovation and Learning, 3*(4), 416–426.

Wickramasinghe, N., & Goldberg, S. (2007). Adaptive mapping to realisation methodology (AMR) to facilitate mobile initiatives in healthcare. *International Journal of Mobile Communications, 5*(3), 300–318.

Wickramasinghe, N., & Bali, R. (2008). Controlling chaos through the application of smart technologies and intelligent techniques. *International Journal of Risk Assessment and Management, 10*(1–2), 172–182.
Wickramasinghe, N., Geisler, E., & Schaffer, J. (2006). Realizing the value proposition for healthcare by incorporating km strategies and data mining techniques with the use of information communication technologies. *International Journal of Healthcare Technology and Management, 7*(3–4), 303–318.
Wickramasinghe, N., Puentes, J., Bali, R. K., & Naguib, R. (2007). Telemedicine trends and challenges: A technology management perspective. *International Journal of Biomedical Engineering and Technology, 1*(1), 59–72.
Wickramasinghe, N., Bali, R., & Schaffer, J. (2008a). The health care intelligence continuum: Key model for enabling KM initiatives and realizing the full potential of SMT in healthcare delivery. *International Journal of Biomedical Engineering and Technology, 1*(4), 415–427.
Wickramasinghe, N., Bali, R., Gibbons, C., & Schaffer, J. (2008b). Realizing the knowledge spiral in healthcare: The role of data mining and knowledge management. *Studies In Health Technology and Informatics, 137*, 147–162.
World Health Organization (WHO). (1998). A health telematics policy in support of WHO's health-for-all strategy for global health development: Report of the WHO group consultation on health telematics, 11–16 December 1997, World Health Organization, Geneva 1998.

Acknowledgements

This book would not have been possible without the cooperation and assistance of numerous people: the contributors, reviewers, our respective institutions, our colleagues, students, and the staff at Springer. In today's networked environment when we are not co-located but distributed across various continents and continually meeting the challenges of the respective local demands on our time, we are especially appreciative to all the contributors and reviewers for not only your timely responses but also the high quality of your submissions and feedback. Finally, we would especially like to thank the production staff at Springer, in particular Khristine Queja, for all their efforts in helping us to make this book possible for our families.

Contents

About the Authors

Dr. Rajeev K. Bali is a Reader in Healthcare Knowledge Management at Coventry University. His main research interests lie in clinical and healthcare knowledge management (from both technical and organisational perspectives). He founded and leads the Knowledge Management for Healthcare (KARMAH) research subgroup (working under BIOCORE). He is well published in peer-reviewed journals and conferences and has been invited internationally to deliver presentations and speeches. He serves on various editorial boards and conference committees and is the Associate Editor for the International Journal of Networking and Virtual Organisations as well as the International Journal of Biomedical Engineering and Technology.

Mr. Steve Goldberg In 1998 INET International Inc. was founded by Steve Goldberg. As INET's President he leads the firm in data collection for international research studies, wireless healthcare programs and INET Mini-conferences. Mr. Goldberg started his 21-year information technology career at Systemhouse Ltd. At Crowntek, he formed an executive collaboration to develop a $30 million IT services business. During his tenure at Cybermation, he transformed the organization from supporting mainframe applications to client/server applications. Prior to INET, at Compugen he successfully built a high-performance team to meet government and corporate e-business needs.

Dr. Indrit Troshani is a Senior Lecturer at the University of Adelaide Business School. He holds a Ph.D. in Computer Science from Edith Cowan University (Western Australia), an MSc in Computer-based Information Systems (Sunderland, UK), and a BBA (Hons) from Malaysia. His research interests and contributions include adoption and diffusion of mobile services and applications in healthcare and network innovations in Business-to-Business (B2B) settings. Dr. Indrit Troshani has been doing research in the area of m-commerce and e-business since he joined the University of Adelaide Business School in July 2003.

Nilmini Wickramasinghe He currently holds the Epworth Chair Health Information Management was appointed in Dec 2009 as a Professor to RMIT University's School of Business IT and Logistics after being a professor in the US for 15 years. She researches and teaches in several areas within information systems including knowledge management, e-commerce and m-commerce, and organizational impacts of technology with particular focus on the applications of these areas to healthcare and thereby effecting superior healthcare delivery. Professor Wickramasinghe is well published with more than 200 referred scholarly articles, several books and an encyclopedia. She has collaborated with many large organizations such as NASA and GE as well as leading healthcare organizations such as the Cleveland Clinic, Johns Hopkins, Kaiser and NorthWestern Memorial Hospital. In addition, she regularly presents her work throughout North America, as well as in Europe and Australia.

Suresh Chalasani is an Associate Professor of Management Information Systems at the University of Wisconsin-Parkside, where he specializes in emerging technologies, supply chain management systems, e-commerce, healthcare management and bioinformatics. He published more than 30 journal articles in these areas. Dr. Chalasani holds a Ph.D. degree in computer engineering from the University of Southern California. Dr. Chalasani was a recipient of multiple research and instructional grants from the National Science Foundation and the University of Wisconsin System. He recently co-edited the IEEE Systems Journal special issue entitled "RFID Technology: Opportunities and Challenges".

Dmitry Chornyi is a researcher at the Department of Information Systems, Technische Universität München, Germany, where he received his bachelor's degree in Information Systems in 2010. He is currently working on his master thesis in human-computer interaction as a visiting researcher at the Stanford University, USA.

Tieh-Chi Chung is a medical doctor and received his Ph.D. from the Graduate Institute of Medicine, Kaohsiung University, Taiwan. He was the Superintendent of Taitung Hospital, Department of Health, Executive Yuan, R.O.C since September 1997 to October 2003; Hualien Hospital, Department of Health, Executive Yuan, R.O.C. since October 2003 to February 2006. Nowadays, he is not only the Administrative Vice President at Meiho University, Taiwan since February 2006 until currently, but also the Head of Graduate Institute of Health Care since August 2009 until now. Since December 2010, he is also the chairman of the Taiwan Society for Adolescent Medicine and Health. His research fields are focused on Epidemiology, Public Health, Healthcare Administration, Health Promotion, Healthcare Quality Management, and Adolescent Medicine and Health.

Bil Davey is a Senior Lecturer at RMIT University Melbourne, Australia. He is an active member of IFIP Working Groups 3.4, 3.7 and 9.7. Bill is associate editor of the IFIP Journal "Education and Information Technologies" and a member of the editorial board of the International Journal of Actor-Network Theory and Technological Innovation." His research interests include e-health, especially as it applies to aging, and the information technology in educational management.

Prof. Dr. Raj Gururajan is the Professor in the School of Information Systems, University of Southern Queensland. He has over 25 years in research, teaching, consultancy, and a proven track record in completing a list of funded projects in Health and Telehealth areas. He has worked as the Associated Dean (Research) in the Faculty of Business and Laws and the member of key university committees and other professional units. He has more than 130 peer-reviewed publications, and was awarded Excellent Journal Article Prizes from the major publishers.

Naffisah Hassan is currently a Ph.D. student under the supervision of Dr. Khin Than Win and Assoc. Prof. Peter Hyland in Health Informatics. She holds MSc. BA (Information Technology) from University of Central Lancashire, England and has been teaching (currently on study leave) in Universiti Teknologi MARA, Malaysia for the past 5 years in Information System and Technology.

Peter Hyland (Ph.D.) is an Associate Professor in the School of Information Systems and Technology, University of Wollongong. He has successfully supervised several Ph.D. students in informatics and has published edited books, and book chapters. He also published over 50 academic papers in area of Human Computer Interaction (HCI) and Community Informatics (CI) in peer reviewed journals and conferences.

Junhua Li is an eHealth researcher in the Asia Pacific ubiquitous Healthcare Research Centre (APuHC) at the University of New South Wales (UNSW), Australia. He received his BIS (Bachelor of Information Systems), MIS (Master of Information Systems) and MPhil in eHealth Evaluation and Healthcare Services. Currently, he is completing his Ph.D. in eHealth and Pandemic Response at the UNSW. His current research areas include eHealth/mHealth applications for healthcare delivery and public health services, eHealth implementation issues and evaluation.

Fatemeh Hoda Moghimi is currently a Ph.D. student in Information Systems in the RMIT University. Through her work experience in different industries as a system developer and analysis, she has acquired skills in fields such as implementing Business Intelligence, Data Mining, Data Warehouse, OLAP, ERP as well as IT solution selection for enterprises. Her academic research interests are in the area of health informatics, intelligent solutions and e-services. She has published in some national and international conference (HICSS, IITA, ICTM, EGMM, e-health symposium Hoehenheim) and journal (Economic & Management Journal, knowledge management) papers. Recently, she received IPRS (international postgraduate research scholarship) award from the Australian government.

Pradeep Ray is a Senior Member of the Academic staff at the University of New South Wales, Australia. He has been the Chair of the IEEE Technical Committee on Enterprise Networking (EntNet) for 2002–2004 (currently a member of the Advisory Committee of EntNet) and the founder of IEEE Healthcom that is now the forum of discussions for the IEEE/ITU-D/WHO initiatives on E-Health and M-Health (see www.ehealthcom.org). Pradeep is now the Vice Chair of eHealth Technical Committee at IEEE Communication Society. He led the WHO Research on the Assessment of eHealth involving four countries (India, China, Vietnam and Philippines) from 2006–2009. As a member of EntNet executive between 1998–2004, Pradeep helped launch a number of multidisciplinary, international events, such as EntNet@SUPERCOMM, Financecom and Healthcom. He has been leading a number of collaborative research projects with international organizations (e.g., WHO, ITU-D, IFMBE) and universities in Europe, North America and Asia. More details are available at Pradeep's home page (www.apuhc.org/pradeep).

Dr. Heng-Sheng (Aaron) Tsai obtained his Ph.D. degree at the University of Southern Queensland in 2008. He also has the Master and Bachelor degrees in Information Management area, and worked as an Assistant Professor at Takming University of Science and Technology in Taiwan. Dr. Tsai has academic publications, including book chapter, conference papers, journal article, and project manuals etc. Since 2010, he worked with Professor Gururajan as the Postdoctoral Research Fellow at the Health Informatics team in the University of Southern Queensland.

Ali Sunyaev is an Assistant Professor at the Department of Information Systems, University of Cologne, Germany. Dr. Sunyaev has (co)-authored several international journal articles (including articles in leading journals such as ACM Journal of Data and Information Quality, IEEE Computer and Communications of the AIS). His research interests include design, management and quality of information systems, development of innovative healthcare applications, and management of information systems security. He is also a visiting professor at the Information Technologies Department, Keldysh Institute of Applied Mathematics (KIAM RAS), Russian Academy of Sciences (RAS).

Yung-Yu Su received his Ph.D. (major in Health Informatics) from the school of Information Systems and Technology at the University of Wollongong, Australia on 2009. He is an Assistant Professor of Graduate Institute of Health Care at Meiho University, Taiwan. His research fields are focused on Health Informatics, Healthcare Administration, Health Information Systems Evaluation, Healthcare Research Methodology, Healthcare Delivery System Research, and Health Promotion.

Dr. Arthur Tatnall is an Associate Professor in the School of Management and Information Systems at Victoria University in Melbourne, Australia. In his Ph.D. he used actor-network theory to investigate curriculum innovation in an Australian university. Arthur's research interests include technological innovation, history of technology, project management and information systems curriculum. Much of his research is based on the use of actor-network theory. Arthur is a Fellow of the Australian Computer Society and active in the International Federation for Information Processing (IFIP) as Chair of WG9.7—*History of Computing* and WG3.4—*ICT in Professional and Vocational Education*.

Khin Than Win (MBBS, DCS, IDCS, MS-CIS, Ph.D.) is a Senior Lecturer in the School of Information Systems and Technology, University of Wollongong. She is a medical doctor with Ph.D. in Information Technology (Health Informatics). She has successfully supervised several Ph.D. students in health informatics and published over 70 academic papers in health informatics in peer reviewed journals and conferences.

Dr. Rajeev K. Bali is a Reader in Healthcare Knowledge Management at Coventry University. His main research interests lie in clinical and healthcare knowledge management (from both technical and organisational perspectives). He founded and leads the Knowledge Management for Healthcare (KARMAH) research subgroup (working under BIOCORE). He is well published in peer-reviewed journals and conferences and has been invited internationally to deliver presentations and speeches. He serves on various editorial boards and conference committees and is the Associate Editor for the International Journal of Networking and Virtual Organisations as well as the International Journal of Biomedical Engineering and Technology.

Raouf NG Naguib is a Professor of Biomedical Computing and Head of BIOCORE. Prior to this appointment, he was a Lecturer at Newcastle University, UK. He has published over 240 journals and conference papers and reports in many aspects of biomedical and digital signal processing, image processing, AI and evolutionary computation in cancer research. He was awarded the Fulbright Cancer Fellowship in 1995–1996 when he carried out research at the University of Hawaii in Mãnoa, on the applications of artificial neural networks in breast cancer diagnosis and prognosis. He is a member of several national and international research committees and boards.

Dr. Vikram Baskaran is an Assistant Professor in the Ted Rogers School of Information Technology Management at Ryerson University. He is an engineer by profession with an interest in biomedical computing. His research interest is on finding a viable application of the KM paradigm in healthcare. His special interest in developing HL7 messaging and healthcare informatics has provided opportunities to excel in these fields. His current activities overlap KM, e-health, AI and healthcare informatics. He has been previously engaged in a wide area of industrial projects (software and engineering at the senior level).

Alan C. Richards is a Senior Lecturer in Information Technology and Systems at Coventry University, UK. His main research areas of interest are business organisations, business strategy, knowledge management, crisis management, urban health and water resource management. He has twenty years experience with Severn Trent Water (UK). He is currently undertaking a Ph.D. with BIOCORE at Coventry University, UK.

Aapo Immonen His work aims to formulate a knowledge-based conceptual model which aims to enhance healthcare professionals' experience and knowledge in post-crisis (and crisis prevention) situations from the public health point of view. Mr. Immonen works as a researcher at the Crisis Management Centre, Finland as well as at the Finnish Emergency Service College. Before this he worked as a researcher at the University of Kuopio (Finland) where his research areas were privacy, confidentiality and data security issues as well as wireless data communication technologies supporting public health. He has extensive experience in the areas of project and development management after working for several years in these areas in the public and private sectors as well as in numerous EU-funded projects. He is also a practising paramedic.

Prof. Ian M. Marshall is Deputy Vice-Chancellor (Academic) at Coventry University. Professor Marshall's applied research interests are focused on the use of games in education and training and on development effort estimation for multimedia and other interactive courseware. He has worked extensively as a computer and information systems consultant, flexible learning material developer and trainer. In addition, he has extensive experience working with small- to medium-sized enterprises as well as with city councils and regional development agencies.

Dr. Mohd Khanapi Abd Ghani is a Senior Lecturer at Universiti Teknikal Malaysia Melaka (UTeM). He had 16 years of experience in implementing and managing commercial and national Information and Communication Technology (ICT) projects before changing his career path from industry to academia in 2003. He earned his MSc in Real-time Software Engineering from Malaysia Technology of University. His research areas of interest include electronic healthcare systems, telemedicine, ICTs, and system architecture and design. He completed his Ph.D. with the BIOCORE Applied Research Group at Coventry University, UK.

Nicola Armstrong is pursuing a Ph.D. at the University of Ulster. She received an Associate Bachelor's degree in Computer Science in 2006, and then went on to receive the Bachelor of Science degree in Information Communication Technology in 2008, both from the University of Ulster. Her areas of research interest include smartphone technology development, smart home environments and the application of information communication technologies in the healthcare domain.

Prof. Christopher Nugent is a Professor of Biomedical Engineering at the University of Ulster. He received a Bachelor of Engineering in Electronic Systems and DPhil in Biomedical Engineering both from the University of Ulster. His research within biomedical engineering addresses the themes of the development and evaluation of technologies to support independent living and medical decision support systems specifically in the domain of computerised electrocardiology. He has published extensively in these areas with work which spans theoretical, clinical and biomedical engineering domains.

Dr. George Moore received both a Bachelor's degree and Ph.D in Computing from the University of Ulster. His recent research has focused on assistive technology to support independent living, with an emphasis on investigating mobile solutions. He also has expertise in user experience design and an interest in natural user interfaces. George Moore is an active member of the British Computer Society and a Chartered IT Professional. His research interests mobile computing, assistive technology, user experience design and natural user interfaces.

Dr. Dewar D. Finlay was born in Northern Ireland in 1977. He received the B.Eng. degree in electronic systems in 1999, and the Ph.D. degree in Computer Science in 2006, both from the University of Ulster. He is currently a Lecturer in Computer Science at the University of Ulster. In particular, his research interests include smart environments, healthcare technology, and computerized electrocardiology.

Dr. John Puentes holds an Electronics Engineering degree and a Master's of Image Processing and Artificial Intelligence, obtained in 1990 and 1992 respectively. He also holds a Ph.D. in Signal Processing and Telecommunications from Rennes 1 University, Rennes, France, received in 1996 and the French Habilitation to Supervise Research obtained in 2009. He is Associate Professor at the Image and Information Processing Department, Telecom Bretagne, Brest, France. His primary research interests are medical decision support, medical information processing and multimedia medical information systems.

Dr. Julien Montagner Julien Montagner holds a Master's degree in Engineering gained in 2000, in the fields of computer sciences and modeling (ISIMA, French "Ecole d'Ingénieur", Clermont-Fd, France). He also holds a Ph.D. in Computer Sciences and Image Processing from the Clermont-Fd I and II Universities, France, gained in 2004. Since 2006, he is assistant professor at the Image and Information Processing Department, Telecom Bretagne. His primary research interests are image and information processing, and systems based on the implementation of information fusion algorithms.

Dr. Laurent Lecornu holds a MSc in Signal Processing and Telecommunications from Rennes 1 University, France gained in 1990. He also holds a Ph.D. in Signal Processing and Telecommunications from the same university, gained in 1995. Since 2002, he is assistant professor at the Image and Information Processing Department, Telecom Bretagne. His primary research interests are information processing, medical information aggregation and medical databases data mining.

Jaakko Lähteenmäki obtained his degrees, Master of Sciences and Licentiate of Sciences in Technology from Helsinki University of Technology in 1986 and 1994 respectively. He is currently a Principal Scientist at the Technical Research Centre of Finland (VTT). His current research interests are focused in ICT-based chronic disease management.

Part I
Why Pervasive Healthcare and KM?

Chapter 1
Introduction

Indrit Troshani and Nilmini Wickramasinghe

Abstract This brief chapter introduces many important concepts and constructs and sets the scene for why a pervasive perspective is a prudent choice for supporting superior healthcare delivery in the current healthcare environment globally.

1.1 Introduction

The need for improvement in the delivery of healthcare is unarguable especially when one looks at the more recent trends of healthcare expenditure for all OECD countries (OECD 2012). In particular, the statistics from the US are most alarming and some scholars and practitioners alike predict that if unchecked US healthcare costs could rise to as much as 20 % of their GNP by 2020 (Porter and Tiesberg 2006).Without a question there is a clear need and urgency for short and long term solutions to this current crisis with regard to delivering cost effective quality healthcare. Naturally, in today's Information Age, such a search has lead to a focus on pervasive information and communication technologies (ICTs). While we clearly believe there is indeed value and merit in applying ICTs to effect superior healthcare delivery, we caution regarding a carte blanche approach and rather advocate a more careful analysis and clear articulation of realizing cost-benefits that are generally promised with ICT implementations. Moreover, we believe that a subset of ICTs, namely, pervasive technologies may indeed hold the key to effecting superior cost effective healthcare delivery.

I. Troshani (✉)
University of Adelaide Business School, The University of Adelaide,
10 Pulteney Street, Adelaide, SA 5005, Australia
e-mail: indrit.troshani@adelaide.edu.au

N. Wickramasinghe
Epworth Chair Health Information Management,
School of Business Information Technology and Logistics,
RMIT University, Melbourne VIC 3001, Australia
e-mail: nilmini.wickramasinghe@rmit.edu.au

R. K. Bali et al. (eds.), *Pervasive Health Knowledge Management,*
Healthcare Delivery in the Information Age,
DOI 10.1007/978-1-4614-4514-2_1, © Springer Science+Business Media New York 2013

1.1.1 Focus of this Section

This section introduces many important concepts and constructs and sets the scene for why a pervasive perspective is a prudent choice for supporting superior healthcare delivery in the current healthcare environment globally. The need for improvement in the delivery of healthcare is unarguable especially when one looks at the more recent trends of healthcare expenditure for all OECD countries (OECD 2012). In particular, the statistics from the US are most alarming and some scholars and practitioners alike predict that if unchecked US healthcare costs could rise to as much as 20 % of their GNP by 2020 (Porter and Tiesberg 2006). Without a question there is a clear need and urgency for short and long term solutions to this current crisis with regard to delivering cost effective quality healthcare. Naturally, in today's Information Age, such a search has lead to a focus on pervasive information and communication technologies (ICTs). While we clearly believe there is indeed value and merit in applying ICTs to effect superior healthcare delivery, we caution regarding a *carte blanche* approach and rather advocate a more careful analysis and clear articulation of realizing cost-benefits that are generally promised with ICT implementations. Moreover, we believe that a subset of ICTs, namely, pervasive technologies may indeed hold the key to effecting superior cost effective healthcare delivery.

1.1.2 The Chapters

The chapters in this section then not only present the case for why pervasive technologies might be appropriate for effecting superior healthcare delivery but also why it is important to also and contemporaneously apply current management principles such as knowledge management to such pervasive technology applications. Specifically, the five chapters that make up this section discuss the following:

Chapter 1 "Pervasive Computing and Healthcare" N. Wickramasinghe. This chapter presents the case that it is only possible to truly leverage the full benefits of pervasive technologies for healthcare delivery, if a network centric perspective is adopted.

Chapter 2 "Implicit and Explicit Knowledge assets in Healthcare" N. Wickramasinghe, introduces the area of knowledge management in the context of healthcare delivery.

Chapter 3 "Regulating Pervasive e-Health Services" I. Troshani and N. Wickramasinghe provides some useful insights relating to implications for regulations and public policy with regard to incorporating pervasive technology solutions into healthcare contexts.

Chapter 4 "e-Health Complexity and Actor-Network Theory" I. Troshani presents an argument why actor-network theory constitutes a suitable methodological approach for improving current understanding of all of the various benefits that pervasive technologies can afford to healthcare delivery given inherent complexity of modern healthcare.

Chapter 5 "e-health Trends" I. Troshani and N. Wickramasinghe, the final chapter in section I provides a discussion of the near future possibilities, and thus, why it behoves healthcare organisations and public policy makers globally to think about incorporating pervasive technology solutions into their healthcare delivery strategies.

References

OECD. (2012). http://www.oecd.org/els/healthpoliciesanddata/oecdhealthdata2012-frequentlyrequesteddata.htm. Accessed Feb 2012.

Porter, M., & Tiesberg, E. (2006). Redefining healthcare. Cambridge: Harvard University Press.

Chapter 2
Pervasive Computing and Healthcare

Nilmini Wickramasinghe

Abstract A confluence of developments has led to the possibility of realizing a vision of pervasive healthcare. These include, but are not limited to, society becoming increasingly mobile, dramatic advances in various areas of technology and computer science, exponentially increasing healthcare costs coupled with workforce issues, the need to provide effective and efficient healthcare, and the change in the makeup of leading diseases most notably the increase in noncommunicable (or chronic) diseases. This is actually a very exciting time in healthcare delivery and one of the major challenges is to prudently adopt and implement appropriate pervasive healthcare solutions. To do this successfully, naturally requires a full appreciation of the key considerations in pervasive computing and healthcare; in particular, an appreciation of network healthcare operations. The objective of this chapter is to provide such a holistic perspective.

Keywords Pervasive computing · Ubiquitous computing · Pervasive healthcare · Network-centric healthcare

2.1 Introduction

The introduction to information communication technologies (ICTs) into healthcare contexts has led to increased access by healthcare providers and patients, more efficient tasks and processes, and a possibility for superior delivery of care (Varshney 2007, 2009; Kern and Jaron 2003; Wells 2003; Lin 1999; von Lubitz et al. 2006). However, contemporaneously we are also seeing an increase in the number of medical errors (US Institute of Medicine Report, o. J) as well as significant cost increases in all OECD countries (Zwicker et al. 2011), which provides significant stress on healthcare systems. In addition, we are also observing a growth in healthcare disparities and the quality of care (Chalassani et al. 2011) Moreover, other important trends include an aging population and a change in the makeup of leading disease and the exponential increase of noncommunicable disease (Wickramasinghe et al. 2011). Simply stated, providing superior healthcare today is indeed challenging.

N. Wickramasinghe (✉)
Epworth Chair Health Information Management, School of Business Information Technology and Logistics, RMIT University, Melbourne VIC 3001, Australia
e-mail: nilmini.wickramasinghe@rmit.edu.au

R. K. Bali et al. (eds.), *Pervasive Health Knowledge Management,*
Healthcare Delivery in the Information Age,
DOI 10.1007/978-1-4614-4514-2_2,

A possible solution appears to lie in the use of mobile and wireless technology (Varshney 2007, 2009; Wickramasinghe and Goldberg 2009). In particular, many have suggested that current and emerging wireless technologies (ibid) could improve quality of healthcare delivery both in urban and rural settings as well as decrease medical errors caused by poor or incomplete information. Moreover, in the area of chronic or noncommunicable disease, several scholars believe wireless technologies can provide superior patient self-care (Wickramasinghe et al. 2011; Wickramasinghe and Goldberg 2009). A vision for pervasive healthcare does indeed appear to be a reality and thus what is important is to understand some of the critical considerations that must be addressed in order to realize such a vision. However, it is the contention of this chapter that without consideration of a network-centric perspective, pervasive healthcare solutions will be unable to deliver their full potential benefits.

2.2 Background

Pervasive or ubiquitous computing (the latter term was coined by Mark Weiser in 1988) is fundamentally a postdesktop model of human–computer interaction in which information processing has been thoroughly integrated into everyday objects and activities. In the course of ordinary activities, someone "using" ubiquitous computing engages many computational devices and systems simultaneously, and may not necessarily even be aware that they are doing so. This model is usually considered advancement from the desktop paradigm and is defined as "machines that fit the human environment instead of forcing humans to enter theirs" (http://en.wikipedia.org/wiki/Ubiquitous_computing). Essentially then, ubiquitous is considered to be "... something that is available anywhere, anytime, while pervasive is something that is permeated in the environment" (Varshney 2009, p. 39); however, in the context of a vision for pervasive healthcare the two terms can be considered interchangeable and both are equally necessary to realize a pervasive healthcare vision. Specifically, there exist four major types or categories for pervasive healthcare; namely implantable, wearable, portable, and environmental (Varshney 2007, 2009).

Some of the immediate challenges in such a context include finding Internet use, supporting context awareness, providing energy access, and protecting privacy and trust (Varshney 2007, 2009). However, current successful initiatives include smart homes, mobile and ubiquitous telemedicine to support medical diagnosis, treatment and patient care especially in rural areas, pervasive patient monitoring services ranging from sensors to mobile phones to monitor particular criteria such as blood sugar for diabetes, or if someone has fallen especially in the case of an elderly individual, intelligent emergency monitoring, health aware mobile devices, pervasive life style management, and medical inventory management systems (ibid).

Taken together, on examination of these current pervasive healthcare initiatives, one cannot be criticized for categorizing them as an extension or subset of e-health; namely, as mobile health or m-health. The key is how to translate m-health into m-healthcare or m-care; i.e., to provide superior care using pervasive technology. To understand this, it is first necessary to understand e-health, its goal and purpose, as well as the doctrine of network-centric healthcare operations.

2.3 e-health

Today, there exist many definitions of e-health but essentially e-health involves the application of ICTs to support and facilitate the range of healthcare functions concerned with the practice and delivery of care (Varshney 2007, 2009; Zwicker et al. 2011). e-health; however, also includes the digitizing of various healthcare processes and tasks including e-billing, e-payment, e-prescription, e-radiology, and e-records (Varshney 2009). Healthcare systems throughout the world are implementing various e-health initiatives in an attempt to gain efficiencies in healthcare delivery and management, improve quality of care, reduce costs and medical errors, and provide more patient-centric healthcare (Zwicker et al. 2011).

Effective conduct of healthcare operations is not only extremely expensive, it is also extremely complex. In fact, most healthcare problems affecting the world have multiple roots involving social, economical, political, and even geographical factors whose combination provides fertile grounds for the spread of illnesses, prevalence of trauma, enhanced mortality, etc. (Akhtar 1991). As a remedy, it has been proposed that, instead of the currently practiced concentration on a specific devastating illness that captures public attention such as HIV/AIDS, a comprehensive "systems approach" offers the best approach to the solution the causative factors of global healthcare problems (Akhtar 1991). Presently, the governments and political bodies of both European Union and of the United States begin to view the "systems approach" as the only viable option (European Institute of Medicine 2003; National Coalition on Healthcare 2004; Kyprianou 2005).

The introduction of ICT into healthcare delivery has changed many aspects of medicine; however, the explosive growth of worldwide healthcare costs indicates that a mere introduction of advanced technology does not solve the problem (von Lubitz and Wickramasinghe 2006b; Onen 2004; Olutimayin 2002; Larson and Society of General Internal medicine (SGIM) Task Force on the Domain of General Internal Medicine 2004). The quest for financial rewards provided by the lucrative healthcare markets of the Western world led to a plethora of dissonant healthcare platforms (e.g., electronic health records) that operate well within circumscribed (regional) networks but fail to provide a unified national or international service (Onen 2004; Olutimayin 2002; Larson and SGIM Task Force on the Domain of General Internal Medicine 2004). In addition, there is a striking lack of standards that would permit seamless interaction or even fusion of nonhealthcare (e.g., economy or local politics) and healthcare knowledge creation and management resources. Thus, despite the massive amount of information that is available to healthcare providers and administrators, despite availability of technologies that, theoretically at least, should act as facilitators and disseminators, the practical side of access to, and the use and administration of healthcare are characterized by increasing disparity, cost, and burgeoning chaos (Larson and SGIM Task Force on the Domain of General Internal Medicine 2004).

Previous work by von Lubitz and Wickramasinghe (Akhtar 1991; von Lubitz and Wickramasinghe 2006a, c) discusses the general principles and applicability of the military concept of network-centric operations and its adaptation to modern worldwide healthcare activities. Succinctly stated, the doctrine of network-centric healthcare operations is defined as "unhindered networking operations within and among the physical, information, and cognitive domains that govern all activities conducted in healthcare space based on free, multidirectional flow and exchange of information without regard to the involved platforms or platform-systems, and utilizing all available means of ICTs to facilitate such operations" (Akhtar 1991, p. 334). The three domains include the (Akhtar 1991):

1. *Information domain*: Contains all elements, which are required for generation, storage, dissemination/sharing, manipulation of information, and in addition its transformation and dissemination/sharing as knowledge in all its forms.
2. *Physical domain*: Encompasses the structure of the entire environment healthcare operations intended to influence indirectly or directly—political environment, fiscal operations, patient and personnel education, etc.
3. *Cognitive domain*: Relates to all human factors, which affect operations—education, training, experience, motivation, and intuition of individuals involved in the relevant activities.

The proposed network-centric healthcare operations are conducted using a World Healthcare Information Grid (WHIG)—a multidimensional communications network connecting all relevant information acquisition entities (sensors) with information processing, manipulating, and disseminating organizations (nodes). The nodes also serve as knowledge gathering, transforming, generating, and disseminating centers (Fig. 2.1).

At the highest level of complexity, healthcare activities are characterized by multidirectional and unrestricted flow of multispectral data deriving not only from research/clinical/administrative sources but also from fields that may appear to be almost entirely unrelated—economy, politics, social structure, etc. (Akhtar 1991). At the interdisciplinary level, the data exist as highly incompatible entities the access to which is frequently virtually impossible. In network-centric operations, raw data, information, and node-generated knowledge exist in fully compatible formats based on standards that allow automated meshing, manipulation, and reconfiguration. Essentially, network-centric healthcare operations are based on the principles of high-order network computing, with the WHIG serving as a rapid distribution system, and the nodes as the sophisticated processing centers whose task is to act as integrated data-/information-/knowledge-generating sites and DSS/ESS platforms providing high-level, query-sensitive network-wide outputs. The nodes are also capable of extracting and analyzing data and information from healthcare-relevant sensors and electronic data sources (e.g., financial, political, military, geological, law enforcement, infrastructure level, etc.), meshing complex inputs into knowledge blocks relevant to both specific and general healthcare issues. Incorporation of

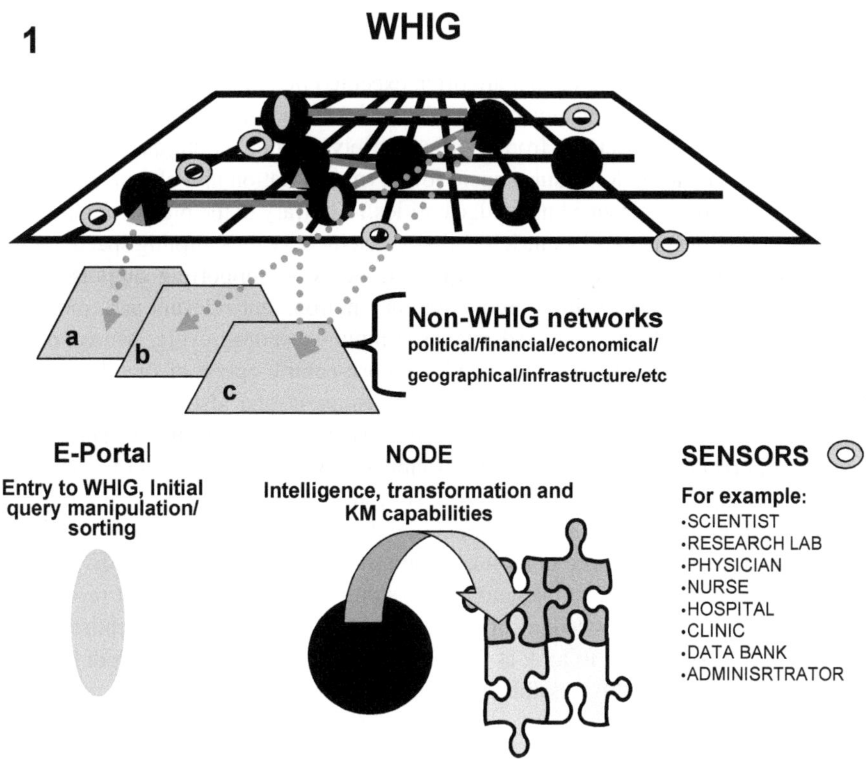

Fig. 2.1 Schematic diagram of a WHIG segment. Sensors feed raw data/information into the network through network-distributed portals. Likewise, data, information, and knowledge queries enter through portals as well. The latter provide entry-level security screening and sorting/routing. Subsequent manipulation, classification, and transformation into information/pertinent knowledge is executed by interconnected nodes. Whenever required, each node can access information/knowledge existing within non-WHIG networks and databases and compare/merge the contents with the contents existing within the WHIG. (Adapted from von Lubitz et al. 2006)

external information in healthcare operations is not only necessary but often critical element that will ultimately determine success of either planned or conducted activities (Olutimayin 2002; Larson and SGIM Task Force on the Domain of General Internal Medicine 2004). The complications resulting either from the failure to include elements external to the essential healthcare activities or consequent to the exclusion caused by either by sheer ignorance or by incompatibility of information/knowledge resource platforms have been amply demonstrated on several occasions (von Lubitz and Wickramasinghe 2006a, c).

The theoretical foundations for the activities characterized by a broad range of multidisciplinary (multispectral) inputs have been synthesized by Boyd as the OODA Loop (Boyd 1987; Akhtar 1991; Larson and SGIM Task Force on the Domain of General Internal Medicine 2004; von Lubitz and Wickramasinghe 2006a) whose practical applications ramify from military activities to global financial/banking operations, lean manufacturing, just-in-time supply chains, medical training, etc. The rules described in Boyd's (OODA) Loop apply particularly well to major international healthcare programs that are often executed in a highly fluid, ultracomplex environments that demand not only rapid, reliable sampling of the environment (data/information collection) from a broad variety of sources but also a very high degree of automation at the subsequent levels (manipulation and classification into larger information/germane knowledge entities.) Contrary to the prevalent platform-centric operations, network centricity allows vast increase in sampling speed, range, and data manipulation speed. Consequently, decision supporting outputs of the network are faster, more situation/operational environment-relevant and, most importantly, allow robustly elevated rate of stimulus–response cycle. Moreover, by increasing reaction relevance and speed, network-centric operations facilitate goal-oriented manipulation of the operational environment and also increase both the level (accuracy) and predictive range of responses to environment-induced pressures. However, in order for such interactions to happen, a well-integrated international system of multitype telecommunications must be in place. While the development of such an umbrella system can be conducted with the greatest ease among the Western countries, it is far more complex among the Less Developed World. The task is, however, not insurmountable and the frequently raised arguments of prohibitive costs or nonexistent knowledge support at the local level may not be entirely true. Moreover, we only need to look at the infrastructures that support modern banking to see that not only is this possible, it can happen on a global scale.

2.4 Summary

Returning to the specific context of pervasive healthcare or m-health, what becomes important then is to incorporate a holistic perspective, i.e., a network-centric perspective into the design and development of any pervasive healthcare intervention. If such a conceptualization occurs, only then will it be possible to provide anytime, anywhere for anyone healthcare delivery that subscribes to a healthcare value proposition of excellence in access, quality, and value. The idea of network-centric healthcare operations may seem at first futuristic and unrealistic; but a question we do need to ask ourselves is can we afford to continue down the track of ineffective, inefficient, and costly healthcare initiatives or should we begin to develop a superior solution?

References

Akhtar, R. (Ed.). (1991). *Health care patterns and planning in developing countries* (pp. 1–336). New York: Greenwood.

Boyd, J. R., COL USAF. (1987). In Patterns of Conflict, unpubl Briefing (accessible as Essence of Winning and Losing, http://www.d-n-i.net).

Chalassani, S., Wickramaisnghe, N., Goldberg, S., & Koritala, S. (2011). Business and IT aspects of Wireless Enabled Healthcare Solutions. AMCIS Detroit, 4–7 Aug.
European Institute of Medicine. (2003). *Health is Wealth: Strategic vision for European healthcare at the beginning of the 21st century*. Salzburg: European Academy of Arts and Sciences.
http://en.wikipedia.org/wiki/Ubiquitous_computing. Accessed 07 Oct 2011.
Kern, S., & Jaron, D. (2003). Healthcare technology, economics and policy: An evolving balance. *IEEE Engineering in Medicine and Biology Magazine, 22,* 16–19.
Kyprianou, M., Commissioner, E.U. Health and Consumer Protection. (2005). The new European Healthcare Agenda—The European Voice conference "Healthcare: Is Europe getting better?".
Larson, E. B., & Society of General Internal medicine (SGIM) Task Force on the Domain of General Internal Medicine. (2004). Healthcare system chaos should spur innovation: Summary of a report of the Society of General Internal Medicine Task Force on the Domain of General Internal Medicine. *Annals of Internal Medicine, 140,* 639.
Lin, J. (1999). Applying telecommunications technology to health care delivery. *IEEE Engineering in Medicine Biology Magazine,* 28–31.
National Coalition on Healthcare. (2004). *Building a better health: Specifications for reform.* Washington, DC: National Coalition on Healthcare.
Olutimayin, J. (2002). Communication in health care delivery in developing countries: Which way out? *Pacific Health Dialog, 9,* 237–241.
Onen, C. L. (2004). Medicine in resource-poor settings: Time for a paradigm shift? *Clinical Medicine, 4,* 355–360.
US Institute of Medicine Report. (o. J). To Err is human: Building a safer health system. http://wwwnap.edu/books/0300906837l/html/.
Varshney, U. (2007). Pervasive healthcare and wireless health monitoring. *Mobile Networks and Applications, 12,* 113–127.
Varshney, U. (2009). *Pervasive healthcare computing*. New York: Springer.
Lubitz, D. von, & Wickramasinghe, N. (2006a). Creating germane knowledge in dynamic environments. *International Journal Innovation and Learning, 3*(3), 326–347.
Lubitz, D. von, & Wickramasinghe, N. (2006b). Healthcare and technology: The doctrine of networkcentric healthcare. *International Journal of Electronic Healthcare, 4,* 322–344.
Lubitz, D. von, & Wickramasinghe, N. (2006c). Networkcentric Healthcare: Applying the tools, techniques and strategies of knowledge management to create superior healthcare operations. *International Journal of Electronic Healthcare (IJEH), 4,* 415–428.
Lubitz, D. von, Wickramasinghe, N., & Yanovsky, G. (2006). Networkcentric healthcare operations: The telecommuniucations structure. *International Journal of Networking and Virtual Organizations, 3*(1), 60–85.
Wells, P. (2003). Can Technology truly reduce healthcare costs. *IEEE Engineering in Medicine Biology Magazine,* 20–25.
Wickramasinghe, N., & Goldberg, S. (2009). The S'ANT approach to facilitate a superior chronic disease self-management model. *IJANTTI, 1*(4), 21–34.
Wickramasinghe, N., Troshani, I., Rao, S., Hague, W., & Goldberg, S. (2011). A transaction cost assessment of a pervasive technology solution for gestational diabetes. *IJHISI* (in press).
Zwicker, M., Seitz, J., & Wickramasinghe, N. (2011). The telematics infrastructure: The backbone of the German e-health card. *International Journal of Healthcare Delivery Reform* (in press).

Chapter 3
Implicit and Explicit Knowledge Assets in Healthcare

Nilmini Wickramasinghe

Abstract Data and information permeate healthcare organizations and more recently are often stored in disparate databases. However, given the voluminous nature of these disparate data assets, it is no longer possible for healthcare providers to process these data without the aid of sophisticated tools and technologies. The goal of knowledge management is to provide the decision maker with appropriate tools, technologies, techniques, and tactics to turn data and information into valuable knowledge assets. In order to leverage the full potential of implicit and explicit knowledge assets in healthcare delivery; it is essential to not only understand the knowledge construct, but also important frameworks and models such as the knowledge management infrastructure (KMI) framework and intelligence continuum (IC) model as discussed in this chapter.

Keywords Knowledge management · Data mining · Business intelligence · Knowledge management infrastructure · Knowledge assets · Intelligence continuum · Healthcare · Healthcare delivery

3.1 Introduction

Knowledge management is management technique aimed at solving the current business challenges to increase efficiency and efficacy of core business processes while simultaneously incorporating continuous innovation and ensuring a sustainable competitive advantage. The premise for the need for knowledge management is based on a paradigm shift in the business environment where knowledge is central to

Material from this chapter has been adapted from Wickramasinghe, N. (2010). Healthcare Knowledge Management: Incorporating the tools technologies strategies and process of KM to effect superior healthcare delivery. In Gibbons et al. (Eds.), *Perspectives of knowledge management in urban health*. New York: Springer.

N. Wickramasinghe (✉)
Epworth Chair Health Information Management,
School of Business Information Technology and Logistics,
RMIT University, Melbourne VIC 3001, Australia,
e-mail: nilmini.wickramasinghe@rmit.edu.au

R. K. Bali et al. (eds.), *Pervasive Health Knowledge Management*,
Healthcare Delivery in the Information Age,
DOI 10.1007/978-1-4614-4514-2_3, © Springer Science+Business Media New York 2013

organizational performance given that we are now operating in a knowledge economy as opposed to an agrarian or industrial economy (Drucker 1993, 1999).

The successful application knowledge management lies in the development of a sound knowledge management infrastructure (KMI) and the systematic and continuous application of specific steps supported by various technologies. This serves to underscore the dynamic nature of knowledge management where the existing extant knowledge base is always being updated. The KMI framework not only helps organizations to structure their knowledge assets but also make explicit the numerous implicit knowledge assets currently evident in healthcare (Wickramasinghe and Davidson 2004), while the intelligence continuum (IC) provides the key tools and technologies to facilitate superior healthcare delivery (Wickramasinghe and Schaffer 2006). Taken together, the KMI and IC can enable healthcare to realize its value proposition of delivering effective and efficient value-added healthcare services.

3.2 Knowledge Management

"Land, labor, and capital now pale in comparison to knowledge as the critical asset to be managed in today's knowledge economy." Drucker (1999, p. 47). The nations that lead the world into the next century will be those who can shift from being industrial economies, based upon the production of manufactured goods, to those that possess the capacity to produce and utilize knowledge successfully. The focus of the many nations' economy has shifted first to information-intensive industries such as financial services and logistics, and now toward innovation-driven industries, such as computer software and biotechnology, where competitive advantage lies mostly in the innovative use of human resources. This represents a move from an era of standardization to an era of innovation where knowledge, its creation, and management hold the key to success (Bukowitz and Williams 1997; Drucker 1993, 1999).

Knowledge management is a key approach to help solve current business problems such as competitiveness and the need to innovate that are faced by organizations today. The premise for knowledge management is based on a paradigm shift in the business environment where knowledge is central to organizational performance (Swan et al. 1999; Newell et al. 2002). In essence, knowledge management not only involves the production of information but also the capture of data at the source, the transmission and analysis of these data, as well as the communication of information based on or derived from the data to those who can act on it (Davenport and Prusak 1998). Thus, data and information represent critical raw assets in the generation of knowledge while successful knowledge management initiatives require a tripartite view; namely the incorporation of people, processes, and technologies (Wickramasinghe 2003).

Broadly speaking, knowledge management involves four key steps of creating/generating knowledge, representing/storing knowledge, accessing/using/reusing knowledge, and disseminating/transferring knowledge (Davenport and Prusak 1998; Markus 2001; Alavi and Leidner 2001; Wickramasinghe 2004a). Knowledge creation, generally accepted as the first step for any knowledge management endeavor, requires an understanding of the knowledge construct as well as its people and technology dimensions. Given that knowledge creation is the first step in any knowledge management initiative, it naturally has a significant impact on the other consequent Knowledge Management (KM) steps, thus making the identification of and facilitating of knowledge creation a key focal point for any organization wanting to fully leverage its knowledge potential.

Knowledge, however, is not a simple construct. Specifically, knowledge can exist as an object, in essentially two forms; explicit or factual knowledge and tacit or "know-how" (Polanyi 1958, 1966). It is well established that while both types of knowledge are important, tacit knowledge is more difficult to identify and thus manage (Nonaka 1994; Nonaka and Nishiguchi 2001). Of equal importance, though perhaps less well defined, knowledge also has a subjective component and can be viewed as an ongoing phenomenon, being shaped by social practices of communities (Boland and Tenkasi 1995). The objective elements of knowledge can be thought of as primarily having an impact on process while the subjective elements typically impact innovation (Wickramasinghe 2003). Enabling and enhancing both effective and efficient processes as well as the functions of supporting and fostering innovation are key concerns of knowledge management.

It is important to note that, organizational knowledge is not static; rather it changes and evolves during the lifetime of an organization. What is more, it is possible to transform one form of knowledge into another; i.e., transform tacit knowledge into explicit and vice versa (Wickramasinghe 2006). This process of transforming one form of knowledge into another is known as the knowledge spiral (Nonaka 1994). Naturally, this does not imply one form of knowledge is necessarily transformed 100 % into another form of knowledge. According to Nonaka (1994):

1. Socialization or tacit to tacit knowledge transformation usually occurs through apprenticeship type relations where the teacher or master passes on the skill to the apprentice.
2. Combination or explicit to explicit knowledge transformation usually occurs via formal learning of facts.
3. Externalization or tacit to explicit knowledge transformation usually occurs when there is an articulation of nuances; for example, if an expert surgeon is questioned as to why he performs a particular surgical procedure in a certain manner, by his articulation of the steps the tacit knowledge becomes explicit.
4. Internalization or explicit to tacit knowledge transformation usually occurs when explicit knowledge is internalized and can then be used to broaden, reframe, and extend one's tacit knowledge. Integral to these transformations of knowledge through the knowledge spiral is that new knowledge is being continuously created (ibid) and this can potentially bring many benefits to organizations. What becomes important then for any organization in today's knowledge economy is to maximize the full potential of all its knowledge assets and successfully make all germane knowledge explicit so it can be used effectively and efficiently by all people within the organization as required (Wickramasinghe 2004b, 2006).

Thus, given the complex nature of knowledge, scholars approach knowledge creation from three major perspectives including a people-oriented perspective, a technology-oriented perspective, and a process-oriented perspective. The preceding has served to highlight central themes within the people-oriented perspective. In addition to Nonaka's conceptualization, other scholars such as Spender and Blackler (Newell et al. 2002) have also presented conceptualizations of knowledge creation that also fall within the people-oriented perspective. For completeness, they are now briefly discussed.

In particular, Spender draws a distinction between individual knowledge and social knowledge (yet another duality), each of which he claims can be implicit or explicit (ibid). From this framework, we can see that Spender's definition of implicit knowledge corresponds to Nonaka's tacit knowledge. However, unlike Spender, Nonaka doesn't differentiate between individual and social dimensions of knowledge; rather he merely focuses on the nature and types of the knowledge itself. In contrast, Blackler (ibid) views knowledge creation from an organizational perspective, noting that knowledge can exist as encoded, embedded, embodied, encultured, and/or embrained. In addition, Blackler emphasized that for different organizational types, different types of knowledge predominate, and highlights the connection between knowledge and organizational processes (ibid). Blackler's types of knowledge can be thought of in terms of spanning a continuum of tacit (implicit) through to explicit with embrained being predominantly tacit (implicit) and encoded being predominantly explicit while embedded, embodied, and encultured types of knowledge exhibit varying degrees of a tacit (implicit)/explicit combination.

3.2.1 Technology-Oriented Perspective

In contrast to the above primarily people-oriented perspectives pertaining to knowledge creation, knowledge discovery in databases (KDD; and more specifically data mining) approaches knowledge creation from a primarily technology-oriented perspective. In particular, the KDD process focuses on how data are transformed into knowledge by identifying valid, novel, potentially useful, and ultimately understandable patterns in data (Fayyad et al. 1996). KDD is primarily used on data sets for creating knowledge through model building, or by finding patterns and relationships in data. How to manage such newly discovered knowledge and other organizational knowledge is at the core of knowledge management. Figure 3.1a summarizes the key steps within the KDD process; while it is beyond the scope of this chapter to describe in detail all the steps, which constitute the KDD process, an important duality to highlight here is that between exploratory and predictive data mining. Typically, Lockean and Leibnizian inquiring systems would subscribe to a technology-oriented perspective for knowledge creation (Malhotra 1997).

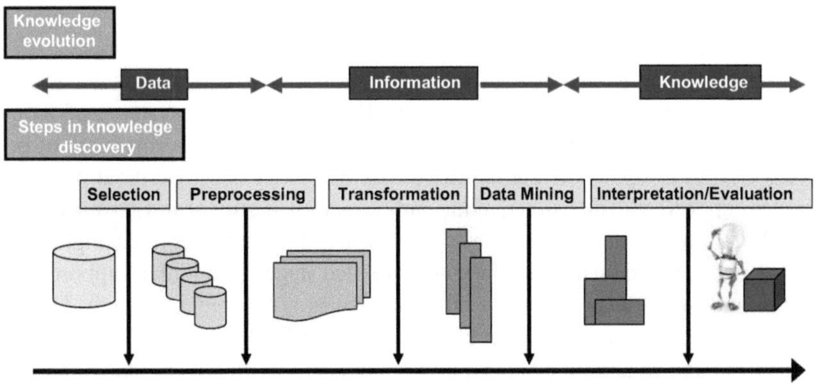

a

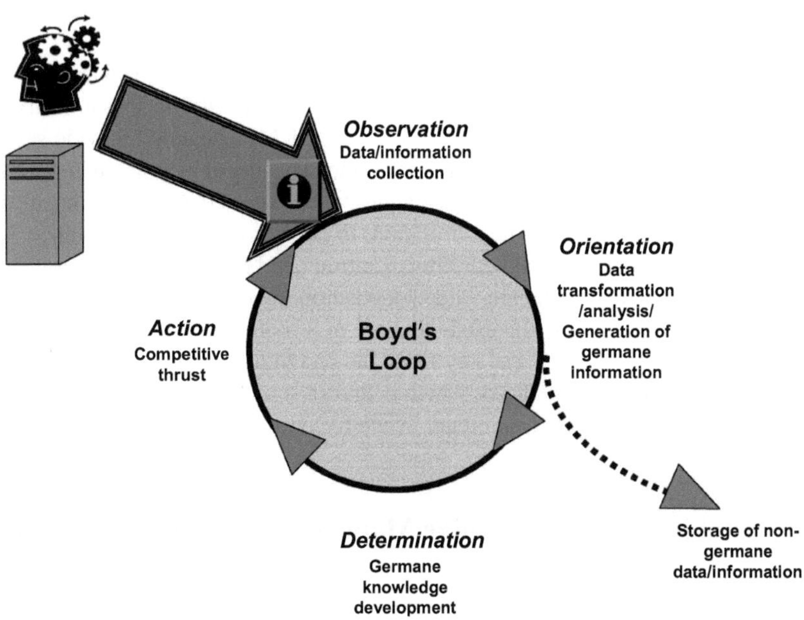

b

Fig. 3.1 **a** Data mining. **b** Process perspective to knowledge generation. (Adapted from Wickramasinghe and von Lubitz 2007)

3.2.2 Process-Oriented Knowledge Generation

A process-centric approach to knowledge creation not only combines the essentials of both the people-centric and technology-centric perspectives but also emphasizes the dynamic and ongoing nature of the process of knowledge creation itself and supports simultaneously the Lokean/Leibnizian and Hegelian/Kantian systems of inquiry. Process-centered knowledge generation is grounded in the pioneering work of Boyd and his OODA Loop, a conceptual framework that maps out the critical process required to support rapid decision making and extraction of critical and germane knowledge (Wickramasinghe and von Lubitz 2007; von Lubitz and Wickramasinghe 2006).

The Loop is based on a cycle of four interrelated stages essential to support critical analysis and rapid decision making that revolve in both time and space: Observation followed by Orientation, then by Decision, and finally Action (OODA). At the Observation and Orientation stages, implicit and explicit inputs are gathered or extracted from the environment (Observation) and converted into coherent information (Orientation). The latter determines the sequential Determination (knowledge generation) and Action (practical implementation of knowledge) steps (ibid.; Fig. 3.1b). The outcome of the Action stage then affects, in turn, the character of the starting point (Observation) of the next revolution in the forward progression of the rolling loop.

Healthcare is an industry currently facing major challenges at a global level (Wickramasinghe and Silvers 2003; Wickramasinghe and Schaffer 2006). This industry has yet to truly embrace knowledge management. Yet, KM appears to provide several viable possibilities to address the current crisis faced by global healthcare in the areas of access, quality, and value (Wickramasinghe and Schaffer 2006). In healthcare, one of the most critical knowledge transformations to effect is that of tacit to explicit; i.e., externalization so that the healthcare organization can best leverage its knowledge potential to realize the healthcare value proposition (Wickramasinghe et al. 2003). Integral to such a process is the establishment of a robust knowledge management infrastructure and the adoption of key tools and techniques. This is achieved by the application of an appropriate KMI, which is in turn supported by the IC (ibid).

Table 3.1 below provides a summary of the five key elements of the KMI.

3.3 Establishing a Knowledge Management Infrastructure

The most valuable resources available to any organization are human skills, expertise, and relationships. KM is about capitalizing on these precious assets (Duffy 2001). Most companies do not capitalize on the wealth of expertise in the form of knowledge scattered across their levels (Hansen et al. 2001). Information centers, market intelligence, and learning are converging to form knowledge management functions. Knowledge management offers organizations many strategies, techniques, and tools to apply to their existing business processes so that they are able to grow and effectively utilize their knowledge assets. The KM infrastructure not only forms the

Table 3.1 The elements of the KMI

Element of the knowledge management infrastructure	Description of element
Infrastructure for collaboration	The key to competitive advantage and improving customer satisfaction lies in the ability of organizations to form learning alliances; these being strategic partnerships based on a business environment that encourages mutual (and reflective) learning between partners (Holt et al. 2000). Organizations can utilize their strategy framework to identify partners and collaborators for enhancing their value chain
Organizational memory	Organizational memory is concerned with the storing and subsequent accessing and replenishing of an organization's "know-how," which is recorded in documents or in its people (Maier and Lehner 2000). However, a key component of knowledge management not addressed in the construct of organizational memory is the subjective aspect (Wickramasinghe 2003). Knowledge as a subjective component primarily refers to an ongoing phenomenon of exchange where knowledge is being shaped by social practices of communities (Boland and Tenkasi 1995), in the tradition of a Hegelian/Kantian perspective where the importance of divergence of meaning is essential to support the "sense-making" processes of knowledge creation (Wickramasinghe and Mills 2001). Thus, strong organizational memory systems ensure the access of information or knowledge throughout the company to everyone at any time (Croasdell 2001)
Human asset infrastructure	This deals with the participation and willingness of people. Today, organizations have to attract and motivate the best people; reward, recognize, train, educate, and improve them (Ellinger et al. 1999) so that the highly skilled and more independent workers can exploit technologies to create knowledge in learning organizations (Thorne and Smith 2000). The human asset infrastructure then, helps to identify and utilize the special skills of people who can create greater business value if they and their inherent skills and experiences are managed to make explicit use of their knowledge
Knowledge transfer network	This element is concerned with the dissemination of knowledge and information. Unless there is a strong communication infrastructure in place, people are not able to communicate effectively and thus are unable to effectively transfer knowledge. An appropriate communications infrastructure includes, but is not limited to, the Internet and Intranets for creating the knowledge transfer network as well as discussion rooms, bulletin boards for meetings and for displaying information
Business intelligence infrastructure	In an intelligent enterprise, various information systems are integrated with knowledge-gathering and analyzing tools for data analysis, and dynamic end-user querying of a variety of enterprise data sources (Hammond 2001). Business intelligence infrastructures have customers, suppliers, and other partners embedded into single integrated system. Customers will view their own purchasing habits, and suppliers will see the demand pattern, which may help them to offer volume discounts, etc. This information can help all customers, suppliers, and enterprises to analyze data and provide them with the competitive advantage. The intelligence of a company is not only available to Internal users but can even be leveraged by selling it to others such as consumers who may be interested in this type of informational intelligence

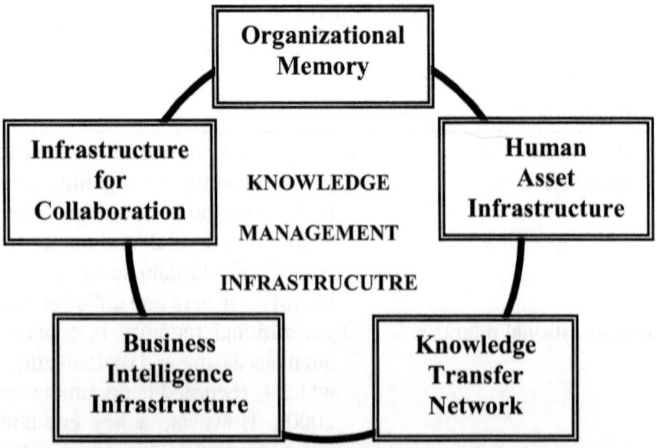

Fig. 3.2 Key elements that constitute the knowledge management infrastructure. (Adapted from Wickramasinghe et al. 2005)

foundation for enabling and fostering knowledge management, continuous learning, and sustaining an organizational memory (Drucker 1999) but also provides the foundations for actualizing the four key steps of knowledge management; namely, creating/generating knowledge, representing/storing knowledge, accessing/using/reusing knowledge, and disseminating/transferring knowledge (discussed in Sect. 3.2). An organization's entire "know-how," including new knowledge, can only be created for optimization if an effective KM infrastructure is established. Specifically, the KM infrastructure consists of social and technical tools and techniques, including hardware and software that should be established so that knowledge can be created from any new events or activities on a continual basis. In addition, the KM infrastructure will have a repository of knowledge, systems to distribute the knowledge to the members of the organization, and a facilitator system for the creation of new knowledge. Thus, a knowledge-based infrastructure will foster the creation of knowledge, and provide an integrated system to share and diffuse the knowledge within the organization (Srikantaiah 2000) as well as support for continual creation and generation of new knowledge (Wickramasinghe 2003). The KMI depicted in Fig. 3.2 contains the five essential elements of organizational memory, human asset infrastructure, knowledge transfer network, business intelligence infrastructure, and infrastructure for collaboration that together must be present for any KM initiative to succeed.

3.3.1 *The Intelligence Continuum*

In addition to the KMI, which provides an organizing framework, in order to capture the dynamic nature of KM, it is important to have an appropriate dynamic model. This is achieved by the Intelligence Continuum. The IC consists of a collection of key tools, techniques, and processes of the knowledge economy; i.e., including data mining, business intelligence/analytics, and knowledge management, which are applied to a generic system of people, process, and technology in a systematic and ordered fashion (Wickramasinghe and Fadlalla 2004; Wickramasinghe and Schaffer

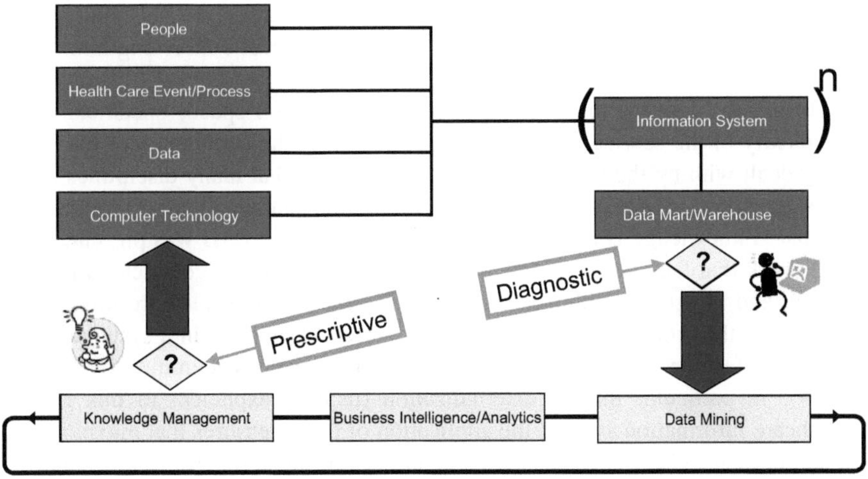

Fig. 3.3 The intelligence continuum

2006; Wickramasinghe and Silvers 2003; Wickramasinghe and Lichtenstein 2006; Wickramasinghe et al. 2005). Taken together, they represent a very powerful system for refining the data raw material stored in data marts and/or data warehouses and thereby maximizing the value and utility of these data assets for any organization (Geisler 1999, 2000, 2001, 2002; Geisler and Wickramasinghe 2006; Kostoff and Geisler 1999). As depicted in Fig. 3.3, the intelligence continuum is applied to the output of the generic healthcare information system. Once applied, the results become part of the data set that are reintroduced into the system and combined with the other inputs of people, processes, and technology to develop an improvement continuum. Thus, the intelligence continuum includes the generation of data, the analysis of these data to provide a "diagnosis," and the reintroduction into the cycle as a "prescriptive" solution. In this way, the next iteration, or "future state" always represents the enhancement of the extant knowledge base of the previous iteration. For the IC to be truly effective, however, the KMI must already be in place so that all data, information, and knowledge assets are explicit and the technologies of the IC can be applied to them in a systematic and methodical fashion.

3.4 Conclusion

Healthcare globally is facing many challenges including escalating costs and more pressures to deliver high-quality, effective, and efficient care. By nurturing knowledge management and making their knowledge assets explicit, healthcare organizations will be more suitably equipped to meet these challenges; since knowledge holds the key to developing better practice management techniques, while data and information are so necessary in disease management and evidence-based medicine. To do this successfully, it is necessary to understand the complex construct of knowledge as well as the people, technology, and process perspectives concerning knowledge creation and generation.

Healthcare delivery takes place in a complex action space; specifically, the complexity of the service delivery process, driven by the complexity of the issues being dealt with by the teams, which in turn requires that many disciplines create and share knowledge to enable the delivery of a high quality of care. Thus, the need for shared knowledge is a fundamental requirement. The KMI was presented as a framework that facilities disparate and often implicit knowledge assets to become explicit and integrated within a larger system, the generic healthcare information system. Furthermore, such a framework in particular supports in a systematic and structured fashion all four key knowledge transformations identified by Nonaka (1994), in particular that of externalization (tacit to explicit). To this generic healthcare information system, the application of the IC ensures that maximization of appropriate and germane knowledge assets occurs and a superior future state will be realized.

Given the challenges faced by healthcare organizations today, the importance of knowledge management, understanding the means available to support knowledge management and explicitly developing and designing an appropriate healthcare information system using the KMI framework, and then applying to this the IC model is indeed of strategic significance, especially as it serves to facilitate the realization of a healthcare value proposition of excellence.

References

Alavi, M., & Leidner, D. (2001). Review: Knowledge management and knowledge management systems: Conceptual foundations and research issues. *MIS Quarterly, 25*(1), 107–136.

Applegate, L., Mason, R., & Thorpe, D. (1986). Design of a management support system for hospital strategic planning. *Journal of Medical Systems, 10*(1), 79–94.

Boland, R., & Tenkasi, R. (1995). Perspective making perspective taking. *Organization Science, 6*, 350–372.

Bukowitz, W. R., & Williams, R. L. (1997). New metrics for hidden assets. *Journal of Strategic Performance Measurement, 1*(1), 12–18.

Croasdell, D. C. (2001). IT's role in organizational memory and learning. *Information Systems Management, 18*(1), 8–11.

Davenport, T., & Prusak, L. (1998). *Working knowledge*. Boston: Harvard Business School Press.

Drucker, P. (1993). *Post-capitalist society*. New York: Harper Collins.

Drucker, P. (1999, October). Beyond the information revolution. *The Atlantic Monthly*, 47–57.

Duffy, J. (2001). The tools and technologies needed for knowledge management. *Information Management Journal, 35*(1), 64–67.

Ellinger, A. D., Watkins, K. E., & Bostrom, R. P. (1999). Managers as facilitators of learning in learning organizations. *Human Resource Development Quarterly, 10*(2), 105–125.

Fayyad, U. M., Piatetsky-Shapiro, G., & Smyth, P. (1996). From data mining to knowledge discovery: An overview. In U. M. Fayyad, G. Piatetsky-Shapiro, P. Smyth, & R. Uthurusamy (Eds.), *Advances in knowledge discovery and data mining*. Menlo Park: AAAI Press, The MIT Press.

Geisler, E. (1999). Mapping the knowledge-base of management of medical technology. *International Journal of Healthcare Technology and Management, 1*(1), 3–10.

Geisler, E. (2000). *The metrics of science and technology*. Westport: Greenwood.

Geisler, E. (2001). *Creating value with science and technology*. Westport: Quorum Books.

Geisler, E. (2002). The metrics of technology evaluation: Where we stand and where we should go from here. *International Journal of Technology Management, 24*(4), 341–374.

Geisler, E., & Wickramasinghe, N. (2006). *Knowledge management: Concepts and cases*. Armonk: M. E. Sharpe Publishers (forthcoming).

Hammond, C. (2001). The intelligent enterprise. *InfoWorld, 23*(6), 45–46.

Holt, G. D., Love, P. E. D., & Li, H. (2000). The learning organization: Toward a paradigm for mutually beneficial strategic construction alliances. *International Journal of Project Management, 18*(6), 415–421.

Kostoff, R., & Geisler, E. (1999). Strategic management and implementation of textual data mining in government organizations. *Technology Analysis and Strategic Management, 11*(4), 493–525.

Maier, R., & Lehner, F. (2000). *Perspectives on knowledge management systems theoretical framework and design of an empirical study*. Proceedings of 8th European Conference on Information Systems (ECIS).

Malhotra, Y. (1997). *Knowledge management for inquiring organizations*. Proceedings of 3rd Americas Conference on Information Systems, pp. 293–295.

Markus, L. (2001). Toward a theory of knowledge reuse: Types of knowledge reuse situations and factors in reuse success. *Journal of Management Information Systems, 18*(1), 57–93.

Newell, S., Robertson, M., Scarbrough, H., & Swan, J. (2002). *Managing knowledge work*. New York: Palgrave.

Nonaka, I. (1994). A dynamic theory of organizational knowledge creation. *Organizational Science, 5*, 14–37.

Nonaka, I., & Nishiguchi, T. (2001). *Knowledge emergence*. Oxford: Oxford University Press.

Polanyi, M. (1958). *Personal knowledge: Towards a post-critical philosophy*. Chicago: University Press.

Polanyi, M. (1966). *The tacit dimension*. London: Routledge, Kegan Paul.

Srikantaiah, T. K. (2000). Knowledge management for information professional. *ASIS Monograph Series*, Information Today, Inc.

Swan, J., Scarbrough, H., & Preston, J. (1999). *Knowledge management—the next fad to forget people?* Proceedings of the 7th European Conference in Information Systems.

Thorne, K., & Smith, M. (2000). Competitive advantage in world class organizations. *Management Accounting, 78*(3), 22–26.

Von Lubitz, D., & Wickramasinghe, N. (2006). Creating Germane knowledge in dynamic environments. *International Journal of Innovation and Learning (IJIL), 3*(3), 326–347.

Wickramasinghe, N. (2003). Do we practice what we preach: Are knowledge management systems in practice truly reflective of knowledge management systems in theory? *Business Process Management Journal, 9*(3), 295–316.

Wickramasinghe, N. (2004a). Actualizing the knowledge spiral through data mining—a clinical example. In J. Schaffer, & A. M. Fadlalla, 7–11 Sept.

Wickramasinghe, N. (2004b). Making explicit the implicit knowledge assets in healthcare. With Davison, G. *Healthcare Management Science, 17*(3), 185–196.

Wickramasinghe, N. (2006). Knowledge creation: A meta-framework. *International Journal of Innovation and Learning, 3*(5), 558–573.

Wickramasinghe, N., & Davison, G. (2004). Making explicit the implicit knowledge assets in healthcare. *Health Care Management Science, 7*(3), 185–196.

Wickramasinghe, N., & Fadlalla, A. (2004). An integrative framework for HIPAA-Compliant I*IQ healthcare information systems. *International Journal of Health Care Quality Assurance, 17*(2), 65–74.

Wickramasinghe, N., & Lichtenstein, S. (2006). Supporting knowledge creation with e-mail. *International Journal of Innovation and Learning, 3*(4), 416–426.

Wickramasinghe, N., & Lubitz, D. von. (2007). *Knowledge-based enterprises*. Hershey: IGI.

Wickramasinghe, N., & Mills, G. (2001). Integrating e-commerce and knowledge management—what does the Kaiser experience really tell us? *International Journal of Accounting Information Systems, 3*(2), 83–98.

Wickramasinghe, N., & Schaffer, J. (2006). Creating knowledge-driven healthcare processes with the intelligence continuum. *International Journal of Electronic Healthcare, 2*(2), 164–174.

Wickramasinghe, N., Sharma, S., & Gupta, J. (2005). A framework for building a learning organization in the 21st century. *International Journal of Innovation and Learning, 2*(3), 261–273.

Wickramasinghe, N., & Silvers, J. B. (2003). IS/IT the prescription to enable medical group practices to manage managed care. *Health Care Management Science, 6*, 75–86.

Wickramasinghe, N., Fadlalla, A., Geisler, E., & Schaffer, J. (2003). *Knowledge management and data mining: Strategic imperatives for healthcare*. 3rd Hospital of the Future Conference at Warwick, U.K.

Wickramasinghe, N., Fadlalla, A., Gesiler, E., & Schaffer, J. (2005). A framework for assessing e-health preparedness. *International Journal of Electronic Healthcare, 1*(3), 316–334.

Chapter 4
Regulating Pervasive e-Health Services

Indrit Troshani and Nilmini Wickramasinghe

Abstract While the development of pervasive e-health services is experiencing growth in many countries worldwide, existing regulatory regimes are ill-equipped for dealing with them. In this chapter, we investigate institutional regulatory factors that can impact pervasive e-health services. These factors are important as they can shape both the nature of these services and their diffusion trajectory. We argue that coregulation, a mixture of direct monitoring and intervention of regulators through legislation and complete industry self-regulation, can be an effective approach for regulating the pervasive e-health services industry. Given the complex and dynamic nature of this industry, coregulation can minimize monitoring costs and enhance compliance.

Keywords e-health · Regulation · Coregulation · Institution-based view

4.1 Introduction

Pervasive e-health constitutes the use of digitally enabled technologies to facilitate and enhance the exchange of clinical, administrative, informational, educational, and transactional data ubiquitously in healthcare settings (Holliday and Tam 2004; Piotti and Macome 2007; Sohn and Lee 2007). Examples of pervasive e-health services include telemedicine and telecare services, virtual reality, computer-assisted surgery, mobile monitoring systems (e.g., for the electronic management of chronic diseases), electronic medical records management including digital imaging and archiving systems, and electronic prescribing (Ferraud-Ciandet 2010). Taken together, pervasive e-health services have the potential to generate enormous efficiencies and services quality as well as to reduce medical errors (Anderson 2007; Hsu et al. 2005).

I. Troshani (✉)
University of Adelaide Business School, The University of Adelaide,
10 Pulteney Street, Adelaide, SA 5005, Australia
e-mail: indrit.troshani@adelaide.edu.au

N. Wickramasinghe
Epworth Chair Health Information Management, School of Business Information Technology and Logistics, RMIT University, Melbourne VIC 3001, Australia
e-mail: nilmini.wickramasinghe@rmit.edu.au

R. K. Bali et al. (eds.), *Pervasive Health Knowledge Management,*
Healthcare Delivery in the Information Age,
DOI 10.1007/978-1-4614-4514-2_4,

Delivering pervasive e-health services requires the integration of diverse technological and organizational resources, which typically cannot be found within individual organizations. The knowledge necessary for developing and deploying these services may involve several heterogeneous stakeholders that are often embedded in various technological, economic, and social settings (Holliday and Tam 2004). In order to succeed, these stakeholders must interact with each other while complying with institutional requirements including legal and societal requirements that balance their diverging interests, motivations, and needs (Camponovo and Pigneur 2003; Kluge 2007; Rao Hill and Troshani 2010; Troshani and Rao Hill 2009). These requirements constitute a regulatory regime, which can operate at either industrial, national, or international levels and can influence, direct, limit, or prohibit any activity undertaken by stakeholders operating in the pervasive e-health services industry (Holliday and Tam 2004; Hsu et al. 2005; Ooijevaar 2010).

Given the nature of healthcare and the sensitivity of healthcare information, it is typically incumbent upon regulatory and legislative government authorities to set up regulatory regimes and mandate their use (Huang et al. 2010). Generally, these regimes can facilitate the exchange of healthcare data and information amongst various healthcare stakeholders while also providing protection of patient rights including privacy (Huang et al. 2010). Credible and transparent regulatory rules can boost much needed investments in the pervasive e-health services industry, promote public confidence and the development of innovative and affordable pervasive e-health solutions and stimulate industry research and development efforts (Kluge 2007; Verikoukis et al. 2006). However, regulation can also impact the industry in a negative way. Increasing the regulatory compliance burden for stakeholders can increase the overall cost of operation, which can impede the development and deployment of pervasive e-health services by acting as a barrier and thus hampering pervasive e-health innovations (Fisher and Harindranath 2004; Folger 2001; Hsu et al. 2005; Ooijevaar 2010; Tongia 2007).

It is not until particular pervasive e-health services have been commercialized that their originators realize the problems that they pose to patients in particular and more broadly to society (MacInnes 2005). Therefore, "one needs to be concerned with societal, legal, and general economic factors" (MacInnes 2005, p. 7) when a service technology has reached a minimum standard of performance and reliability. This is a stage that is generally overlooked. That is, answers are needed for potential legal, societal, and general economic concerns that pervasive e-health solutions may introduce (Goggin and Spurgeon 2005; MacInnes 2005; Parente 2000).

Even though regulation has been attracting the attention of policy makers as e-health matures, regulatory regimes around the globe are ill-equipped and moving slowly for dealing with these technologies (Hsu et al. 2005; Ooijevaar 2010). In fact, there are growing concerns in extant literature that regulatory agencies have failed to keep abreast with developments in the pervasive e-health realm (Fried et al. 2000; Goldsmith 2000). Yet, extant research also shows that regulatory issues including legal barriers have been identified as a major force in the development and deployment of pervasive e-health services (Holliday and Tam 2004; Min et al. 2007). In fact, because extant policy frameworks that are inherited from specific national and international settings are "not well-placed to deal with contemporary communications technologies that blur the boundaries among these" (Goggin and Spurgeon 2005, p.181), pervasive e-health services may not always fit within traditional healthcare regulation models (Ooijevaar 2010). For example, while in some regulatory regimes there may be legal obstacles that influence the reimbursement structures and payments when treatments are carried out in the e-health realm (e.g., Internet), in others there are limitations that mandate physical face-to-face physician–patient consultation thereby restricting the use of corresponding emerging e-health opportunities (Holliday and Tam 2004). These examples suggest that regulation can shape the form pervasive e-health solutions will (or will not) take (Ooijevaar 2010; Parente 2000).

In this chapter, we aim to address these concerns by developing an institutional regulatory framework. Our objective is to leverage on extant literature by using the institution-based view as a tool to investigate how regulation can affect pervasive e-health solutions. This chapter is structured as follows. First, we examine the institution-based view as a theoretical base after which we address prominent regulatory issues as they apply to pervasive e-health services. The chapter culminates with an institutional regulatory framework for pervasive e-health services. We conclude by discussing managerial implications and proposing directions for future research.

4.2 Institution-Based View

The institution-based view suggests that institutions interact with organizations or networks of organizations by indicating which choices can be acceptable and supportable, that is, institutions reflect "humanly devised constraints that structure human interaction" (North 1990, p. 3). These constraints take the shape of "regulative, normative, and cognitive structures and activities that provide stability and meaning to social behavior" (Scott 1995, p.33).

In providing constraints and establishing the "rules of the game" (Peng et al. 2009, p. 64), institutional frameworks can help minimize uncertainty in the environment in which organizations operate. Institutional frameworks can comprise both formal and informal constraints. While formal constraints are regulatory, and thus coercive in nature, and include laws (e.g., economic liberalization), regulations (e.g., regulatory regime), and political rules (e.g., transparency and/or corruption), informal constraints include socially accepted norms of behaviors that are entrenched in culture, ethical standards, and ideology (North 1990; Peng et al. 2009; Scott 1995).

There is agreement amongst scholars that institutions are more than background conditions (Ingram and Silverman 2002; Peng et al. 2008, 2009) in that they "directly determine what arrows a firm has in its quiver as it struggles to formulate and implement strategy" (Ingram and Silverman 2002, p. 20). That is, actions that are carried out and outcomes that are sought by organizations and networks of organizations must conform to formal and informal rules of what can and cannot be done (Lu et al. 2003). Thus, the manner in which organizational stakeholders behave in their environment and their strategic choices are a reflection of the formal and information constraints of the institutional context that practitioners and decision-makers face (Oliver 1997; Peng 2002; Scott 1995).

In the healthcare industry, all stakeholders operate within the boundary of a regulated environment (Peng et al. 2008, 2009). In extant literature, both formal and informal aspects of the institutional context have been taken for granted and have been assumed away as "background" (Peng et al. 2008, p. 922) conditions (Barney 2001; Barney et al. 2001; Narayanan and Fahey 2005). Further research is required examining the interactions between institutions and organizations in the healthcare industry, particularly in contexts where pervasive e-health services are growing (Kluge 2007; Narayanan and Fahey 2005; Ooijevaar 2010). However, understanding of these interactions and the institutional context is important, particularly in complex knowledge-intensive settings, such as healthcare and e-health as it can help deepen current understanding concerning ensuing strategic behaviors of stakeholders (Ingram and Silverman 2002). Institutional settings can create a conducive (or restrictive) atmosphere that determines an organization's behavior in its market. It follows that the development of pervasive e-health solutions may be better understood with a full examination of the institutional setting where organizations interact in attempts to achieve their objectives. Furthermore, institutional frameworks can also determine the nature of the networks that organizations build (Meyer et al. 2009). Cost and risks of being involved in organizational networks for developing pervasive e-health solutions are likely to decrease (Meyer et al. 2009) as transparency and predictability increase and information asymmetry is reduced (Peng and Heath 1996). Conversely, where institutional frameworks are weaker and information asymmetries exist, their presence maybe "conspicuous," which can increase both the costs and risks of becoming involved in the development of e-health solutions (Meyer et al. 2009).

In this chapter, we focus on the formal aspects of the institution-based view in the healthcare industry with particular reference to pervasive e-health. These aspects are encapsulated in a regulatory regime, which is "a form of public policy" (Wilks 1996) that includes monitoring and intervention in order to remedy any form of perceived social injustice (Benoliel 2003; Fisher and Harindranath 2004). Thus, a regulatory regime is meant to protect patients, but also to be reactive to market dynamics in order not to over- or underregulate. On the one hand, overregulation can bring several adverse outcomes to the industry including high engagement costs and possible duplicative and confusing rules for all stakeholders including patients (AMTA 2005; Benoliel 2003). On the other hand, underregulation can also lead to adverse outcomes for the healthcare industry including patient exposure to unfair and illicit practices (Benoliel 2003). The manner in which stakeholder interactions are influenced by the regulatory regime has direct implications on the healthcare industry and on the manner in which pervasive e-health solutions are developed and deployed.

4.3 Regulatory Issues

In this section, we discuss prominent regulatory issues as they impact pervasive e-health services including privacy, quality of online health content, and access to development resources.

4.3.1 Privacy

Privacy is the right of individuals to be left alone. It includes information privacy, which represents the individual's desire to have access to and exercise control over their personal information that is collected, held, and used by healthcare providers (Minch 2004; Newman and Bach 2004; Ng-Kruelle et al. 2001). Privacy has been and still is one of the core issues in healthcare generally and pervasive e-health services more specifically (Boulding 2000). Because many pervasive e-health services rely on the Internet and/or wireless networks as data delivery infrastructures, there is unease and concerns of possible patient privacy violations amongst many stakeholders particularly when data are sensitive in nature (e.g., private patient data and health information; Wen and Tan 2002).

Privacy regulation as it pertains to pervasive e-health services needs to establish that special security measures are undertaken by healthcare providers to ensure that patient information is not inadvertently disclosed or leaked to or even shared with any stakeholder without the patient's explicit agreement or advance consent (e.g., "opt in"; Boulding 2000; Jones et al. 2004). Such obligation of healthcare providers that hold personal identifiable health information to protect a person's privacy is commonly referred to as confidentiality (Lumpkin 2000). That is, holders of personal identifiable health information can only share such information on the basis of fair information practices and established regulations (Lumpkin 2000).

Ineffective and inadequate regulatory conditions can be exploited for illicit purposes by unethical stakeholders that interface with patients (Ubacht 2004). Consequently, the patients' perceived credibility and trust on pervasive e-health solutions and more broadly in the healthcare system can be adversely affected, if undesirable opportunistic behaviors occur (Rao and Troshani 2007; Troshani and Rao Hill 2008). Specific legislation and regulation is, therefore, required for safeguarding patients' rights to privacy (Boulding 2000).

Another important concept related to privacy and confidentiality is that of security, which concerns the extent to which "information can be stored with access limited to those who are authorized" (Lumpkin 2000). With security, personal identifiable health information needs to be protected while it is in storage (e.g., in a hard-disk drive or backup devices) or in transit from one location to another via networked computers or the Internet (i.e., being e-mailed). Whether in storage or in transit health information needs to be protected against vulnerabilities (e.g., hacker attacks) using technologies such as encryption, which have been proven to help achieve confidentiality, authentication, and message integrity (Galanxhi-Janaqi and Nah 2004;

Lu et al. 2003; Lumpkin 2000). For example, public key infrastructure and certification authorities, which commonly use public key cryptography to encrypt and decrypt mobile transmissions and authenticate both patients and healthcare providers.

Privacy and the manner in which it is achieved by way of confidentiality and security are critical to create a trusting healthcare environment as well as patient confidence in pervasive e-health services. Trust determines the patients' expectations in their relationships with their healthcare providers, and it increases their perceived certainty concerning the provider's expected behavior. More generally, trust is essential in all economic activities where undesirable opportunistic behavior is likely to occur (Gefen et al. 2003). Trust becomes particularly vital in healthcare settings where pervasive e-health solutions are in use and where situational factors such as uncertainty or risk and information asymmetry are present (Ba and Pavlou 2002). On the one hand, patients may be unable to judge the trustworthiness of healthcare providers, and on the other, the latter can also easily take advantage of the former by engaging in harmful opportunistic behaviors. For example, healthcare providers can engage in illicit behaviors including selling or sharing the personal information of its patients.

Ironically, the same information practices, which provide value to both patients and healthcare providers also cause privacy concerns. Some of these concerns include: the type of information that can be collected about patients and the ways in which it will be protected; the stakeholders and entities that can access this information and their accountability; and the ways in which the information will be used (Galanxhi-Janaqi and Nah 2004). In healthcare settings where pervasive e-health services are used, a trusting environment can be encapsulated in perceived credibility (Lin and Wang 2005; Lin and Lee 2005; Wang et al. 2003). Evidence shows that there is a significant direct relationship between perceived credibility and the intention to adopt pervasive e-health services (Lin and Wang 2005).

4.3.2 *Quality of Online Health Content*

Online health content quality concerns websites that provide medical advice or distribute medical information or healthcare education to patients ubiquitously (Bodkin and Miaoulis 2007; Houston et al. 2003). Patients demand and can have both synchronous and asynchronous access to scientific evidence, online doctors, educational materials, support groups, and online counseling (Cudore and Bobrowski 2003; Paris and Ferranti 2001). Typically, online health content sites offer free information concerning disease treatments, wellness, and lifestyle management programs. Quality health content is important because well-informed patients can become productive participants and take responsibility in their healthcare and treatment regimen. There are, however, growing concerns that this information might be incomplete, incorrect, biased, or even misleading since the sites that offer it often rely heavily on sponsorship and advertising revenues from sponsoring organizations such as pharmaceutical companies or even private hospitals (Eysenbach 2000).

While there are debates in the literature supporting both forms of outright government regulation and industry self-regulation, there is general agreement that the perceived quality of online health content can impact on patient trust, which can, in turn, adversely affect patient's confidence in these websites, and their intentions to interact with them (McKnight et al. 2002). This suggests that some form of regulation that attempts to rate content quality is necessary (Huang et al. 2010). Whether implemented by government regulators, industry associations, or third party accreditation agencies, online health content quality should be measured against quality assurance and compliance criteria that are set by credible and authoritative bodies that aim at filtering content for compliance and quality assurance before it is made publicly available (Terry 2002). For example, filtering can ensure that: (1) editorially independent health content is not unduly influenced by sponsorship and advertising content, and that website design and layout clearly and unambiguously indicates the differences between these two types of content; (2) websites clearly explain to online patients the limitations and risks of using online health advice exclusively to address their medical problems; and (3) websites provide convenient mechanisms for patients to provide feedback (Boulding 2000; Eysenbach 2000). While additional functionality can be tested for compliance, the general purpose is to protect patients from dubious practices and educate content providers about their responsibilities.

4.3.3 Access to Development Resources

Government organizations and industry associations can also facilitate the regulation of pervasive e-health services by assisting with knowledge development and deployment, subsidies, and standardization. These can assist health content providers and e-health services developers create compliant applications and content repositories.

Knowledge Development The creation of technical and business knowledge underlying the development of pervasive health content and services is essential for the success of emerging areas such as e-health. Currently, while evidence suggests that many e-health content providers have exhibited a huge interest for distributing e-health content electronically via the Internet or mobile channels, the knowledge concerning the ways that such content can be adequately formatted is limited. Funding research or coordinating taskforces that build this knowledge are two possible options for e-health industry stakeholders (Choudhrie et al. 2003; Damsgaard and Lyytinen 2001; King et al. 1994).

Knowledge Deployment Once built, development knowledge and technical knowhow needs to be deployed and this is important not only for building awareness amongst stakeholders, but also for showing them how e-health business models operate. Government organizations and industry associations could become proactive in undertaking additional knowledge deployment measures including education and training. These measures can help pervasive e-health service developers acquire the necessary knowledge and learn about the ways that they can format and structure e-health content and services for various channels (e.g., mobile), and to distribute to patients. As part of knowledge deployment, many argue the need for publicizing success stories of exemplar e-health services providers in the local media and industry newsletters. Publicized success stories set examples and could help new entrants in the industry learn about critical success factors and lessons learnt from past experiences.

Subsidies Often governments, industry associations, and other powerful players in the market may provide subsidies to players in emerging industries such as e-health, which can help fund innovative pervasive e-health services, and research and development initiatives (Choudhrie et al. 2003; Damsgaard and Lyytinen 2001; King et al. 1994; Muzzi and Kautz 2004).

Standardization Involves developing standards or local practices that can be adopted by all stakeholders involved in the provision of pervasive e-health services and limiting the use of other options (Choudhrie et al. 2003; Damsgaard and Lyytinen 2001; King et al. 1994; Lyytinen and Damsgaard 2001). This is essential for the development and widespread diffusion of these services. The lack of industry standards can make the development of pervasive e-health services prohibitively costly.

4.4 An Institutional Framework for Pervasive e-Health Services

An institutional regulatory setting is generally implemented by organizations with legislative powers, such as regulatory bodies. These regulate the context in which pervasive e-health services are developed, deployed, and used. It is vital for such a framework to be well understood by all stakeholders that operate in a healthcare system. Compliance failure can have serious consequences that can range from fines, to reputation damage or even operation license loss (Fisher and Harindranath 2004). Therefore, the institutional framework can provide regulatory certainty and predictability, which is essential for all healthcare stakeholders (Fisher and Harindranath 2004; Niemeyer 2001). However, for emerging industries such as the pervasive e-health solutions, regulatory authorities have to deal with a multitude of heterogeneous networked stakeholders. Furthermore, as pervasive e-health services are dynamic and still undergoing rapid changes, regulatory definitions become a moving target, which implies that regulators should constantly acquire industry-specific knowledge over time (Tallberg et al. 2007; Ubacht 2004). Consequently, the institutional regulatory context in the domain of pervasive e-health services can become extremely complex and achieving regulatory certainty may be an elusive undertaking or even unrealistic (Fisher and Harindranath 2004).

We argue that a coregulation approach may be adopted for regulating pervasive e-health services. Accordingly, coregulation represents close collaboration between regulatory bodies, including government organizations, industry associations and third party accreditation bodies, and the e-health industry in terms of a mixture

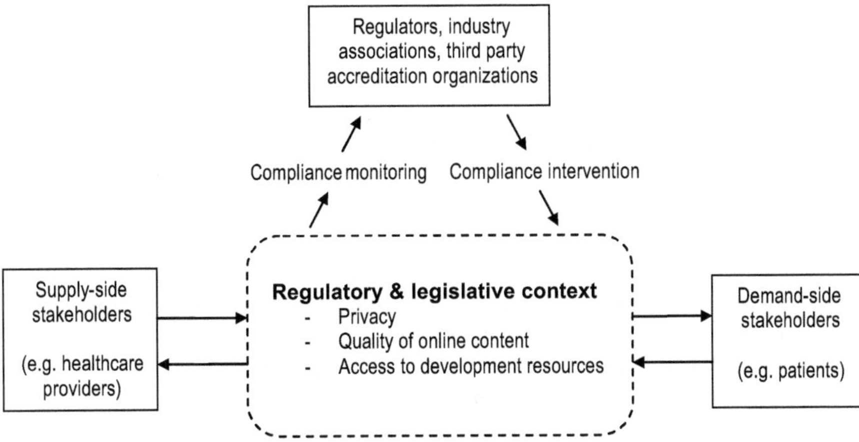

Fig. 4.1 Institutional regulatory framework for pervasive e-health services

of direct monitoring and intervention through legislation, on the one hand, and complete self-regulation, on the other. There is no direct regulation, nor is there pure self-regulation. Regulatory bodies can provide the e-health industry with some parameters concerning the regulatory issues discussed in the previous section in which key problems are to be solved. It is, subsequently, the responsibility of the pervasive e-health services industry to work out the details that best suit the specific technologies used and business models adopted. The role of the regulator is, thus, to allow the industry to apply its own codes in the first instance and to monitor the effectiveness and enforcement of those codes.

The diagram in Fig. 4.1 integrates the regulatory issues discussed previously with the notion of coregulation to form the proposed institutional regulatory framework for the pervasive e-health services industry. This constitutes a contribution to the existing body of knowledge as it provides an integrative view of regulatory issues concerning the emerging pervasive e-health services industry. The issues included in this framework are consistent with the ideas presented in the work of Boulding (2000) and Terry (2002). The institutional context issues covered by the proposed framework are feasible for two reasons. First, they feature heavily in the literature as important prerequisites for the effective regulation of the pervasive e-health services industry. Second, these issues have been implemented in various forms in other industries.

Figure 4.1 also shows that the institutional regulatory framework operates via compliance monitoring and intervention. First, monitoring may be implemented by establishing suitable reporting mechanisms. Second, intervention should only occur in cases of compliance violations or market failure. Regulatory issues included in our framework impact all stakeholders in the pervasive e-health services industry. It follows that during compliance, stakeholder interaction is likely to be frictionless.

However, if conflicts do occur, regulators, industry associations, or third party accreditation organizations can intervene. In any case, the development and operation of the proposed institutional regulatory framework should not interfere with or distort future market or industry developments.

With coregulation, the pervasive e-health services industry is empowered to take responsibility for participating in the development of its own regulation. Three major benefits emerge with this approach: first, regulation costs are likely to be significantly reduced; second, compliance is likely to occur naturally, and therefore, regulation in itself is likely to be perceived to be less restrictive and onerous than in traditional regulation models; and third, industry-driven coregulation also has the advantage to ensure that it is likely to remain appropriate and be responsive to changing market conditions and technology development and capable of delivering timely and transparent outcomes. Taken together, these advantages are likely to promote business activity, market integrity, and patient confidence in emerging pervasive e-health services.

4.5 Conclusion, Implications, and Future Research

Creating a solid institutional regulatory context in the fast evolving pervasive e-health services industry can be an extremely difficult task. There are many reasons for this, including the highly complex nature of the networks and stakeholder relationships required to provide pervasive e-health services as well as the constantly evolving underlying technologies. There are growing calls from both scholars and practitioners alike for further research in this area. In response to these calls, this chapter draws on existing literature and it proposes an institutional regulatory framework suitable for the pervasive e-health services industry. We have first provided the motivation for further work in this area. We have subsequently discussed the proposed framework, which comprises three major components: first, privacy, including confidentiality and security, second, quality of online health content, and third, access to development resources, including knowledge development and deployment, subsidies, and standardization. We argue that these encompass the interests of the main stakeholders operating in the pervasive e-health services industry and given its dynamic and complex nature, coregulation is the most effective approach to minimize costs and enhance compliance.

We believe that this framework is the first of its kind, and, thus, it contributes to the existing body of knowledge, which can be employed by both academics and practitioners alike. First, it can be invaluable to stakeholders in the pervasive e-health services industry in helping them improve their understanding of the institutional factors that enhance or constrain their positions in their value chain and industry. A deeper understanding of such factors can help stakeholders in many ways in: (1) achieving a valuable competitive advantage. Stakeholders that exhibit compliance with regulatory rules that benefit e-health services users may achieve their trust more effectively than those who do not (Killström et al. 2006; Meyer et al. 2009);

(2) providing stakeholders the opportunity to "achieve knowledge on legal issues, to stay away from legal areas in which processes are unclear, and to avoid related risks" (Kijl et al. 2005, pp. 66–67), which decreases potential transaction costs (Kijl et al. 2005; Woolfson 2005); and (3) helping avoid unbalanced legal rights amongst stakeholders, which can severely threaten businesses by causing otherwise innovative business practices to be illicit (Kijl et al. 2005; Killström et al. 2006; Meyer et al. 2009; Woolfson 2005). Second, regulatory and legislative influences can have direct implications on how pervasive e-health services and related business practices are designed and how they operate at organizational, industry, and institutional levels. Furthermore, these influences can determine the nature of pervasive e-health services that can be offered and their diffusion trajectories amongst end-users or patients (MacInnes 2005; Meyer et al. 2009; Spiller and Zelner 1997).

There are certain practical implications that can be derived from this discussion. First, the framework shows that critical dependencies exist amongst stakeholders in their networks and the institutional context in which they operate. A deep understanding of the institutional context is critical for enabling the development and deployment of pervasive e-health services. Knowledge and appreciation of the importance of the institutional context factors discussed in this chapter may help healthcare providers to both design new services or enhance existing ones in order to both help patients and gain competitive advantage (Feldmann 2002). Second, our analysis also offers insights to proactive and reactive stakeholders about the manner in which they can interact with others without violating the existing institutional context. Third, understanding of institutional context factors in the pervasive e-health services industry can provide insights to marketers in designing high-quality and effective promotional campaigns for their new service offerings and by doing so promote the establishment of a trusting environment (Feldmann 2002; Xu 2007). For instance, marketing campaigns may emphasize privacy protection, etc. as a way of establishing and strengthening trust in the emerging pervasive e-health services industry.

While we have used extant research as a primary basis to make a contribution to current understanding of institutional regulatory factors operating in the pervasive e-health services, we also recognize that this review can be more comprehensive. We appreciate that a limitation of this study is that the institutional factors examined in this chapter were sourced by using secondary data, which suggest that the proposed framework may not be generalizeable or even exhaustive. Therefore, we propose that for using our institutional framework as a starting point further research is needed to both validate these factors and extend them further. In addition, further work should focus on enforcement mechanisms of the components of the framework. Third, different countries represent different regulatory jurisdictions (Verikoukis et al. 2006). As various supply-side stakeholders (e.g., healthcare providers) increasingly offer pervasive e-health services across national borders, further research is required for developing regulatory interfaces for transnational healthcare (Rao Hill and Troshani 2010; Troshani and Rao Hill 2009).

References

AMTA. (2005). *AMTA Response to regulation taskforece isues paper 2005*. Australian Capital Territory: Australian Mobile Telecommunications Association.

Anderson, J. G. (2007). Social, ethical and legal barriers to e-health. *International Journal of Medical Informatics, 76*(5–6), 480–483.

Ba, S., & Pavlou, P. A. (2002). Evidence of the effect of trust building technology in electronic markets: Price premiums and buyer behavior. *MIS Quarterly, 26*(3), 243–268.

Barney, J. B. (2001). Is the resource-based "view" a useful perspective for strategic management research? Yes. *Academy of Management Review, 26*(1), 41–56.

Barney, J. B., Wright, M., & Ketchen, D. J. J. (2001). The resource-based view of the firm: Ten years after 1991. *Journal of Management, 27,* 625–641.

Benoliel, D. (2003). Cyberspace technological standardization: An institutional theory retrospective. *Berkeley Technology Law Journal, 18*(4), 1259–1339.

Bodkin, C., & Miaoulis, G. (2007). eHealth information quality and ethics issues: An exploratory study of consumer perceptions. *International Journal of Pharmaceutical and Healthcare Marketing, 1*(1), 27–42.

Boulding, M. E. (2000). Self-regulation: Who needs it? *Health Affairs, 19*(6), 133–139.

Camponovo, G., & Pigneur, Y. (2003). *Business model analysis applied to mobile business*. Paper presented at the 5th International Conference on Enterprise Information Systems (ICEIS 2003), Angers, France, 23–26 April.

Choudhrie, J., Papazafeiropoulou, A., & Lee, H. (2003). A web of stakeholders and strategies: A case of broadband diffusion in South Korea. *Journal of Information Technology, 18*(4), 281–290.

Cudore, B. A., & Bobrowski, P. E. (2003). How effective are healthcare web sites for marketers? *Marketing Health Services, 23*(3), 37–41.

Damsgaard, J., & Lyytinen, K. (2001). The role of intermediating institutions in the diffusion of electronic data interchange (EDI): How industry associations intervened in Denmark, Finland, and Hong Kong. *The Information Society, 17*(3), 195–210.

Eysenbach, G. (2000). Towards ethical guidelines for e-health: JMIR theme issue on eHealth Ethics. *Journal of Medical Internet Research, 2*(1), 1–7.

Feldmann, V. (2002). Competitive strategy for media companies in the mobile internet. *Schmalenbach Business Review, 54,* 351–371.

Ferraud-Ciandet, N. (2010). Privacy and data protection in ehealth: Aa comparative approach between South African and French legal systems. In P. Cunningham & M. Cunningham (Eds.), *IST-Africa 2010 Conference Proceedings*: IIMC International Information Management Corporation.

Fisher, J., & Harindranath, G. (2004). Regulation as a barrier to electronic commerce in Europe: The case of the European fund management industry. *European Journal of Information Systems, 13*(4), 260–272.

Folger, M. (2001). *Conduct of business and e-regulation*. Paper presented at the Second Annual Conference on E-Regulation of Financial Services, Westminster and City Programmes.

Fried, B. M., Weinreich, G., Cavalier, G. M., & Lester, K. J. (2000). E-health: Technologic revolution meets regulatory constraint. *Health Affairs, 19*(1), 124–131.

Galanxhi-Janaqi, H., & Nah, F. F.-H. (2004). U-commerce: Emerging trends and research issues. *Industrial Management & Data Systems, 104*(9), 744–755.

Gefen, D., Karahanna, E., & Straub, D. W. (2003). Trust and TAM in online shopping: An integrated model. *MIS Quarterly, 27*(1), 51–90.

Goggin, G., & Spurgeon, C. (2005). Mobile message services and communications policy. *Prometheus, 23*(2), 181–193.

Goldsmith, J. (2000). How will the Internet change our health system? *Health Affairs, 19*(1), 148–156.

Holliday, I., & Tam, W.-K. (2004). E-health in the East Asian tigers. *International Journal of Medical Informatics, 73*(11–12), 759–769.

Houston, T. K., Sands, D. Z., Nash, B. R., & Ford, D. E. (2003). Experiences of physicians who frequently use email with patients. *Health Communication, 15*(4), 515–525.

Hsu, J., Huang, J., Kinsman, J., Fireman, B., Miller, R., Selby, J., et al. (2005). Use of e-health services between 1999–2002: A growing digital divide. *The Journal of the American Medical Association, 12*(2), 164–171.

Huang, W., Seitz, J., & Wickramasinghe, N. (2010). *Manifesto for e-health success*. Proceedings of the 14th Pacific Asia Conference on Information Systems (PACIS 2010), Taipei, Taiwan, July 9–12.

Ingram, P., & Silverman, B. (2002). Introduction. In P. Ingram & B. Silverman (Eds.), *The new institionalism in strategic management* (pp. 1–30). Amsterdam: Elsevier.

Jones, R., Rogers, R., Roberts, J., Gaunt, N., Campbell, J., Thorogood, M., et al. (2004). *E-health stakeholder consultation and policy context review. Report for the National Co-ordinating Centre for NHS Service Delivery and Organisation R & D (NCCSDO) programme of research on e-health*. Plymouth: University of Plymouth.

Kijl, B., Bouwman, H., Haaker, T., & Faber, E. (2005). *Dynamic business models in mobile service value networks: A theoretical and conceptual framework (FRUX/D2.2-II)*. The Netherlands: TU Delft.

Killström, U., Galli, L., Haaker, T., Immonen, O., Kijl, B., Pitkänen, O., et al. (2006). *Initial marketplace dynamics (incl. business models) analysis (IST-2004-511607 MobiLife)*. Finland: Information Society Technologies.

King, J. L., Gurbaxani, V., Kraemer, K. L., McFarlan, F. W., Raman, K. S., & Yap, C. S. (1994). Institutional factors in information technology innovation. *Information Systems Research, 5*(2), 139–169.

Kluge, E.-H. W. (2007). Secure e-health: Managing risks to patient health data. *International Journal of Medical Informatics, 76*(5–6), 402–406.

Lin, H. F., & Lee, G. G. (2005). Impact of organizational learning and knowledge management factors on e-business adoption. *Management Decision, 43*(2), 171–188.

Lin, H., & Wang, Y. (2005). Predicting consumer intention to use mobile commerce in Taiwan. In W. Brookes, E. Lawrence, R. Steele, & E. Chang (Eds.), *International Conference on Mobile Business*. July 11–13, 2005, Sydney, Australia: IEEE Computer Society.

Lu, J., Yu, C., Liu, C., & Yao, J. E. (2003). Technology acceptance model for wireless internet. *Internet Research: Electronic Networking Applications and Policy, 13*(3), 206–222.

Lumpkin, J. R. (2000). E-health, HIPAA, and beyond. *Health Affairs, 19*(6), 149–151.

Lyytinen, K., & Damsgaard, J. (2001). *What's wrong with the diffusion of innovation theory: The case of a complex and networked technology*. Paper presented at the IFIP 8.6, Banff, Canada.

MacInnes, I. (2005). Dynamic business model framework for emerging technologies. *International Journal of Services Technology and Management, 6*(1), 3–19.

McKnight, D., Choudhury, V., & Macmar, C. (2002). The impact of initial consumer trust on intentions to transact with a web site: A trust building model. *Journal of Strategic Information Systems, 11*, 297–323.

Meyer, K. E., Estrin, S., Bhaumik, S. K., & Peng, M. W. (2009). Institutions, resources, and entry strategies in emerging economies. *Strategic Management Journal, 30*(1), 61–80.

Min, S. D., Lee, B. W., Yoon, S. W., Lee, Y. B., Kim, J. K., Lee, M., et al. (2007). *Actual condition of Korean e-health: What do enterprisers want for developing e-health industry?* Proceedings of the 9th International Conference on e-Health Networking, Application and Services, Taipei, Taiway, June 19–22.

Minch, R. P. (2004). *Privacy issues in location-aware mobile devices*. Proceedings of the 37th Hawaii International Conference on System Sciences, Hawaii, January 5–8.

Muzzi, C., & Kautz, K. (2004). Information and communication technologies diffusion in industrial districts. In J. Damsgaard & H. Z. Henriksen (Eds.), *Networked information technologies: Diffusion and adoption* (pp. 19–38). Dordrecht: Kluwer.

Narayanan, V. K., & Fahey, L. (2005). The relevance of the institutional underpinning of Porter's five forces framework to emerging economies: An epistemological analysis. *Journal of Management Studies, 42*(1), 207–223.

Newman, A. L., & Bach, D. (2004). Privacy and regulation in a digital age. In B. Preissl, H. Bouwman, & C. Steinfield (Eds.), *E-life after the Dot.Com bust*. Heidelberg: Physica-Verlag.
Ng-Kruelle, G., Swatman, P. A., Rebne, D. S., & Hempe, J. F. (2001). The price of convenience: Privacy and mobile commerce. *Quarterly Journal of Electronic Commerce, 3*(4), 273–285.
Niemeyer, J. (2001). *An economic analysis of securities market regulation and supervision: Where to go after the Lamfalussy Report? Stockholdm School of Economics/EFI Working Paper Series in Economics and Finance*. Stockholm: Stockholm School of Economics.
North, D. C. (1990). *Institutions, institutional change, and economic performance*. Cambridge: Harvard University Press.
Oliver, C. (1997). Sustainable competitive advantage: Combining institutional and resource-based views. *Strategic Management Journal, 18*, 679–713.
Ooijevaar, J. R. (2010). *The influence of national healthcare regulation on e-health business models: An exploratory comparative case study of four European healthcare markets*. Unpublished Masters Thesis, University of Twente, Enschede.
Parente, S. T. (2000). Beyond the hype: A taxonomy of e-health business models. *Health Affairs, 19*(6), 89–102.
Paris, J., & Ferranti, J. (2001). The changing fact of medicine: Health care on the internet. *Journal of Perinatology, 21*(1), 34–39.
Peng, M. W. (2002). Towards an institution-based view of business strategy. *Asia Pacific Journal of Management, 19*(2/3), 251–267.
Peng, M. W., & Heath, P. (1996). The growth of the firm in planned economies in transition: Institutions, organizations, and strategic choices. *Academy of Management Review, 21*, 492–528.
Peng, M. W., Wang, D. Y. L., & Jiang, Y. (2008). An institution-based view of international business strategy: A focus on emerging economies. *Journal of International Business Studies, 39*(5), 920–936.
Peng, M. W., Sun, S. L., Pinkham, B., & Chen, H. (2009). The institution-based view as a third leg for a strategy tripod. *Academy of Management Perspectives, 23*(3), 63–81.
Piotti, B., & Macome, E. (2007). Public healthcare in Mozambique: Strategic issues in the ICT development during managerial changes and public reforms. *International Journal of Medical Informatics, 76*(1), 185–194.
Rao, S., & Troshani, I. (2007). A conceptual framework and propositions for the acceptance of mobile services. *Journal of Theoretical and Applied Electronic Commerce Research, 2*(2), 61–73.
Rao Hill, S., & Troshani, I. (2010). Factors influencing the adoption of personalisation mobile services: Empirical evidence from young Australians. *International Journal of Mobile Communications, 8*(2), 150–168.
Scott, W. R. (1995). *Institutions and organizations*. Thousand Oaks: Sage.
Sohn, M., & Lee, J. (2007). *U-health in Korea: Opportunities and challenges*. Proceedings of the Portland International Center for Management of Engineering and Technology (PICMET 2007), Portland, Oregon, August 5–9.
Spiller, P. T., & Zelner, B. A. (1997). Product complementarities, capabilities and governance: A dynamic transaction cost perspective. *Industrial and Corporate Change, 6*(3), 561–594.
Tallberg, M., Hämmäinen, H., Töyli, J., Kamppari, S., & Kivi, A. (2007). Impacts of handset bundling on mobile data usage: The case of Finland. *Telecommunications Policy, 31*(10/11), 648–659.
Terry, N. (2002). Regulating health information: A US perspective. *British Medical Journal, 324*(7337), 602–605.
Tongia, R. (2007). Connectivity in emerging regions: The need for improved technology and business models. *IEEE Communications Magazine, 45*(1), 96–103.
Troshani, I., & Rao Hill, S. (2008). A proposed framework for mobile services adoption: A review of existing theories, extensions, and future research directions. In G. C. Karmakar & L. S. Dooley (Eds.), *Mobile multimedia communications: Concepts, applications and challenges* (pp. 85–108). Hershey: Idea Group Publishing.

Troshani, I., & Rao Hill, S. (2009). Linking stakeholder salience with mobile services diffusion. *International Journal of Mobile Communications, 7*(3), 269–289.

Ubacht, J. (2004). Regulatory practice in telecommunications markets: How to grasp the 'real world of public action'? *Communications & Strategies, 54*(2nd Quarter), 219–242.

Verikoukis, C., Konstas, I., Anastasiadou, D., & Angelidis, P. (2006). Overview on telecommunications regulation framework in south-eastern Europe. *Telecommunication Systems, 32*(2/3), 209–221.

Wang, Y.-S., Wang, Y.-M., Lin, H.-H., & Tang, T.-I. (2003). Determinants of user acceptance of Internet banking: An empirical study. *International Journal of Service Industry Management, 14*(5), 501–519.

Wen, H. J., & Tan, J. (2002). *The evolving face of telemedicine & e-health: Opening doors and closing gaps in e-health services: Opportunities & challenges*. Proceedings of the 36th Hawaii International Conference on System Sciences, Hawaii.

Wilks, S. (1996). Regulatory compliance and capitalist diversity in Europe *Journal of European Public Policy, 3*(4), 536–559.

Woolfson, M. (2005). Can self-regulation protect the mobile industry from crooks? *New Media Age, 17/03/2005*, 16.

Xu, D. J. (2007). The influence of personalization in affecting consumer attitudes toward mobile advertising in China. *Journal of Computer Information Systems, Winter 2006–2007,* 9–19.

Chapter 5
e-Health Complexity and Actor–Network Theory

Indrit Troshani

Abstract e-health constitutes the use of digitally enabled technologies to facilitate the exchange of clinical, administrative, and transactional healthcare data ubiquitously and has the potential to offer enormous value to all actors operating in healthcare. Delivering healthcare benefits by way of e-health solutions, however, remains an elusive goal for e-health entrepreneurs. The inherent complexity of modern healthcare settings has much to answer for this. In attempts to improve current understanding, this chapter argues how e-health research can be enhanced using actor–network theory (ANT) as an appropriate and powerful tool that can enable researchers to "follow the actors" and, in the process, tackle the underlying complexities of modern healthcare environments.

Keywords e-health · ICT · Healthcare · Complexity · Actor–network theory (ANT)

5.1 Introduction

Recent developments in information and communications technology (ICT) have created enormous opportunities for healthcare, which is information-intensive in nature. e-health is one of these opportunities, which constitutes the use of digitally enabled technologies to facilitate the exchange of clinical, administrative, and transactional data ubiquitously in healthcare settings (Sohn and Lee 2007). It has the potential to create enormous value for all healthcare actors generally, and patients and healthcare providers in particular. It can enable patients to use pervasive healthcare services conveniently and effectively as need arises, while also significantly facilitating healthcare services delivery for providers (Ha and Lee 2008).

Although investments in pervasive e-health have grown recently, growth has lagged behind other industries (Menon et al. 2000; Chiasson and Davidson 2004; Cho et al. 2008). In fact, taking advantage of ICT benefits to efficiently deliver effective and quality services in healthcare remains elusive for e-health entrepreneurs, which suggests that pervasive e-health is a challenging undertaking (Cho et al. 2008). In

I. Troshani (✉)
University of Adelaide Business School, The University of Adelaide,
10 Pulteney Street, Adelaide SA 5005, Australia
e-mail: indrit.troshani@adelaide.edu.au

R. K. Bali et al. (eds.), *Pervasive Health Knowledge Management*,
Healthcare Delivery in the Information Age,
DOI 10.1007/978-1-4614-4514-2_5,

addition to the technical complexity inherent in the hardware and software components of pervasive e-health solutions, these challenges can be also attributed to numerous other factors including the intrinsic complexity of the healthcare industry as it pertains to social issues and communication patterns (Davidson 2000; Kaplan 2001), high levels of leadership and resource commitments (Garabaldi 1998), organizational culture and structure (Bangert and Doktor 2003), institutional changes (Schriger et al. 1997), anticipated and unanticipated healthcare practice changes (Massaro 1993), and inconsistent and potentially incompatible interests and agendas of constituent stakeholders (Constantinides and Barrett 2006). In addition, e-health complexity can also be attributed to the fact that healthcare is multidisciplinary in nature as it builds on various disciplines, including medicine, biomedical engineering, computer and information science, statistics, health promotion and marketing, and management science (Anderson 1997; Chiasson and Davidson 2004; Wickramasinghe et al. 2007).

In this context, Chiasson and Davidson (2004) argue that although there is an increasing number of contributions to e-health research, knowledge in this area remains limited. In particular, extant studies have provided limited coverage of the contextual industry settings that contribute to complexity, which constitutes a limitation since such settings can help understand why pervasive e-health solutions emerge and how they are shaped. In fact, pervasive e-health solutions affect or are affected by configurations of interacting industry and broader environment and societal factors (Atkinson 2000; Benbasat and Zmud 2003; Cho et al. 2008). In relation to this, Chiasson and Davidson (2005) argue that "accounting for industry will help researchers determine the technical and social boundaries of IT artifacts and IS theories" (p. 592). In fact, the resulting IT artifacts generally, and pervasive e-health solutions in particular "encapsulate[s] the structures, routines, norms, and values implicit in the rich contexts within which the artifact is embedded" (Benbasat and Zmud 2003, p. 186).

The objective of this chapter is to enhance current understanding concerning underlying contextual e-health complexity. It culminates with an argument concerning how e-health complexity can be tackled using actor–network theory (ANT) as an appropriate and solid tool to address this complexity. It is hoped that by achieving this objective, e-health research can be extended in ways that systematically capture the contextual and social aspects that support the complex interactions and collaborations, which occur in modern healthcare settings (Timpka et al. 2007). This can be invaluable in designing and implementing pervasive e-health solutions and in informing policy-making at both organizational and broader industry and national levels. There is agreement in the literature that there is paucity of research in this area (Lorenzi et al. 1997, 1998; Timpka et al. 2007).

This chapter is structured as follows. First, we explain why healthcare is complex after which we provide an overview of ANT. Then, we explain why ANT might be a suitable approach for researching e-health and tackling its intrinsic complexities before identifying some challenges that can be encountered in the process.

5.2 Healthcare Complexity

In relation to healthcare complexity, Wilson and Holt (2001) argue that "effective clinical decision making requires a holistic approach that accepts unpredictability and builds on subtle emergent forces within the overall system" (p. 688). It follows that developing and implementing pervasive e-health solutions is also a complex social and technological undertaking (Sohn and Lee 2007), which stems from a range of challenges including creating a new healthcare culture, achieving compatibility with legacy systems, and tailoring pervasive e-health solutions to address complex expectations and needs of heterogeneous stakeholders that have different and even incompatible objectives and agendas.

Healthcare systems are characterized by fuzzy boundaries, in that, actors can change or, at the same time, be members of other systems (Plsek and Greenhalgh 2001). For example, typical healthcare systems are characterized by two broad categories of heterogeneous actors including healthcare service consumers (i.e., patients) and service providers. Consumers are the end-users of particular healthcare services such as personal care or healthcare-related content. Service providers supply services to manage specific health problems that consumers are experiencing and include experts such as clinicians, nurses, dietitians, health information managers, and hospital administrators.

Consumers and providers are connected through communication flows and services requirements and their interaction and communication can be facilitated by pervasive e-health applications and their underlying infrastructures, which are typically supplied by the providers. The e-health applications and infrastructure are created and maintained by network operators, database managers, system administrators and include nonhuman actors such as specialized software, information processing algorithms, and storage devices. Taken together, pervasive e-health applications attempt to facilitate the delivery of healthcare services to patients at the right time and place (Sohn and Lee 2007). In addition to these actors, government regulators and insurance organizations play important roles in creating legal and regulatory frameworks for guiding the manner in which pervasive e-health applications operate. Thus, healthcare settings are characterized by complex webs of interactions of heterogeneous actors that have different and potentially incompatible objectives.

As actors operate in healthcare settings, they adopt sets of their own "internalised rules" (Plsek and Greenhalgh 2001, p. 625), which are driven by mental models, instincts, and potentially inconsistent rules and guidelines, and are not necessarily shared by or even logical to various participating actors in the system. Consequently, actor interactions can lead to "continually emerging, novel behaviour" (Plsek and Greenhalgh 2001, p. 626), and potentially, even unpredictability (Lane and Maxfield 1996), which results when "interactions among parts of a complex system produce variable, new, and unpredictable capabilities that are not inherent in any of the parts acting alone" (Plsek and Wilson 2001, p. 746).

In addition, actor behavior in healthcare settings is not necessarily linear (Wilson and Holt 2001). For instance, using linear assumptions that are governed by textbook rules, guidelines, and protocols as a basis to provide advice to diabetes patients (e.g., if X then Y), may result in chaotic glucose levels and potentially harmful outcomes without considering wider illness history and specific personal circumstances (Plsek and Wilson 2001; Wilson and Holt 2001).

Finally, healthcare systems can be described as networks of networks, in that, they comprise multiple networked systems, which in turn embed or nest yet other (microlevel) systems. This suggests that each system cannot be fully understood in isolation unless other interacting systems at the macro- and microlevels are fully considered. For example, patients' visit patterns at a healthcare center, in addition to their specific illness conditions are also driven by the specific center's locality and wider society and regulatory rules and regulations (Plsek and Greenhalgh 2001). Thus, taken together, these factors can potentially result in adaptive actor behavior, which can ultimately create a fluid reality consisting of a multiplicity of different potentially incompatible realities that pervasive e-health solutions operate in and need to address simultaneously, thereby, resulting in substantial healthcare complexity (Fraser and Greenhalgh 2001; Plsek and Wilson 2001; Sohn and Lee 2007; Broer et al. 2010; Cresswell 2010).

5.3 Actor–Network Theory

ANT offers a framework for investigating how technical artifacts come into being (Bijker et al. 1987; Callon 1991; Latour 1999a; Allen 2004). It addresses the role of technology in social settings and the processes by way of which it influences or is influenced by social elements in a setting over time (Mähring et al. 2004). It focuses on actors and their attempts to secure their interests by forming and strengthening alliances in actor networks, which in turn generate technical artifacts (e.g., an application, a code of practice, hardware components; Akrich 1992). As the actor networks that generate these artifacts become stabilized, the technical artifacts are said to become taken for granted or "irreversible" (Denis et al. 2007).

Actors represent human or nonhuman entities that are able to make their presence individually felt by other actors (Law 1987). ANT provides a symmetrical treatment between the technical and the social aspects of technology, in that both human and nonhuman actors are treated alike. That is, technical artifacts are treated as genuine actors, in that, while just merely physical, technical artifacts constitute a dynamic embodiment of human actors' subjectivities, including their motives, intentions, interests, and prejudices (Faraj et al. 2004). Using the ANT approach can be advantageous particularly for investigating the development of complex technology. It allows investigation to be focused on the nature of an actor network as a representation of complex social interactions consisting of entrepreneurial political activities and negotiations that occur in order to enroll supporting actors or allies. Successful enrollment in a network represents the alignment of the otherwise diverse interests of its actors (McLoughlin 1999), which suggests that to maintain network stability actors must be willing to participate in specific ways of thinking and acting (Walsham 1997).

There are two pivotal concepts underpinning ANT, namely, inscription and translation. Inscription means that actors that develop an artifact seek to embody or inscribe their interests into it. When inscribed, interests may be manifested as specific anticipations and restrictions concerning future usage patterns of the artifact (Hanseth and Monteiro 1997). The artifact, thus, becomes a genuine actor that has the ability to impose the inscribed interest onto other actors, i.e., the users of the artifact. Therefore, the technical aspects of artifacts, their roles, and constitutions are profoundly social (Mähring et al. 2004).

Translation constitutes a variety of negotiation methods whereby different actors' interests are continually aligned to achieve a stable actor network that is dedicated to constructing a technical artifact (Callon 1986a; Rodon et al. 2008). Translation comprises four stages: problematization, interessement, enrollment, and mobilization. During problematization one (or more) initiating actor(s), also known as a focal actor, defines and constructs a problem and articulates the manner in which it affects its interests (Lee and Oh 2006). The focal actor also identifies other actors whose interests are consistent with its own and attempts to establish itself as an indispensable resource and an obligatory passage point for them to resolve the identified problem (Callon 1986b). Problematization is not a singular event, rather a set of dynamic processes whereby the problem emerges and is constructed as a result of following other actors (Broer et al. 2010).The aim of problematization is to frame the identified problem in a way such that different actors draw mutually compatible understandings concerning the way the problem (or its solution) affects their interests rather than make all interests the same (Callon 1986b; Denis et al. 2007; Troshani and Lymer 2010).

Interessement consists of processes that attempt to "lock in" other actors as allies or supporters in the actor network. During interessement, the focal actor attempts to convince others that the interests defined during problematization are aligned with its own. Successful interessement "confirms (more or less completely) the validity of the problematization and the alliances it implies" (Callon 1986b, pp. 209–210). During enrollment, focal actors attempt to define and coordinate roles aiming to stabilize and strengthen the emerging network. It involves "multilateral negotiations, trials of strength and tricks that accompany the interessement and enable them [focal actor(s)] to succeed" (Callon 1986b, p. 211). Successful enrollment in networks represents the alignment of the otherwise diverse interests of its actors, which suggests that to maintain network stability actors must be willing to participate in specific ways of thinking and acting (Walsham 1997).

During mobilization, the focal actor employs methods for ensuring that allies operate in accordance with their agreement and do not betray its interests (Callon 1997). Although temporarily, stability may be achieved in an actor network when allies are mobilized at which point "the underlying ideas have become institutionalized and are no longer seen as controversial" (Mähring et al. 2004, p. 214). Translation and inscription have been summarized in Fig. 5.1 (Troshani and Lymer 2010).

While using distinct translation stages facilitates theoretical discourse, analysis, and understanding, in practice, these stages can be interwoven and fluid (Mähring et al. 2004). In addition, complete translation does not necessarily have to traverse all stages, it may, in fact, fail or stop at any stage (Callon 1986b).

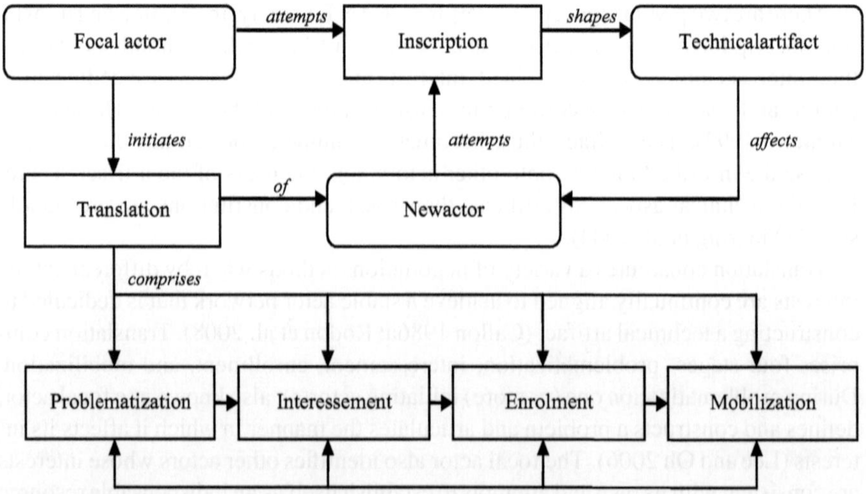

Fig. 5.1 ANT: Inscription and translation. (Adopted from Troshani and Lymer 2010)

With ANT analyses, researchers "follow the actors" and explore how these actors themselves define unfolding events in their attempts to develop technology solutions (e.g., e-health applications) to solve healthcare problems (Latour 1987b, 2005). When an actor network achieves stability or agreement with respect to a technical solution, network actors are said to be aligned. In the healthcare settings, this means that relevant human actors, including patients, clinicians, policy makers , and non-human actors, including diagnostic equipment and software, codes of practice, have become aligned and their network solidified. That is, the emerging e-health applications that these actor networks are attempting to generate have become taken for granted or "irreversible" (Denis et al. 2007; Timpka et al. 2007; Greenhalgh and Stones 2010; Steen 2010).

5.4 Why ANT Can Be Useful in Addressing e-Health Complexity

As previously argued, healthcare generally and e-health in particular are highly complex. For example, a small change in a specific healthcare context can potentially result in a change of actors, their relationships and roles. ANT provides a useful vehicle to capture actor involvement in healthcare processes for many reasons (Sohn and Lee 2007).

First, by focusing on actor networks as the fundamental building blocks in developing pervasive e-health solutions, ANT looks at the relationships between actors as complex social interactions comprising entrepreneurial and political activities and negotiations (Latour 1987a; Garud and Rappa 1994). That is, it examines the manner in which actors form, strengthen, and maintain networks of actor alliances in relation to pervasive e-health solutions, and how their goals are locked into patterns of interactions and in processes of continuous alignment of dynamic interests (Mähring et al. 2004). By focusing on the evolving process of their construction, as opposed to predefined or fixed elements, insights can be gained concerning the effectiveness of the operation of pervasive e-health solutions and the shape that they will (or will not) take in addition to drawing attention to both anticipated and unanticipated consequences of their use in healthcare settings (Broer et al. 2010; Robert et al. 2010). Therefore, ANT allows investigating such questions as how and why pervasive e-health solutions "come into being and how users and other actors conform, ignore, modify, or usurp the original designers' interests" (Faraj et al. 2004, p. 189). In doing so, ANT can help investigate the fluidity of the healthcare reality and the underlying complex actor interactions as they unfold, which might otherwise be missed in postdevelopment assessments (Latour 1987a; Walsham 1997; Hanseth et al. 2004; Lee and Oh 2006; Cresswell 2010).

This is important for two reasons: (1) ANT takes a "action-oriented or formative" (Broer et al. 2010) process-based qualitative approach, which opens up the healthcare "black-box," which is critical if the requirements of e-health solutions are to be fully understood; and (2) there is agreement in the literature that there is a "need to recognize that different actors can play multiple roles in multiple networks at multiple time points" (Cresswell 2010, pp. 4–5). Thus, by recognizing healthcare fluidity, ANT facilitates formative qualitative assessments to studying pervasive e-health solutions while recognizing the coexistence of multiple realities in actor networks thereby challenging predictability assumptions of traditional summative outcome-oriented or causal approaches (Mol 1998; Bate and Robert 2002; Broer et al. 2010; Cresswell 2010).

Second, ANT offers a rich language that allows e-health researchers "not to distinguish a priori between [the] social and technical" (p. 185), thereby encouraging "a detailed description of the concrete mechanisms at work which glue the [actor] network together—without being distracted by the means, technical or non-technical, of actually achieving this" (Hanseth and Monteiro 1997, p. 185). That is, by considering nonhuman actors in healthcare settings, such as e-health hardware devices or pervasive e-health software applications, ANT examines how these can affect the behavior of human actors and are affected by them. This is important because technical objects are "no longer viewed as passive 'black box' containers of information, but as playing an active role that is determined by their position in the ever-changing network" (Cresswell 2010, p. 4). By providing a lexicon that blurs the boundaries between the (nonhuman) technical and human actors, ANT helps achieve depth and richness in capturing the true complexity of healthcare relationships, and consequently, crystallize requirements of pervasive e-health solutions (McLean and Hassard 2004).

Third, ANT can be particularly useful in helping direct analysis toward improving the understanding of unfolding action. This includes identifying and distinguishing the categories of participating actors and their interests, as well as crucial developments concerning pervasive e-health solutions and actions undertaken by actors based on their interests to react to and affect such developments (Ramiller 2005,

2007). Furthermore, with ANT, multiple human actors belonging to the same organization can be collectively deemed as a single actor and their underlying stable networks can be included or excluded from analysis as necessary. According to Hanseth and Monteiro (1997), this is justified as ANT "has a scalable notion of an actor" (p. 190), meaning that it "does not distinguish between a macro- and micro-actor because opening one (macro) black-box, there is always a new actor network" (p. 190). Actors enrolled in and committed to the (microlevel) actor networks within actant organizations can be considered to be spokespersons and representative of the interests of other actors in their organizations. That is, effective translation of actors in an actor network also entails representation (Ramiller 2007), meaning that one actor has the ability to claim the "authority to speak ... on behalf of another actor" (Callon and Latour 1981).

This is consistent with ANT assumptions concerning the use of sociological levels (e.g., individual, group, organization) as units of analysis. Specifically, "ANT focuses on the identification of networks of actors, where the networks themselves are seen to become actors, as the scope of analysis widens. This affords a flexible framework that makes the 'levels' in implementation research a matter of empirical discovery rather than stipulation, and that helps thereby to foster a greater realism in capturing the action that takes place" (Ramiller 2005, p. 53). This approach enables researchers to draw together actors from both micro- and macrocontexts. In doing so, ANT focuses on microcontexts, i.e., how actors interact with one another to shape pervasive e-health solutions, and uses findings to draw conclusions about macrocontexts, i.e., political and institutional environments where actors are embedded (Cresswell 2010).

5.5 Challenges of Using ANT in e-Health

Generally, ANT is criticized for its inherent limited capability for providing empirically verifiable evidence, hence adversely impacting on its ability to provide generalizations (Cresswell 2010). Nevertheless, by providing a rich vocabulary, ANT can help both with explanation and interpretations of healthcare phenomena, which can be information requirements specification of e-health solutions (Law and Hassard 1999). In this section, we discuss critical issues concerning the valid production of ANT accounts. These issues concern the achievement of symmetry, which is necessary in order to strengthen explanation and interpretation in ANT accounts (McLean and Hassard 2004).

The Inclusion/Exclusion Issue With ANT, one must closely "follow the actors" in order to understand how actor network negotiations influence the form that technical artifacts will or will not take (Callon 1986a; Latour 1987a; Law 1991). To address this in practical terms, snowballing can be used to identify actors in e-health solutions networks (Aaker and Day 1990). To decide "who to include and who to exclude" (McLean and Hassard 2004, p. 499), investigative work can be directed at contextualizing a particular pervasive e-health solution as the assemblage that researchers wish to chart (Miller 1996). That is, while following the actors, one can stop when the contextualizers (e.g., e-health solutions negotiations, interactions, alliances) stop, i.e., as references to these contextualizers or specific actors "melt from view" (Law 1991, p. 11).

The Humans/Nonhumans Issue All actors, social or technical, rely on spokespersons to speak on their behalf (Pels 1995). Spokespersons can symmetrically speak for both "people and things, but only humans can act (can be permitted to act) as spokespersons" (Pels 1995, p. 138). Focusing on human interpretations only can provide a social focus or bias of the technical, which may affect symmetry between the two (Collins and Yearley 1992). To minimize this risk, researchers can follow Callon (1986b) who argues that "no point of view is privileged and no interpretation is censored" (p. 200). Thus, researchers can follow all those involved in doing relevant work concerning pervasive e-health solutions, no matter how many and heterogeneous they are (Latour 1987a). Heterogeneous actors can provide different perspectives, which account for multiple realities. In addition to providing triangulation of qualitative data, this also reduces the possibility of interpretations being locked into one mindset. Furthermore, data can be collected from multiple sources. That is, while interviews can be conducted with human actors and spokespersons, technical e-health documentation (e.g., user manuals, data flow diagrams [DFDs], entity relationship diagrams [ERDs], use cases) can also be examined for triangulation and support.

The Privileging and Status Issue Technical actors (e.g., e-health applications or hardware) can be conceptualized as those whose interests they represent and inscribe (Walsham 1997) and which are shaped as "a consequence of the relations in which they are located and performed; that is, in, by and through these relations" (McLean and Hassard 2004, p. 507). e-health researchers can follow Callon and Latour (1981) who argue that in the process of developing e-health solutions, both the social and the technical are "analytically composite" (p. 348) and "twin results" (p. 348) of network building processes and thus, no attempts should be made to analytically favor these solutions (Collins and Yearley 1992). Therefore, the emerging pervasive e-health solutions are indeed actors, but in same manner as other actors, they are susceptible to shaping and constraint (Ramiller 2007).

The Agency Issue Once operational, the developed e-health solutions can act autonomously. While these may facilitate some aspects of human agency, they may also constrain others, in that, "[h]umans try to marshal the agency of the machines to serve their own purposes, but cannot always anticipate and control the consequences" (Rose et al. 2005, p. 147). Where pervasive e-health solutions do not meet requirements, remedies can be identified and implemented for unanticipated consequences suggesting that these solutions have the power of agency (Latour 1999b; Rose et al. 2005). However, with ANT "agency is assumed not to be limited to individuals, objects or social determinants, but as emerging as an effect of interactions of network components" (Cresswell 2010, p. 5).

Heterogeneous Engineering and the Political Issue Law (1991) argues that: "No one, no thing, no class, no gender, can have power unless a set of relations is constituted and held in place: a set of relations that distinguishes between this and that (distribution [of power]), and then goes on to regulate the relations between this and that … power, whatever form it may take, is recursively woven into the intricate dance that unites the social and the technical" (p. 18). On this basis, with ANT, e-health solutions are examined in terms of organizational processes, negotiations, power plays, and political decision making that determine sets of relations and hierarchies between and amongst heterogeneous actors in networks (Winner 1993; Bowker and Star 1999). This helps unearth "political biases that can underlie the spectrum of choice that surface for relevant actors" (Winner 1993, p. 370).

5.6 Conclusions

e-health constitutes the use of digitally enabled technologies to facilitate the exchange of clinical, administrative, and transactional data ubiquitously in healthcare settings and has the potential to offer enormous value for all actors operating in healthcare including patients and healthcare providers (Sohn and Lee 2007; Ha and Lee 2008). Yet, taking advantage of the benefits that e-health can provide to improve the delivery of effective quality services in healthcare remains elusive for e-health entrepreneurs. At least, in part, this is attributed to the complexity of modern healthcare settings where e-health applications are expected to operate (Cho et al. 2008). In attempts to enhance current understanding concerning underlying contextual e-health complexity factors, this chapter argues how e-health complexity can be tackled using ANT as an appropriate and powerful tool. Specifically, it can help specify the requirements of pervasive e-health services that are expected to operate in fluid healthcare settings with fuzzy boundaries where causal and predictable behaviors can be elusive. This is important because ANT can help capture the multiple realities of actor networks thereby potentially enhancing e-health effectiveness.

References

Aaker, D. A., & Day, G. S. (1990). *Marketing research* (4th ed.). New York: Wiley.

Akrich, M. (1992). The de-scription of technical objects. In W. E. Bijker & J. Law (Eds.), *Shaping technology/building society: Studies in sociotechnical change* (pp. 205–224). Cambridge: MIT Press.

Allen, J. P. (2004). Redefining the network: Enrollment strategies in the PDA industry. *Information Technology & People, 7*(2), 171–185.

Anderson, J. G. (1997). Clearing the way for physicians' use of clinical information systems. *Communications of the ACM, 40*(8), 83–90.

Atkinson, C. J. (2000). The 'soft information systems and technologies methodology' (SISTeM): Actor network contingency approach to integrated development. *European Journal of Information Systems, 9*(2), 104–123.

Bangert, D., & Doktor, R. (2003). *The role of organizational culture in the management of clinical e-health systems*. Proceedings of Hawaii International Conference of Systems Sciences (pp. 163–171). Big Island: Computer Society Press.

Bate, P., & Robert, G. (2002). Studying health care "quality" qualitatively: The dilemmas and tensions between different forms of evaluation research within the U.K. National Health Service. *Qualitative Health Research, 12*(7), 91–96.

Benbasat, I., & Zmud, R. W. (2003). The identity crisis within the IS discipline: Defining and communicating the discipline's core properties. *MIS Quarterly, 27*(2), 183–194.

Bijker, W. E., Hughes, T. P., & Pinch, T. J. (1987). *The social construction of technological systems*. Cambridge: MIT Press.

Bowker, G., & Star, L. (1999). *Sorting things out: Classification and its consequences*. Cambridge: MIT Press.

Broer, T., Nieboer, A. P., & Bal, R. A. (2010). Opening the black box of quality improvement collaboratives: An actor-network theory approach. *BMC Health Services Research, 10,* 1–9.

Callon, M. (1986a). The sociology of an actor-network: The case of the electric vehicle. In M. Callon, J. Law, & A. Rip (Eds.), *Mapping the dynamics of science and technology* (pp. 19–34). London: Macmillan.

Callon, M. (1986b). Some elements of sociology translation: Domestication of the scallops and the fishermen of St Brieuc Bay. In J. Law (Ed.), *Power, action & belief. A new sociology of knowledge?* (pp. 196–229). London: Routledge, Kegan Paul.

Callon, M. (1991). Techno-economic network and irreversability. In J. Law (Ed.), *A sociology of monsters. Essays on power, technology and domination* (pp. 132–164). London: Routledge.

Callon, M., & Latour, B. (1981). Unscrewing the Big Leviathan: How actors macrostructure reality and how sociologists help them to do so. In K. D. Knorr-Cetina & A. V. Cicourel (Eds.), *Advances in social theory and methodology: Toward an integration of micro- and macro-sociologies* (pp. 277–303). Boston: Routledge, Kegan Paul.

Chiasson, M., & Davidson, E. (2004). Pushing the contextual envelope: Developing and diffusing IS theory for health information systems research. *Information and Organization, 14*(3), 155–188.

Chiasson, M., & Davidson, E. (2005). Taking industry seriously in information systems research. *MIS Quarterly, 29*(4), 591–605.

Cho, S., Mathiassen, L., & Nilsson, A. (2008). Contextual dynamics during health information systems implementation: An event-based actor-network approach. *European Journal of Information Systems, 17*(6), 614–630.

Collins, H., & Yearley, S. (1992). Epitemological chicken. In A. Pickering (Ed.), *Science, practice and culture*. Chicago: University of Chicago Press.

Constantinides, P., & Barrett, M. (2006). Negotiating ICT development and use: The case of a telemedicine system in the healthcare region of Crete. *Information and Organization, 16*(1), 27–55.

Cresswell, K. M. (2010). Actor-network theory and its role in understanding the implementation of information technology developments in healthcare. *BMC Medical Informatics & Decision Making, 10*(67), 1–11.

Davidson, E. (2000). Analyzing genre of organizational communication in clinical information systems. *Information Technology & People, 13*(3), 196–209.

Denis, J.-L., Langley, A., & Rouleau, L. (2007). Strategizing in pluralistic contexts: Rethinking theoretical frames. *Human Relations, 60*(1), 179–215.

Faraj, S., Kwon, D., & Watts, S. (2004). Contested artifact: Technology sensemaking, actor networks, and the shaping of the web browser. *Information Technology & People, 17*(2), 186–209.

Fraser, S. W., & Greenhalgh, T. (2001). Complexity science: Coping with complexity: Educating for capability. *British Medical Journal, 323*(7316), 799–804.

Garabaldi, R. (1998). Computers and the quality of care-a clinician's perspective. *New England Journal of Medicine, 338*(4), 232–238.

Garud, R., & Rappa, M. A. (1994). A socio-cognitive model of technology evolution: The case of cochlear implants. *Organization Science, 5*(3), 344–362.

Greenhalgh, T., & Stones, R. (2010). Theorising bit IT programmes in healthcare: Strong structuration theory meets actor-network theory. *Social Science & Medicine, 70*(9), 1285–1294.

Ha, K., & Lee, J.,(2008). *U-health and regulatory implications in Korea*. Proceedings of Portland International Center for Management of Engineering and Technology (PICMET 2008) (pp. 351–355). Cape Town: IEEE.

Hanseth, O., & Monteiro, E. (1997). Inscribing behavior in information infrastructure standards. *Accounting, Management & Information Technology, 7*(4), 183–211.

Hanseth, O., Aanestad, M., & Berg, M. (2004). Actor-network theory and information systems. What's so special? *Information Technology & People, 17*(2), 116–123.

Kaplan, B. (2001). Evaluating informatics applications-social interactionalism and call for methodological pluralism. *International Journal of Medical Informatics, 64*(1), 39–56.

Lane, D., & Maxfield, R. (1996). Strategy under complexity: Fostering generative relationships. *Long Range Planning, 29*(2), 215–231.

Latour, B. (1987a). *Science in action*. Cambridge: Harvard University Press.

Latour, B. (1987b). *Science in action: How to follow scientists and engineers through society*. Cambridge: Harvard University Press.

Latour, B. (1999a). On recalling ANT. In J. Law & J. Hassard (Eds.), *Actor network theory and after*. Oxford: Blackwell, Sociological Review.

Latour, B. (1999b). *Pandora's hope: Essays on the reality of science studies*. Cambridge: Harvard University Press.

Latour, B. (2005). *Reassembling the social: An introduction to actor-network theory*. Oxford: Oxford University Press.

Law, J. (1987). Technolong and heterogenous engineering: The case of Portugese expansion. In W. E. Bijker, T. P. Hughes, & T. J. Pinch (Eds.), *The social construction of technological systems: New directions in the sociology and history of technology* (pp. 111–134). Cambridge: MIT Press.

Law, J. (1991). Introduction. In J. Law (Ed.), *A sociology of monsters: Essays on power, technology, and domination*. London: Routledge.

Law, J., & Hassard, J. (1999). *Actor network theory and after*. Oxford: Blackwell.

Lee, H., & Oh, S. (2006). A standards war waged by a developing country: Understanding international standard setting from the actor-network perspective. *Journal of Strategic Information Systems, 15*(3), 177–195.

Lorenzi, N. M., Riley, R. T., Blyth, A. J. C., Southon, G., & Dixon, B. J. (1997). Antecedents of the people and organizational aspects of medical informatics. *Journal of American Medical Association (JAMA), 4*(2), 79–83.

Lorenzi, N. M., Riley, R. T., Blyth, A. J. C., Southon, G., & Dixon, B. J. (1998). People and organizational aspects of medical informatics. In B. Cesnik, A. T. Mccray, & J. R. Scherrer (Eds.), *MEDINFO '98 Proceedings of the Ninth World Congress on Medical Informatics* (pp. 1197–1200). Seoul: IOS Press.

Mähring, M., Holmström, J., Keil, M., & Montealegre, R. (2004). Trojan actor-networks and swift translation: Bringing actor-network theory to IT project escalation studies. *Information Technology & People, 17*(2), 210–238.

Massaro, T. (1993). Introducing physician order entry at a major academic medical center: Impact on organizational culture and behavior. *Academic Medicine, 68*(1), 20–35.

Mclean, C., & Hassard, J. (2004). Symmetrical absence/symmetrical absurdity: Critical notes on the production of actor-network accounts. *Journal of Management Studies, 41*(3), 493–519.

Mcloughlin, I. (1999). *Creative technological change: The shaping of technology and organisations*. London: Routledge.

Menon, N. M., Lee, B., & Eldenburg, L. (2000). Productivity of information systems in the healthcare industry. *Information Systems Research, 11*(1), 83–92.

Miller, P. (1996). The multiplying machine. *Accounting, Organizations and Society, 21*(7/8), 615–630.

Mol, A. (1998). Ontological politics. A word and some questions. *The Sociological Review, 46*(S), 74–89.

Pels, D. (1995). The politics of symmetry. *Social Studies of Science, 26*(2), 277–304.

Plsek, P. E., & Greenhalgh, T. (2001). Complexity science: The challenge of complexity in health care. *British Medical Journal, 323*(7313), 625–628.

Plsek, P. E., & Wilson, T. (2001). Complexity science: Complexity, leadership, and management in healthcare organisations. *British Medical Journal, 323*(7315), 746–749.

Ramiller, N. C. (2005). Applying the sociology of translation to a system project in a lagging enterprise. *Journal of Information Technology Theory and Application, 7*(1), 51–76.

Ramiller, N. C. (2007). Constructing safety: System designs, system effects, and the play of heterogeneous interests in a behavioral health care setting. *International Journal of Medical Informatics, 76S*(Suppl. 1), S196–S204.

Robert, G., Greenhalgh, T., Macfarlane, F., & Peacock, R. (2010). Adopting and assimilating new non-pharmaceutical technologies into health care: A systematic review. *Journal of Health Services Research and Policy, 15*(4), 243–250.

Rodon, J., Pastor, J. A., Sese, F., & Christiaanse, E. (2008). Unravelling the dynamics of IOIS implementation: An actor-network study of an IOIS in the seaport of Barcelona. *Journal of Information Technology, 23,* 97–108.

Rose, J., Jones, M., & Truex, D. (2005). Socio-theoretic accounts of IS: The problems of agency. *Scandinavian Journal of Information Systems, 17*(1), 133–152.

Schriger, D., Baraff, L., Rogers, W., & Cretin, L. (1997). Implementation of clinical guidelines using a computer charting systems. *The Journal of the American Medical Association, 278,* 1585–1590.

Sohn, M., & Lee, J. (2007). *U-health in Korea: Opportunities and challenges.* Proceedings of Portland International Center for Management of Engineering and Technology (PICMET 2007) (pp. 2791–2794). Oregon: IEEE.

Steen, J. (2010). Actor-network theory and the dilemma of the resource concept in strategic management. *Scandinavian Journal of Management, 26*(3), 324–331.

Timpka, T., Bång, M., Delbanco, T., & Walker, J. (2007). Information infrastructure for inter-organizational mental health services: An actor-network theory analysis of psychiatric rehabilitation. *Journal of Biomedical Informatics, 40*(4), 429–437.

Troshani, I., & Lymer, A. (2010). Translation in XBRL standardization. *Information Technology & People, 23*(2), 136–164.

Walsham, G. (1997). Actor-network and IS research: Current status and future prospects. In A. S. Lee, J. Liebenau, & J. I. Degross, (Eds.), *Information systems and qualitative research* (pp. 466–480). London: Chapman & Hall.

Wickramasinghe, N., Bali, R. K., & Tatnall, A. (2007). Using actor network theory to understand network centric healthcare operations. *International Journal of Electronic Healthcare, 3*(3), 317–328.

Wilson, T., & Holt, T. (2001). Complexity science: Complexity and clinical care. *British Medical Journal, 323*(7314), 685–688.

Winner, L. (1993). Upon opening the black box and finding it empty: Social constructivism and the philosophy of technology. *Science, Technology and Human Values, 18*(3), 362–378.

Chapter 6
e-Health Trends

Indrit Troshani and Nilmini Wickramasinghe

Abstract The use of Information and Communications Technologies (ICT) to support the achievement of health outcomes has the potential to transform the manner in which health services are delivered. Although there is an increasing number of contributions in e-health research, knowledge in this area remains limited. In this chapter, we discuss current trends in pervasive e-health with the hope that this endeavor will assist e-health scholars channel their research efforts. Having extensively reviewed extant research, we focus on health education, electronic health records (EHR), standardization, and m-health.

Keywords e-health · Trends · Health education · Electronic health records (EHR) · Standardization · m-health

6.1 Introduction

The use of digitally enabled technologies such as information and communications technologies (ICT) to support the achievement of health goals has the potential to transform the manner in which health services are delivered (WHO 2011). e-Health is defined as the use of ICT to improve health and health care outcomes (Lintonen et al. 2007; Mackert et al. 2009). e-Health is an emerging field, which comprises the intersection of numerous disciplines, including medicine, biomedical engineering, computer and information science, statistics, health promotion and marketing, and management science (Anderson 1997; Chiasson and Davidson 2004; Wickramasinghe et al. 2007). ICT are touted to offer a huge potential to raise the quality, increase the efficiency, and decrease the costs of primary, secondary, and tertiary healthcare (Heinzelmann et al. 2005). In addition, these technologies can empower

I. Troshani (✉)
University of Adelaide Business School, The University of Adelaide,
10 Pulteney Street, Adelaide SA 5005, Australia
e-mail: indrit.troshani@adelaide.edu.au

N. Wickramasinghe
Epworth Chair Health Information Management,
School of Business Information Technology and Logistics,
RMIT University, Melbourne VIC 3001, Australia
e-mail: nilmini.wickramasinghe@rmit.edu.au

R. K. Bali et al. (eds.), *Pervasive Health Knowledge Management*,
Healthcare Delivery in the Information Age,
DOI 10.1007/978-1-4614-4514-2_6, © Springer Science+Business Media New York 2013

patients to better understand their medical conditions and take responsibility by making informed decisions about such conditions (Raisinghani and Young 2008). More specifically, the espoused benefits of e-health include preventing and controlling of diseases by way of facilitating health information acquisition (Baker et al. 2003), customizing and personalizing information dissemination (Tate et al. 2006), detecting and treating diseases (Thomas et al. 2002), and encouraging the adoption of healthy lifestyles including weight control, physical activity, and quitting smoking (Tate et al. 2003).

For example, chronic diseases such as diabetes, in addition to having a huge impact on the diabetes sufferers themselves, as previously illustrated, can also be very costly to treat (AIHW 2007, 2008). Yet, pervasive diabetes monitoring solutions can offer enormous benefits, which include efficient and accurate monitoring and control of glucose levels and minimizing unnecessary hospitalizations or even just doctor visits (Wickramasinghe et al. 2009). These solutions have also been shown to improve patients' quality of life by preventing and controlling disease progress and instilling preventative behaviors amongst diabetes sufferers (Koch 2006; Wickramasinghe et al. 2010).

In this context, Chiasson and Davidson (2004) argue that although there is an increasing number of contributions to e-health research, knowledge in this area remains limited and underdeveloped. In addition, as Koch (2006) and WHO (2011) argue, most modern developed healthcare systems are experiencing many challenges such as:

- Increasing demand for healthcare services due to increasing aging populations and changed lifestyles resulting often in chronic diseases.
- Increasing demand for healthcare accessibility (e.g., home care).
- Increasing need for efficiency, personalization, and quality equity in healthcare.
- Increasing and chronic staff shortages.
- Limited budgets.

There is widespread agreement in the literature that e-health can help in addressing these challenges. Thus, knowledge and understanding of current e-health trends can be useful in assisting researchers address these challenges since it can help understand why pervasive e-health solutions emerge and how they are shaped. In addition, it can assist e-health scholars channel their research efforts. Thus, the aim of this chapter is to identify existing trends in e-health research. Having extensively reviewed extant research, we first discuss health education, electronic health records (EHR), standardization, and m-health. The chapter is subsequently concluded with a discussion of research directions.

6.2 Health Education

Recent research has stressed the need for improving health literacy and education, particularly, because it can have a huge impact on individual quality of life, public health, and even more broadly, on national economies (Ball and Lillis 2001;

Gazmararian et al. 2005; Mackert et al. 2009). Many organizations around the world are using pervasive e-health technologies to address health literacy and education problems. The main reason for this is attributed to the fact the e-health technologies offer adaptability, cost-effectiveness, and accessibility (Eysenbach 2007). In addition to this, findings reported in Ball and Lillis (2001) concerning a study conducted by Deloitte & Touche and VHA Inc. reveal that two-thirds of the US patients do not receive any literature in relation to their medication conditions. At least in part, this is getting patients to take matters into their own hands and look for medical information online (Ball and Lillis 2001).

One of the technologies that is receiving much attention is Web 2.0. It offers online activities that encourage interactivity and collaboration through interpersonal networking and personalization while also fostering a sense of community amongst users (Abram 2005). There are many Web 2.0 applications that offer a huge potential for health literacy and healthcare education (Boulos and Wheeler 2007) including wikis, blogs, podcasting, RSS feeds, social networking applications, and instant messaging (IM). We explain these in turn and illustrate them with examples about how they are being used in relation to health literature and education.

A *wiki* is a collaborative application that allows users to provide content while also enabling that content to be edited by anybody (Boulos et al. 2006). In healthcare settings, wikis can be used for knowledge sharing (e.g., http://www.wikisurgery.com). In addition, wikis offer strong localization capabilities enabling non-English posts as well. For example, DiabetesPost at http://www.diabetespost.com/ enables posts to be made in Arabic. *Blogs* enable users to provide online journals or web diaries that can be easily published and updated chronologically on issues of interest or on common themes including health literacy and education (Boulos et al. 2006). Some of the most notable health education blogs include http://drugscope.blogspot.com and http://biographyofbreastcancer.blogspot.com. As blog users are not necessarily professionals, there is a substantial risk for misinformation, although, according to Boulos et al. (2006) inherent "collaborative intelligence" acts as a built-in quality control and assurance mechanism for blogs.

Podcasts are location and time-independent digital files that can be downloaded automatically by free software on portable devices, such as Apple iPods/iPads or MP3/MP4 players and played by users at their leisure (Boulos and Wheeler 2007). Notable examples of health education podcasts include http://healthliteracyoutloud.com.

Really Simple Syndication (RSS) feeds are protocols that are used to indicate updates or additions to content to websites or blogs as per user-defined queries or requirements (Boulos and Wheeler 2007). Typically, RSS works when users subscribe to RSS feeds using RSS aggregators that are typically supported in modern browsers. Aggregators crawl selected websites regularly and display feeds to users enabling them to conveniently and quickly overview updates on specific topics at any point in time at the selected websites (Boulos and Wheeler 2007).

Social Networking Applications enable forming of groups of individuals that share common interests or circumstances. For example, http://www.depressionnet.com.au is an Australian online community that provides comprehensive information for people living with depression. A similar social networking application is the CURE DiABETES group at http://groups.myspace.com/cureDiABETES, which is run by patients and supporters in order to help and support diabetes sufferers.

Instant messaging (IM) Instant Messaging constitutes real-time online interaction between two or more users who can share text, audio, video, and other types of files. A nurse-led web chat application enabling the public to interact with qualified nurses was well received by patients (Emin ovic et al. 2004).

As patients wish to interact and exchange increasingly more information with healthcare providers, opportunities are existing for using Web 2.0 tools and applications to enable or facilitate these interactions for literacy development and education purposes. By emphasizing education, these tools empower patients to take responsibility for their conditions, thereby making them active and responsible participants in their treatment regimen (Boulos et al. 2006; Boulos and Wheeler 2007; Mackert et al. 2009; Nicholas et al. 2001).

6.3 Electronic Health Records

EHRs represent medical information concerning patients, which is meant to support healthcare-related activities and evidence-based medical decision support both directly or indirectly. This information is collected longitudinally during patient visits at any healthcare delivery setting (Raghupathi and Kesh 2009). In addition to patient demographics, EHRs also include past medical history such as medications, problems, immunizations, radiology and laboratory results, and progress notes (Raghupathi and Kesh 2009). It is anticipated that in the future EHRs will offer rich medically relevant information in addition to text. EHRs will include still images, echocardiograms, endoscopies, and even video recordings of patient interviews or visits, which will enable convenient access to expertise that is located remotely and even facilitate training of medical practitioners (Heinzelmann et al. 2005).

EHRs can offer many benefits including complete, accurate, error-free universally accessible lifetime patient health information (Raghupathi and Kesh 2009). They also offer significant productivity improvements in the healthcare industry (von Lubitz and Wickramasinghe 2006). In a healthcare setting where healthcare costs are steadily increasing while pressures are growing to satisfy unmet needs and increasing competition, the promises of EHRs to offer quality and productivity constitute the main driving forces for developing them.

There are a number of risks that need to be mitigated as EHR development progresses and design issues addressed. Although EHRs offer many benefits, healthcare professionals may find with EHRs they may be exchanging a set of issues with another. For example, issues experienced with traditional manual paper-based patient record systems such as lost patient charts, poor handwriting, and missing information may be exchanged with issues with data capture problems, computer crashes, programming errors, and susceptibility for viruses and other malware, which are likely to affect EHRs and potentially render them useless (Glaser and Aske 2010; Goldschmidt 2005).

Another major issue with EHRs concerns the privacy and security of confidential personal medical and health information (Rao Hill and Troshani 2010; Troshani and Rao Hill 2009). For example, unethical use of such information for personal gain by disgruntled or unethical employees or even legislated use of private information without an individual's prior consent constitute serious risks that need to be mitigated as EHRs are developed (Goldschmidt 2005). Thus, the question that needs further research is if the espoused benefits of EHRs will indeed outweigh their risks and development costs (Rash 2005).

Extant research shows that EHR design and development have been constrained by major challenges (Raghupathi and Kesh 2009). First, the literature suggests that existing EHRs seem to be driven by specific vendors or technologies and ignore the diverse and complex nature of modern healthcare settings and processes (Blobel 2006). For example, driven by specific vendors, existing EHRs do not appear to comply with portability standards (Hippisley-Cox et al. 2003). In addition, almost all exiting EHRs are based on relatively simple relational database applications, which consist of patient data entry forms and report generation capabilities, but which lack the capacity to be interoperable in large-scale distributed environments and to inexpensively scale up to fully functional applications (Hippisley-Cox et al. 2003; Raghupathi and Kesh 2009). One possible way to address these issues is to take a holistic network-centric view to EHR design (von Lubitz and Wickramasinghe 2006).

6.4 Standardization

Standardization entails developing standards in the development and provision of pervasive e-health applications and limiting the use of other options (Choudrie et al. 2003; Damsgaard and Lyytinen 2001; King et al. 1994). Standards constitute conventions that are needed for the structure and behavior of computing functions, formats, and processes (Engel et al. 2006). Standards play a critical role in the transmissions of electronic information, and as such, standard development, that is, standardization, is essential for the development and widespread diffusion of pervasive e-health applications. Lack of standardization can create interoperability issues adversely impacting information exchange between and amongst various e-health applications, that is, e-health applications can become "information islands" and thus present difficulties to integrate with larger healthcare systems (Tang et al. 2006).

For example, standards developed for electronic payments in the finance and banking sectors worldwide have been highly successful and have become widely diffused due to the national and international standardization approaches adopted and coordination amongst key stakeholders (WHO 2011). Similarly, governments and industry associations are collaborating by way of the Global Harmonization Task Force in order to develop standards for medical technologies (WHO 2011).

Standardization facilitates both integration and interoperability thereby enabling industry growth and development while lack thereof can make the development of pervasive e-health applications and their integration prohibitively costly (Engel et al.

2006; Koch 2006; Lee et al. 2009). Standardization can include many aspects of e-health, ranging from terminology, text/image communications, health hardware devices, and even security and privacy (Lee et al. 2009). For example, South Korean e-health initiatives are considering the US Health Insurance Portability and Accountability Act (HIPAA) as a security standard for medical data and the International Classification of Diseases (ICD) for terminology standardization (Lee et al. 2009).

6.5 m-Health

Mobile health or simply m-health is defined as a component of e-health whereby medical practice is supported by mobile devices including mobile phones and personal digital assistants (PDAs) or any other wireless devices (WHO 2011). According to the International Telecommunications Union (ITU), there are over 5 billion wireless subscribers in the world, over 70 % of which reside in low- to middle-income countries (ITU 2010). The widespread accessibility and availability of mobile phones makes these devices very powerful media for reaching individuals generally (e.g., with general health promotion messages) and patients suffering from various medical conditions, in particular, by way of mobile health applications.

Evidence collected in a recent World Health Organization (WHO) study shows that there are numerous activities of m-health services that are currently being offered in member countries including health call centers, emergency toll-free telephone services, managing emergencies and disasters, mobile telemedicine, appointment reminders, community mobilization and health promotion, treatment compliance, mobile patient records, information access, patient monitoring, health surveys and data collection, surveillance, health awareness raising, and decision support systems (ITU 2010). While 83 % of WHO member states offer at least one of these m-health services, many offer four to six with the most popular m-health services being health call centers (59 %), emergency toll-free telephone services (55 %), managing emergencies and disasters (54 %), and mobile telemedicine (49 %; WHO 2011). As might be expected, the WHO study also shows that counties in the high-income group have implemented a greater range of m-health initiatives than those in the lower-income groups while m-health call centers and healthcare help lines appear to be popular across all income groups (WHO 2011). In addition, all income categories identified competing m- and e-health priorities was one of the greatest barriers to m-health adoption (WHO 2011).

A recent study carried out by PriceWaterhouseCoopers's Health Research Institute (HRI) presents the case for the market for m-health applications and services. For example, in a recent survey they conducted, they found that 40 % of respondents are willing to pay for remote health monitoring devices and monthly service fees to send data automatically to their doctors while based on these respondents, HRI estimates that the annual market for mobile health monitoring devices ranges between $7.7 and $43 billion (PWC 2010).

The PWC study also identifies three main business models that can be viable in the m-health market (PWC 2010). First, the *operational/clinical business model* enables all healthcare stakeholders including providers, payers, medical device and drug companies to use m-health applications to run their operations more efficiently. Second, the *consumer products and services model* provides unique value-added m-health applications to individuals. Third, the *infrastructure business model* offers connecting secure infrastructures that enable m-health information and services (PWC 2010). Further research is required to evaluate the viability and effectiveness of these models in practice.

6.6 Conclusion and Future Research

The healthcare industry is under increasing pressure worldwide from many challenges including quality improvements, chronic staff shortages, and limited resources including financial and human resources. The use of ICT to enable healthcare and improve health outcomes, e-health, is touted to transform the healthcare industry and help address these challenges. Although the number of contributions in e-health research is steadily growing, knowledge in this area remains still at an embryonic stage (Chiasson and Davidson 2004). Having extensively reviewed extant research, we have discussed current e-health trends including health education, EHR, standardization, and m-health. We believe that this discussion can assist e-health scholars hone in their efforts and extend existing limited research in these areas.

For successful implementations to become a reality in the identified areas, adoption of corresponding e-health applications by both patients and healthcare providers is necessary (Raisinghani and Young 2008). In order for adoption to occur, coordinated campaigns are needed to establish public awareness and understanding concerning the value of e-health applications. These campaigns can encourage open learning and information sharing. In addition, given the complexity of e-health applications and diversity of stakeholders that they may ultimately affect, partnerships should be fostered between the different stakeholders including vendors, patients, providers, insurers, drug and medical device companies, as well as between public and private sectors (Raisinghani and Young 2008).

New research directions can extend the areas identified in the previous sections in many ways. First, controlled studies can focus on longitudinal analyses and investigations targeting the adoption of e-health applications and services in the identified areas (Cline and Haynes 2001). Second, cost/benefits evaluations can be carried out to assess whether the costs involved in developing e-health applications can be offset by espoused benefits that these applications promise to offer (Halkias et al. 2008). Third, further research needs to investigate the demographics of the patients seeking to use e-health applications, how they use them, the information they seek and its quality, and how their behaviors can be affected (Wyatt 1997). This can also help identify underserved communities, thereby, address equity concerns. Finally, further research can also examine the manner in which public policy can assist the development of e-health applications (e.g., subsidies, training; Cline and Haynes 2001).

References

Abram, S. (2005). Web 2.0-huh? Library 2.0, librarian 2.0. *Information Outlook, 9*(1), 44–45.

AIHW. (2007). *National indicators for monitoring diabetes: Report of the Diabetes Indicators Review Subcommittee of the National Diabetes Data Working Group: AIHW cat. no. CVD 38.* Canberra: AIHW.

AIHW. (2008). *Diabetes: Australian facts 2008.* Canberra: Australian Institute of Health and Welfare.

Anderson, J. G. (1997). Clearing the way for physicians' use of clinical information systems. *Communications of the ACM, 40*(8), 83–90.

Baker, L., Wagner, T. H., Singer, S., & Bundorf, M. K. (2003). Use of the Internet and e-mail for health care information: Results from a national survey. *Journal of American Medical Association (JAMA), 289*(18), 2400–2406.

Ball, M. J., & Lillis, J. (2001). E-health: Transforming the physician/patient relationship. *International Journal of Medical Informatics, 61*(1), 1–10.

Blobel, B. G. M. E. (2006). Advanced EHR architectures-promises or reality. *Methods of Information in Medicine, 45*(1), 95–101.

Boulos, M. N. K., & Wheeler, S. (2007). The emerging Web 2.0 social software: An enabling suite of sociable technologies in health and health care education. *Health Information and Libraries Journal, 24*(1), 2–23.

Boulos, M. N. K., Maramba, I., & Wheeler, S. (2006). Wikis, blogs and podcasts. A new generation of web-based tools for virtual collaborative clinical practice and education. *British Medical Journal, 6,* 41. http://www.biomedcentral.com/1472-6920/6/41.

Chiasson, M., & Davidson, E. (2004). Pushing the contextual envelope: Developing and diffusing IS theory for health information systems research. *Information and Organization, 14*(3), 155–188.

Choudrie, J., Papazafeiropoulou, A., & Lee, H. (2003). A web of stakeholders and strategies: A case of broadband diffusion in South Korea. *Journal of Information Technology, 18,* 281–290.

Cline, R. J. W., & Haynes, K. M. (2001). Consumer health information seeking on the Internet: The state of the art. *Health Education Research, 16*(6), 671–692.

Damsgaard, J., & Lyytinen, K. (2001). The role of intermediating institutions in the diffusion of electronic data interchange (EDI): How industry associations intervened in Denmark, Finland, and Hong Kong. *The Information Society, 17*(3), 195–210.

Eminovic, N., Wyatt, J. C., Tarpey, A. M., Murray, G., & Ingrams, G. J. (2004). First evaluation of the NHS direct online clinical enquiry service: A nurse-led web chat triage service for the public. *Journal of Medical Internet Research, 6,* e17. http://www.jmir.org//2/e17/.

Engel, K., Blobel, B., & Pharow, P. (2006). Standards for enabling health informatics interoperability. In A. Hasman, R. Haux, J. Van Der Lei, E. De Clercq, & F. H. R. France (Eds.), *Ubiquity: Technologies for better health in aging societies* (Studies in Health Technology and Informatics, Vol. 124) (pp. 145–150). Amsterdam: IOS Press.

Eysenbach, G. (2007). Credibility of health information and digital media: New perspectives and implications for youth. In B. E. Metzger & A. J. Flanagin (Eds.), *Digital media, youth, and credibility*. Cambridge: MIT Press.

Gazmararian, J., Curran, J., Parker, R., Bernhardt, J., & DeBuono, B. (2005). Public health literacy in America: An ethical imperative. *American Journal of Preventative Medicine, 28*(3), 317–322.

Glaser, J., & Aske, J. (2010, July). Healthcare IT trends raise bar for information security. *Healthcare Financial Management,* 40–44.

Goldschmidt, P. G. (2005). HIT and MIS: Implications of health information technology and medical information systems. *Communications of the ACM, 48*(10), 69–74.

Halkias, D., Harkiolakis, N., & Thurman, P. (2008). Internet use for health-related purposes among Greek consumers. *Telemedicine and e-Health, 14*(3), 255–260.

Heinzelmann, P. J., Lugn, N. E., & Kvedar, J. C. (2005). Telemedicine in the future. *Journal of Telemedicine and Telecare, 11,* 384–390.

Hippisley-Cox, J., Pringle, M., Cates, R., Wyna, A., Hammersley, V., Coupland, C., et al. (2003). The electronic patient record in primary care—regression or progression? A cross sectional study. *British Medical Journal, 326,* 1439–1443.
ITU. (2010). *The world in 2010: ICT facts and figs*. Geneva: International Telecommunications Union (ITU). http://www.itu.int/ITU-D/material/FactsFigures2010.pdf.
King, J. L., Gurbaxani, V., Kraemer, K. L., McFarlan, K. L., Raman, K. S., & Yap, C. S. (1994). Institutional factors in information technology innovation. *Information Systems Research, 5*(2), 139–169.
Koch, S. (2006). Home telehealth-current state and future trends. *International Journal of Medical Informatics, 75,* 565–576.
Lee, M., Min, S. D., Shin, H. S., Lee, B. W., & Kim, J. K. (2009). The e-health landscape: Current status and future prospects in Korea. *Telemedicine and e-Health, 15*(4), 362–369.
Lintonen, T. P., Konu, A. I., & Seedhouse, D. (2007). Information technology in health promotion. *Health Education Research, 23*(3), 560–566.
Mackert, M., Love, B., & Whitten, P. (2009). Patient education on mobile devices: An e-health intervention for low health literate audiences. *Journal of Information Science, 35*(1), 82–93.
Nicholas, D., Huntington, P., Williams, P., & Blackburn, P. (2001). Digital health informatin provision and health outcomes. *Journal of Information Science, 27*(4), 265–276.
PWC. (2010). *Healthcare unwired: New business models delivering care anywhere.* Health Research Institute and PriceWaterhouseCoopers.
Raghupathi, W., & Kesh, S. (2009). Designing electronic health records versus total digital health systems: A systemic analysis. *Systems Research and Behavioural Science, 26*(1), 63–79.
Raisinghani, M. S., & Young, E. (2008). Personal health records: Key adoption issues and implications for management. *International Journal of Electronic Healthcare, 4*(1), 67–77.
Rao Hill, S., & Troshani, I. (2010). Factors influencing the adoption of personalisation mobile services: Empirical evidence from young Australians. *International Journal of Mobile Communications, 8*(2), 150–168.
Rash, M. C. (2005, April 4). Privacy concerns hinder electronic medical records. *The Business Journal of the Greater Triad Area,* 4–6.
Tang, P. C., Ash, J. S., Bates, D. W., Overhage, J. M., & Sands, D. Z. (2006). Personal health records: Definitions, benefits, and strategies for overcoming barriers to adoption. *The Journal of the American Medical Informatics Association, 13*(2), 121–126.
Tate, D. F., Jackvony, E. H., & Wing, R. R. (2003). Effects of Internet behavioral counseling on weight loss in adults at risk for type 2 diabetes. *Journal of American Medical Association (JAMA), 289*(14), 1563–1571.
Tate, D. F., Jackvony, E. H., & Wing, R. R. (2006). A self-regulation program for maintenance of weight loss. *New England Journal of Medicine, 355*(15), 1563–1571.
Thomas, B., Stamler, L. L., Lafreniere, K. D., Out, J., & Delahunt, T. D. (2002). Using the Internet to identify women's sources of breast health education and screening. *Women Health, 36*(1), 33–48.
Troshani, I., & Rao Hill, S. (2009). Linking stakeholder salience with mobile services diffusion. *International Journal of Mobile Communications, 7*(3), 269–289.
Lubitz, D. von, & Wickramasinghe, N. (2006). Healthcare and technology: The doctrine of networkcentric healthcare. *International Journal of Electronic Healthcare, 2*(4), 322–344.
WHO. (2011). *mHealth: New horizons for health through mobile technologies*. Geneva: World Health Organization (WHO).
Wickramasinghe, N., Bali, R. K., & Tatnall, A. (2007). Using actor network theory to understand network centric healthcare operations. *International Journal of Electronic Healthcare, 3*(3), 317–328.
Wickramasinghe, N., Troshani, I., & Goldberg, S. (2009). Supporting diabetes self-management with pervasive wireless technology solutions. *International Journal of Healthcare Delivery Reform Initiatives, 1*(4), 17–31.

Wickramasinghe, N., Troshani, I., & Goldberg, S. (2010). An investigation into the use of pervasive wireless technologies to support diabetes healthcare. In A. Coronato & G. De Pietro (Eds.), *Pervasive and smart technologies for healthcare: Ubiquitous methodologies and tools* (pp. 114–129). New York: IGI Global.

Wyatt, J. C. (1997). Commentary: Measuring quality and impact of the World Wide Web. *British Journal of Medicine, 314,* 1879–1881.

Part II
KM and Pervasive Health

Chapter 7
Making Sense of Pervasive Healthcare: The Role of Knowledge Management

Rajeev K. Bali

Abstract This brief chapter serves as an introduction to the section of the book dealing with KM aspects of pervasive health. It may well be that, to some, the notion of pervasive healthcare conjures images, which depict the following terms: wireless, technology, infrastructure, protocols, and standards. This overtly technical focus is then applied to the *patient* and their (improved) healthcare. However, the true power of pervasive computing for health lies not so much with the technology itself but rather with its judicious application to the healthcare (patient) domain. What improvements and efficiencies can it bring about in this regard?

7.1 Introduction

This brief chapter serves as an introduction to the section of the book dealing with KM aspects of pervasive health. It may well be that, to some, the notion of pervasive healthcare conjures images, which depict the following terms: wireless, technology, infrastructure, protocols and standards. This overtly technical focus is then applied to the *patient* and their (improved) healthcare. However, the true power of pervasive computing for health lies not so much with the technology itself but rather with its judicious application to the healthcare (patient) domain. What improvements and efficiencies can it bring about in this regard?

7.2 KM and Pervasive Health

The delivery of relevant and quality information to healthcare professionals is important to ensure enhanced patient care. Facilitated by contemporary technologies, healthcare professionals have rapid access to a growing plethora of clinical and medical information, be this in the form of instant second opinions (validation)

R. K. Bali (✉)
Biomedical Computing and Engineering Technologies (BIOCORE)
Applied Research Group, Coventry University, CV1 2TT, Coventry, UK
e-mail: r.bali@ieee.org

R. K. Bali et al. (eds.), *Pervasive Health Knowledge Management*,
Healthcare Delivery in the Information Age,
DOI 10.1007/978-1-4614-4514-2_7,

or cross-checking established statistics (verification). Transforming this information into knowledge (via human-led processes) leads to exponential advantages (Wickramasinghe et al. 2009).

Knowledge is the enemy of disease (National Knowledge Service 2006) and serves ultimately to protect the patient from harm. As skills and knowledge exist in both individuals and organizations, the essence of KM for healthcare is how best to identify and capture knowledge and experience in order to disseminate it further throughout relevant organizations and, by extension, to the individuals operating within them. There have been several attempts to bring various forms of clinical information to the clinician at the point of care, which include: to develop computer applications that stand alone, although which are often network accessible, and are available to the clinician upon his/her request; to incorporate the clinical knowledge directly into clinical information systems used by clinicians while giving care (once there, the computer-based system can automatically prompt the clinician or the clinician can request help) or to request help from an outside source (Sittig 2005).

The movement to make sense of knowledge came about from unhappiness with the somewhat outdated understanding of KM, which depicted a linear relationship between data, information, knowledge, and wisdom. Several researchers have suggested other ideas including the notion that the effective transition to knowledge should also include an element of sensemaking (Snowden 2005): how can we make sense of the world so we can act in it? Sensemaking has been an area of interest and research for some time; researchers have concentrated on individual sensemaking and the "cognitive gap" experienced when attempting to make sense of observed data (Dervin 1996) while others (Weick et al. 2005) have focussed on sensemaking at the organizational level. Sensemaking also needs to include considerations of data privacy and security; balancing these aspects with functionality and usability remains the focus of continued research and development.

"*Ipsa scientia potestas est*" (knowledge itself is power)—Sir Francis Bacon first wrote this in 1597 and its relevance to contemporary organizations remains true to this day. The required multidisciplinary approach to pervasive healthcare will encompass the required (and ever evolving) technologies (ubiquitous, "always on," "always ready") combined with refined processes and suitably empowered healthcare professionals and their patients. The effective mix of people, process, and technology—the very essence of KM—will bring about integrated advances for pervasive healthcare delivery. When combined with due consideration of the necessary sensemaking aspects (including "proof of concept"), the future efficacy of pervasive healthcare would appear to be sound.

7.3 The Chapters

The chapters in this section focus on knowledge-based issues surrounding pervasive healthcare delivery and management. *Bali et al.* explain the efficacy of knowledge-based pervasive technologies for crisis scenarios. The requirement for greater information sharing, collaboration, leadership, and transparency is highlighted. *Abd Ghani et al.* outline the design of a pervasive health record as applied to the Malaysian health context. A pervasive health record would allow healthcare professionals to have better knowledge in order to provide accurate and more efficient treatment protocols.

Puentes et al. propose a scheme for sensor-based data quality characterization adapted to a pervasive scenario. Using mobile devices as intermediation interfaces, the potential for successful pervasive healthcare is detailed.

Finally, *Armstrong et al.* discuss smartphone application design for people with dementia. Smartphone technologies offer promise to assist people with dementia regarding their unmet needs and also relieve caregiver's burden.

Acknowledgments An expanded version of this chapter appears as a Working Paper from the *Biomedical Computing and Engineering Technologies (BIOCORE) Applied Research Group*, Coventry University, UK; reproduced with permission. I would like to thank all chapter authors for their valuable and interesting contributions to this section.

References

Dervin, B. (1996). *Given a context by any other name: Methodological tools for taming the unruly beast*. Keynote paper, ISIC 96: Information Seeking in Context, 1–23.

National Knowledge Service. (2006). NHS National Knowledge Service homepage. http://www.nks.nhs.uk/. Accessed 11 Sept 2009.

Sittig, D. F. (2005). An overview of efforts to bring clinical knowledge to the point of care. In R. K. Bali (Ed.), *Clinical knowledge management: Opportunities and challenges*. USA: IGP.

Snowden, D. (2005). Multi-ontology sense making; a new simplicity in decision making. http://www.cognitive-edge.com/ceresources/articles/40_Multi-ontology_sense_makingv2_May05.pdf. Accessed 19 July 2008.

Weick, K. E., Sutcliffe, K. M., & Obstfeld, D. (2005). Organizing and the process of sensemaking. *Organization Science, 16*(4), 409–421.

Wickramasinghe, N., Bali, R. K., Lehaney, B., Schaffer, J. L., & Gibbons, M. C. (2009). *Healthcare knowledge management primer*. USA: Routledge.

Chapter 8
Managing Knowledge in Crisis Scenarios: The Use of Pervasive Technologies

Rajeev K. Bali, Vikraman Baskaran, Aapo Immonen, Alan C. Richards, Ian M. Marshall and Raouf NG Naguib

Abstract This chapter will examine why contemporary pervasive tools and technologies in conjunction with established knowledge management methods are vital to crisis scenarios. We discuss how such technologies can be used as an effective mechanism to transfer often complex information in as efficient a manner as possible. Three case studies are presented, followed by a discussion, which illustrate the challenges faced during different crises situations and how the use of technologies can make a difference in those contexts.

Keywords Complex information · Crisis management · Disaster scenarios · Preparedness · Critical knowledge · Leadership

8.1 Pervasive Technologies

The unprecedented aging of the global population is one of the driving forces behind this international pervasive healthcare effort. The United Nations (UN) state that the amount of people above the age of 60 will increase from 10 % of the global population

---

R. K. Bali (✉) · A. Immonen · A. C. Richards · I. M. Marshall · R. N. G. Naguib
Biomedical Computing and Engineering Technologies (BIOCORE) Applied Research Group,
Coventry University, CV1 2TT, Coventry, UK
e-mail: r.bali@ieee.org

A. Immonen
e-mail: immonena@coventry.ac.uk

A. C. Richards
e-mail: a.richards@coventry.ac.uk

I. M. Marshall
e-mail: i.marshall@coventry.ac.uk

R. N. G. Naguib
e-mail: r.naguib@coventry.ac.uk

V. Baskaran
Ted Rogers School of Information Technology Management,
Ryerson University, 350 Victoria Street, M5B 2K3, Toronto, Canada
e-mail: vikraman@ryerson.ca

A. Immonen
Emergency Services College, Kuopio, Finland

R. K. Bali et al. (eds.), *Pervasive Health Knowledge Management*,
Healthcare Delivery in the Information Age,
DOI 10.1007/978-1-4614-4514-2_8,

in the year 2000 to 21 % of the global population in the year 2050 (United Nations 2002).

One proposed solution to the current crisis is pervasive healthcare. The wide-scale deployment of wireless networks will improve communication among patients, physicians, and other healthcare workers as well as enable the delivery of accurate medical information anytime and anywhere thereby reducing errors and improving access (Varshney 2005).

Pervasive healthcare is an emerging technological field of great interest with the potential to improve the quality of life for patients and improve the efficiency of healthcare institutions (Salvador et al. 2007). The technologies within pervasive healthcare include monitoring and body sensor networks, assistive technologies, computing for hospitals, and preventive and persuasive technologies (Bardram 2008).

8.2 Knowledge Management

The term "knowledge" is often misunderstood and misinterpreted as it exhibits both physical and mental characteristics (Miller 2002; Breen 1997). All organizational domains, including healthcare, have embraced the concept of managing knowledge as the primary way of effective management for the future (Paul and Kimble 2002). Domains predominantly focused on the aspect of service provision are more directly influenced and affected by "right or wrong" choices made towards implementing Knowledge Management (KM). Service-based domains (such as healthcare) are more influenced by these choices as such domains are "knowledge rich." They are therefore prone to become breeding grounds for the creation of knowledge gaps (often referred to as "islands" or "silos"). Eventually, this can lead to knowledge deprivation at the required point of delivery, ultimately losing the competitive edge (Rodrigo 2001; Smith and Preston 2000).

The fact that modern-day organizations are facing a deluge of data and information whilst simultaneously lacking knowledge is very well documented (Liebowitz and Beckman 1998; Sieloff 1999). Technological innovations relating to workflow and such technologies as groupware systems have brought about a radical transformation in the way organizations can interact both internally and externally. These new ways of collaboration have resulted in organizations being inundated with information to an unprecedented degree resulting in data and information overload (Sieloff 1999; Cothrel and Williams 1999; Drucker 1998).

Crisis situations require a rapid response and the ability to sustain an unhindered flow of resources to critically affected areas. Such areas are primed for effective KM as this may make the difference between life and death for a sizeable population. Adoption of KM approaches and integrating the inherent tools and technologies with pervasive technologies will not only help to better manage crisis situations but may also better predict oncoming crises, allowing stakeholders to take proactive actions that minimize further damage to life, infrastructure, and so forth. The following three crisis scenarios are related to natural disasters, which occurred in different geographical areas. The cases identify impediments and challenges experienced in such situations and the need for working KM-based solutions.

8.3 Crisis Scenario #1: Haiti Earthquake (2010)

On 12 January 2010, an earthquake of magnitude 7.0 struck the Haitian capital of Port au Prince. The quake left up to 230,000 people dead and another 200,000 injured. In addition, up to a million people were left homeless (Bilham 2010). Six months on from the disaster those affected continue to be in dire need of support and the aid process has been heavily criticized in many quarters. This case study aims to understand the issues, which have made the delivery of aid so difficult. The arrival of aid to Haiti was prompt and abundant. However, this created its own problems. Due to a lack of preparedness, the arrival of aid was described as incredibly disorganized (BBC 2010). As increasing numbers of aid agencies arrived bringing with them drastically needed supplies, vital equipment was left sitting next to the runway for a number of days. In the immediate aftermath of the disaster when healthcare equipment was most needed, a lack of organization disrupted its distribution.

Médecins Sans Frontières complained of delays to supplies arriving at the expense of foreign troops. GOAL blamed the UN and the United States for the delay, claiming it was their failure to work together, which caused such disruption. The UN responded by blaming what it termed as underestimated logistical problems (BBC 2010). One of the reasons behind some of the chaotic beginnings to the aid situation can be attributed to a loss of personnel and systems belonging to the UN during the earthquake. The Inter Agency Standards Committee (IASC), however, who produced a report on the disaster in July 2010 criticized the early lack of coordination whilst praising subsequent efforts to improve this.

The IASC reserves its biggest criticism in its report for the lack of leadership that organization displayed, highlighting the lack of coordination between aid agencies in the early stages. This is blamed upon the high number of independent agencies involved and the shortage of available information. However, the report goes on to suggest that the cluster approach taken towards the development enabled communication to significantly improve. The report also highlights the failure of some aid agencies to engage with the authorities hence restricting their strategic effectiveness. Furthermore, other organizations were hampered by their inability to access and thus benefit from the knowledge base possessed by these agencies (IASC 2010).

IASC identifies two barriers to interorganizational knowledge sharing; one being the language barrier, the other a restricted access to coordination centers' headquarters (IASC 2010). In addition, incompatible systems may have prevented agencies from working together effectively. The report further highlights the failure of inexperienced, well-intentioned agencies to share and coordinate relief operations. A report carried out by the Disaster Accountability Project on aid agencies working in Haiti was also highly critical of the lack of transparency displayed. Of 200 organizations interviewed, only six regularly provided factual updated reports (Smilowitz 2010). This report calls for increased transparency in all aid agencies in order to ensure accountability and monitoring and proposed that policies should be put in place as a matter of course to ensure the enforcement of such guidelines. Many of the problems have been blamed on ineffective coordination strategies caused by the sheer scale of such a relief effort (Smilowitz 2010).

8.4 Crisis Scenario #2: Asian Tsunami (2004)

On 26 December 2004, an earthquake of magnitude 9.0 struck 250 km off the coast of the Indonesian city of Banda Aceh (Pickrell 2005). The subsequent tsunami caused substantial damage to towns and cities in 13 countries as far away as Somalia. The death toll was estimated to be around 225,000 with a further 500,000 injured. An additional 150,000 people were killed by the resultant spread of infectious disease (Pickrell 2005). The subsequent after effects of the disaster left 5 million homeless and a further 1 million unable to make a living. The estimated total cost of the disaster was placed at approximately $7.5 billion.

Such previously unprecedented geographical dispersion of the disaster made the distribution of effective aid a near impossible prospect and proved a huge drain on resources, particularly to large organizations like the UN. Takeda and Helms discussed how the United Nations Disaster Relief Agency managed the situation (Takeda and Helms 2006) and argued that the highly bureaucratic system employed for disaster preparedness actually added to the complexity of the disaster relief efforts due to its failure to include any scope for adaptability. The same authors argue that a system was in place to coordinate the work of Nongovernmental Organizations (NGOs) and aid agencies under the UN umbrella (Takeda and Helms 2006) and argue that the rational approach employed by these systems is unworkable in an irrational situation. They additionally call for the use of a more fluid system capable of changing according to the needs of the situation (a holistic management system). They state their belief that, whilst management information systems are vital for sharing information, in an ever-changing world it is equally important that these systems are fluid and able to adapt to change.

The general consensus as to the relief efforts experienced following the tsunami is largely positive, which has resulted in a belief that much has been learnt from the situations encountered (Shaw et al. 2010). However, some reports suggest that similar errors to those made during the tsunami relief effort are still being made today. This indicates that mistakes are not being appropriately engineered out of the relative organizations' relief strategies.

In the immediate aftermath of the tsunami, the UN elected to set up Humanitarian Information Centers (HICs), which contained information on ownership, maps, surveys, meetings, and funding. The HIC was largely considered a success and currently remains operable in some affected countries. One point of note, which has arisen from the UN's work in Indonesia, is the reported change in the relationship between the UN and NGOs. Whereas previously NGOs acted as a "subcontractor" to the UN, increasingly NGO funding has changed the dynamic. The United Nations Development Programme (UNDP) reports one NGO asking the UN to carry out work on their behalf (UNDP 2005). This blurring of established relationships sets a precedent, which could compromise the UN's ability to influence government policy making. The UNDP also reports success in collaborations between Islamic and Western NGOs (UNDP 2005), which had previously been an area of much sensitivity. The mass geographic dispersion of aid agencies during the tsunami relief effort created unprecedented problems for the UN in coordinating an efficient response.

8.5 Crisis Scenario #3: Gujarat Earthquake (2001)

On 26 January 2001, a major earthquake measuring 6.9 on the Richter Scale struck the Western Indian state of Gujarat. Reports suggested the earthquake killed in excess of 20,000 people and left a further 165,000 injured. Over 16 million people were affected by the disaster, which left around 7,000 homes destroyed (BBC 2001). In the immediate aftermath of the disaster, relief work was largely undertaken by bilateral agencies and NGOs. United Nations Disaster and Coordination (UNDAC) reported that nearly 250 agencies were active in the region by February. The UN response to the disaster was relatively minor with the organization endeavoring to develop a coordination center. The center became operational a week after the initial disaster, which by the UN's own concession, proved largely ineffective. The UN also confesses that the team sent was largely ill-equipped and insignificant (Harland and Wahlstrom 2001).

A distinct lack of management capacity and good relations with the Indian government further hampered attempts to develop successful strategies. This was attributed to India's longstanding directive of managing disasters internally. The result was a slow response by the UN to the disaster and a subsequent lack of information sharing between the state and the UN. A slow response to the disaster and the UN's late entry into the situation resulted in UN departments being forced to spend much of the early days catching up. Harland and Wahlstrom reiterated the need for leaders to be appointed and how fast they should respond to a given crisis situation: "*Leadership can only be provided if the aspiring leader is the first on-site*" (Harland and Wahlstrom 2001). Failure to produce field reports was put down to a problem in centralized decision making.

8.6 Application of Knowledge-Based Pervasive Technologies

The scenarios above highlight various knowledge gaps and how the lack of coordination, leadership, ownership, and basic information flow reduced the efficiency and effectiveness of relief efforts delivered to these situations. Whilst local culture, people, and processes are vital for tackling such situations, knowledge-based pervasive technologies can be viewed as enablers, which assist recovery and stabilization efforts.

Under normal organizational circumstances, technologies such as data integration, document and content management (support applications enabling users to have personalized access to the organizational knowledge base) continue to grow at an exponential rate (Bali et al. 2005). This has implications for decision makers across all sectors including healthcare as they have to deal with large amounts of data (Bali 2005). One of the major challenges that face healthcare managers is how to make effective decisions based on the data at hand.

It is acknowledged that the selection of a particular direction is both constrained and influenced by the availability of data, the ability to transform data into information and then to make recognition of it by deriving knowledge from the information. Practitioners then have to decide on how best to effectively transfer this knowledge on an organization-wide basis. For the healthcare setting, knowledge deprivation can result in a loss of resources making the care process inefficient (Baskaran et al. 2006).

As crisis and postcrisis situations often involve geographically dispersed personnel, knowledge-based tools (such as pervasive technologies) are ideally suited as they allow for flexible and robust mobile communication. This allows the crisis to be handled in the most efficient and effective manner possible. Natural or man-made disasters often encompass a large healthcare component to address their aftermaths and access to good quality healthcare is often a big factor in deciding how fast the affected area can return to its normal state. Effective Crisis Response Systems (CRS) need to support collaborative knowledge-based environments, which facilitate timely information exchange supporting successful resolution of the crisis. A CRS encompasses six essential phases (Yuan and Detlor 2005): monitoring and reporting, identification, notification, organization, operation, and assessment and investigation.

Well-executed KM initiatives to improve this cycle offer many benefits, which could be reaped by aid agencies during the management of crisis situations. Such benefits include: establishment of better working relationships, reduction of organizational competitiveness, increased transparency, identification of strong stakeholders, improved performance measurement, establishment of a shared vision, stronger partnerships, increase coordination and reduction of duplicated efforts, and increased information flow.

With the advent and continued popularity of social networking websites (such as Facebook and Twitter), healthcare information can be communicated during crisis situations much more quickly than could be imagined only a few years ago. When this information is validated, it transforms into knowledge. Such knowledge can be most effective in the "weak signals" and "early warnings" phases of crisis and disasters (Immonen et al. 2009). The "always on" nature of some pervasive technologies have strong parallels with contemporary social networking technologies. Judiciously combining these may result in exponential productivity gains in terms of transfer of required knowledge.

For the three given case studies, the usefulness of a publicly available pervasive system would have been useful (Kostakos and O'Neill 2004). Globalization is driven by information and communication technologies (ICTs) with the Internet at its core. Universal access to the internet needs to be combined with "adequate and unbiased information" (Kostakos and O'Neill 2004) in the public domain. This allows the public to make informed decisions. Interaction with pervasive systems may take the form of early warning systems (for tsunamis and earthquakes) as well as rapidly communicated information regarding first responders, emergency evacuation procedures, rendezvous points, and so forth.

8.7 Conclusion

The incorporation and effective use of knowledge-based pervasive technologies could assist healthcare stakeholders involved in crisis scenarios in overcoming many of the issues, which they currently face. However, before such tools and technologies can become a fundamental aspect of crisis management, there is a pressing need to overcome the current causes of problems and impediments to knowledge sharing, which currently exist (Immonen et al. 2009).

We believe that continuing to couple KM with pervasive technologies will enhance and advance crisis management approaches. There is a requirement for making provision to encourage greater information sharing, collaboration, leadership, and transparency among the multiple stakeholders involved. Wider acceptance of KM could help achieve this; it has borne witness to some outstanding achievements in recent years and has helped to make significant progress in the world of healthcare (Bali et al. 2009). The effective use of KM-enabled pervasive technologies in crisis management can help to retain expertise, train new employees, and analyze and disseminate vital statistics and information to operatives working in the field (Wickramasinghe and Bali 2008).

Acknowledgments Case studies appear courtesy of the Biomedical Computing and Engineering Technologies (BIOCORE) Applied Research Group, Coventry University, UK (http://www.coventry.ac.uk/biocore).

References

Bali, R. K. (Ed.). (2005). *Clinical knowledge management: Opportunities and challenges*. USA: IGP.

Bali, R. K., Feng, D. D., Burstein, F., & Dwivedi, A. (2005). Advances in clinical and health-care knowledge management. *IEEE Transcations on Information Technology in Biomedicine, 9*(2), 157–161.

Bali, R. K., Wickramasinghe, N., & Lehaney, B. (2009). *Knowledge management primer*. USA: Routledge.

Bardram, J. E. (2008). Pervasive healthcare as a scientific discipline. *Methods of Information in Medicine, 47*(3), 178–185.

Baskaran, V., Bali, R. K., Arochena, H., Naguib, R. N. G., Wheaton, M., & Wallis, M. (2006). Improving uptake of a breast screening programme: A knowledge management approach for opportunistic intervention. In L. Bos, et al. (Ed.), *Medical and care compunetics 3* (pp. 191–197). Netherlands: IOS.

BBC. (2001). Gujarat earthquake. http://news.bbc.co.uk/1/hi/uk/1139081.stm. Accessed 25 July 2010.

BBC. (2010). Haiti Earthquake. http://news.bbc.co.uk/1/hi/in_depth/americas/2010/haiti_earthquake/default.stm. Accessed 25 July 2010.

Bilham, R. (2010). Lessons from the Haiti earthquake. *Nature, 463,* 878–879. http://www.nature.com/nature/journal/v463/n7283/full/463878a.html. Accessed 25 Dec 2010.

Breen, M. (1997). Information does not equal knowledge: Theorizing the political economy of virtuality. *Journal of Computer-Mediated Communication, 3,* 3. http://www.ascusc.org/jcmc/vol3/issue3/breen.html. Accessed 10 March 2004.

Cothrel, J., & Williams, R. (1999). On-line communities: Helping them form and grow. *Journal of Knowledge Management, 3*(1), 54–60.

Drucker, P. (1998). *The coming of the new organization. Harvard Business Review on Knowledge Management* (pp. 1–19). USA: Harvard Business School Press.

Harland, D., & Wahlstrom, M. (2001). *The role of OCHA in emergency United Nations operations following the earthquake in Gujarat, India—26 Jan. 2001*. Geneva: United Nations.

IASC. (2010). *Response to the humanitarian crisis in Haiti: Achievements, challenges, and lessons to be learned*. Final Draft. IASC.

Immonen, A., Bali, R. K., Naguib, R. N. G., & Ilvonen, K. (2009). *Towards a knowledge-based conceptual model for post-crisis public health scenarios*. Proceedings IEEE International Conference on Humanoid, Nanotechnology, Information Technology, Communication and Control, Environment, and Management, Manila, Philippines, 185–189.

Kostakos, V., & O'Neill, E. (2004). *Pervasive computing in emergency situations*. Proceedings of the Thirty-Seventh Annual Hawaii International Conference on System Sciences (CD/ROM), 5–8 Jan. 2004. Computer Society Press, Nos. 1–2, 172–182.

Liebowitz, J., & Beckman, T. (1998). *Knowledge organizations: What every manager should know*. USA: St. Lucie Press.

Miller, F. J. (2002). I = 0 (Information has no intrinsic meaning). *Information Research: International Electronic Journal, 8*, 1. http://informationr.net/ir/8-1/paper140.html. Accessed 11 Sept 2012.

Paul, M. H., & Kimble, C. (2002). The duality of knowledge. *Information Research: International Electronic Journal, 8*(1). http://informationr.net/ir/8-1/paper142.htm. Accessed 11 Sept 2012.

Pickrell, J. (2005). Facts and figures: Asian tsunami disaster. *New Scientist*. http://environment.newscientist.com/channel/earth/tsunami/dn9931-facts-and-figures-asian-tsunami-disaster-html. Accessed 15 Dec 2010.

Rodrigo, B. C. (2001). Using information technology to support knowledge conversion processes. *Information Research: International Electronic Journal, 7*(1). http://informationr.net/ir/7-1/paper118.html. Accessed 11 Sept 2012.

Salvador, Z., Larrea, M., & Lafuente, A. (2007). *Infrastructural software requirements of pervasive health care*. Proceedings of the IADIS International Conference Applied Computing 2007, Salamanca, Spain [CD-ROM].

Shaw, J., Mulligan, M., Nadarajah, Y., Mercer, D., & Ahmed, I. (2010). *Lessons from tsunami recovery in Sri Lanka and India*. Australia: Monash University.

Sieloff, C. (1999). If only HP knew what HP knows: The roots of knowledge management at Hewlett-Packard. *Journal of Knowledge Management, 3*(1), 47–53.

Smilowitz, B. (2010). *Report on the transparency of relief organizations responding to the 2010 Haiti Earthquake*. Disaster Accountability Project.

Smith, L., & Preston, H. (2000). Information management and technology strategy in healthcare: Local timescales and national requirements. *Information Research: International Electronic Journal, 5*(3). http://informationr.net/ir/5-3/paper74.html. Accessed 11 Sept 2012.

Takeda, M., & Helms, M. (2006). Bureaucracy, meet catastrophe: Analysis of the tsunami disaster relief efforts and their implications for global emergency governance. *International Journal of Public Sector Management, 19*(2), 631–656.

UN Department of Economic and Social Affairs, World Population Ageing 1950–2050. (2002). http://www.un.org/esa/population/publications/worldageing19502050/.

UNDP. (2005). *The Millennium Development Goals Report 2005*. New York: United Nations Development Program. http://millenniumindicators.un.org/unsd/mi/mi_dev_report.asp. Accessed 22 Feb 2012.

Varshney, U. (2005). Pervasive healthcare: Applications, challenges and wireless solutions. *Communications of the Association for Information Systems, 16*, Article 3. http://aisel.aisnet.org/cais/vol16/iss1/3. Accessed 11 Sept 2012.

Wickramasinghe, N., & Bali, R. (2008). Controlling Chaos through the application of smart technologies and intelligent techniques. *International Journal of Risk Assessment and Management, 10*(1–2), 172–182.

Yuan, Y., & Detlor, B. (2005). Intelligent mobile crisis response systems. *Communications of the ACM, 48*(2), 95–98.

Chapter 9
The Analysis and Design of a Pervasive Health Record: Perspectives From Malaysia

Mohd Khanapi Abd Ghani, Rajeev K. Bali, Raouf NG Naguib and Ian M. Marshall

Abstract This chapter will outline the design of an innovative and pervasive Lifetime Health Record (LHR) dataset for the Ministry of Health Malaysia (MOHM). The dataset was developed after an analysis of clinical consultation workflows and the usage of patient demographic and clinical records in a typical outpatient clinic. Common LHR components, structures, and messages are proposed. The proposed dataset and associated framework are crucial for achieving prompt access to a patient's LHR and for the provision of seamless and continuous care. Implications for management of health information and knowledge and pervasive access are provided.

Keywords Clinical record · Patient demographic · Knowledge management · Telehealth · Malaysia

9.1 The Need for Pervasive Health Records in Healthcare Services

Portable devices and wireless technology applications in healthcare can be recognized as both emerging and enabling technologies that have been applied in various countries for improving patient care services. For example, a variety of wireless technologies such as mobile computing, wireless networks, and global positioning systems (GPS) have been applied to ambulance care in Sweden (Geier 2001) and emergency trauma care in the Netherlands (Lua et al. 2005).

M. K. A. Ghani (✉)
Faculty of Information and Communication Technology (FTMK),
University Teknikal Malaysia Melaka (UTeM) 76100 Melaka, Malaysia
e-mail: khanapi@utem.edu.my

R. K. Bali · R. N. G. Naguib · I. M. Marshall
Biomedical Computing and Engineering Technologies (BIOCORE) Applied Research Group,
Coventry University, CV1 2TT, Coventry, UK
e-mail: r.bali@ieee.org

R. N. G. Naguib
e-mail: r.naguib@coventry.ac.uk

I. M. Marshall
e-mail: i.marshall@coventry.ac.uk

R. K. Bali et al. (eds.), *Pervasive Health Knowledge Management*,
Healthcare Delivery in the Information Age,
DOI 10.1007/978-1-4614-4514-2_9,

The four different implementations of the pervasive technologies are: implanted, wearable, portable, and environmental. The level of indistinguishableness varies for each of these as implantable technologies may be completely invisible; wearable technologies may be somewhat visible, whilst portable technologies may be more visible. Environmental technologies, depending on the level of integration (such as using television for smart display), could also become indistinguishable (Upkar 2009).

With the emergence of information and communication technologies (ICT) and healthcare practices, there is now a variety of daily used items upon which medical records can be stored and displayed. These include items such as Personal Digital Assistants (PDAs), mobile phones, smart cards, and laptops, which are readily available at all times (Abd Ghani et al. 2007). Applied to a healthcare context, these devices are useful for continuity of care purposes such as storage of health records and clinical decision support systems.

In the context of a typical episodic doctor–patient consultation, a substantial portion of the healthcare provider's time is spent in obtaining the patient's medical history and subsequently recording, dictating, transcribing, and arranging the information in an organized manner before a diagnosis can be made or before an appropriate treatment can be prescribed and administered (Abd Ghani et al. 2008b).

If the patient needs to be referred to another medical provider for an expert opinion or second opinion, the entire procedure of information collection may have to be repeated. Any necessary pathological (and perhaps radiological) data collection process is a laborious task, one, which cannot be delegated to another professional (Maheu et al. 2001). Crucially, the absence or incompleteness of such data may lead to inappropriate diagnosis and treatment or one that is contrary with the person's physiological condition, for example: allergies (Chaudhry et al. 2006). According to a study conducted by the Institute of Medicine (Williams and Moore 1995), the situation is quite worrying as 30 % of physicians find great difficulty in accessing patients' records at the right time and 70 % of hospital records are found to be incomplete. Pervasive medical records are therefore important for continuing care and these efforts are currently progressing in many countries such as Canada, the United Kingdom, and countries in mainland Europe (Ingeborg and Volker 2001).

The government of Canada is committed to the development of a web-based interoperable enterprise health records solution by integrating approximately 40,000 existing health information systems in use across the country (Canada Health Infoway 2006). This is to enable the health records of patients to be available and accessible anywhere at any point of time. Similar efforts are also being undertaken in the United Kingdom's National Health Service (NHS) through its extensive health ICT project *Connecting for Health* (National Health Services 2006) where the Electronic Health Records (EHR) service is the most integral component among the applications and an important backbone of the NHS health infostructure (National Health Services 2007).

Many of the above discussions suggest that disparate health records and health information systems may not be sustained in the long term. Healthcare will not be improved if the services are still episodic and if access to health records is always restricted within a healthcare facility and an application system. Pervasive computing would enable the disparate electronic medical record (EMR) systems to be integrated through pervasive health records that could interact with portable devices anywhere at any point of time. Good care is dependent on access to the previous health records, which should be a feature of future healthcare systems.

9.2 Analysis and Design Methodology

This work outlined in this chapter is based on data obtained from the outpatient clinic of the Ministry of Health Malaysia (MOHM) to conduct, explore, and analyze use of patient health records. Two methods contributed to the proposition for the Lifetime Health Record (LHR) components and structure: (1) system analysis and (2) analysis of patient demographic and clinical data.

System analysis was explored through case study analysis, accessing archival records, discussions, and interviews. Key patient demographic and health records were identified and obtained through the collection of secondary data from various sources including documents and archival records (paper-based consultation templates and administrative and clinical forms). A pilot telemedicine application was investigated and analyzed by means of open-ended interviews, discussions, and reviews of archived records. The telemedicine contractor was contacted in order to access essential information and data, such as technical reports and application implementation experiences, which could provide invaluable input and a clearer understanding of the blueprint for the pilot telemedicine application.

For the analysis of patient demographic and clinical data, outpatient clinic personnel were contacted for accessing and obtaining the primary source of evidence through structured interviews. Based upon responses and feedback from the initial case study, detailed questionnaires were created for collecting the primary evidence and data. Through the main personnel contact of the case study organization, 30 respondents (medical officers or GPs) from different health clinics and polyclinics were identified for the interview. According to Naiburg and Maksimchuk (Naiburg and Maksimchuk 2001), the best way to understand business processes and information obtained from many stakeholders and sources is to start by modeling their descriptions. In our case, this was achieved through an analysis of an outpatient clinic business model, which described the activities, users, and stakeholders involved in the workflow.

The interviews were carried out by ten assistant researchers who were appointed to conduct the interviews with 30 doctors in outpatient clinics. The assistant researchers were all medical graduates with extensive knowledge in the clinical domain. By selecting this group, the discussion between interviewer and respondent was conducted smoothly.

9.3 Background to Outpatient Clinics

The outpatient clinic department reports (administratively) to the Family Health Development Division of the Public Health Services of MOHM. Healthcare services are provided through various health centers and community polyclinics strategically

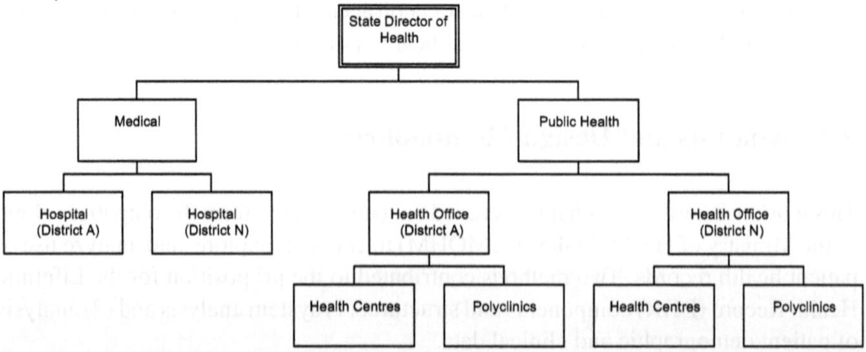

Fig. 9.1 State health organizational structure. (Adapted from Ministry of Health Malaysia 2008)

located in the most populated areas in the district. Health centers and community polyclinics comprise the first level of health services made available to the community. The services provided are comprehensive at this level, including maternal health, child health, acute and chronic care of diseases, mental health, geriatric care, community-based rehabilitation, well-person services, and health promotion. These services are provided as outpatient treatments with laboratory and radiological services supporting these functions. Pharmaceutical services are also provided in-house. Figure 9.1 below gives the organizational structure of medical and public health at the state and district level.

9.4 Analyzing the Current Health Information System

The aim of analyzing the current system was to evaluate the minimum number of application systems and data/objects needed to be captured, manipulated, and stored for creating the LHR dataset. The consultation and medical consultation workflow in which the medical records were viewed, captured, and generated in outpatient clinics were analyzed and examined.

The analysis began with the description of the workflow, relevant parts of which were mapped onto the corresponding application systems. This provided an outline of how the application systems would support or contribute towards enhancing continuous and seamless access to patient health records.

9.5 Architectural Overview of the Malaysian Telemedicine Application

In order to understand the scope of the project and fully appreciate the functional requirements of the Malaysian telemedicine application, it would be beneficial to depict the overall view of the pilot telemedicine project, the gathering of EMRs, and the generation of the LHR repository (Fig. 9.2).

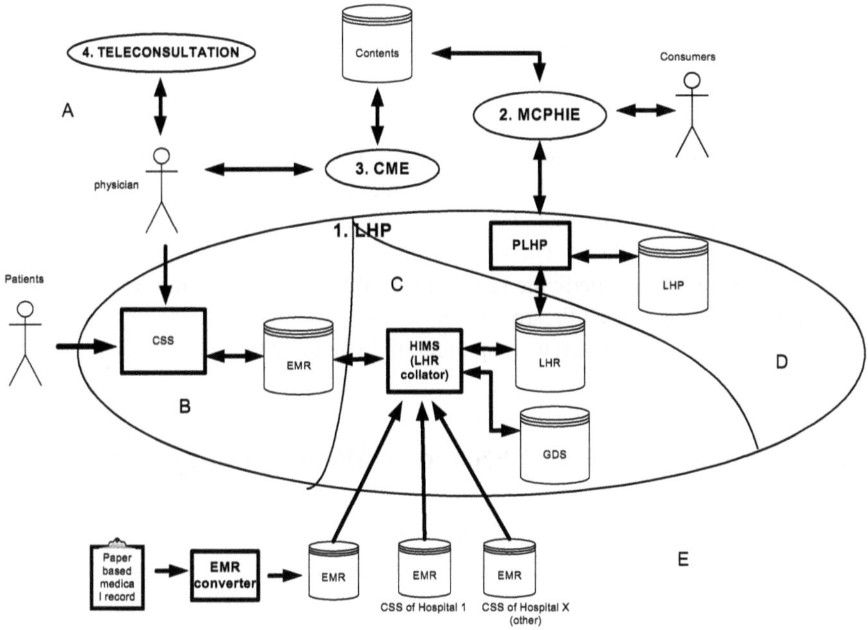

Fig. 9.2 A visualization of the entire scope of the telemedicine pilot project. (Adapted from Harun 2002, 2007; Ministry of Health Malaysia 1997c)

The top (A) of the diagram shows the three components of the Malaysian integrated telemedicine projects: mass-communication personalized health information and education (MCPHIE), continuing medical education (CME), and Teleconsultation. The bottom (E) part of the diagram shows the nontelemedicine projects or external systems, including paper-based medical records and other clinical support systems (CSS) from various hospitals that link to the lifetime health plans (LHP; LHR collator) for forming the LHR repository. The middle part of the diagram, LHP (B, C, and D) has to interface with Part A for formulating, generating, and providing a complete and integrated set of past medical records for the individual. Some of the important points that can be derived from this overall diagram include:

1. CSS (B) component has to link/collect data from teleconsultation applications to form EMRs; this has to occur even if the CSS applications are not part of the telemedicine projects. Examples are the legacy clinical information system (CIS), paper-based medical records, and other types of CIS.
2. HIMS-LHR Collator (C) has to collect all EMRs from a single healthcare center or from other healthcare centers using CSS applications and from paper medical records, converted to EMRs, to form LHRs in the LHR repository. This repository then generates and delivers group data services for central agencies and various institutions for statistical analysis and health plans.

3. Personalized lifetime health plan (PLHP; D) components may use the contents of the MCPHIE and CME module and LHR repository to formulate a generic plan called LHP.

Given these points, the LHR repository, which correlates each episode of care of an individual into a continuous health record, is the central key delivery function of the Malaysian integrated telemedicine application. The CSS and HIMS are the core components of the project and they principally collect the EMRs for generating the LHRs of individuals. The key question was whether the current framework (the Malaysian pilot telemedicine project) was able to provide continuous access to the LHR for pervasive healthcare services. In order to address this, the functional requirements for modeling each component (CSS and HIMS) will now be presented.

9.6 Critical Analysis of CSS and HIMS for Maintaining LHRs

This section explores the activities involved from CSS (the creation and collection of EMRs) to HIMS (the generation of LHRs). First, the workflow involved in providing clinical services during a doctor–patient encounter (in healthcare facilities) and the collection and distribution of LHRs at the central system are analyzed. The basic definitions of the application systems within the component (CSS and HIMS) are examined at which point it should be possible to map the relevant parts of the workflow to the corresponding application systems. This provides us with the required data objects (or information) and how the application systems will support the pervasive healthcare services. For this purpose, the analysis will continue to discuss the CSS and HIMS workflow in the next section. In each component, the analysis process will focus on the workflow and map it to appropriate applications and discover the suitable data objects for developing the LHR components and structure.

9.7 The CSS and Source of EMRs

Clinical services refer to the process of providing medical diagnosis and treatment for the patient who visits the healthcare centers for treatment. The clinical support system provides support for clinical and administrative services at healthcare centers and for creating EMRs, which directly contribute to the creation of LHRs.

The clinical support system is crucial to providing decision support for the clinician during a consultation and diagnosis process (Hovenga et al. 1996). Support is required by the clinician in order to provide a high level of professional care and accurate diagnosis and treatment. Timely and seamless access to a patient's past medical record would ensure a continuum of care. Hence, the major requirement of the CSS is to be able to retrieve past medical records seamlessly from the same healthcare center, as well as from other healthcare providers.

9.8 Consultation and Medical Diagnosis Workflow

Since the 1980s, continuous efforts have been made to exploit technology to enhance the collection, distribution, and interpretation of patient data (Szirbika et al. 2006). These have involved a process of consultation and medical diagnosis during a doctor–patient encounter. The consultation and medical diagnosis process is important for building up and collecting the patient's medical record. It is essential to explore this process in order to provide inputs for evaluating and identifying LHR datasets. A typical workflow for the process is shown in Fig. 9.3.

The above workflow is based on a typical consultation process in outpatient clinics of MOHM. The workflow is a combination of processes from various levels of healthcare facilities that include primary care centers, health clinics and polyclinics, secondary or state hospitals, and tertiary hospitals. Some healthcare facilities have fewer processes but the basic processes are covered for facilitating the consultation and medical diagnosis process.

In summary, the clinical consultation and diagnosis workflow starts when the patient arrives for a clinical visit. The patient first has to register at the counter before (s)he gets to see the doctor in the consultation room. The doctor performs an examination and, if necessary, orders tests so that an interpretation can be made. These tests and investigations are normally carried out by histopathology laboratories and/or a radiologist, with the results/interpretation being returned to the doctor. The doctor makes a diagnosis and recommends the appropriate treatment based on the results and recommendations made by the pathologist or radiologist. Once the patient's diagnosis is decided upon, drugs may be prescribed if the patient is an outpatient, otherwise the patient will be admitted into hospital for acute treatment. After receiving treatment, the patient may be billed or the treatment may be free of charge. Any follow-up appointments are scheduled before the patient is discharged.

9.9 The CSS Application Systems Workflow

There are two principal roles of the CSS applications. One is to assist in the workflow of practitioners at tertiary centers, polyclinics, and primary care centers. The second is to build up the EMRs, which will then contribute towards building the LHRs (Ministry of Health Malaysia 1997c). These roles would be realized by replacing all paper-based medical records with EMRs. The records must be made available at all times and anywhere. In this section, we will continue to identify the candidate application systems by mapping the workflow to appropriate applications. The basic definitions of the various CSS components will be described according to the workflow depicted in Fig. 9.4.

Patient Management System The first (1), seventh (7), and eighth (8) stages of the workflow for the consultation can be mapped into the patient management system (PMS). This component takes care of all administrative functions at the registration

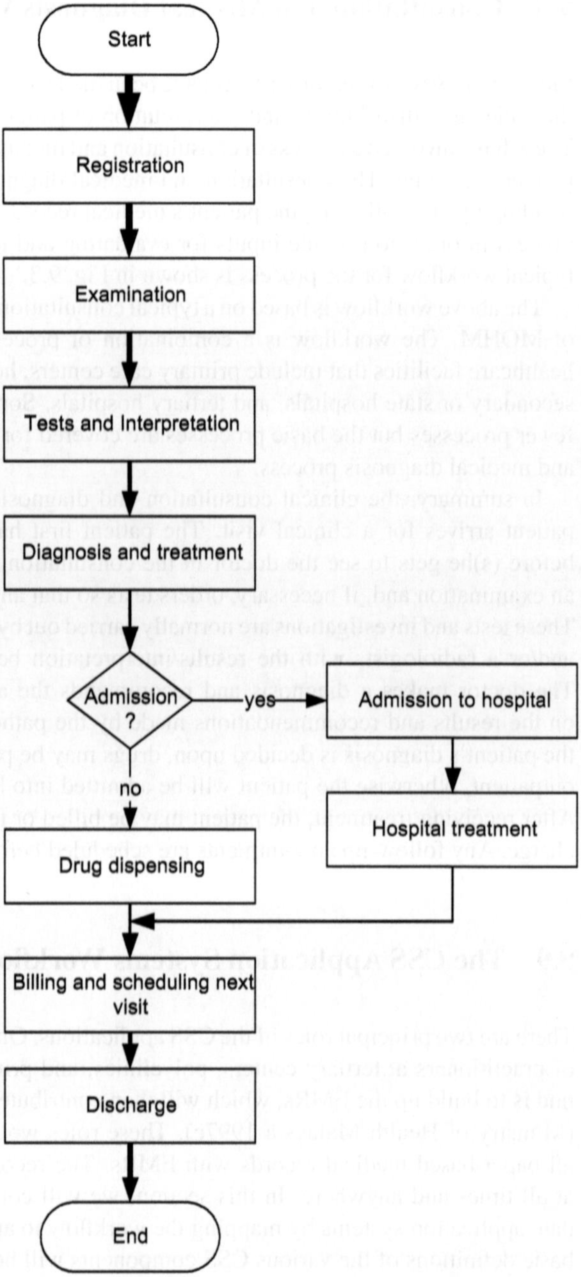

Fig. 9.3 Typical clinical consultation and diagnosis workflow

center, such as registering the patient's visit for the day, maintaining the patient's profile, scheduling of appointments, and billing. This component covers the patient's entire demographic information and provides the necessary information for clinical consultation and diagnosis.

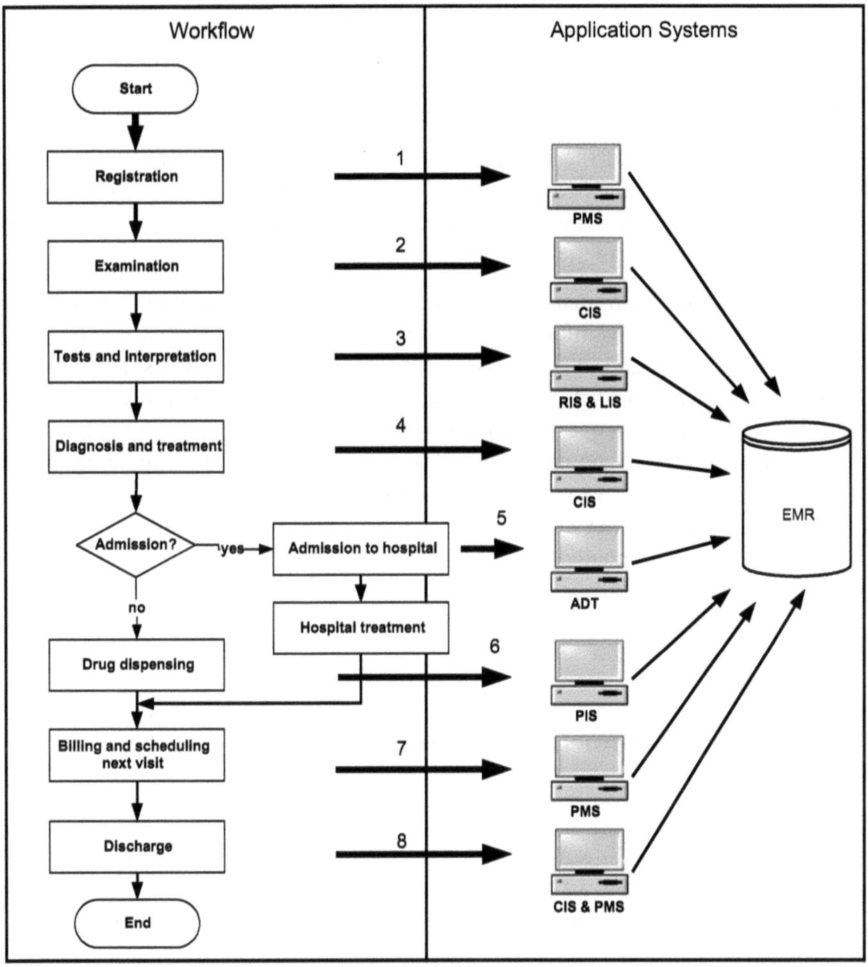

Fig. 9.4 Consultation workflow to application systems

Clinical Information System The next processes, second (2) and fourth (4) stages of the workflow can be mapped into the CIS. The CIS component mainly supports the administrative routines of the clinical processes in the workflow. This is where the data entry and retrieval of the patient's health record are carried out for viewing past visits, medical history, physical examinations, tests, interpretation, diagnosis, and treatment. At the end of the consultation and diagnosis process, the clinical findings and discharge summary will be stored in the EMR repository.

Laboratory Information System and Radiology Information System The third (3) process supports all the tasks of the clinical laboratories and of the radiology department. The laboratory information system (LIS) and radiology information system (RIS) carry out tests on samples and examination orders delivered to them. The systems receive test orders via CIS and return the results of the requested analysis through the local area network (LAN) channel of the hospital.

Admission, Discharge, and Transfer Information System In certain circumstances, the patient from a serious illness (critical disease) requires intensive treatment. The doctor recommends that the patient is admitted into the ward. This stage of the workflow (5) can be mapped onto the admission, discharge, and transfer (ADT) information system. This component basically supports the administrative routines of the inpatient process in the workflow.

Pharmacy Information System Finally, the sixth (6) stage of the workflow could be mapped to the pharmacist information system (PIS). PIS supports pharmacists at the level of tertiary care and in hospitals, healthcare centers, polyclinics, and primary care centers. The pharmacists receive prescriptions from healthcare professionals via CIS, prepare the drugs requested, and check drug interactions and compatibilities.

It is also clear from the discussion above that the CIS is the main role within the group of CSS applications that houses the EMRs and then creates LHRs. The important point here is that a suitable framework is required to ensure that the LHRs or EMRs can be continually and seamlessly accessed at appropriate times during the consultation and diagnosis process anytime and anywhere. The functions and data objects of the CSS applications to be stored and manipulated for creating LHR datasets will now be discussed.

9.10 Analyzing Functions and Data Objects

In this section, the suitable and critical datasets required during the consultation and diagnosis processes will be identified and defined. The identified datasets will be used to form the standard LHR structure. In Table 9.1, the minimal functions and datasets for CSS are listed in a high-level format (by indicating the attribute's name).

In order to enable the LHRs to be accessed anytime and anywhere, the LHR repository should be hosted and managed centrally by the application system, namely the health information management and support.

9.11 The HIMS and Source of Electronic Medical Records

Like the CSS, the HIMS is also a set of applications and has essentially two roles:

1. To create LHRs, which are critical for the basis of pervasive health information services
2. To create a health group data warehouse for policy makers and various healthcare institutions.

To achieve the goal of global information sharing and pervasive healthcare services, the health information systems must be capable of integration and communication

Table 9.1 Minimal functions and datasets for CSS

Minimal functions and data objects for CSS		
Application	Possible functions	Data objects
PMS	Patient registration Appointment Billing	The administrative component of EMRs comprising minimum the following: – Basic attributes of patient demographics including *name, identification certificate, date of birth, gender, race, religion, occupation, address, telephone number,* etc. – Next-of-kin information including *emergency contact person, relationship, address, telephone number,* etc. – Appointment information including *date and time of visit, doctor's name, type of case,* etc. – Billing information including *government servant, insurance, self-paid*
CIS	Consultation Order investigation/ test Order prescription	The clinical component of EMRs, comprising minimum the following: – *Diagnosis or problem* – *Signs and symptoms* – *Blood information* – *Allergy information* – *Onset date of problem* – *Lab test information* – *Radiology report* – *Medication information* – *Social history* – *Immunization record* – *Family history* – *Disability information* – *Recent vital signs, etc.*
LIS	Manage test orders Manage data entry for laboratory test results and retrieval of EMRs	The laboratory component of EMRs comprising minimum the following: – *Date and time of test* – *Test result* – *Test report* – *Type of test* – *Number of test taken* – *Place and location of test done*
RIS	Manage radiology order Manage radiology data entry and retrieval of EMRs	The radiology component of EMRs comprising minimum the following: – *Date and time of studies done* – *Study reports* – *Parts of body examined* – *Name of interpreter* – *Number of pictures taken* – *Place and location of studies done*

Table 9.1 (continued)

Minimal functions and data objects for CSS		
Application	Possible functions	Data objects
PIS	Manage prescription order Manage drug dispensing Manage drug stock and retrieval of EMRs	The prescription component of EMRs comprising minimum the following: – *Start date for taking the drug* – *Drug's name* – *Dosage* – *Frequency of taking the drug* – *Place and location where the drug is taken*
ADT	Manage ward Manage patient discharge and retrieval of EMRs	The ADT component of EMRs comprising minimum the following: – *Ward information* – *Date admitted* – *Date discharged, etc.*

with one another (Roman et al. 2006). The medical records generated from different applications and locations should be hosted at a central location for accessibility anytime and anywhere. The creation of LHRs will be carried out by means of linking and integrating the summary of EMRs from various CSS applications as well as from paper medical records converted to EMRs.

The LHR repository requires an information system to ensure the completeness of an individual's medical history in a health data warehouse. Hence, a principal target for the HIMS applications is to create as many LHRs as possible in order to provide access to LHRs from CSS users thus providing the full set of integrated patient health records (for any given patient) regardless of time and location. This should assist healthcare professionals to make better diagnoses and provide better treatment when compared to episodic medical records alone, which are essentially restricted to data available at the same healthcare centers only.

9.12 The HIMS Workflow

As explained earlier, HIMS is responsible for managing the collection and the distribution of LHRs. This summary of medical data will be used by medical practitioners at healthcare centers. Policy makers and health planners would prefer to see final reports such as health indicators and statistics. The workflow of HIMS therefore refers more to the process of EMR collection for the generation of an LHR repository than to the workflow at healthcare centers. Within this context, three activities are involved in the HIMS workflow:

- LHR collection
- LHR management
- Health data warehousing

LHR Collection The workflow starts with the collection of LHRs from various healthcare facility centers such as hospitals and primary care centers. The LHR is the central key delivery point of the Malaysian integrated telemedicine application (Ministry of Health Malaysia 1997b). The LHR consists of all episodes and encounters of an individual from all healthcare centers since birth and correlates each episode of care into a continuous health record. Therefore, it is a summarized health record of every individual compiled from their electronic medical records.

The records refer to a patient's medical history cumulatively derived from the clinical support system (such as the clinical information system, laboratory information system, pharmacy information system, and patient management system) and can be collected and gathered from the various spectra of health information systems and healthcare levels (EMRWorld 2006; Coiera 2003; Bates et al. 2001). The most important consideration is that the LHR should not only contain longitudinal health summary information but also incorporate the online retrieval of a patient's health history whenever required. When the LHRs are generated and stored in a proper data store system, the LHR repository has to be managed and maintained.

LHR Management The LHR repository will have to be managed by HIMS in terms of security, data integrity, and the retrieval and storage processes. This is an important activity as the LHR repository is the nerve center of the Malaysian telemedicine project; issues such as data integrity and security are imperative.

Health Data Warehouse The useful and effective delivery of healthcare services depends on the ability to deliver appropriate and proactive value-added services to different client segments on a timely basis. Irrespective of the access enablers, distribution channels, and technology employed, the services need to be packaged according to usage patterns, demographics, and behavioral psychographics (Ministry of Health Malaysia 1997a). Such studies can be part of the services offered by the health data warehouse.

At this point, it should be understood that the creation process of LHR depends mainly on the availability of EMRs from various healthcare centers. In fact, the LHR is not only a subset of the EMR but also provides the possibility of online retrieval of all the details of the EMRs. As such, crucial patient health summaries need to be analyzed and identified for developing a pervasive LHR dataset. This is required to ensure the continuous and seamless upkeep of patient health records.

The next section will map the HIMS workflow to appropriate applications that can be used as important inputs for identifying data objects and proposing the alternative LHRs datasets.

9.13 Workflow and Possible Application Systems

The HIMS workflow can be made up of the following set of applications. First, the LHR collection can be mapped to the LHR collator application where it puts together an episode summary of EMRs to form a single fully integrated LHR for each individual. The final LHR will contain all EMR summaries for that person in chronological order from birth to the current date as well as some form of summary (lifetime health summary) that is required for easy reference (Abd Ghani et al. 2007).

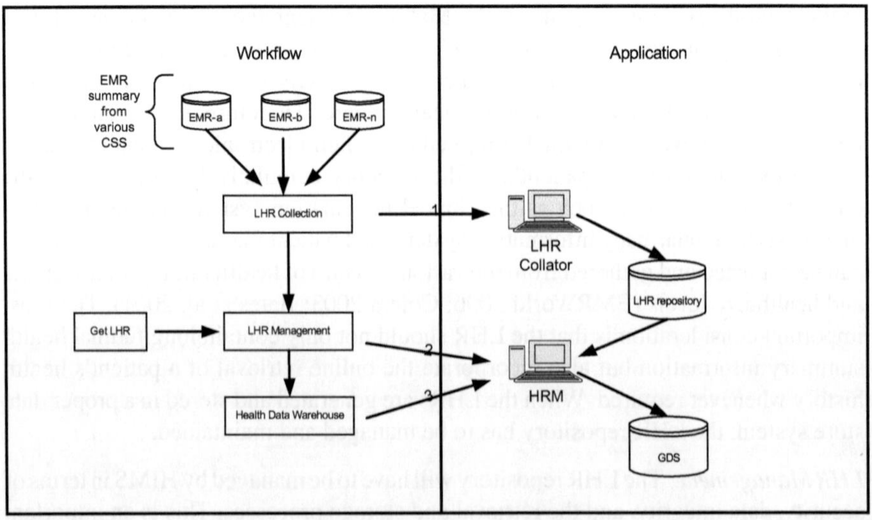

Fig. 9.5 Conceptual workflow of EMR to LHR and the applications

HIMS needs to be active at all times because the LHR contents need to be updated with every new encounter at various healthcare centers.

Second, the LHR management should be mapped to the health record management application (HRM) where its major concern is managing the data retrieval and distribution from the LHR repository to CSS's users at healthcare facilities (healthcare professionals, nurses, etc.). In addition, the HRM is also responsible for managing the integration services, reference datasets, transactions and access.

Finally, data mining can also be mapped to a HRM module where it makes use of data in the LHR repository to produce value-added health group data services for researchers, policy makers and health planners. Figure 9.5 depicts the HIMS workflow mapped to the application systems.

9.14 Functions and Data Objects

This section presents and gives an indication of the functional requirements of the LHR collator and HRM and defines the suitable datasets for forming the LHR components and structure. The format for this Table 9.2 is slightly different from that for the CSS applications mainly because this cluster of applications requires many other types of support to ensure success. The format of the table is explained as follows.

- Functions
- Support needs
- Enablers
- Technical
- Data object.

Table 9.2 Minimal functions and data objects for HIMS

Function	Support needs	Enablers	Technical	Data objects for LHR datasets
LHR repository, LHR collection, storage, archiving	Data center organization, network communication infrastructure, security, policy, and enforcement group	Enterprise management system, network management system, database management system, performance management system	Data entry at source, dataset guidelines, protocols and format (e.g., DICOM, HL7, CTV3, etc.)	Patient identification number, patient demographics, discharge summary/clinical notes
HRM—acce ss capabilities and data distribution, who/how/what/when/where, management of user groups	24 h online, network communication infrastructure	Network management system	Online 24 h, open system standards, telecommunication network infrastructure, dataset guidelines, protocols and format, possible portable storage devices	Patient demographics (name, identification number, DOB, allergy, blood type/rhesus), patient problem summary (disease, e.g., hypertension, diabetes; chief complaint, e.g., fever; condition, e.g., pregnant; disability, e.g., deaf, blind; social problem, e.g., smoking, substance abuse; date of onset; date of resolution), patient episode summary (episode list, date of visit, healthcare facility name, test ordered, treatment ordered)
LHR integration/ link	Network communication infrastructure, security, policy and enforcement group	Network management system, broadband, GSM	Online 24 h, open system standards, telecommunication network infrastructure, dataset guidelines, protocols and format, possible portable storage devices	Patient demographics (name, identification number, DOB, allergy, blood type/rhesus), patient problem summary (disease, e.g., hypertension, diabetes; chief complaint, e.g., fever; condition, e.g., pregnant; disability, e.g., deaf, blind; social problem, e.g., smoking, substance abuse; date of onset; date of resolution), patient episode summary (episode list, date of visit, healthcare facility name, test ordered, treatment ordered)

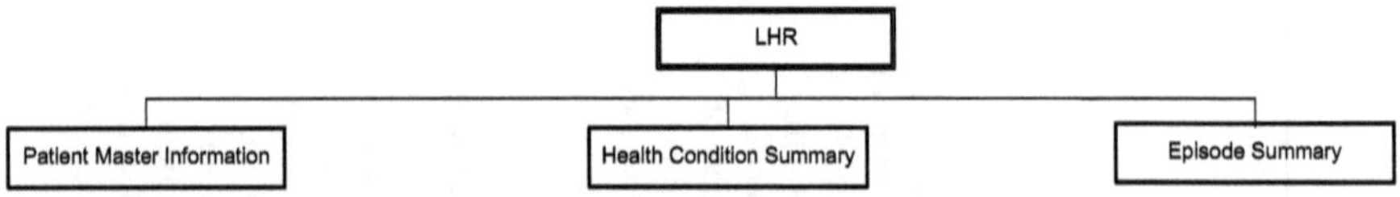

Fig. 9.6 Proposed LHR components

9.15 Summary of System Analysis

At this point, the overall picture of the consultation and medical diagnosis workflow in outpatient clinics (CSS-EMRs) and LHR (HIMS-LHRs) collection processes have been described and presented. It is critical to maintain the patient health records or EMRs because they are a source of information for other health record structures, especially for generating the LHR repository. Therefore, the continuity and the integrity of EMRs and linkages to the LHRs have to be established first. According to Coiera (Coiera 2003), the more the doctor knows about his/her patient, the more knowledge (s)he will gain to identify his/her patient's problems and the more accurate will be the treatment given. As a result of the system analysis, the applications system and data objects have been introduced and identified. This information would be used to design the LHR components and structure for pervasive health information.

With all the previous discussions in mind, the following section presents the proposed LHR datasets for pervasive health information.

9.16 A Proposed Pervasive LHR Dataset

Based on inputs and evidences obtained from the case study, the LHR was divided into three components (refer to Fig. 9.6).

1. Patient master information
2. Health condition summary
3. Episode summary.

9.17 Patient Master Information (PMI)

The Patient Master Information comprises administrative records and the required information to identify and distinguish the patient across healthcare facilities and levels (Health Level 7 2008; Ministry of Health Malaysia 2003). It is often used to locate the patient identifier, including patient demographic data and the related health administration information. The Patient Master Information includes a demographic record, next-of-kin record, birth record, family health record, medical insurance record, employment record, and organ donor record.

It was noted from the findings of the primary data collection that a patient's demographic information to be viewed by doctors during consultation is highly regarded. Such information is indicated as compulsory due to the fact that it is a key identifier for the patient. Analysis shows that only eight data elements (with total size of 162 bytes) were identified as crucial and available at the point of doctor patient consultation (see Table 9.3). The administrative records detailed above could be included in the patient information as optional records.

9.18 Health Condition Summary (HCS)

The Health Condition Summary consists of records, which summarize the illness and wellness condition of the patient. Each condition has a status indicator to indicate either an active or inactive status. This summary of the patient's condition will enhance the continuity of care by providing a method for communicating the most relevant information about a patient and providing support for the generation of LHRs (Ministry of Health Malaysia 1997c; Medical Record Institute 2006). It was noted from the primary data collection that the first step of patient care or treatment was that the doctor gathers information about the patient's current health status. Here, many types of information can be collected about the patient and placed in portable devices or web databases in the form of the patient's LHR. By giving the latest health condition summary of the patient at the start of a first doctor–patient encounter, the accuracy, quality, safety, and continuity of care can be ensured.

The Health Condition Summary component could be added and enhanced in the future. The set of information provided below is the result of initial analysis revealed from the primary data collection (see Fig. 9.3). The Health Condition Summary comprises such information as chronic disease, allergy, immunization/vaccination, social history, surgical medical procedure, disability, and obstetric record.

9.19 Episode Summary

The episode summary consists of data for a particular episode or visit. If required, it provides the necessary data for reference to the source of the information where details of the episodes are stored. It comprises the following information: episode record, encounter record, symptoms record, diagnosis record, lab test record, radiology record, medication record, vital sign record, and health plan record.

These LHR components provide the conceptual structure for pervasive LHR information and it is envisaged that many LHRs could be collected and generated continuously from various health information systems.

Table 9.3 Patient demographic data elements and requirements

No.	Data element	Description	Format	Length	Priority (R/O)
1.	PMI number	A unique person identification number used throughout life for healthcare purpose	Alphanumeric	9	R
2.	Name	Name of the patient	Alphanumeric	80	R
3.	Alias name	Other name of the patient	Alphanumeric	80	O
4.	IC no	National registration identification number	Alphanumeric	12	O
5.	Old IC no	Old personal identification that was used before 1990	Alphanumeric	80	O
6.	ID type	Type of the other ID number such as military number	Alphanumeric	10	O
7.	ID number	Identification number other than new and old IC No	Alphanumeric	12	O
8.	Birth date	Date of birth	Date (ddmmyyyy)	8	R
9.	Sex	Patient gender	Alphanumeric	1	R
10.	Race code	Individual race code	Alphanumeric	4	R
11.	Blood type	Blood group [A/B/AB/O]	Alphanumeric	2	O
12.	Blood rhesus	Positive or negative	Alphanumeric	1	O
13.	Marital status code	Individual marital status code	Alphanumeric	1	O
14.	Religion code	Individual religion code	Alphanumeric	2	O
15.	Nationality code	Nationality code	Alphanumeric	3	O
16.	Home address 1	Address line 1	Alphanumeric	30	R
17.	Home address 2	Address line 2	Alphanumeric	30	O
18.	Home address 3	Address line 3	Alphanumeric	30	O
19.	Home town code	Town code	Alphanumeric	4	O
20.	Home state code	State code	Alphanumeric	2	O
21.	Home country code	Country code	Alphanumeric	3	O
22.	Home postcode	Postcode number	Alphanumeric	5	O
23.	Home phone	Home phone number	Alphanumeric	15	R
24.	Postal address 1	Address line 1	Alphanumeric	30	O
25.	Postal address 2	Address line 2	Alphanumeric	30	O
26.	Postal address 3	Address line 3	Alphanumeric	30	O
27.	Postal town code	Town code	Alphanumeric	4	O
28.	Postal state code	State code	Alphanumeric	2	O
29.	Postal country code	Country code	Alphanumeric	3	O
30.	Postal postcode	Postcode number	Numeric	5	O
31.	Office phone	Office phone number for working patient	Alphanumeric	15	O
32.	Mobile phone	Personal phone number	Alphanumeric	15	R
33.	E-mail	Electronic mail address	Alphanumeric	50	O
34.	Organ donor indicator	This denotes that the patient is an organ donor	Alphanumeric	1	O
35.	Chronic diseaseIndicator	This denotes that the patient has a chronic disease	Alphanumeric	1	O

Table 9.3 (continued)

No.	Data element	Description	Format	Length	Priority(R/O)
36.	Allergy indicator	This denotes that the patient has allergy to any medication	Alphanumeric	1	O
37.	Death certified indicator	Death medical certified	Alphanumeric	1	O

Total size of patient demographic record (O + R): 612 bytes
Total size of required data elements (R): 162 bytes

9.20 Discussion

It was noted from the findings that doctors in outpatient clinics have a limited time to consult patient problems; the average consultation period is 20 minutes. This demonstrates that the patient health records required by the doctors should be simplified (in terms of number of attributes and size in bytes) for facilitating the consultation process in an efficient and effective manner. The simplified version of LHR could be stored and accessed from portable devices such as smart phones. This would enhance prompt access to health records and could improve the diagnosis process. The impact of this pervasive LHR for knowledge management, contact, and practice will now be elaborated.

Platform for Research and Development Malaysia's integrated telehealth system (or other health information system), via its role as the premier database repository for patient's LHRs in the country, will function as the health knowledge platform from which a variety of research and development activities can be launched (Harun 2002). These activities will spearhead the development and establishment of initiatives, which may produce innovative healthcare products and services of national and international significance.

Health Group Data Services The standard datasets of LHRs would ensure that data, information, and knowledge within it could be mined and applied to various applications transcending geographical and service-level constraints. The LHR repository would be a premier source of health knowledge and could effectively feed back into the LHR purposes (Ministry of Health Malaysia 1997b; Wickramasinghe et al. 2006).

Health Knowledge Communication Protocol The benefits of standard LHR datasets are numerous. The LHR datasets ensure that many applications could be integrated, thus increasing the interoperability of the telehealth system and its subsequent assimilation into other health information systems. The patient's health records could be written to and displayed from portable devices within the patient's possession.

Personalized Lifetime Health Plan The LHR datasets enable the many records of individuals to be mined incrementally. The LHR repository contains the medical records of a person for his/her lifetime on a chronological basis. Through proper knowledge management applications, with standardized practices, personalized health plans could be created and/or tailored to the specific needs of the individual based on the person's complete and integrated LHR (Abd Ghani et al. 2008b). The health plans and health records created by the patients and healthcare professionals would generate a personalized lifetime health plan for the individual and provide crucial healthcare knowledge for quality healthcare (Wickramasinghe and Schaffer 2006; Abd Ghani et al. 2008a).

9.21 Conclusion

The analysis of patient demographic and clinical data usage in public outpatient clinics across Malaysia supported the need for patient health summaries (and records). Such records provide invaluable information to healthcare professionals during doctor–patient consultation episodes. The analysis concluded that a simplified version of patient health records should be developed. This was to be achieved by developing and proposing lifetime health record components and structures tailored to Malaysian telehealth perspectives and needs. By judicious use of three major LHR dataset components, a pervasive LHR could easily be created for use in portable devices. Where doctors have better knowledge to provide accurate and more efficient treatment protocols, healthcare services offered to the patient could therefore be improved.

References

Abd Ghani, M. K., et al. (2007). *The design of flexible front end framework for accessing patient health records through short message service.* IEEE Asia-Pacific Conference on Applied Electromagnetics. Melaka: IEEE.

Abd Ghani, M. K., et al. (2008a). *A flexible telemedicine framework for the continuous upkeep of patient health record.* Proceedings of the Fourteenth Americas Conference on Information Systems, Toronto, Canada.

Abd Ghani, M. K., et al. (2008b). Electronic health records approaches and challenges: A comparison between Malaysia and four East Asian countries. *International Journal of Electronic Healthcare, 4*(1), 78–104.

Bates, D., Cohen, M., & Leape, L. (2001). Reducing the frequency of errors in medicine using information technology. *Journal of the American Medical Informatics Association, 8*, 301–308.

Canada Health Infoway. (2006). EHRS blueprint—an interoperable EHR framework: Executive overview. http://knowledge.infoway-inforoute.ca/en/. Accessed 19 Mar 2007.

Chaudhry, B., et al. (2006). Systematic review: Impact of health information technology on quality, efficiency, and costs of medical care. *Annals of Internal Medicine, 144*, 742–752.

Coiera, E. (2003). *Guide to health informatics* (2nd ed.). London: Hodder Arnold.

EMRWorld. (2006). Electronic medical records—EMR vs EHR. http://www.emrworld.net/emr-research/emr.php. Accessed 23 Feb 2008.

Geier, J. (2001). Saving lives with roving LANs. Network World. http://wireless.itworld.com/4246/NWW0205bgside/pfindex.html. Accessed 30 Mar 2007.

Harun, M. H. (2002). *Integrated telehealth: What does it all mean?* DTP Enterprise Sdn Bhd.

Harun, M. H. (2007). Early experience of integrated telehealth—lessons learned.

Health Level 7. (2008). HL7 electronic health record. http://www.hl7.org/ehr/. Accessed 27 Mar 2008.

Hovenga, E., Kidd, M., & Cesnik, B. (1996). *Medical informatics: An overview*. Melbourne VIC: Churchill Livingstone.

Ingeborg, S., & Volker, W. (2001). Incremental EHR introduction considering the situation in health care and the current standards under development. *International Congress Series, 1230*, 889–894.

Lua, Y. C., et al. (2005). A review and a framework of handheld computer adoption in healthcare. *International Journal of Medical Informatics, 74*, 409–422.

Maheu, M. M., Whitten, P., & Allen, A. (2001). *E-health, telehealth and telemedicine: A guide to start-up and success*. San Francisco: Jossey-Bass, Wiley.

Medical Record Institute. (2006). Continuity of Care Record (CCR)—The Concept Paper of the CCR—Version 3. http://medrecinst.com/pages/about.asp?id=54. Accessed 02 Apr 2008.

Ministry of Health Malaysia. (1997a). *Concept request for proposal for lifetime health plan—schedule 3: Network infrastructure*. Copyright 1997 Government of Malaysia.

Ministry of Health Malaysia. (1997b). *Concept request for proposal for lifetime health plan: Telemedicine flagship application*. Copyright 1997 Government of Malaysia.

Ministry of Health Malaysia. (1997c). *Telemedicine blueprint: Telemedicine flagship application*. Copyright 1997 Government of Malaysia.

Ministry of Health Malaysia. (2003). *Business Process Reengineering Workshop Report: National Consensus Meeting for Standard Operating Procedure of Patient Management*. Copyright 2003 Government of Malaysia.

Ministry of Health Malaysia. (2008). Ministry of health Malaysia—organisation structure. http://www.moh.gov.my/opencms/opencms/moh/carta.html. Accessed 29 Apr 2008.

Naiburg, E. J., & Maksimchuk, R. A. (2001). *UML for database design*. Boston: Addison-Wesley.

National Health Services. (2006). Connecting for health—fact sheets: N3. http://www.connectingforhealth.nhs.uk/publications/toolkitaugust05/factsheet_n3.doc. Accessed 17 May 2006.

National Health Services. (2007). The NHS care records service better information for better, safer care. http://www.nhscarerecords.nhs.uk/patients/what-do-i-need-to-do-now/how-can-i-find-out-more/nhs-crs-summary-leaflets/summary_leaflet_online.pdf. Accessed 19 July 2007.

Roman, I., et al. (2006). Demographic management in a federated healthcare environment. *International Journal of Medical Informatics, 75*(9), 671–682.

Szirbika, N. B., Pelletier, C., & Chaussalet, T. (2006). Six methodological steps to build medical data warehouses for research. *International Journal of Medical Informatics, 75*, 683–691.

Upkar, V. (2009). *Pervasive healthcare computing: EMR/EHR, wireless and health monitoring*. New York: Springer.

Wickramasinghe, N., & Schaffer, J. (2006). Creating knowledge driven healthcare processes with the intelligence continuum. *International Journal of Electronic Healthcare, 2*(2), 164–174.

Wickramasinghe, N., Geisler, E., & Schaffer, J. (2006). Realizing the value proposition for healthcare by incorporating KM strategies and data mining techniques with the use of information communication technologies. *International Journal of Healthcare Technology and Management, 7*(3/4), 303–318.

Williams, F., & Moore, M. (1995). Telemedicine: Its place on the information highway. http://www.csua.berkeley.edu/~utsai/Telemed.html. Accessed 20 Apr 2005.

Chapter 10
Quality Analysis of Sensors Data for Personal Health Records on Mobile Devices

John Puentes, Julien Montagner, Laurent Lecornu and Jaakko Lähteenmäki

Abstract Data collected by multiple physiological sensors are being increasingly used for wellness monitoring or disease management, within a pervasiveness context facilitated by the massive use of mobile devices. These abundant complementary raw data are challenging to understand and process, because of their voluminous and heterogeneous nature, as well as the data quality issues that could impede their utilization. This chapter examines the main data quality questions concerning six frequently used physiological sensors—glucometer, scale, blood pressure meter, heart rate meter, pedometer, and thermometer—as well as patient observations that may be associated to a given set of measurements. We discuss specific details that are either overlooked in the literature or avoided by data exploration and information extraction algorithms, but have significant importance to properly preprocess these data. Making use of different types of formalized knowledge, according to the characteristics of physiological measurement devices, relevant data handled by a Personal Health Record on a mobile device, are evaluated from a data quality perspective, considering data deficiencies factors, consequences, and reasons. We propose a general scheme for sensors data quality characterization adapted to a pervasive scenario.

Keywords Knowledge for data validation · Quality estimation of heterogeneous data · Pervasive health monitoring · Data understanding · Physiological sensors · Mobile devices

10.1 Introduction

Usually, patients make direct requests to the physicians, in order to obtain answers about their health condition in a face to face interaction. During these exchanges, patient observations that may provide valuable complementary information are only communicated verbally to the physician, who may or may not take them into account.

J. Puentes (✉) · J. Montagner · L. Lecornu
Institut Telecom, Département Images et Traitement de l'Information,
Telecom Bretagne, Technopôle Brest-Iroise, CS 83818 29238 Brest Cedex 3, France
e-mail: John.Puentes@telecom-bretagne.eu

J. Lähteenmäki
Knowledge Intensive Services, VTT Technical Research Center of Finland,
Otaniemi, Finland

R. K. Bali et al. (eds.), *Pervasive Health Knowledge Management*,
Healthcare Delivery in the Information Age,
DOI 10.1007/978-1-4614-4514-2_10,

With the increasing use of multiple physiological sensors and the associated patient observations combined within a Personal Health Record (PHR) managed using a mobile device, the patient–physician interaction is likely to change in some cases. Consider, for instance, a heart failure patient, who after an hour of moderate physical activity feels unusually tired, with a sensation of arrhythmia. In this case, collected data could permit to analyze the symptoms severity, to determine if it is pertinent to ask for an appointment or rush to the closest healthcare center. Another case to examine could be the follow-up of disease treatments, given that after hospital discharge, outpatient clinic consultation hours are limited, and as a consequence, such lack of time delays the optimization of patient medication significantly. In this case, periodical assessment of longitudinal PHR data could reduce the delay of medication evaluation. In both contexts, assuming that a Decision Support (DS) system will be capable of analyzing stored data and provide appropriate information to better understand each situation, it is fundamental to determine initially the appropriateness of available data in terms of quality.

The notion of data quality is essential in order to estimate if collected data from sensors and patient observations, can be properly processed to extract the required information, given that data acquisition conditions are uncontrolled and depend mainly on how the user respects a given protocol, the type of sensors and vendor, as well as the collected data volume. Moreover, sensors measurements are subject to various limitations like resolution errors, calibration variability, response time, noise, variable accuracy, and precision depending on working conditions, signal artifacts, use discomfort, and battery lifetime. On the other hand, observations are patient-dependent, need to be structured and documented, besides being somewhat subjective. In addition, data can be manually entered by the individual, or automatically transferred from sensors. In this last context, the sensor can generate continuous data streams without human intervention (fully automatic) or even if the measurement and the transmission are automatic, only a single measurement is carried out at a time (semi-automatic). All these elements may contribute differently to alter the expected data quality and should be evaluated before the application of data exploration or information extraction algorithms. Our work intends to examine some essential data quality questions related to six commonly used physiological sensors, namely, glucometer, scale, blood pressure meter, heart rate meter, pedometer, and thermometer, along with patient observations, to determine raw data usability potential, in accordance with stipulated processing goals. Such considerations are expected to facilitate patient follow-up and DS, in the areas of wellness monitoring and disease management.

Data from physiological sensors and personal observations are the components of a PHR for DS that, stores, exchanges, and displays the data considered to be a complement to the Electronic Health Record (EHR), with the goal of endorsing individuals' active role in their own healthcare. The use of this PHR for DS implies, nevertheless, that it is critical to understand how to handle and evaluate data imperfections before information extraction takes place. This chapter examines the initial required knowledge to cope with physiological sensors data quality issues within a context of pervasive PHR, to facilitate data exploration and information extraction under deficient data conditions.

PHRs on mobile devices are a nascent pervasive application trend in healthcare (Sect. 10.2) around which there are still multiple issues and questions. Nonetheless, the examined physiological sensors (Sect. 10.3) data that can be handled in a PHR using a mobile device are expected to become a common component of the PHR in scenarios like the two described previously, and therefore sensors data quality analysis (Sect. 10.4) is necessary to determine the usability of the collected data for information extraction. Results are discussed to identify processing requirements according to the quality estimation approach (Sect. 10.5), before summarizing our work (Sect. 10.6).

10.2 Personal Health Records on Mobile Devices

Physicians are slowly but progressively loosing the complete control they once had over patient data and information. Besides having increasing access to parts of their own data organized as summaries (Civan et al. 2006), individuals are also boosting the collection of their physiological signals to follow-up some health conditions (Coughlin and Pope 2008; Korhonen et al. 2003; Pantelopoulos and Bourbakis 2010). Even though such initiatives are not formally advocated by physicians, their growing popularity driven in part by the availability of portable, wearable, or implantable physiological sensors and multifunction mobile devices (phones, tablets, and personal digital assistants), is leading to study the potential usefulness of collected data beyond wellness monitoring or disease management, to provide appropriate DS (Stead and Lin 2009). Some reported applications include: automatic arrhythmias detection (Leijdekkers and Gay 2006), semiautomatic hypertension management in diabetic patients (Logan et al. 2007), manual medication adherence support (Silva et al. 2009), outpatient cardiac rehabilitation using varied types of data acquisition procedures (Walters et al. 2010), manually feed wellness diary (Mattila et al. 2010), and multipurpose platforms with semiautomatic inputs (Laakko et al. 2008), among others. Figure 10.1 illustrates a recent example of user interfaces to manually input sensors data for remote patient monitoring system, which provides automatic feedback to patients and alerts to health professionals when the support system estimates that patient data should be reviewed (Lähteenmäki et al. 2011).

Despite their pervasiveness and efficiency as distributed terminals, mobile devices are not capable of hosting computational intensive applications like handling large databases, study voluminous data quality, or properly integrate masses of data to produce an information extraction workflow. Although those devices were not specifically designed to manipulate large sets of medical data and information, they can be used as intermediation interfaces to communicate data, partially visualize it, and handle DS requests.

PHRs are basically understood as a personalized summary of personal health data, around which several services can be connected according to patient needs and decisions (Eysenbach 2008; Kaelber et al. 2008; Pagliari et al. 2007). However, given the implicit and nonformalized variability of existing PHRs approaches, multiple

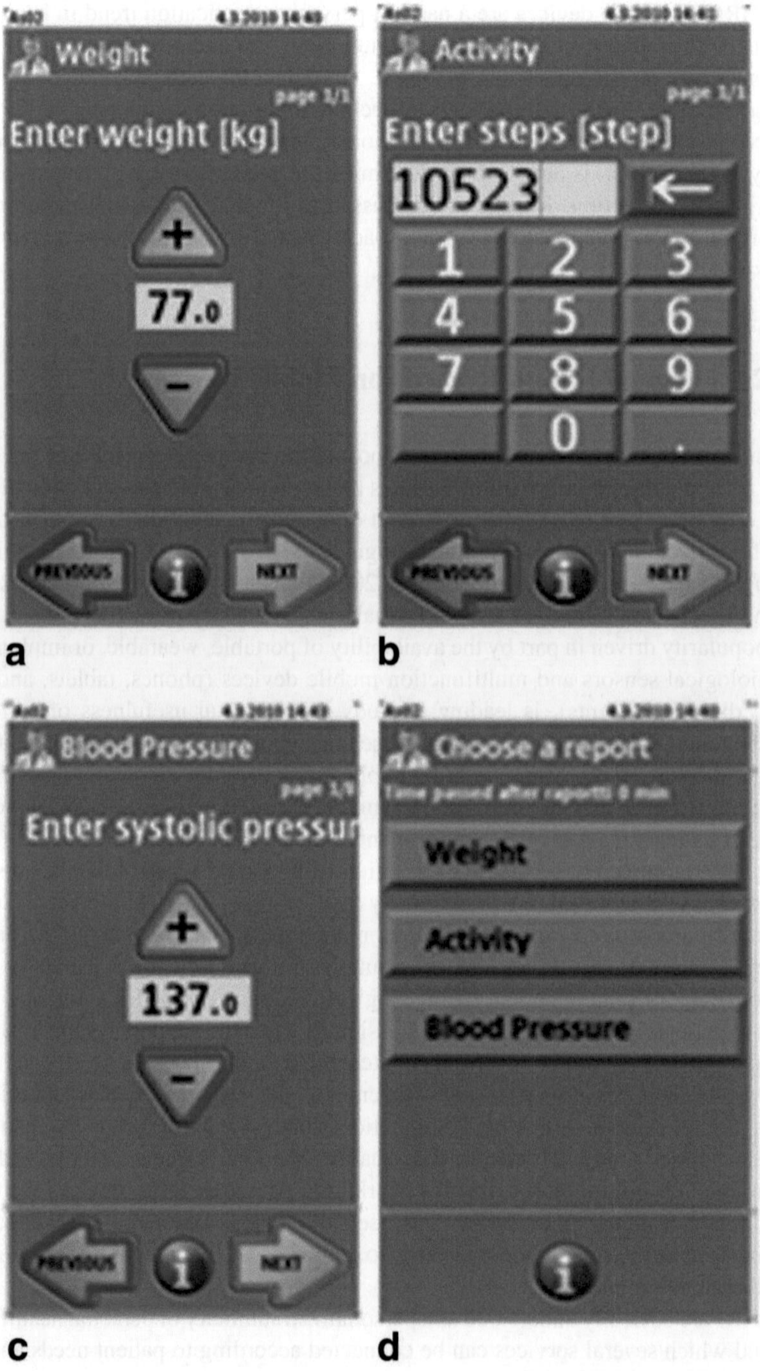

Fig. 10.1 Examples of physiological sensors data input interface on a mobile phone (Lähteenmäki et al. 2011): **a** for weight measurements, **b** for amount of steps, **c** for systolic pressure values, and **d** to request a specific values set report

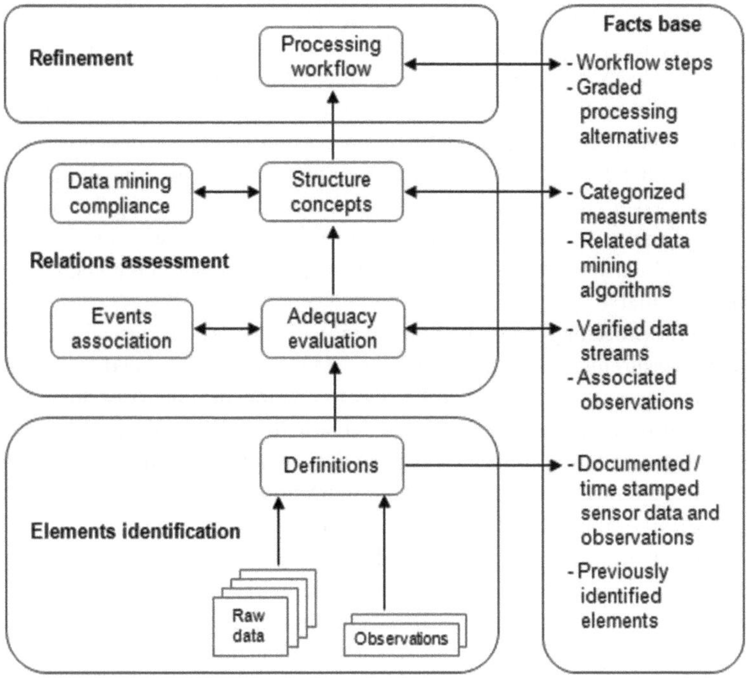

Fig. 10.2 Schematic description of the knowledge-based integration model proposed to structure the PHR data, formed by the interactions between three layers (Puentes and Lähteenmäki 2011): elements identification, relations assessment, and refinement

definitions as well as a wide range of complexity characterize PHR concept, without a definition based on consensus (Kaelber et al. 2008; Pagliari et al. 2007; Tang et al. 2006). In addition, the PHR has been rarely incorporated to medical care flows, mainly because its adoption raises a wide variety of questions and challenges (Halamka et al. 2008; Pagliari et al. 2007). The PHR used in this work is restricted to sensors data and personal observations, periodically uploaded to a server, to be available for visualization and/or processing. Such data can be acquired by the patient throughout the day or night, without the intervention of medical personnel, as part of wellness supervision or disease follow-up. This PHR also contains personal observations related to the occurrence of events like dizziness, weakness, dyspnea, arrhythmias, or other anomalies, conveying additional elements that properly documented have the potential to reinforce DS. Supplementary data like medications, laboratory tests, medical history, and allergies that can be either accessed from the patient EHR or copied from it to the PHR are not taken into account for this analysis. Our definition of PHR implies therefore that it is a complement to the health care professionals-oriented EHR, and does not include summaries or subsets of data originally stored and handled within the EHR. Otherwise, sensors data recorded in the PHR can be structured according to a knowledge-based integration model (Puentes and Lähteenmäki 2011) that evaluates data appropriateness to extract information (Fig. 10.2).

The abstracted integration of three data processing layers basically relies on the initial data definitions according to their identification, characterization, and structure (bottom layer), combined with data validation, taking into account the coherence of collected values and unusual events, along with their relations through time (middle layer). Results obtained lead to define a processing workflow, depending on grading the available data quality, and suggesting processing workflow alternatives (top layer). Each layer generates a set of extracted facts that enable to guide the processing steps of the next layer. Documented and time-stamped elements from previous physiological sensors measure sessions uploads, are also part of the first layer output whenever available.

Even if the preceding integration model globally verifies data streams, categorizes recorded measurements, and examines the compliance with related data mining algorithms, those analysis alone do not assess completely the quality of processed data. In general, it is commonly accepted that data quality relies mainly on accuracy and completeness, leading to disregard data sets on which one of these quality estimations is not appropriate. Such data quality definition applies when the sensors work under ideal conditions and if the user handles correctly all the sensing devices. That is not necessarily the case on practical conditions, when the device's operation may be interrupted or altered by multiple factors and the users could inappropriately place, read, or activate the sensors. Under those circumstances some parts of the collected data will correspond to the accepted data quality elements, while others need further interpretation according to complementary data quality knowledge, before deciding if the concerned data set should be deleted from the database or can be used with certain constraints. To this end, relevant data stored in PHR is evaluated from a quality point of view making use of different types of formalized knowledge, according to the characteristics of diverse physiological measurement scenarios and devices.

10.3 Physiological Sensors Data and Personal Observations

In order to determine the required knowledge to evaluate physiological sensors data quality, this section presents the initial elements to be considered before deciding if collected data are adequate or not. These basic concepts allow formulating the data quality framework discussed in Sect. 10.4. The following definitions are considered at the first data integration level (Sect. 10.2) to verify raw data characteristics.

10.3.1 Time Concepts

Temporal data are the core reference that enable data studies through time, for both separated and combined sensors data sets. This is the most critical global reference, because its absence means that one or several data sets could not be properly used to extract information, regardless of their accuracy and completeness. The main time concepts concern:

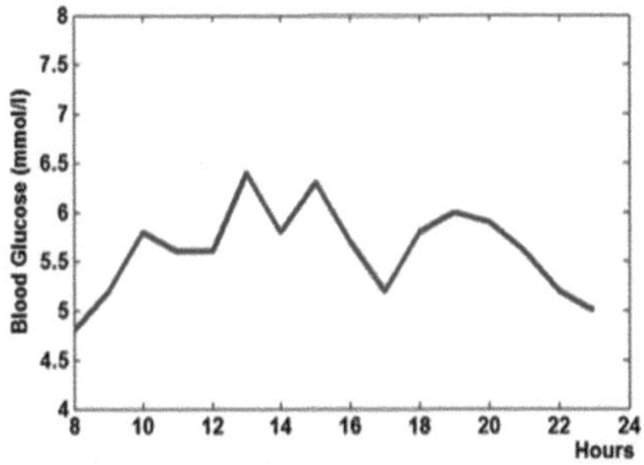

a

Item	Attributes
Glucose measurement definition	Sugar concentration in the blood
Units	mmol/L or mg/dL
Glucometer	Brand, model, glucose measurement definition, values ordering, accuracy (0.1 mmol/L or 1 mg/dL), validity range (20-500mg/dL), acquisition conditions (10-40°C) and file type
Valid glucose measurements	3.6 to 5.8 mmol/L or 64.8 to 104 mg/dL

b

Fig. 10.3 Example of blood glucose data measurements during 1 day (**a**) and the table of associated items and attributes to be verified at the elements identification level (**b**)

1. Time reference to be used when analyzing the integrated data—date, hour, minutes, seconds, and related measurement sessions. It is taken as the starting point in time to evaluate a group of measurement sessions.
2. Time measurement definitions and related units—instant and interval. Values can vary from a specific moment, to intervals of minutes, hours, days, weeks, or months.
3. Time stamps during a measurement session can be sequential or fragmented in continuous subintervals. When the second case is detected, a list of subintervals is generated.
4. Elements of a session—measurement, user and session identification, date, start time, duration, type of sensor, and/or observation report.

10.3.2 Glucose

Devices to measure glucose concentration in the blood apply an electrochemical sensing procedure, namely: a reproducible amount of blood absorbed by capillary test strips reacts with an enzyme electrode containing glucose oxidase or dehydrogenase; this enzyme is reoxidized with an excess of a reoxidized mediator reagent at the electrode that generates an electrical current; the amount of glucose in the blood that has reacted with the enzyme is proportional to the total charge passing through the electrode. The frequency of measures varies from 1 to several times per day (Fig. 10.3), to a measure per minute depending on the sensor type. For such continuous monitoring, a tiny sensor under the skin is preferred, with a transmitter to send information to a wireless mobile device receiver.

Required basic knowledge to validate and document raw glucose data is listed in Fig. 10.3b. It consists of the measurement definition, units, glucometer features, and the intervals of valid measurements. Use of glucometers is fundamental for diabetes follow-up. Currently, glucose measurements management can be facilitated by the use of pervasive applications running on mobile devices, which can make automatic and continuous measurements (Cho et al. 2009; Tatara et al. 2009).

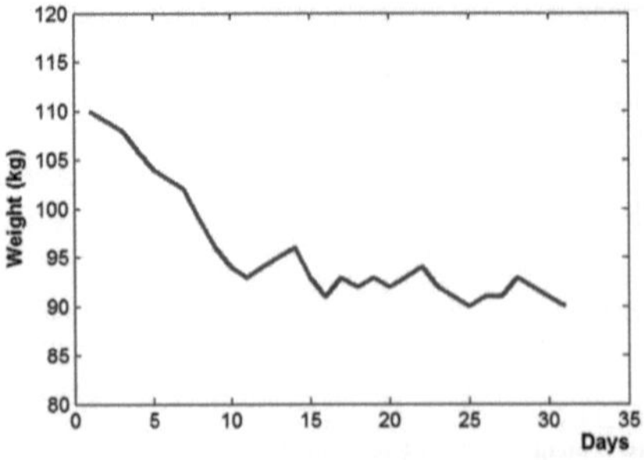

Item	Attributes
Weight measurement definition	Subject's body mass
Units	Kg and gr
Scale	Brand, model, weight measurement definition, values ordering, accuracy (0.2 Kg), validity range (10-150 Kg), and file type
Valid weight measurements	Table of values according to age, height and clinical condition

b

Fig. 10.4 Example of weight data measurements during 1 month (**a**) and the table of associated items and attributes to be verified at the elements identification level (**b**)

10.3.3 Weight

Weighting scales measure the vertical pressure of the standing body on a sensor using either mechanical or digital approaches. In the case of medical weighting scales, specific models integrated for beds and wheel chairs have been also developed. Advanced designs include wireless monitoring combined with other sensors like body mass index, height rod and data transfer to the EHR. Normally, an individual's weight is measured once a day in the morning before breakfast (Fig. 10.4a).

Relevant knowledge needed to validate and document raw weight data is presented in Fig. 10.4b. It encompasses the weight measurement definition, units, scale features, and the descriptions of valid measurements. Weight measurements are frequently used in longitudinal studies to detect risk factors associated to pathologies on which weight is a significant variable. Periodic measurements monitor individual's weight through time in different contexts like dietary follow-up, personal fitness, and when recovering from or making the follow-up of a clinical condition. Except for some recent models, it is not possible to save automatically the data, but to make manual data inputs (Lähteenmäki et al. 2011; Yon et al. 2007).

10.3.4 Blood Pressure

Blood pressure originates from the force exerted by blood on the arterial walls, as the heart contractions make it circulate on the body. Commonly, arterial pressure is measured in a noninvasive way placing a manometer on the left arm, since blood pressure is slightly higher in the left side near the aorta. The manometer is integrated to an inflatable cuff that maintains it in contact with the arm skin, minimizing pressure loss. Reduced-form and cuffless sensors (Hung et al. 2004) have also been included in small-sized devices like pulse-pens (Salvi et al. 2004). To facilitate frequent measurements at home, wearable forms (wrist-worn, attached to finger) of

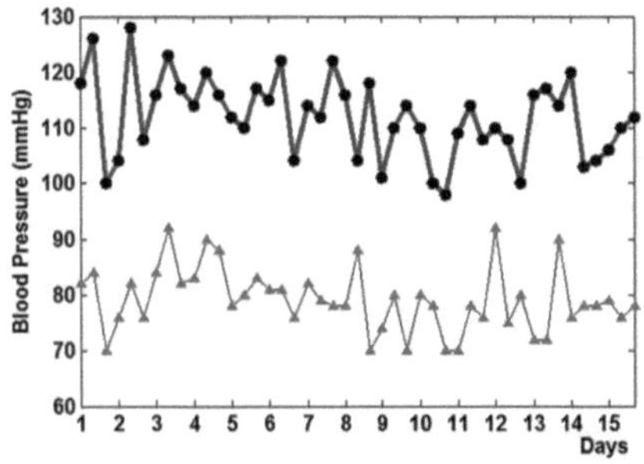

a

Item	Attributes
Blood pressure measurement definition	Systolic and diastolic blood pressure measured at the upper arm
Units	mmHg
Blood pressure meter	Brand, model, blood pressure measurement definition, values ordering, accuracy and file type
Valid blood pressure measurements	Normal systolic 120/140 mmHg Normal diastolic 80/90 mmHg

b

Fig. 10.5 Example of systolic (*round points*) and diastolic (*triangular points*) blood pressure data measurements during 15 days with three values per day (**a**) and the table of associated items and attributes to be verified at the elements identification level (**b**)

such system have been also proposed (Anliker et al. 2004; Mundt et al. 2005). More invasive methods like the insertion of an intravascular cannula exist, but are inappropriate for self-measurement. Two different pressure values synchronized on heart rate are acquired simultaneously: systolic and diastolic pressure. The first corresponds to pressure during contraction of the heart ventricles (higher value), and the second during the relaxation phase of blood inflow (lower value). Measures are acquired at periodic intervals several times a day by automated sensors, while the basic blood pressure control might involve only one measurement per day, and manual data feed. An example of systolic and diastolic pressure measurements is shown in Fig. 10.5a.

Basic blood pressure meter knowledge necessary to validate and document raw data is described in Fig. 10.5b. It includes a definition of measurement definition, used pressure units, information provided by the sensor manufacturer, and ranges of normal pressure values. Positioning the pressure sensor is simple and moderate position variations do not highly affect the measurements. However, other activities (speaking, moving, walking, etc.) during the measurement can modify arterial pressure, and therefore it is recommended to remain seated.

10.3.5 Heart Rate

Heart rate is often measured simultaneously with blood pressure, given the very close nature of these physiological phenomena. For instance, heart rate can be estimated using the periodicity of systolic blood pressure values. There are also other measurement methods: electrodes attached to the chest skin to monitor the electrocardiogram; or noninvasive approaches as placing a visible-light sensor on anatomical parts like the fingers characterized by thin skin, to measure periodical blood color variations due to changes in oxygen level as indicators of heart activity. Since heart rate sensors are rather small-sized, integration to wearable devices as

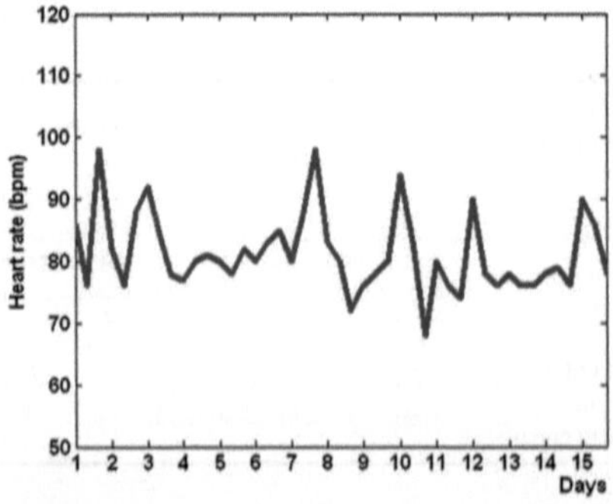

a

Item	Attributes
Heart rate measurement definition	Pulse
Units	Beats per minute (bmp)
Heart rate meter	Brand, model, heart rate measurement definition, values ordering, accuracy and file type
Valid heart rate measurements	At rest 40-60 bmp, in moderate activity 60-80 bmp, walking 76-108 bmp, during exercise 109-160 bmp These magnitudes vary depending on age, weight, height and clinical condition

b

Fig. 10.6 Example of three daily heart rate data measurements during 15 days (**a**) and the table of associated items and attributes to be verified at the elements identification level (**b**)

a finger-ring have been experienced (Asada et al. 2003). Moreover, such sensors have also been connected to portable electronic devices, like a smart phone, for continuous measurement and data transmission purposes (Worringham et al. 2011). Analyzed data are usually obtained by measuring heart rate several times a day, assuming that the integration time necessary to count heart beats is constant. An example of heart rate measurements is presented in Fig. 10.6a.

Basic knowledge necessary to validate and document raw heart rate data is described in Fig. 10.6b, including used units (in relation with the measurement integration time), information provided by the sensor manufacturer about the equipment, commonly accepted ranges of normal heart rate values in several conditions, and patient data that have to be known to determine normal ranges. At low levels of blood pressure, there is a risk of confusion between the central rate (heart) and radial rate (rhythm of blood flow in peripheral arteries). Theoretically, these rates are the same, but mixing them up in a unique measurement session could lead to irregular signals.

10.3.6 *Activity*

There are basically three types of devices to infer the activity level: step counter, pedometer, and accelerometer. The step counter enumerates the amount of steps, while the pedometer also estimates the distance and the accelerometer additionally estimates the speed. Pedometers are at the moment the most commonly used devices to measure activity, by detecting the vertical motion of a mechanical sensor. Although wireless activity measurement devices have been available in the last years, data transfer to the mobile devices is in general carried out manually or semiautomatically. Studied data consists of the distribution of steps per minute during arbitrary periods of time (Fig. 10.7a).

Basic pedometer knowledge necessary to validate and document raw activity data is described in Fig. 10.7b. It includes the activity measurement definition, units,

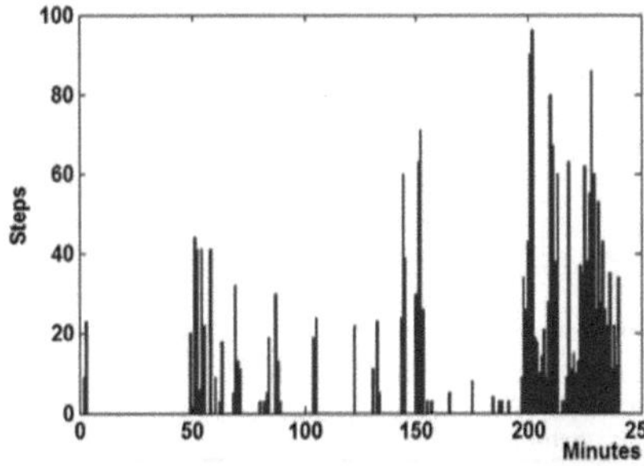

a

Item	Attributes
Activity measurement definition	Movement in termes of walking steps
Units	Amount of steps per time unit Depends on the pedometer characteristics and can be expressed also as distance
Pedometer	Brand, model, activity measurement definition, values ordering, accuracy and file type
Valid activity measurements	0 to 180 steps per minute and up to 10 000 steps per day

b

Fig. 10.7 Example of activity data measurements during 4 hours (**a**) and the table of associated items and attributes to be verified at the elements identification level (**b**)

pedometer features, and the interval of valid measurements. From the data interpretation and information extraction viewpoint, to define activity as a sum of walking steps is rather restrictive, because it excludes any other activities (like, for instance, skating, climbing, dancing, weight lifting, etc.), but it is a universal human motion mode that can be quantified in a simple and inexpensive manner. The main interest of using pedometers concerns the link between physical activity related to changes in body mass, blood pressure, and heart rate (Bravata et al. 2007).

10.3.7 Temperature

Several technologies have been developed to measure the body temperature, for instance, mercury in glass, digital mercury and infrared, placing the corresponding sensor at different anatomical places, like mouth, temporal artery, ear, or armpit (Crawford et al. 2011). Each method has its specific variability and error ranges, which must be taken into account when analyzing data sets. Measurements can be obtained at irregular or regular moments as well as continuously (Fig. 10.8a).

Body temperature measurement is usually the initial part of a full clinical examination and in a pervasive health scenario, if it is measured continuously could be an early warning of a developing symptom, or give information about treatment and pathology evolution. Some continuous temperature monitors have been developed that are able to record temperature data with a variable periodic acquisition interval from 1 minute to 24 hours (Sessler 2008).

10.3.8 Observations

Conventionally, nurses or healthcare assistants make observations about patients' status under particular circumstances (Wheatley 2006). Such exercise implies

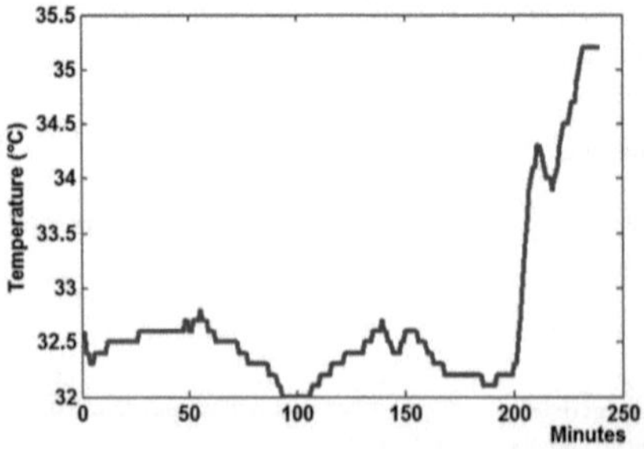

a

Item	Attributes
Temperature measurement definition	Superficial skin heat
Units	Heat in degree Celsius; Depends on the thermometer characteristics and can be expressed in other units
Thermometer	Brand, model, temperature measurement definition, values ordering, accuracy (0.05°C to 0.1°C) and file type
Valid temperature measurements	From 10 to 42°C

b

Fig. 10.8 Example of skin temperature data measurements during 4 hours (**a**) and the table of associated items and attributes to be verified at the elements identification level (**b**)

certain training not commonly acquired by individuals making use of pervasive health systems. In addition, individuals' subjectivity plays a nonnegligible role when describing the degree of certain situations. Nevertheless, if properly formulated, these data can provide additional useful information (Strömgren et al. 2001), suggesting that personal observations should be added to sensors data in the PHR. For that reason, a structured and simple ergonomic application can record at any time the observations description on a mobile device, limiting as much as possible the use of free text. The main elements to be taken into account are:

1. *Observations source description*. Source application, time stamp, and file type.
2. *Observations definition and description*. Dizziness (confusion, loss of stability and perception), weakness (discomfort, fatigue), and dyspnea (distress, breathlessness), quantified to levels such as "none," "occasionally," and "frequently."
3. *Observation report content*. Observations definitions, rank on a scale given by the patient to the sensation, circumstance that provoked it, frequency, additional comments, and source application.
4. *Valid observation report*. Applications to create observations reports must comply with the required observation report content.

10.4 Sensors Data Quality Analysis

Support to decision making has been identified as a relevant challenge related to the use of physiological sensors for personalized care (Gatzoulis and Iakovidis 2007). A significant part of DS success depends on sensors data quality beyond the conventional accuracy and completeness assumptions. Taking as reference concepts described in Sect. 10.3, the proposed analysis is based on essential data features related to each type of sensor or observations generation, which can alter unexpectedly data exploration and information extraction results, if those features are not properly taken into account. We focus on data quality analysis in sensors operational phase without including preliminary sensor design and testing considerations. At the basic knowledge level, criteria to define data deficiencies are:

Inconsistent Values Given the constrains fixed by an absolute definition rage, other data range or possible physiological interactions between two signals, analyzed data do not respect any of them appearing out of bounds with respect to the expected behavior. Inconsistency can also arrive when sudden changes in amplitude of some isolated values occur producing outliers. Those changes can be followed by lighter periodic variations, revealed by first or higher statistical order moments processed locally using sliding windows, inducing internal data set coherence defaults.

Irrelevant Values These appear, for instance, as very significant signal amplitude variations at relative high frequencies, and can be thus interpreted as noise when they are properly identified, considering that pertinent information about the studied situation is not provided. Other form of noise appears when amplitude variations are smaller than the sensor resolution indicated by the manufacturer, or are too small with respect to the expected measurement level.

Unavailable Values During a data acquisition session, single or multiple values can be missing due to improper sensor operation or because the sensor is not capable of acquiring values out of its range of measurement. Data can also be considered as inexistent when there is no complementary information to properly explain a particular deficiency and as a consequence the concerned values cannot be used.

At a higher knowledge level, each one of these data deficiencies descriptions is formulated as algorithms to automatically detect their appearance in a data set and decide how to handle it, depending on its potential impact on the quality of conveyed information. Since conventionally the notion of extracted information emerges when data are interpreted to find a sense to it in a given context, additional knowledge is necessary to examine more complex features of data quality. The following criteria are thus directly linked to an assumed available predetermined reference, necessary to formalize the measurement context, and represent essentially the cumulated consequences of values deficiencies on collected data sets:

Coherence Acquired data sets are expected to consistently represent the physiological measured parameter (physical reference) and to do it within the proper time frame (temporal reference) repetitively for the same individual. When data sets with deficiencies are compared, the resulting degree of coherence evaluates the internal data set compatibility with the measurement context as part of the associated data quality.

Proximity to Real Value Recorded data sets relative quality also depends on how close they are to the corresponding reference physiological measurement gold standard represented by the sensor calibration. These measurements are affected by other factor as noise and sensibility limits. Independently, or associated to dispersion estimations, the accuracy criterion illustrates the data set variability with respect to the used reference. Precision is also considered to be significantly affected when multiple measures of the same phenomenon under identical conditions are characterized by extensive values dispersion compared to the assumed sensors response modeled under controlled conditions.

Pertinence Even if none of the previous deficiencies are detected in the data sets, the manner data acquisition was carried out could make them irrelevant. Such lack of data quality is produced when the measurement sessions do not follow the required acquisition periodicity; when different signals that must be synchronized are acquired separately, or when values represent different integration intervals; when despite periodicity and synchronicity, acquisition conditions differ between sessions (physical, emotional, or environmental conditions). Pertinence issues are also produced when the sensor is not adequate to measure the studied phenomenon because it is partially incompatible with measurement references.

When data deficiencies are found at either single values or entire data sets, it is also necessary to identify the potential deficiency cause in order to solve it, because otherwise most of the data acquisition effort will be wasted. For that reason, some possible interpretations should be associated to the previous evaluations. That knowledge concerning the interpretation labels can be described as:

Data Management Error Generated by a human operator that wrongly assigned the measurement session within the PHR, or incorrectly grouped data sets at the preprocessing stage. It could also be associated to manual, semiautomatic, or automatic transmission errors, as well as postoperational inappropriate data manipulations.

Limited Sensor Even if the sensor measures the physiological parameter correctly, its sensibility, resolution, and/or periodicity of measurements are not compatible with some situations of the intended study. It also concerns the application to input patient observations, which can be unsuitable sometimes because considered items do not fit patient sensations.

Calibration Error The sensor does not behave as expected because it has not been properly calibrated, the utilization conditions do not fit calibration limits, the calibration was not verified when it was necessary, or the calibration is gradually lost through time. Analogously, observations can be reported using an application that does not structure correctly all expected sensations.

Measurement Error Produced by sensors that do not work properly because of a temporal malfunction, inappropriate acquisition conditions, functional degradation of the sensor, and/or because the sensor has changed its position without the user noticing it.

User Negligence Caused by user voluntary or involuntary carelessness at a given instant or period of time despite having demonstrated previously correct understanding of how to apply the measurement protocol.

Unsuitable Protocol Because of difficulties to understand and correctly apply the measurement protocol, acquired values may not represent the indicated periodicity and/or expected values range, not being therefore significant for the intended study. This situation can also happen when acquisition conditions change during a measurement session.

Table 10.1 Data quality characterization common to most of the PHR signals

	Coherence			Proximity to real value			
	Physical	Temporal	Internal	Accuracy	Precision	Pertinence	Possible interpretation
Outliers and sudden changes in statistical moments				•	•		Calibration error Measurement error User negligence Unsuitable protocol
Position of measures with respect to physical value ranges	•			•			Data management error Calibration error Measurement error
Relations with other PHR data	•		•				Data management error Measurement error User negligence
High frequency variations hiding pertinent information	•				•	•	Limited sensor Measurement error Unsuitable protocol
Values' dynamic range inferior or near to sensor precision					•	•	Limited sensor Unsuitable protocol
Missing data		•					Data management error Measurement error User negligence Unsuitable protocol

The rest of the section examines how observed data quality deficiencies at separate values or data sets levels for the different data sources can be characterized according to data quality deficiencies indications, impact on data quality, and which reasons could explain the given situation.

10.4.1 Common Data Quality Criteria

Data deficiencies are closely related to the measured physiological parameter, sensor characteristics and performance, measurement conditions, and user behavior. However, there are basic general data deficiencies that can be spotted in every signal only considering the information stored in the PHR, and characterized by plain inspection or applying simple signal processing algorithms. Table 10.1 lists the main data deficiency indicators (1st column), produced data deficiencies (2nd to 7th columns) and possible interpretation (8th column) that can be identified. The same scheme is applied throughout this section.

At this basic global level, high frequency variations are likely to have the higher impact, followed by outliers, the position of measures with respect to physical value ranges, the relations with other PHR data, and a values' dynamic range

Table 10.2 Characterization of time concepts data quality

	Coherence			Proximity to real value			
	Physical	Temporal	Internal	Accuracy	Precision	Pertinence	Possible interpretation
Inappropriate time resolution	•	•	•			•	Limited sensor Unsuitable protocol
Different time resolutions of two or more signals	•	•	•			•	Limited sensor Unsuitable protocol
Different time resolutions for the same signal	•	•	•			•	Calibration error
Same time units with different reference time intervals		•	•			•	Data management error Calibration error
Contradictory time stamps		•	•			•	Data management error Calibration error Measurement error
Missing start and/or end measurement time reference		•	•			•	Measurement error

inferior or near to sensor precision. The most frequent data deficiencies are physical incoherence and precision defaults. There are multiple reasons to explain those deficiencies with a prevalence of measurement errors and unsuitable protocol.

10.4.2 Time Concepts Data Quality

Time tracking is inherent to any of the intended portable sensor-based physiological measurements and in most of the cases, it is automatically associated to the given data set or personal observations. There are, nevertheless, situations on which the time reference quality can be altered with consequences for all or some of the related values (Table 10.2).

Since time concepts do not relate directly to the sensor measurement performance, i.e., accuracy and precision, the most penalizing factors are the difference of time resolutions for a signal, a set of different physiological signals, or for data sets of the same signal. The other indicators, same units but different references, contradictory time stamps, and lack of start or end reference, do not necessarily influence the physical measurement reference. Moreover, the most relevant deficiencies when quality issues emerge have an impact, by order of relative importance, on: temporal and internal coherence, pertinence, physical coherence. Also, calibration error could be the most common possible interpretation, followed by limited sensor, unsuitable protocol, data management error, and measurement error. Data transmission errors independently of the transmission modality are considered as data management errors.

Table 10.3 Characterization of glucose measurements data quality

	Coherence			Proximity to real value			
	Physical	Temporal	Internal	Accuracy	Precision	Pertinence	Possible interpretation
Measurement bias	•	•		•		•	Calibration error Measurement error
Unjustified high variation between successive values				•		•	Measurement error User negligence
Invalid or unexpected time stamp				•		•	Unsuitable protocol
Incoherence between a measured glucose rate variation compared to a reference glucose variation	•	•		•		•	Measurement error Unsuitable protocol

10.4.3 Glucose Data Quality

Glucose measurements can be acquired individually at home or in a pervasive mobile monitoring manner, with or without direct analysis. Given that the glucose rate is not constant in the human body, data validity depends on how error limits relate to the reference values. Measurements accuracy is therefore determined according to procedural recommendations (Sacks et al. 2002) or norms (ISO 15197 2003). For instance, the DIN EN ISO 1597 norm requires 95 % of all results to be within ±15 mg/dl of the reference values for glucose levels less than 75 mg/dl, and within ±20 % of the reference values for glucose results greater than or equal to 75 mg/dl. A recent study (Krouwer and Cembrowski 2010) divides the analytical error in four categories—device imprecision, random patient interference, protocol-independent bias, and protocol-dependent bias—to define grids of blood glucose monitoring performance for clinical purposes. By comparison, Table 10.3 lists the main deficiencies considered to characterize glucose measurements data quality.

The emergence of measurement bias and incoherencies when comparing to reference variations produce most of the identified data deficiencies, followed by unjustified high variation between successive values and invalid or unexpected time stamps. Identified data quality deficiencies have mainly consequences on accuracy and pertinence, while measurement errors and unsuitable protocol are frequent possible interpretation. Data deficiencies could augment as new devices for continuous glucose monitoring (pervasive or not) besides alerts generation, intend to anticipate glucose imbalances, and regulate insulin doses progressively.

10.4.4 Weight Data Quality

Regardless of its apparent simplicity, the measurement of body weight is relatively complex given its high variability during the day. In addition, self-reported weight

Table 10.4 Characterization of weight measurements data quality

	Coherence			Proximity to real value			
	Physical	Temporal	Internal	Accuracy	Precision	Pertinence	Possible interpretation
High variation between consecutive measures		•		•	•	•	Calibration error User negligence Unsuitable protocol
Offset appearance		•		•		•	Calibration error
Time stamps variation		•		•		•	User negligence Unsuitable protocol
Incoherent data set trend	•	•	•	•		•	Data management error
Weak periodic variations with respect to precedent values		•				•	Measurement error User negligence
Progressive near constant measurement offset	•	•		•		•	Calibration error

measurements are prone to be underestimated (Taylor et al. 2006) and the difficulties to calibrate hospital scales (Pedrolli et al. 2009) certainly could be mirrored in the use of personal scales, which are more popular but less suitable. Nevertheless, the accuracy and precision of scales are not being examined by specific recommendations or norms. Some of the most common weight data deficiencies are described in Table 10.4.

Weight measurements data volume is reduced compared to other physiological signals. As a consequence, data quality may be relatively more vulnerable than when the amount of values is significantly higher. High variations between consecutive measures, incoherent data set trends, and progressive near constant measurement offsets are the main data deficiencies indicators, followed by the appearance of offsets, time stamps variations, and weak periodic variations. Data quality deficiencies are very significant at the temporal coherence, pertinence, and accuracy levels. Calibration errors, user negligence, and unsuitable protocol are the most common possible interpretations.

10.4.5 Blood Pressure Data Quality

Measurements of blood pressure have the specificity of presenting two values for each time stamp: systolic and diastolic pressure. The blood pressure signal is thus composed of two curves holding complementary pieces of information. On the other hand, data quality problems are also double, since the validity of measures depends not only on normal value ranges, but is also linked to relations between the two curves. Table 10.5 lists possible data deficiencies due to this composed nature and relations with related signals of the record.

Table 10.5 Characterization of blood pressure measurements data quality

	Coherence			Proximity to real value			
	Physical	Temporal	Internal	Accuracy	Precision	Pertinence	Possible interpretation
Synchronization between diastolic/systolic signals		•	•			•	Limited sensor Calibration error Measurement error
Correlation between diastolic/systolic signals			•	•	•		Data management error Measurement error
Relative position and gap between diastolic/systolic curves	•		•	•			Data management error Measurement error
Relations with heart rate values	•		•				Data management error Measurement error

Synchronization problems between blood pressure curves are difficult to spot if only signal values are studied, except when a strong correlation is supposed to exist. Within such context, all relations (temporal, magnitude, and correlation) between diastolic/systolic signals appear as the most critical factors. As a result, data defaults of blood pressure measurements have a strong impact on internal and physical coherence, followed by accuracy. Data management errors and measurement errors are the more frequent possible interpretations.

10.4.6 Heart Rate Data Quality

The close relation of heart rate and blood pressure measurements makes the data quality considerations to be partially linked. Moreover, some abnormal values of blood pressure can cause irregularities in the heart rate signal (central/radial rate), with consequences for the combined coherence of the two phenomena. On the other hand, heart rate is, along with temperature, one of the vital signals that is rapidly influenced by subjective reasons as the psychological and emotional state of the patient. Other external influences that could explain anomalies in heart rate data, for instance, undocumented type of effort, are supposed to be avoided by instructions of the measurement protocol. Table 10.6 summarizes heart rate data quality deficiencies.

The coherence of heart rate values is very complex to assess, given that some apparent defaults could not be caused by any of the proposed interpretations, but is part of the physiologic behavior. The main indicators of data defaults are the existence of abnormal values or outliers that can be explained in the specific case of heart rate by a confusion between central and radial rates (e.g., after a too low blood pressure), as well as variations of statistical moments that can be the result of a change in patient's emotional states. Data defaults of heart rate measurements have particular consequences on physical and internal coherence and accuracy, as

Table 10.6 Characterization of heart rate measurements data quality

	Coherence			Proximity to real value			
	Physical	Temporal	Internal	Accuracy	Physical	Pertinence	Possible interpretation
Abnormal values			•	•		•	Limited sensor Measurement error
Sudden changes	•			•		•	Limited sensor Unsuitable protocol
Relations with blood pressure values	•		•				Data management error Measurement error

Table 10.7 Characterization of activity measurements data quality

	Coherence			Proximity to real value			
	Physical	Temporal	Internal	Accuracy	Precision	Pertinence	Possible interpretation
Negative values	•				•		Measurement error
Out of bounds counts with respect to individual's condition	•		•	•	•	•	Limited sensor Measurement error Unsuitable protocol
Long sequences of constant positive values	•			•		•	Measurement error
High variability for repeated similar activity patterns	•		•	•	•	•	Calibration errors Measurement error
Monotonic decreasing or increasing counts for repeated similar activity patterns	•			•	•	•	Measurement error

well as pertinence. Possible interpretations are mostly related to limited sensor and measurement errors.

10.4.7 Activity Data Quality

Pedometers are known to have considerable variable performance between brands and models (Schneider et al. 2003, 2004; Steele et al. 2003). Besides, the user's age and activity dynamism are likely to induce unwanted activity measurement errors (Pagels et al. 2011; Strycker et al. 2007; Tudor-Locke et al. 2004). Table 10.7 summarizes most of these deficiencies and how they affect the quality of activity measurements.

Table 10.8 Characterization of temperature measurements data quality

	Coherence			Proximity to real value			
	Physical	Temporal	Internal	Accuracy	Precision	Pertinence	Possible interpretation
Progressive near constant measurement offset	•	•		•		•	Calibration error Measurement error
Rapid data variation				•	•	•	Measurement error User negligence
Unexpected reference values for a type of thermometer	•		•			•	Measurement error User negligence Unsuitable protocol

It is important to note that missing values are difficult to detect in activity measurements and are not considered for simplicity reasons. High variability for repeated similar activity patterns and out of bounds counts appear as the most critical factors, followed by monotonic decreasing or increasing counts for repeated similar activity patterns, negative values, and long sequences of constant values. Data defaults of activity measurements have a strong impact on the physical coherence of values and direct consequences on their accuracy and pertinence. Measurement errors are the most common possible interpretation.

10.4.8 Temperature Data Quality

Several factors such as level of activity, time of the day, what and how it is measured, influence temperature data. Depending on the technology and sensed part of the body, measurements variability is considerable even for the same patient (Crawford et al. 2011; Fortuna et al. 2010; Paes et al. 2010). As a result, the thermometer choice is determined by the clinical context and the patient condition. Table 10.8 summarizes the main identified temperature data quality factors.

For temperature measurements, progressive near constant measurement offset has the highest impact on data quality followed by rapid data variation and unexpected reference values. Effects of data deficiencies are notable on pertinence, physical coherence, and accuracy. Measurement errors and user negligence are the most frequent possible interpretations.

10.4.9 Observations Data Quality

Patient observations input in a pervasive health application are guided by the use of an application to record the essential information using a structured short

Table 10.9 Characterization of patient observations data quality

	Coherence			Proximity to real value			
	Physical	Temporal	Internal	Accuracy	Precision	Pertinence	Possible interpretation
Lack of synchronization with sensors measurements	•	•				•	User negligence Unsuitable protocol
Absence of circumstance	•	•		•		•	Limited sensor User negligence Unsuitable protocol
Absence of sensation intensity	•			•			Limited sensor User negligence Unsuitable protocol
Absence of frequency estimation	•	•	•	•		•	Limited sensor User negligence Unsuitable protocol
Absence of duration estimation	•	•				•	Limited sensor User negligence Unsuitable protocol
Mistaken sensation identification	•			•		•	Limited sensor User negligence
Contradictory reports					•	•	Data management error Calibration error User negligence

report made out of selected key terms and a comment. Although the absence of observations will not invalidate sensors data sets, observations deficiencies could add unexpected bias to information extraction (Table 10.9).

At the deficiencies factors level, the absence of frequency estimation and circumstance are the most critical. In addition, a large amount of common deficiencies appear to affect the pertinence and the coherence of the described observations, followed by the temporal coherence and the accuracy. Consequently, patient observations data quality could be significantly diminished by user negligence, unsuitable protocols, and limited applications. Patient observations data quality seems to rely for these reasons on a strong human behavior component, independently of the corresponding applications suitability. Despite such apparent functional fragility to properly collect patient observations, their symptomatology content is consistent with the patient record content in some contexts (Strömgren et al. 2001).

10.5 Discussion

This work analyzes the first stage of sensors data preprocessing (Sriram et al. 2009) in a wide sense considering the links between indicators of data inappropriateness, data deficiencies, and possible interpretations for each type of measurement, to be able to determine if sensor signals are reliable or not. The proposed sensors data quality characterization scheme intends to qualitatively define most of the required prior knowledge, preceding a more specific statistical-oriented modeling application, to identify additional knowledge that will be necessary to solve the different issues. Preliminary results indicate that within the context of pervasive self-monitoring using mobile devices as intermediation interfaces, there are still many indispensable improvements.

10.5.1 Towards Improvements in Data Quality

Direct evidence of data acquisition problems can be found when abnormal situations are noticed on data amplitude and relative positions of two linked signals. An example of such situation can be found examining blood pressure signals. Because of well-known physiological reasons, diastolic blood pressure is always lower than systolic values. Crossing or inverted position of these two curves could turn into either an acquisition problem (bad synchronization or sensor malfunction) or a human error when assigning data to the record, in the case of a manual data transfer. Furthermore, even when the relative signals positions are coherent, values gap between two simultaneously acquired measurements can also be representative of acquisition errors. Nevertheless, implicit interpretation ambiguities should be ruled out, particularly with respect to possible unknown physiological causes available as symptomatic information, in order to properly compare values gap to normality values ranges. Another example is temperature measurements, where evidence of data acquisition problems on continuous automatic temperature monitors can be identified at the accuracy level, when a bias appears. Even so, it can be assumed that if the bias is relatively constant, the temporal evolution of the signal can still be valid.

The connection between researched information and available data depends strongly on the medical situation. For example, some tests measure instantaneous glucose levels, whereas others estimate the values rate after glucose absorption, needing temporal follow-up, as well as a test adapted to the patient morphology. In other cases, signals like blood pressure and heart rate that are physiologically coupled to the heart dynamics must show a measurable correlation and compatible multidimensional valid values ranges, which are influenced by some key patient characteristics as age, weight, clinical condition, etc. Studying the position of measured values with respect to such patient-relative validity ranges can be considered as a good indicator of internal data incoherence due to, e.g., data acquisition errors or data management problems.

How to correctly take into account physiological parameters variability is another source of difficulties. When glucose measurements are taken using blood samples obtained from body parts different than the usual one, artifacts are generated in the glucose measurement, given that glucose levels are not the same in different zones of the body. Weight changes can be questionable in some cases, depending on the moment of the day when the measurement was done because the protocol conditions should be carefully followed to avoid misleading values. On the other hand, signals synchronicity is critical to correctly aggregate data from several sensors. In the case of systolic/diastolic blood pressure, the problem is not supposed to happen since signals are acquired simultaneously, with an automated synchronization using as reference the heart rate, except in case of sensor failure. For larger time range synchronization problems (e.g., successive values of a given measurement session acquired at different times of the day), it is also difficult to know if a change is due to an acquisition protocol inconvenient, or if it expresses a physiological fact in relation with the medical context. The only way to face this ambiguity is then to compare other PHR data when available as the session time stamps. Temperature may vary during the day because of ambient conditions and emotional estates, besides being naturally variable in different parts of the body. The assessment of activity characterization thresholds (Tudor-Locke et al. 2004) is not necessarily adapted to all clinical conditions, and should be adjusted to the patient assuming that the pedometer calibration is periodically verified.

Self-reporting could also be a doubtful input. For example, at the exception of dietary protocols, individuals tend to underestimate the actual scale readings. In manual temperature measurements, data can be wrong or missed. Personal observations can also be prone to lack of accuracy and pertinence, considering that reports could be completed without essential details once the uncomfortable sensation has ended, involuntarily because of tiredness or voluntarily if the patient prefers to conceal some information. Moreover, the question about up to what point the patient should gather information related to subjective reactions is also at stake. Typically, heart rate is susceptible to be highly influenced by the emotional state of the patient during measurement. Even if some data fields are present in the PHR interface to attach such information to acquired signals, self-evaluating objectively one's emotional and psychological state is very difficult.

For measurements on which the individuals' intervention is considerable, the nature of certain protocols remains a rich source of data deficiencies. To carry out glucose measurements, the patient should follow few steps, some of them being potentially troubling for data quality like cleaning the finger with a solution that may dilute the blood sample afterwards if not properly done. Furthermore, notwithstanding careful respect of the measurement protocol, glucometer compatibility with a norm like ISO 1597 is not sufficient to assure a high degree of measurement accuracy, compared to higher quality clinical glucometers. An equivalent issue appears in temperature measurements because there are different categories of thermometers, each with a different normal temperature reference expected to be used in specific conditions. If the utilization conditions are not respected, temperature variability when different sensors are used could exceed one degree for the same patient.

Otherwise, self-monitoring sensors calibration is not periodically verified throughout the sensor utilization span. Sensors like personal bathroom scales that are not professional medical products and do not function according to a specific recommendation or norm, provide an acceptable accuracy and precision for daily weight estimations. However, unchecked calibration can introduce important measurement bias of several kilograms, sometimes superior to the original precision of the scale.

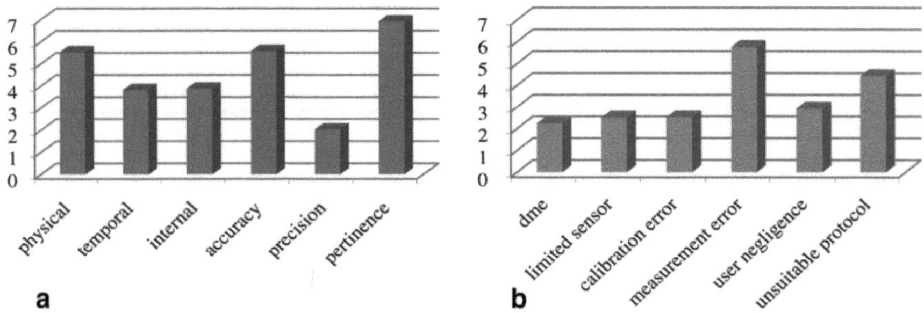

Fig. 10.9 Histograms of data quality deficiencies (**a**) and possible interpretations (**b**) data management error (DME)

Some of the physiological phenomena represented by acquired data cannot be measured instantaneously. Their measurement principle relies thus on the notion of integration time, i.e., the duration required to either process a valid average, or to simply count occurrences of a periodical activity like heart beats per minute. This parameter is essential to measurement precision, given that too short integration times would generate poor estimations of the value to be measured, and raises the question of measurement automation. Beyond the problems generated by sensors utilization and control, most measurements parameters have to be fixed according to medical knowledge and practical experience, which frequently are not accessible to patients. Two complementary solution axes can be envisaged to support the application of measurement protocols entrusting patients with self-measurement tasks: specific patient education and fully automated intelligent measurement procedures.

10.5.2 Data Quality Deficiencies and Possible Interpretations

Whereas indicators of potential data quality deficiencies are proper to each one of the examined parameters and sensors, their impact on data quality as well as the related possible interpretations to explain the origin of such data quality deficiencies, are common to all examined cases for the purpose of our study. This approach enables to make a comparative analysis between cumulative counts of the impacted data deficiencies dimensions and their possible interpretations.

Histograms of the resulting quality deficiencies and possible interpretations are depicted in Fig. 10.9. To obtain these results, the number of identified data deficiencies per column and possible interpretations were separately counted on each data quality analysis table (Tables 10.1–10.9), before dividing those totals by the amount of indicators in each table to avoid favoring sensors with higher amounts of indicators. Final results were calculated summing those partial totals per table, 9 being the maximum value that could be reached for any column.

Among the most common data quality deficiencies (Fig. 10.9a), we find, in descending order of importance: pertinence, accuracy, and physical coherence, which

Table 10.10 Links between data deficiencies and possible interpretations

	Coherence			Proximity to real value		Pertinence
	Physical	Temporal	Internal	Accuracy	Physical	
Data management error	1.33	0.67	1.75	0.83	0.39	0.64
Limited sensor	1.75	1.01	1.26	1.44	0.53	2.35
Calibration error	1.28	1.83	0.95	1.62	0.51	2.18
Measurement error	3.50	1.75	2.90	3.58	1.55	3.80
User negligence	1.36	1.24	0.64	1.65	0.64	2.27
Unsuitable protocol	2.33	1.65	1.01	1.96	0.70	2.94

concern the informative level of acquired data in the medical context, the sensor measurement quality, and the adequacy of measured parameters with the studied physical object or phenomenon. The two most frequently indicated possible interpretations are measurement error and unsuitable protocol. While the first one is trivial, the second one raises the question of measurement protocols suitability to the objective of the measurements. Note that several interpretations can completely or partially explain a data quality default, and therefore which one may be predominant depends on varied factors.

Another comparative analysis was carried out to identify the most common "data deficiency-possible interpretation" links, applying the same principles used to calculate the histogram values of Fig. 10.9. Each result corresponds to the amount of found "data deficiency-possible interpretation" pairs per table, divided by the associated total of indicators per table. Partial totals were added afterwards (Table 10.10).

Without surprise, measurement error is the most common possible interpretation associated to the main data deficiencies in four (pertinence, accuracy, physical, and internal coherence) of the five strongest links. However, the pair pertinence–unsuitable protocol also appears frequently. These results are presented as histograms in Fig. 10.10 to facilitate their visualization.

Finally, a quite complex question related to sensors data quality evaluation is to appropriately distinguish between data characteristics that provide diagnostic information and those that only express a problem hindering access to such pertinent information. Considering the example of detecting sudden changes in a given signal (Hodge and Austin 2004), e.g., blood pressure or heart rate, it is necessary to automatically determine if these outliers or changes in the expected mean value are due to a brutal evolution of the patient medical condition, or to a change in acquisition conditions, or a sensor malfunction. Two strategies to answer these questions could be envisaged: search for additional clues of health condition sudden change, or detect additional consequences of the potential signal acquisition trouble in other signals. In the case of blood pressure, where systolic and diastolic signals are acquired simultaneously, such changes should have a comparable influence on both curves. If not, outliers should probably be considered as the expression of a data quality problem. Except for this particular case of highly correlated signals, the second strategy will face multiple inconvenience given that a sensor malfunction will not mandatorily affect other signals. It is necessary therefore to look for the traces of probable

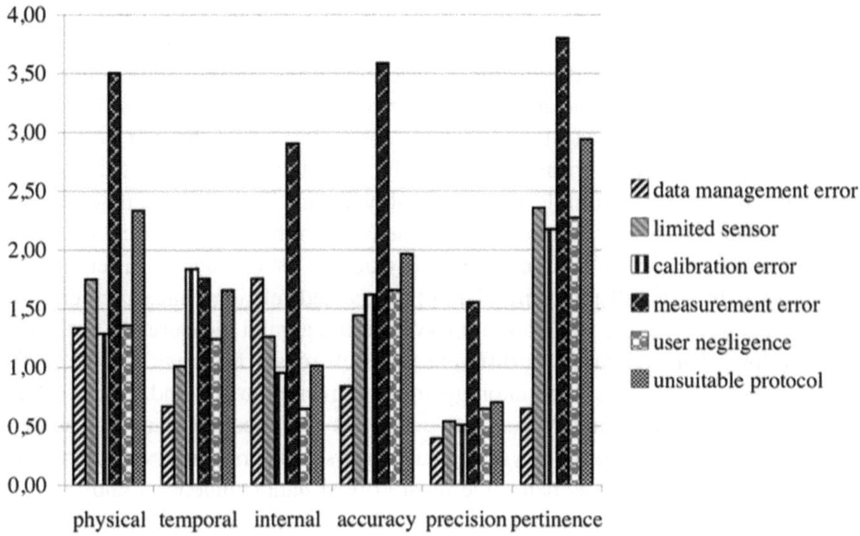

Fig. 10.10 Histograms of the links between data deficiencies and possible interpretations

physiological explanations that will affect other vital signs according to other available data in the EHR, before assuming that it is related to data quality.

10.6 Summary

PHR endorses individuals' active role in their own healthcare providing means to acquire, store, and exchange health data like physiological measurements collected by sensors and personal observations, related to specific associated symptoms or sensations, experienced often while the measurements were being taken. Using mobile devices as intermediation interfaces, pervasive healthcare could have a considerable potential for success if, among crucial aspects, data quality factors, consequences, and reasons are thoroughly examined to reinforce system robustness. This work proposes physiological sensors (glucose, weight, blood pressure, heart rate, activity, and temperature) and patient observations data quality characterization, taking into account the related indications or factors that point to data deficiencies, the impact of such indicators on data coherence (physical, temporal, and internal), data proximity to the real value (accuracy and precision), and pertinence, which could be explained by means of several possible interpretations (data management error, limited sensor, calibration error, measurement error, user negligence, and unsuitable protocol).

The most frequently identified data quality deficiencies were pertinence, accuracy, and physical coherence, which concern the informative level of acquired data in the medical context, the sensor measurement quality, and the adequacy of measured parameters with the studied physical object or phenomenon. Among the two most frequently indicated possible interpretations are, measurement error and unsuitable protocol, the second one raises the question of measurement protocols suitability to the objective of the measurements. Concerning links between data deficiencies and possible interpretations, measurement error exhibits the strongest links with pertinence, accuracy, physical, and internal coherence, while the pair pertinence–unsuitable protocol also appears frequently. Improvements in physiological sensors data quality depend on multiple aspects, notably, the medical situation that connects available data and researched information, sensors calibration practices, measured physiological parameters' inherent variability during the day and in different parts of the body, bias of self-reporting, data sets expected relations, measurement protocol characteristics, and integration interval to find a valid measure. As indicated, the resulting characterization is different for each sensor and may change in the future, depending on sensors technology, measurement protocol, and patient behavior evolutions. Our preliminary qualitative analysis identified the main indicators of data deficiencies for different physiological sensors and personal observations, and compared separately and as pairs, the most critical data deficiencies and possible interpretations, applying an original approach that will serve as reference method for a more statistically focused data quality analysis.

Acknowledgments This work was supported in part by Telecom Bretagne and in part by VTT and the Finnish Funding Agency for Technology and Innovation (Tekes) in the framework of the ITEA2/Care4Me project.

References

Anliker, U., Ward, J. A., Lukowicz, P., Troster, G., Dolveck, F., Baer, M., Keita, F., Schenker, E. B., Catarsi, F., Coluccini, L., Belardinelli, A., Shklarski, D., Alon, M., Hirt, E., Scmid, R., & Vuskovic, M. (2004). AMON: A wearable multiparameter medical monitoring and alert system. *IEEE Transactions on Information Technology in Biomedicine, 8*(4), 415–427.

Asada, H. H., Shaltis, P., Reisner, A., Rhee, S., & Hutchinson, R. C. (2003). Mobile monitoring with wearable photoplethysmographic biosensors. *IEEE Engineering in Medicine and Biology Magazine, 22*(3), 28–40.

Bravata, D. M., Smith-Spangler, C., Sundaram, V., Gienger, A. L., Lin, N., Lewis, R., Stave, C. D., Olkin, I., & Sirard, J. R. (2007). Using pedometers to increase physical activity and improve health. A systematic review. *Journal of the American Medical Association, 298*(19), 2296–2304.

Cho, J. H., Lee, H. C., Lim, D. J., Kwon, H. S., & Yoon, K. H. (2009). Mobile communication using a mobile phone with a glucometer for glucose control in Type 2 patients with diabetes: As effective as an Internet-based glucose monitoring system. *Journal of Telemedicine and Telecare, 15*(2), 77–82.

Civan, A., Skeels, M. M., Stolyar, A., & Pratt, W. (2006). *Personal health information management: Consumers' perspectives*. Proceedings of the Annual Symposium of the American Medical Informatics Association, 156–160.

Coughlin, J. F., & Pope, J. (2008). Innovations in health, wellness, and aging-in-place. *IEEE Engineering in Medicine and Biology Magazine, 27*(4), 47–52.

Crawford, D. C., Hicks, B., & Thompson, M. J. (2011). Which thermometer? Factors influencing best choice for intermittent clinical temperature assessment. *Journal of Medical Engineering and Technology, 30*(4), 199–211.

Eysenbach, G. (2008). Medicine 2.0: Social networking, collaboration, participation, apomediation, and openness. *Journal of Medical Internet Research, 10*(3), e22.

Fortuna, E. L., Carney, M. M., Macy, M., Stanley, R. M., Younger, J. G., & Bradin, S. A. (2010). Accuracy of non-contact infrared thermometry versus rectal thermometry in young children evaluated in the emergency department for fever. *Journal of Emergency Nursing, 36*(2), 101–104.

Gatzoulis, L., & Iakovidis, I. (2007). Wearable and portable ehealth systems. *IEEE Engineering in Medicine and Biology Magazine, 26*(5), 51–56.

Halamka, J. D., Mandl, K. D., & Tang, P. C. (2008). Early experiences with personal health records. *Journal of the American Medical Informatics Association, 15*(1), 1–7.

Hodge, V., & Austin, J. (2004). A survey of outlier detection methodologies. *Artificial Intelligence Review, 22*(2), 85–126.

Hung, K., Zhang, Y. T., & Tai, B. (2004). *Wearable medical devices for tele-home healthcare.* EMBC 04. Proceedings of the 26th Annual International Conference of the IEEE Engineering in Medicine and Biology Society, 2004 Sep 1–5, San Francisco, California, 5384–5387.

ISO 15197. (2003). *In vitro diagnostic test systems–requirements for blood-glucose monitoring systems for self-testing in managing diabetes mellitus.* Geneva: International Organization for Standardization.

Kaelber, D. C., Jha, A. K., Johnston, D., Middleton, B., & Bates, D. W. (2008). A research agenda for personal health records (PHRs). *Journal of the American Medical Informatics Association, 15*(6), 729–736.

Korhonen, I., Pärkä, J., & Van Gils, M. (2003). Health monitoring in the home of the future. *IEEE Engineering in Medicine and Biology Magazine, 22*(3), 66–73.

Krouwer, J., & Cembrowski, G. (2010). A review of standards and statistics used to describe blood glucose monitor performance. *Journal of Diabetes Science and Technology, 4*(1), 75–83.

Laakko, T., Leppanen, J., Lähteenmaki, J., & Nummiaho, A. (2008). *Multipurpose mobile platform for telemedicine applications.* Proceedings 2nd International Conference on Pervasive Computing Technologies for Healthcare, Tampere, Finland, 245–248.

Lähteenmäki, J., Leppänen, J., Orsama, A. L., Salaspuro, V., Pirinen, J., Sormunen, M., Kaijanranta, H., & Ermes, M. (2011). *Remote patient monitoring system with decision support.* BIOMED 11. Proceedings of the 8th IASTED Conference on Biomedical Engineering, 2011 Feb 16–18, Innsbruck, Austria. (in press).

Leijdekkers, P., & Gay, V. (2006). *Personal heart monitoring system using smart phones to detect life threatening arrhythmias.* CBMS 06. Proceedings of the 19th IEEE Symposium on Computer-Based Medical Systems, Salt Lake City, Utah, 157–164.

Logan, A. G., McIsaac, W. J., Tisler, A., Irvine, M. J., Saunders, A., Dunai, A., Rizo, C. A., Feig, D. S., Hamill, M., Trudel, M., & Cafazzo, J. A. (2007). Mobile phone-based remote patient monitoring system for management of hypertension in diabetic patients. *American Journal of Hypertension, 20*(9), 942–948.

Mattila, E., Korhonen, I., Salminen, J. H., Ahtinen, A., Koskinen, E., Sarela, A., Parkka, J., & Lappalainen, R. (2010). Empowering citizens for well-being and chronic disease management with wellness diary. *IEEE Transactions on Information Technology in Biomedicine, 14*(2), 456–463.

Mundt, C. W., Montgomery, K. N., Udoh, U. E., Barker, V. N., Thonier, G. C., Tellier, A. M., Ricks, R. D., Darling, R. B., Cagle, Y. D., Cabrol, N. A., Ruoss, S. J., Swain, J. L., Hines, J. W., & Kovacs, G. T. A. (2005). A multiparameter wearable physiological monitoring system for space and terrestrial applications. *IEEE Transactions on Information Technology in Biomedicine, 9*(3), 382–391.

Paes, B. F., Vermeulen, K., Brohet, R. M., Ploeg, T. van der, & Winter, J. P. de. (2010). Accuracy of tympanic and infrared skin thermometers in children. *Archives of Disease in Childhood, 95*(12), 974–978.

Pagels, P., Boldemann, C., & Raustorp, A. (2011). Comparison of pedometer and accelerometer measures of physical activity during preschool time on 3- to 5-year-old children. *Acta Paediatrica, 100*(1), 116–120.

Pagliari, C., Detmer, D., & Singleton, P. (2007). Potential of electronic personal health records. *British Medical Journal, 335,* 3330–3333.

Pantelopoulos, A., & Bourbakis, N. G. (2010). A survey on wearable sensor-based systems for health monitoring and prognosis. *IEEE Transactions on Systems, Man, and Cybernetics, Part C: Applications and Reviews, 40*(1), 1–12.

Pedrolli, C., Cereda, E., & Costa, A. (2009). Fighting hospital malnutrition: Let's start by calibrating hospital scales! *Mediterranean Journal of Nutrition and Metabolism, 2,* 145–147.

Puentes, J., & Lähteenmäki, J. (2011). *Towards knowledge-based integration of personal health record data from sensors and patient observations*. HealthInf 11. Proceedings 4th International Conference on Health Informatics, 2011 Jan 26–29, Rome, Italy, 280–285.

Sacks, D. B., Bernhardt, P., Dunka, L. J., Goldstein, D. E., Hortin, G. L., & Mueller, P. (2002). *Point-of-care blood glucose testing in acute and chronic care facilities; Approved Guideline* (2nd ed.). C30-A2, 22(17).

Salvi, P., Lio, G., Labat, C., Ricci, E., Pannier, B., & Benetos, A. (2004). Validation of a new non-invasive portable tonometer for determining arterial pressure wave and pulse wave velocity: The PulsePen device. *Journal of Hypertension, 22*(12), 2285–2293.

Schneider, P. L., Crouter, S. E., Lukajic, O., & Basset, D. R. (2003). Accuracy and reliability of 10 pedometers for measuring steps over a 400-m walk. *Medicine & Science in Sports & Exercise, 35*(10), 1779–1784.

Schneider, P. L., Crouter, S. E., & Basset, D. R. (2004). Pedometer measures of free-living physical activity: Comparison of 13 models. *Medicine & Science in Sports & Exercise, 36*(2), 331–335.

Sessler, D. I. (2008). Temperature monitoring and perioperative thermoregulation. *Anesthesiology, 109*(2), 318–338.

Silva, J. M., Mouttham, A., & El Saddik, A. (2009). *UbiMeds: A mobile application to improve accessibility and support medication adherence*. Proceedings of the 1st ACM SIGMM International Workshop on Media Studies and Implementations that Help Improving Access to Disabled Users, 71–78.

Sriram, J., Shin, M., Kotz, D., Rajan, A., Sastry, M., & YarvisInt, M. (2009). *Challenges in data quality assurance in pervasive health monitoring systems*. Proceedings of Future of Trust in Computing, 129–142.

Stead, W. W., & Lin, H. S. (2009). Computational technology for effective health care: Immediate steps and strategic directions. National Research Council of the national Academies. Washington, DC: National Academies Press.

Steele, B. G., Belza, B., Cain, K., Warms, C., Coppersmith, J., & Howard, J. (2003). Bodies in motion: Monitoring daily activity and exercise with motion sensors in people with chronic pulmonary disease. *Journal of Rehabilitation Research & Development, 40*(5), 45–58.

Strömgren, A. S., Groenvold, M., Pedersen, L., Olsen, A. K., Spile, M., & Sjøgren, P. (2001). Does the medical record cover the symptoms experienced by cancer patients receiving palliative care? A comparison of the record and patient self-rating. *Journal of Pain and Symptom Management, 21*(3), 189–196.

Strycker, L. A., Duncan, S. C., Chaumeton, N. R., Duncan, T. E., & Toobert, D. J. (2007). Reliability of pedometer data in samples of youth and older women. *International Journal of Behavioral Nutrition and Physical Activity, 4,* 4.

Tang, P. C., Ash, J. S., Bates, D. W., Overhage, J. M., & Sands, D. Z. (2006). Personal health records: Definitions, benefits, and strategies for overcoming barriers to adoption. *Journal of the American Medical Informatics Association, 13*(2), 121–126.

Tatara, N., Arsand, E., Nilsen, H., & Hartvigsen, G. (2009). *A review of mobile terminal-based applications for self-management of patients with diabetes*. eTELEMED 09. Proceedings of the International Conference on eHealth, Telemedicine, and Social Medicine, 166–175.

Taylor, A. W., Grande, E. D., Gill, T. K., Chittleborough, C. R., Wilson, D. H., Adams, R. J., Grant, J. F., Phillips, P., Appleton, S., & Ruffin, R. E. (2006). How valid are self-reported height and weight? A comparison between CATI self-report and clinic measurements using a large cohort study. *Australian and New Zealand Journal of Public Health, 30*(3), 238–246.

Tudor-Locke, C., & Bassett, D. R. (2004). How many steps/day are enough? Preliminary pedometer indices for public health. *Sports Medicine, 34*(1), 1–8.

Tudor-Locke, C., Bassett, D. R., Swartz, A. M., Strath, S. J., Parr, B. B., Reis, J. P., Dubose, K. D., & Ainsworth, B. E. (2004). A preliminary study of one year of pedometer self monitoring. *Annals of Behavioral Medicine, 28*(3), 158–162.

Walters, D. L., Sarela, A., Fairfull, A., Neighbour, K., Cowen, C., Stephens, B., Sellwood, T., Sellwood, B., Steer, M., Aust, M., Francis, R., Lee, C. K., Hoffman, S., Brealey, G., & Karunanithi, M. (2010). A mobile phone-based care model for outpatient cardiac rehabilitation: The care assessment platform (CAP). *BMC Cardiovascular Disorders, 10,* 5.

Wheatley, I. (2006). The nursing practice of taking level 1 patient observations. *Intensive and Critical Care Nursing, 22*(2), 115–121.

Worringham, C., Rojek, A., & Stewart, I. (2011). Development and feasibility of a Smartphone, ECG and GPS based system for remotely monitoring exercise in cardiac rehabilitation. *PLoS One, 6*(2), e14669.

Yon, B., Johnson, R., Harvey-Berino, J., Gold, B., & Howard, A. (2007). Personal digital assistants are comparable to traditional diaries for dietary self-monitoring during a weight loss program. *Journal of Behavioral Medicine, 30*(2), 165–175.

Chapter 11
Smartphone Application Design and Knowledge Management for People with Dementia

Nicola Armstrong, Christopher Nugent, George Moore and Dewar D. Finlay

Abstract As the number of old and older people living worldwide increases, the number of age-related impairments and prevalence of chronic diseases is also rising. One of the most challenging chronic diseases is Alzheimer's disease (AD). AD is a chronic progressive brain disease, which is a result of the death of brain cells. This in turn impacts on a person's memory, thought and judgment. With the number of AD cases globally predicted to double in the next 20 years, there will be a significant increased burden placed on health and social care provision. The aim of this work has been to identify and alleviate a set of problems associated with AD using smartphone technology, while in addition focusing on the various levels of user support provided in managing the technology. In order to help support persons with AD (PwAD), the current work has considered the design and evaluation of both smartphone-based applications for PwAD and computer-based applications for the PwAD's caregiver. These smartphone-based applications, based on the top unmet needs of PwAD include an activity of daily living reminder, a photo album application for reminiscence, a picture dialing telephone and short messaging service (SMS) and a geo-fencing with 1-hour reminder application. In addition to this, the chapter will also investigate the knowledge management issues within the technical infrastructure required to support all stakeholders in the care provision of the PwAD. This chapter provides details of two pre-study evaluations conducted on a cohort of healthy adult users. Results from both studies are included alongside details of how each of the smartphone application user interfaces have been re-developed.

11.1 Introduction

As the number of old and older (aged 65 and above) people increase within today's ageing society, average life expectancy, risk of chronic disease and age-related impairments are all also rising (Communication from the Commission to the European Parliament 2009). According to figures published by the Office for National Statistics, the estimated number of older people increased 1 % between 1984 and 2009, resulting in an increase of 1.7 million older people within the United Kingdom alone

N. Armstrong (✉) · C. D. Nugent · G. Moore · D. D. Finlay
Computer Science Research Department, University of Ulster, Jordanstown, Northern Ireland
e-mail: Armstrong-n1@email.ulster.ac.uk

R. K. Bali et al. (eds.), *Pervasive Health Knowledge Management*,
Healthcare Delivery in the Information Age,
DOI 10.1007/978-1-4614-4514-2_11, © Springer Science+Business Media New York 2013

(Office for National Statistics o. J.). Globally, the population of older people is expected to double by the year 2040 reaching 1.3 billion, from 506 million older people in the year 2008. An expected increase of 7 % is forecast bringing the total worldwide older population to 14 % (Kinsella and He 2009).

Along with ageing come age-related impairments, for example, slower motor responses, diminished hearing, memory impairments and an increased risk of chronic disease. Chronic diseases are "diseases of long duration and generally slow progress" (World Health Organisation o. J.). Estimates suggest that at least 90 million Americans are affected by a chronic disease (World Health Organisation o. J.). As there is no cure for chronic disease, a person's condition will usually deteriorate over a period of time. This in turn can have a negative effect on a person's day to day activities and very often leads to an overall decreased quality of life, impacting on both the person with the chronic disease, in addition to their family and friends.

11.2 Alzheimer's Disease

One of the most common chronic diseases later in life is dementia (Alzheimer's Association 2009), a descriptive name for a range of brain diseases. The number of people with dementia (PwD) alone in the United Kingdom in 2009 was estimated at 750,000 (Alzheimer's Society o. J) and this figure is expected to rise within the next 30 years to over 1.5 million (CARDI online o. J.). The most common form of dementia is Alzheimer's disease (AD), accounting for two-thirds of all dementia cases. In 2010, the global number of PwD was recorded at 35 million (At Dementia o. J.).

AD is a chronic brain disease (Alzheimer's Association 2010). Throughout the development of the disease, plaques and tangles develop within the structure of the brain and lead to the death of cells. This then leads to a decline in memory, a decreased ability to learn new things and the loss of judgment to reason (Longley et al. 2002). Symptoms of the disease will vary depending on which stage of the disease a person is experiencing. Alongside the impact on a persons with AD (PwAD)'s quality of life, the disease also impacts on healthcare provision. It has been reported that the cost of care for a PwAD within the United Kingdom is on average £25,472 per person each year (o. A. 2010).

Taking all of these factors into consideration, it is evident that efforts need to be made in order to lessen the burden of the disease and reduce healthcare costs. A potential solution to these increased demands for care provision is the use of assistive technology in the form of a cognitive prosthetic utilising smartphone technology. This chapter presents the details of the development and evaluation of both smartphone-based applications for PwAD and computer-based applications for PwAD's caregivers. In addition to this, issues surrounding the knowledge management within the technical infrastructure linking all of the stakeholders are also considered. The remainder of the chapter is structured as follows: Sect. 11.3 provides an overview of smartphone technology. Section 11.4 provides an overview of assistive technologies used to support PwAD. Section 11.5 describes the methods used within the current study and Sect. 11.6 describes the approach adopted to develop the smartphone applications and the results from evaluations along with details of how the applications have been revised following analysis of the evaluation. Section 11.7 presents the details of the caregiver interface application design, Sect. 11.8 presents the results from the caregiver interface evaluation phase, Sect. 11.9 cover knowledge management issues and Further Work and Conclusions are drawn in Sect. 11.10.

11.3 Smartphone Technology

Usage of smartphone technology has gradually become part of daily life and is one of the fastest growing communication technologies within today's society (Boretos 2007). In 2010, the smartphone sales market rose by a massive 72.1 % from 2009. Figures released by Gartner indicated that 297 million smartphone handsets were sold in 2010 and accounted for 19 % of the 1.6 million mobile phones sold that year (Gartner Newsroom 2010). Smartphones are mobile phones, which offer highly advanced capabilities beyond that of a standard mobile phone. Smartphone handset features typically include always-on Internet access including email, short messaging service (SMS), multi-media messaging service (MMS), photographic and video recording, built-in GPS hardware and software, Wi-Fi, bluetooth and the ability to read and edit a variety of files in various formats. Essentially, smartphone handsets can now be viewed as handheld computers that can be used on the go, 24 hours a day 7 days a week with the additional ability to connect with family and friends in real time.

Due to these advancements and the fast evolution in the use of Information Technology (IT), smartphone technology is being used within the healthcare domain in various ways including e-health, telehealth and telemedicine (Singh and Kaur 2010). Examples of this trend include the use of Electronic Health Records (EHR) (Dwivedi et al. 2002b) and clinician's often assessing medical data from a handheld communication device (Dwivedi et al. 2002a). A specific example of this is the Personal Health Monitor, a piece of software that runs on a mobile smartphone. Through the use of sensors, patient data such as ECG readings can be collected and stored within the patient's phone (Leijdekkers and Gay 1986). These data can then be transferred to specialist clinicians who can monitor the patient's vital signs. Alongside the ability for patients to manage a chronic condition at home (Zheng et al. 2010) and the opportunity for better healthcare services, smartphone technology also provides a cost-effective way of reducing healthcare expenditure spent on care home and formal caregiver costs.

11.4 Alzheimer's Disease and Assistive Technologies

Currently within the market place, there are a number of assistive technologies that aim to help PwAD on a daily basis, these devices range from basic aids such as item locator devices and voice recorders including smartfinder locator and Memo Minder

Table 11.1 Smartphone applications previously developed and evaluated. (Armstrong et al. 2009)

Smartphone application	Smartphone application function
Activity of daily living reminder	Reminder messages are delivered to the PwAD via SMS previously set by the caregiver in order to remind the PwAD to carry out activities of daily living. For example, medication reminders and meal preparation
Picture dialing telephone/SMS	Allows PwADs to quickly contact family and friends without having to enter any numbers via a voice call or SMS
Geo-fencing application	A PwAD will be set geographical boundaries (user specified). When a PwAD exits the designated area, an alert is triggered via SMS to remind the PwAD that they have gone too far. If the PwAD fails to acknowledge this reminder, an alert will then be sent to caregivers/family members containing information on the PwAD's whereabouts within a 10-m radius
One-hour reminder system	Reminder by means of SMS sent to the PwAD via mobile smartphone in order to remind them of how long they have been away from their home (user specified). The PwAD can then provide a response to this reminder by pressing an accept button. If the accept button is not pressed, an instant message/alert will then be sent to the PwAD's caregiver

MK 11, to more advanced aids such as wandering devices, for example, the BIME Wander reminder (At Dementia o. J.). Nevertheless, it has recently been reported that there is no one single device that meets core unmet needs of PwAD as presented by Lauriks et al. (2007):

1. The need to remember
2. The need for social contact
3. The need for safety
4. The need for support regarding activities of daily living

The aim of our research, based on the above identified unmet needs, is to recognise and diminish a set of problems associated with AD using smartphone-based technology and their associated services. Another focus within our work will be to compare various levels of user support provided while training both PwAD and their caregivers in technology use. Lastly, we will also be investigating the use of knowledge management issues with regards to smartphone technology.

11.5 Methods

Based on the identified needs for PwAD as identified by Laurkis et al., a suite of smartphone applications were previously developed (Armstrong et al. 2010a). These applications included an activity of daily living reminder application, a picture dialing telephone and short messaging service application, a geo-fencing application and a 1-hour reminder application (refer to Table 11.1). The smartphone used was an HTC Touch HD with a Windows Mobile Operating System. This particular handset was chosen due to its large screen size and portability. In order to create the smartphone

Table 11.2 Participant information

Age group	Female	Male
20–40 years old	4	10
40–60 years old	1	0
60 > years old	0	0

applications, Visual Studio 2008 software was used, along with the programming language Visual Basic .NET.

In order to evaluate the smartphone applications previously created, we conducted a pre-study evaluation on a control group, which consisted of 15 healthy adult participants from various age groups (refer to Table 11.2). Participants were asked firstly to complete a pre-study questionnaire. After this step was complete, participants were then asked to navigate their way around the smartphone interface, commenting openly about what they liked and disliked about the applications.

Participant's hand movements were also recorded at this time. Hand movements were recorded in order to monitor a participant's interaction with the device and also for analysis after the evaluation phase to determine rate of error. When the evaluation process was complete, participants were then asked to complete a post-study questionnaire regarding the applications design and functionality. Example questions within the post-study questionnaire included "Did you feel comfortable using a mobile smartphone with a touch screen interface?", "Did you feel comfortable with the text size on the mobile smartphone?" and "Did you find it difficult to interact with the smartphone applications?"

11.6 Smartphone Application Evaluation and Re-design

Feedback from the smartphone evaluation phase (refer to Table 11.3) suggested that although participants were more than happy to use a touch screen mobile smartphone, and found the applications easy to use, the keyboard and overall text size within the applications was too small and using a stylus to enter the relevant data was inconvenient.

When asked what they liked about the smartphone applications, example comments included, "Easy to use and understand", "Easy navigation and large buttons" "Pictures for voice and call+ option to send message—good mix of apps". Likewise, when asked what they disliked about the applications, participants made the following comments, "The use of stylus", "to many sub menus sometimes", "The response to the touch screen is not very quick". Based on the feedback received from the evaluation phase, each smartphone applications user interface was then re-designed.

11.6.1 Home Screen Re-design

Originally, the home screen interface on the smartphone was designed for both the PwAD and their caregiver (refer to Fig. 11.1). Nevertheless, feedback from the

Table 11.3 User feedback from smartphone applications. (Adapted from Singh and Kaur 2010)

Liked about the applications	Disliked about the applications
Easy to use and understand (15)	Response to touch screen was slow (3)
Phone call application—icons (10)	Message box—too small (7)
Large buttons (4)	Colours not great in pastel (5)
Touch screen (1)	GPS button too small + very detailed (5)
Reminders (4)	No feedback from buttons (4)
Good choice of applications (2)	Don't like to use the stylus (2)
	Keyboard too small—touch screen (4)

Figures within brackets indicate the number of participants out of 15 who made the same comment

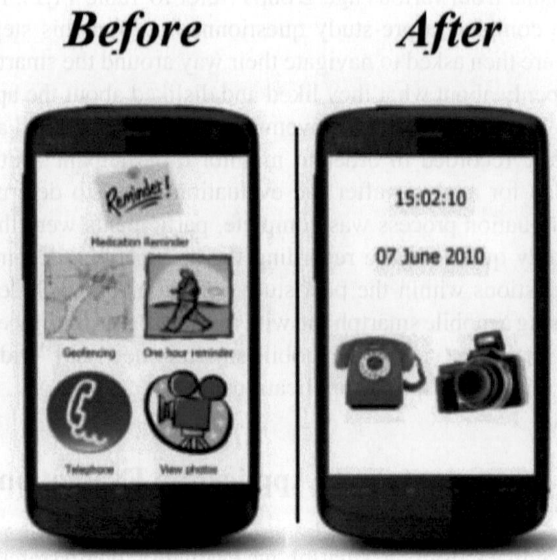

Fig. 11.1 Before (*left*) and after re-design (*right*) home screen

evaluation phase suggested that this could become confusing for the PwAD, as they would be presented with too many options. Taking this into account, the home screen was subsequently re-designed, giving the PwAD only two options, one to make a phone call and one to view photographs.

11.6.2 Activity of Daily Living Reminder Re-design

While evaluating the activity of daily living reminder, participants noted that although they found the application easy to use and navigate throughout, the choice of pastel colour was not overly liked (refer to Fig. 11.2). The small keyboard size to enter messages was also noted as a dislike and participants felt uncomfortable using a stylus to input information.

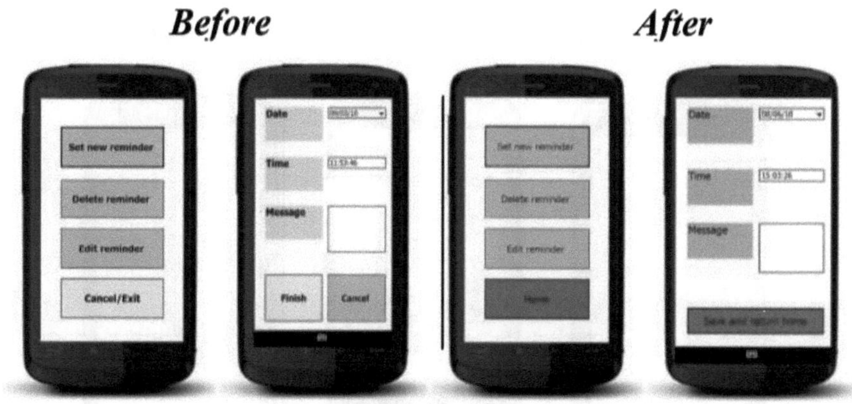

Fig. 11.2 Before (*left*) and after re-design (*right*) reminder application

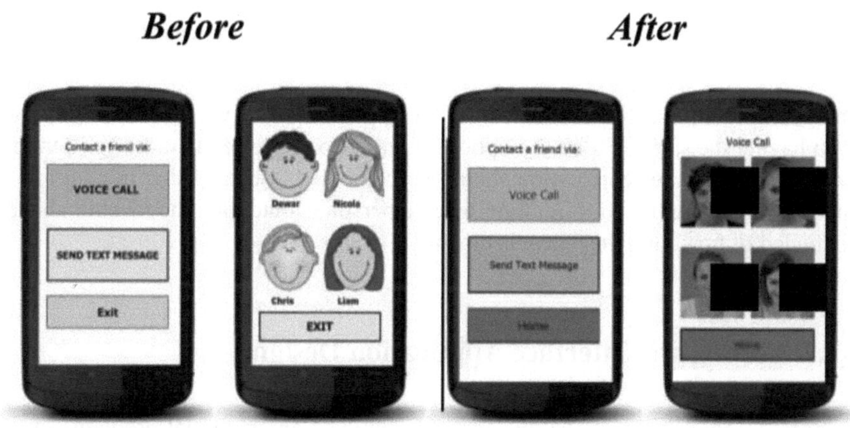

Fig. 11.3 Before (*left*) and after re-design (*right*) picture dialing (images have been modified in order to avoid personal disclosure)

11.6.3 Picture Dialing Telephone/SMS Re-design

Results from the evaluation phase showed that participants found the picture dialing application very useful and easy to use. Suggestions to improve on this application included changing the cartoon picture on the phone to real-life photographs (refer to Fig. 11.4) in order to avoid a PwAD becoming confused (Fig. 11.3).

11.6.4 Geo-fencing Application/1-Hour Reminder System Re-design

Participants noted that the geo-fencing application was too detailed and may cause confusion for a PwAD (refer to Fig. 11.4). It was also noted that the GPS start function

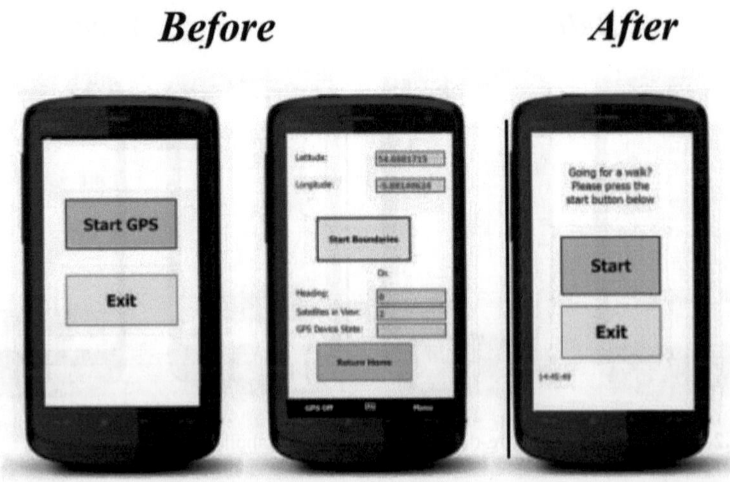

Fig. 11.4 Before (*left*) and after re-design (*right*) geo-fencing and 1-hour reminder application

should be automatically activated once the application was up and running, rather than having the start GPS button option. It was also suggested that the geo-fencing and 1-hour reminder application should be combined, meaning that in addition to the geo-fencing application running when a person is outdoors, they would also be reminded of how long they have been out.

11.7 Caregiver Interface Application Design

In order to combat the above dislikes and eliminate any potential problems in the future, a new solution to the smartphone application was proposed and subsequently implemented. This solution involved caregivers interacting with a large touch screen computer interface as opposed to a smartphone handset in order to enter relevant information and pre-configure the functionality of the cognitive prosthetic. This solution attempted to not only combat the problems associated with the use of the small display on the screen of the smartphone, however, also enabled caregivers to have more flexibility to easily and quickly set reminder messages, upload new photographs, edit phone contacts and set specific boundaries and reminders with regards to distance and time.

Based on the above, a number of computer-based applications were subsequently developed and specifically designed to be used on an all-in-one computer with a large touch screen interface. The computer-based applications developed offer the same services as before, providing caregivers the same options as those on the mobile smartphone. These include an add/edit/delete reminder application, add/edit/delete contacts application, add/edit/delete boundaries application and lastly an add/edit/delete photo album application.

Table 11.4 Participant information

Age Group	Female	Male
20–40 years old	2	7
40–60 years old	1	0
60 > years old	0	0

The sole purpose of the e-top interface and associated applications is to enable caregivers to enter various information regarding, for example, reminder messages and boundaries, on a large touch screen interface rather than on a small smartphone screen. Once the caregiver has entered the relevant information, the data are then transferred onto the smartphone handset. In order to transfer the relevant information, the handset is simply connected to the e-top computer. The interface was created using Adobe Flash software.

In order to evaluate the interface design, a control group of ten healthy adult participants (refer to Table 11.4) tested the touch screen interface applications created. Participants were asked to navigate their way around the system in order to evaluate interface design and functionality. Participants were also asked to complete both pre- and post-study questionnaires and comment openly on what they liked and disliked about the interface. Example questions within the post-study questionnaire included, "Did you feel comfortable using a computer with a touch screen interface?", "What did you like about the computer applications you tested?" and "What did you dislike about the computer applications you tested?"

11.7.1 Home Screen

Feedback suggested that participants found the home screen easy to understand and navigate. The general census suggests that the options were clear and well laid out, however, it was suggested that the photographs/icons on the home screen should also be incorporated as buttons in order to give a participant/caregiver more space/room for fault. A few participants did try and press the icons mistaking them as buttons (Fig. 11.5).

11.7.2 Reminder Screen

From the reminder application, caregivers have the option to add, edit or delete a reminder. Participants found the edit/delete/add reminder screen easy to understand due to the lack of options. Nevertheless, it was suggested that instead of one large photograph in the centre, three smaller separate images also as buttons may be a better choice. It was also suggested that previously set reminders should be flagged within the calendar as soon as the page is accessed. Other notes included the small text size on the actual button and within the drop down list (Fig. 11.6).

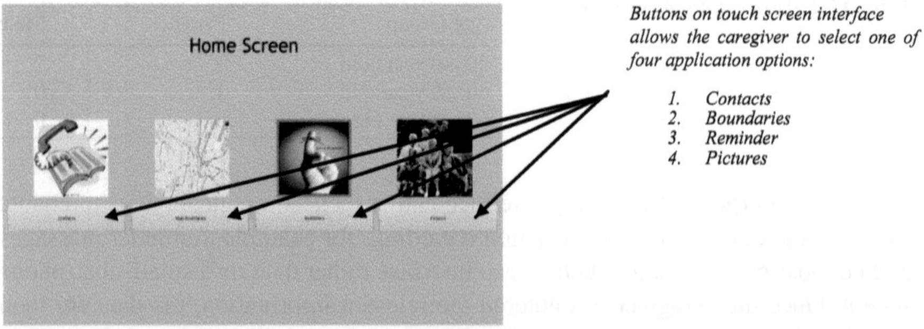

Fig. 11.5 Home screen interface prior to re-design

11.7.3 Contact Screen

Although participants found the contact information screen easy to use, they did find that the text size within the add contact information was too small and expressed that older caregivers may find it difficult to input/read the text displayed. Suggestions for other changes here also included an option to view all currently saved contacts at the same time on one page (Fig. 11.7).

11.7.4 Boundaries Screen

Participants found the boundaries interface and application easy to understand. Participants particularly liked the fact that the map was visible when selecting various boundaries. More than one participant suggested that all boundaries (1, 2 and 3 mile) should be shown on the map/interface at all times. They felt this would benefit the caregiver when selecting various options. Another suggestion was to also change 1-, 2- and 3-mile names to more personal names, for example, the shop, the park or the city centre (Fig. 11.8).

11.7.5 Pictures Screen

Participants found the add picture interface easy to understand and all but one found uploading pictures straight forward. Suggestions for this application included the option to view all currently saved photos at the same time (Fig. 11.9).

11.8 Results from Caregiver Interface Evaluation

The overall feedback from the evaluation of the e-top interface study demonstrated that although participants felt the touch screen interface was easy to use and navigate (refer to Table 11.5) they did have issues with the small text size and felt that the interface, colors and pictures could have been more personal and user-friendly.

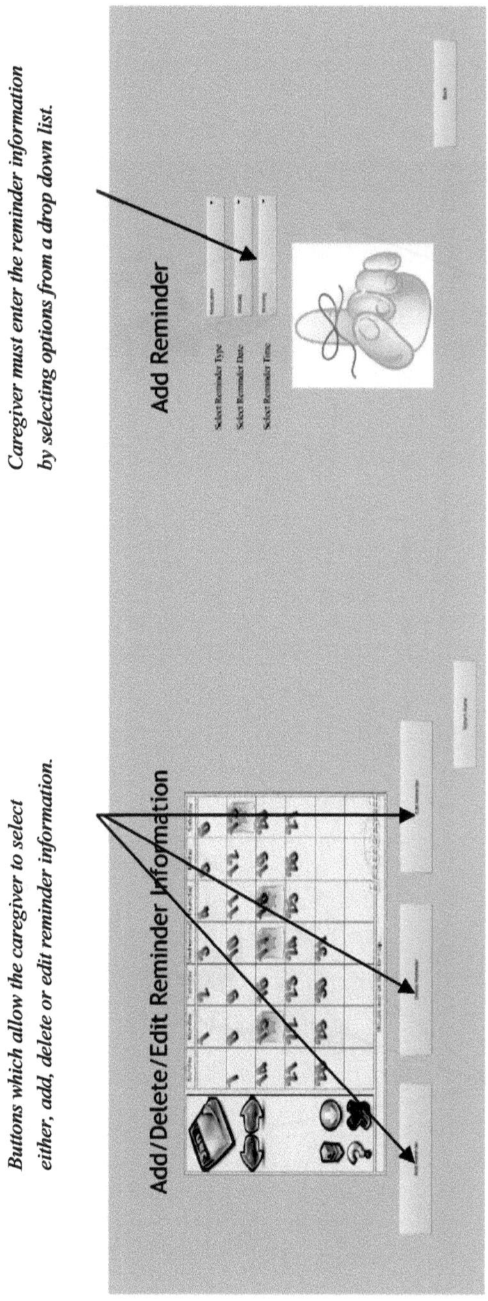

Fig. 11.6 Reminder interface prior to the re-design

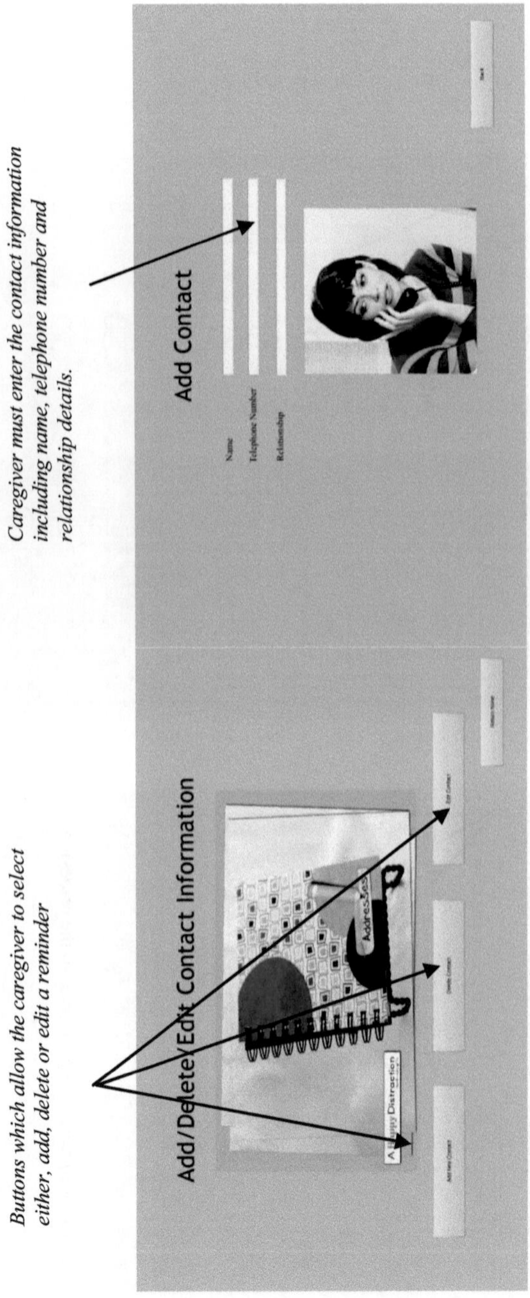

Fig. 11.7 Contacts interface prior to re-design

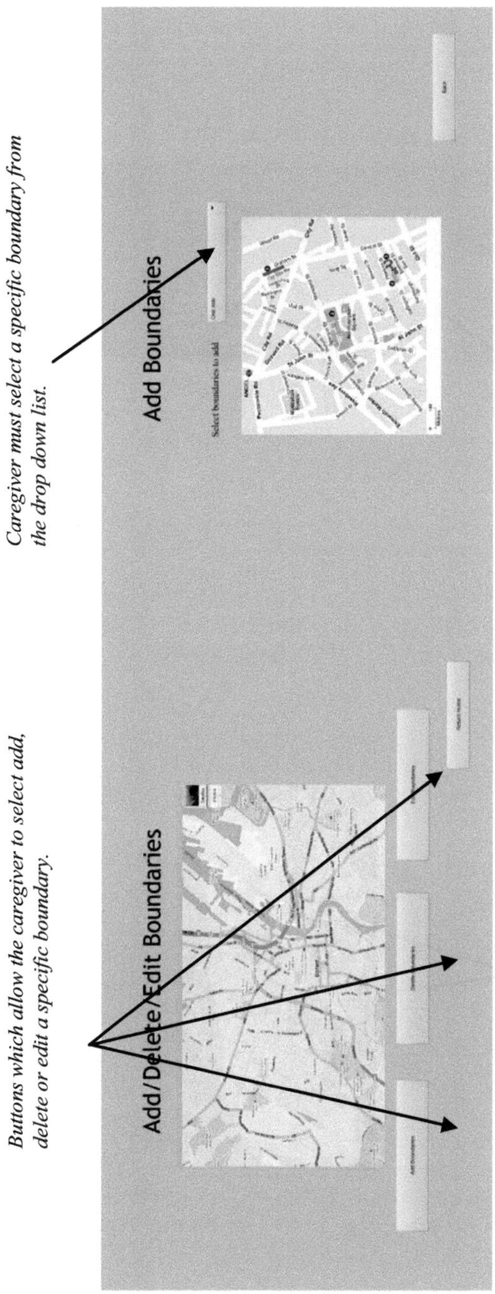

Fig. 11.8 Boundaries interface prior to re-design

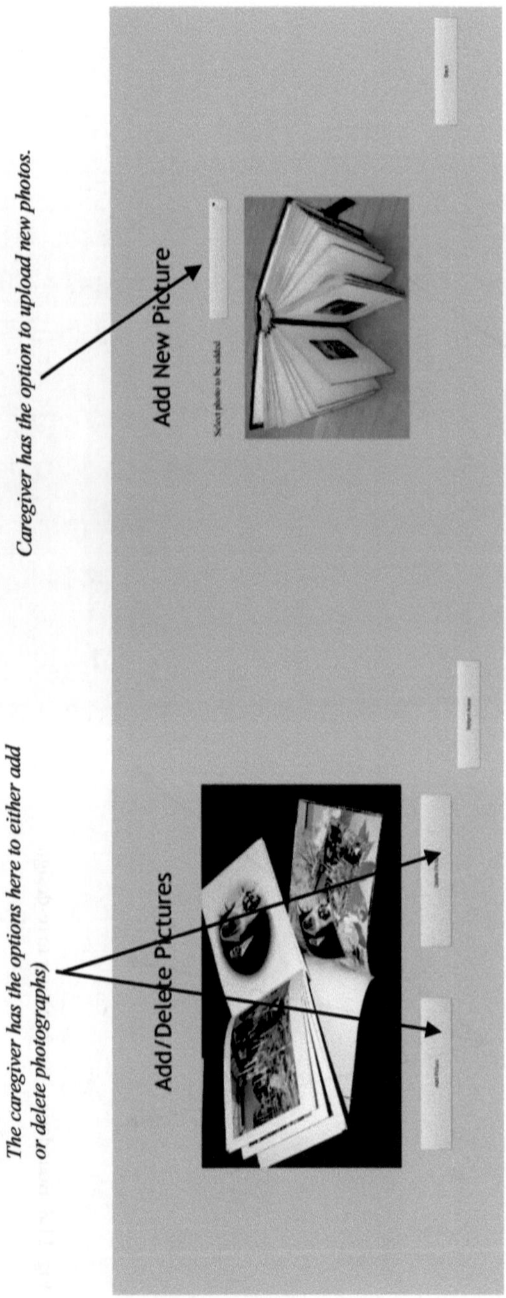

Fig. 11.9 Pictures interface prior to re-design

Table 11.5 User feedback from use of caregiver interface

Liked about the interface	Disliked about the interface
Large button size (3)	Size of text within button too small (4)
Touch screen quick to respond (3)	Drop down text too small (2)
Not too many steps/options to choose from (3)	Buttons slow to respond (1)
Easy to navigate throughout (4)	Images not clickable (3)
Nice use of pictures (1)	Colours are not very personal (1)
Headers on each page (1)	No option to view all saved contacts (1)
Good use of colour (2)	No save button (1)
Very visual (1)	

Figures in brackets indicate number of participants out of the ten who made the same comment

When asked what they liked about the touch screen computer interface application they tested post-study, example comments included, "*Response to touch screen*", "*large button*" and "*common look and theme throughout*". When asked about dislikes, the following example comments were included, "*Images not clickable*", "*small text size*", "*colours (personal preference)*". Based on this feedback, the design of a more personalised end-user interface is currently being developed.

Plans are to make the system user-/caregiver-specific. The caregiver will have the option to design and personalise their own personal user interface. Choices include background color, text size and font style, button size and colour, button position and background images. While testing the newer system, we also intend to investigate whether the level of user support given to the PwAD and their caregiver impacts on technology use (Armstrong et al. 2010b).

Park and Chen reported in 2007 that "millions of dollars are spent on new technologies that eventually are not accepted and adopted" (Park and Chen 2007), due to perceived usefulness. We believe that although there is no one solution that fits all user requirements, devices and assistive technologies currently in the market are not personalised devices and cannot be easily incorporated into everyday life. We also believe that through the use of ICT and personalised user-friendly interfaces coupled with appropriate levels of user training and support this trend may be eliminated.

11.9 Knowledge Management

Knowledge Management (KM) can be described as "a paradigm, which uses technology to support the acquisition, generation, codification and transfer of knowledge" (Dwivedi et al. 2001). Dwivedi et al. (2003) state that a KM strategy is a key factor in managing data within healthcare domains. They believe that the three main components, i.e. people, processes and technology are vital within healthcare information systems.

As the key aim of the smartphone application suite is to transfer data in the form of reminder messages, it is important that the relevant data required/collected within the suite of mobile smartphone applications is properly managed. In order to do this,

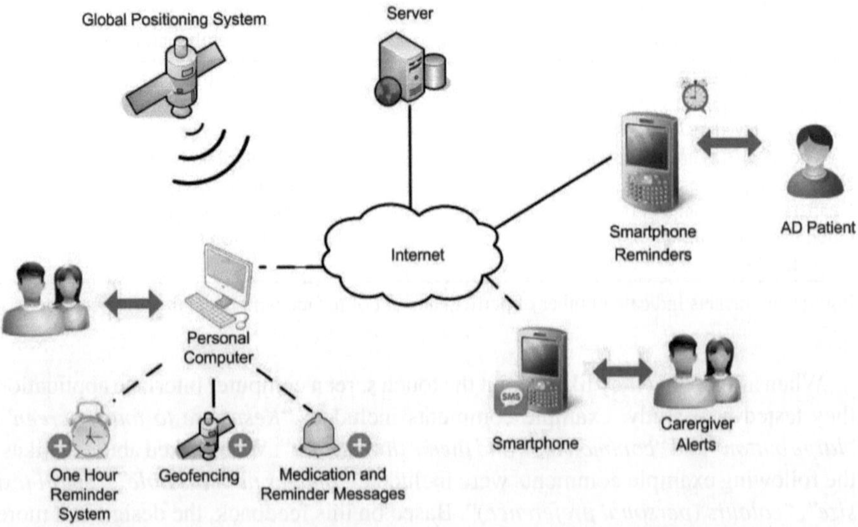

Fig. 11.10 System infrastructure for both smartphone- and computer-based applications. (Adapted from Singh and Kaur 2010)

we have created a database to store such information, within a dedicated server (refer to Fig. 11.10). In order to gather patient-specific information, data are collected from the PwAD or their caregiver. These data are then entered into a password protected, solely dedicated computer via a touch screen by the PwAD caregiver or a nurse and stored within the computer's database. Only the PwAD, their caregiver/nurse or researcher will have access to these data.

Figure 11.10 presents the infrastructure for the current system. In order to communicate and inform all stakeholders involved of any change in circumstance, the communication between them is of the upmost importance. The transfer of knowledge and communication between research staff, PwAD and their caregivers/nurses must be easily obtained in real time. When the relevant data are then obtained from the PwAD's caregiver (this information includes reminder details, contact details and specific boundaries) as previously mentioned, they are stored within the computer's database. This information is then obtained from the database at specific times. When the information is downloaded, a reminder is created and transmitted (reminder) to the smartphone. Information obtained from the PwAD/caregiver with regards to reminder messages include, date, time, reminder type and message displayed. When a reminder message is triggered, the PwAD is then alerted to the smartphone handset, where the reminder should then be acknowledged. If a reminder message is not acknowledged, this information is then sent back to the server. From here, another reminder is then created in order to make the caregiver aware that the reminder has not been acknowledged.

11.9.1 Knowledge Management Issues

As the system is preferably kept within a PwAD's own home, the data are easily accessible to both the PwAD's nurse/caregiver and research staff from the computer. Ideally, it is the preference to be able to view all data input into the database and from the smartphone handset at various locations in order to support all stakeholders involved. As the system is deployed solely on the mobile smartphone handset, gaining information from this can be difficult.

In order to combat this issue, we used mobile KM. Grimm et al. (2005) state that the concept of mobile KM is "the context-aware information processing". This means that a system should have some knowledge about a person's activities/whereabouts and the ability to help with specific activities that may need carried out. Through the use of our context-aware-based applications, for example, the geo-fencing application, we are currently exploiting these advantages and looking at ways to assist the PwAD when they are both inside and outside of the home.

11.10 Further Work and Conclusion

In order to test the smartphone-based applications on the intended target group, PwAD, further effort is required in the re-design of the caregiver interface on the touch screen computer, in order to make it more personalised. When this task has been completed, the system will be suitable to support the evaluation of the end system on our target cohort in order to determine if smartphone technology can help assist PwAD and their caregivers both inside and outside the home environment.

Within the market place today, there are a number of assistive technology aids/devices that may be purchased to help assist PwAD and their caregivers on a daily basis. These aids are simply bought off-the-shelf technology and while they do provide support, the devices tend to target one problem in particular. In order to support PwAD live at home independently for a longer period of time, a more generic solution is required.

We believe that smartphone technology coupled with in-home technology may offer the ability to assist PwADs with regards to their unmet needs and also relieve caregiver's burden. It may also provide PwAD with the opportunity to live independently at home for longer, reduce the costs of healthcare provision and support a user both within their home environment and beyond.

References

Alzheimer's Association. (2009). Alzheimer's disease facts and figures. *Alzheimer's & Dementia, 5*(3).

Alzheimer's Association. (2010). Alzheimer's disease facts and figures. *Alzheimer's & Dementia, 6*.

Alzheimer's Society. (o. J.). What is dementia. http://www.alzheimers.org.uk/site/scripts/documents_info.php?documentID=106. Accessed May 2011.

Armstrong, N., et al. (2009). *Wellness mobile phone, using technology to assist persons with Alzheimer's disease and their carers*. "Ambient Assistive Health and Wellness Management in the Heart of the City: 7th International Conference on Smart Homes and Health Telematics", ICOST, 2009, Tours, France, July 1–3, Proceedings, 5597, 25.

Armstrong, N., et al. (2010a). Developing Smartphone applications for people with Alzheimer's disease. 10th IEEE international Conference on Information Technology and Applications in Biomedicine, ITAB, 2010, Corfu, 3–5 Nov 2010, 1–5.

Armstrong, N., Nugent, C. D., Moore, G., & Finlay, D. D. (2010b). Using smartphones to address the needs of persons with Alzheimer's disease. *Annals of Telecommunications*.

At Dementia. (o. J.). Information on assistive technology for people with dementia, Products. http://www.atdementia.org.uk/productSearch.asp?page_id=16.

Boretos, G. P. (2007). The future of the mobile phone business. *Technological Forecasting & Social Change, 74*,331–340.

CARDI online. (o. J.). Dementia facts and figures. http://www.cardi.ie/news/dementiafactsandfigures. Accessed May 2011.

Communication from the Commission to the European Parliament, the Council, the European Economic and Social Committee and the Committee of the Regions—Ageing well in the Information Society—A i2010 Initiative—Action Plan on Information and Communication Technologies and Ageing {SEC811}/* COM/2007/0332 final (2007).

Dementia. (o. J.). In E. S. Krishnamorrthy, M. J Prince, & J. L. Cummings (Eds.), *A global approach*. Cambridge: Cambridge University Press. ISBN: 13: 9780521857765.

Dwivedi, A., et al. (2001). *Telehealth Systems: Considering Knowledge Management and ICT issues*. Proceedings of the IEEE-EMBC 23rd annual International Conference of the IEEE Engineering in Medicine and Biology Society (EMBS), Turkey, October 2001.

Dwivedi, A., et al. (2002a). *A practical mobile computing solution for healthcare institutions*. Engineering in Medicine and Biology, 2002, 24th Annual Conference and the Annual Fall Meeting of the Biomedical Engineering Society, EMBS/BMES conference, Oct 23–26, 3, 1883–1884.

Dwivedi, A., Bali, R. K., James, A. E., & Naguib, R. N. G. (2002b). *Knowledge management—an enabling paradigm for healthcare stakeholders in realising the vision of Holistic and integrated healthcare management*. In C. J James, et al. (Ed), Proceedings of the IEEE EMBS UK and RI postgraduate Conference on Biomedical Engineering and Medical Physics, Birmingham, UK, p. 6, July 2002.

Dwivdei, A., Bali, R. K., Naguib, R. G., & Nassar, N. S., et al. (2003). *Clinical knowledge management for healthcare*. Proceedings IEEE International Conference Information Technology Applications in Biomedicine, 90–93.

Gartner Newsroom. (2010). Gartner Says Worldwide Mobile Device Sales to End Users Reached 1.6 Billion Units in 2010; Smartphone Sales Grew 72 % in 2010. http://www.gartner.com/it/page.jsp?id=1543014.

Grimm, M., Tazari, M., & Balfanz, D. (2005). *A reference model for mobile knowledge management*. Proceedings of I-KNOW, 05, Graz, Austria, June 29–July 1, 2005.

(o. A.). Improving Dementia service in Northern Ireland: A regional strategy. September 2010.

Kinsella, K., & He, W. (2009). An Ageingworld: 2008. International Population reports, US Census Bureau, published June 2009.

Lauriks, S., et al. (2007). Review of ICT-based services for identified unmet needs of people with dementia. *Ageing Research Reviews, 6*(3), 223–246.

Leijdekkers, P., & Gay, V. (1986). Personal health monitor. United States Patent. http://personalhealthmonitor.net/.

Longley, M., et al. (2002). *Alzheimer's disease, policy and practise across Europe* (p. 1).

Office for National Statistics. (o. J.). Ageing, "Fastest increase in the 'oldest old'". http://www.statistics.gov.uk/cci/nugget.asp?id=949. Accessed May 2011.

Park, Y., & Chen, J. V. (2007). Acceptance and adoption of innovation use of smartphone. *Industrial Management & Data Systems, 107*(9), 1349–1365.

Singh, B., & Kaur, M. (2010). *IT applications in healthcare*. International Conference and Workshop on Emerging Trends (ICWET 2010)—TCET, Mumbai, India, Feb. 2010.

World Health Organisation. (o. J.). Health and chronic disease. http://www.who.int/topics/chronic_diseases/en/.

World Health Organisation. (o. J.). 10 facts on chronic disease. http://www.who.int/features/factfiles/chp/01_en.html.

Zheng, H., et al. (2010). Smart self management: Assistive technology to support people with chronic disease. *Journal of Telemedicine and Telecare,* 224–227.

Part III
The INET Solution and Diabetes Self-Care

Chapter 12
Critical Perspectives on a Possible Solution

Steve Goldberg and Nilmini Wickramasinghe

Abstract Government agencies at all levels have been grappling with the challenges of the healthcare delivery system form several decades (Wickramasinghe et al. 2011; Geisler and Wickramasinghe 2009; Bush 2004; Institute of Medicine 2001). Exponentially increasing costs and declines in quality, access, and availability to the population have and continue to be perplexing and problematic (ibid).Mobile solutions have the possibility to ameliorate the situation however such solutions need to be critically evaluated.

12.1 Introduction

Government agencies at all levels have been grappling with the challenges of the healthcare delivery system form several decades (Wickramasinghe et al. 2011; Geisler and Wickramasinghe 2009; Bush 2004; Institute of Medicine 2001). Exponentially increasing costs and declines in quality, access, and availability to the population have and continue to be perplexing and problematic (ibid).

The figures and trends are alarming and irrespective of all attempts to date continue to rise exponentially (Geisler and Wickramasinghe 2009). Specifically, healthcare delivery costs are approaching 16 % of the gross national product (GNP) and some estimate will reach 20 % of GNP by 2020 if unchecked. Over 45 million Americans are uninsured or underinsured while various government agencies and offices are increasingly overburdened by the arduous tasks of providing care for the underserved segments of their population as well as keeping up with the rising demands of providing affordable and available care to their populations (Centers for Medicare and Medicaid Services 2007; Rachlis 2006; Ramani et al. 2008).

S. Goldberg (✉)
131 Glen Crescent, L4J 4W4, Ontario, Canada,
e-mail: sgoldberg@inet-international.com

N. Wickramasinghe
Epworth Chair Health Information Management, School of Business Information Technology and Logistics, RMIT University, Melbourne VIC 3001, Australia
e-mail: nilmini.wickramasinghe@rmit.edu.au

R. K. Bali et al. (eds.), *Pervasive Health Knowledge Management,*
Healthcare Delivery in the Information Age,
DOI 10.1007/978-1-4614-4514-2_12,

12.2 Background

Today, chronic diseases have replaced infectious diseases as the top global causes of deaths and morbidity (Centers for Disease Control and Prevention 2006; Zimmet 2000; Zuvekas and Cohen 2007). Noncommunicable diseases—such as cardiovascular disorders and strokes, respiratory illnesses such as asthma, arthritis, and diabetes —now account for more deaths and for a disproportionate burden on healthcare budgets of governments, than infectious diseases such as tuberculosis, HIV/AIDS, and malaria (Geisler and Wickramasinghe 2009). This trend is magnified by the demographic realities of this century: The aging of the population and the increased longevity of major segments of the American population are key contributors to the emerging picture of a crisis in the delivery of health services. More patients afflicted by chronic diseases will continue to be a burden on an already drained healthcare delivery system (Windrum 2008; Wickramasinghe and Geisler 2008). It is important to note that the picture in the United States is similar (perhaps not as severe) for all OECD countries; hence all OECD countries must find lasting solutions to address this untenable situation.

It is unsurprising then that governments and practitioners are turning to technology as the panacea. The following serves to highlight the potential of technology for indeed providing a possible solution to this current and serious dilemma. Specifically, the chapters in this section all discuss different critical aspects connected with the INET solution; a particular pervasive technology solution developed for a wireless/mobile environment.

Chapter 13 "Facilitating Superior Chronic Disease Management": A Pervasive Technology Solution to Support Diabetes Self-Care by Wickramasinghe, Troshani, and Goldberg serves to introduce the INET solution and its pervasive technology nature.

Chapter 14 "Achieving m-Health Excellence" by Wickramasinghe and Goldberg further explores the INET solution and the critical factors necessary to make it successful and sustainable.

Chapter 15 "Using Wireless to Monitor Chronic Disease Patients: The Case of Diabetes" by Wickramasinghe and Goldberg provides an evaluation of the INET solution and provides important recommendations and lessons learnt.

Chapter 16 "An Examination of the Business and IT Aspects of Wireless-Enabled Healthcare Solutions" by Chalasani, Goldberg, and Wickramasinghe. The final chapter in this section provides an examination of the business and IT aspects of the INET solution and thereby highlights the strengths and weaknesses of this solution.

Chapter 17 "Applying the IPM Framework to Improve Remote Management in the Context of Chronic Disease Care" by Mogimi, Goldberg, and Wickramasinghe presents a framework to measure the performance and thereby ongoing benefits to care of the pervasive wireless solution.

Taken together, the four chapters in this section then provide a detailed discussion of the INET solution. This is done neither to endorse nor to discredit the specific solution but rather to illustrate all the key considerations that must be understood when trying to design and develop an appropriate pervasive technology solution to better facilitate superior healthcare delivery. These lessons and recommendations are applicable to all and any solutions that might be developed for this niche.

References

Bush, G. W. (2004). State of the union address. http://whitehouse.gov/news/relkease/2004/01/20040120-7.html.

Centers for Disease Control and Prevention. (2006). *Estimating the cost of chronic diseases*. Washington, DC: Centers for Disease Control and Prevention. (In cooperation with the National Center for Chronic Disease Prevention and Health Promotion, and the Agency for Healthcare Research and Quality).

Centers for Medicare and Medicaid Services. (2007). National health expediting data. http://www.cms.hhs.gov/nationalhealthexpendata/.

Geisler, E., & Wickramasinghe, N. (2009). *The role and use of wireless technology in the management and monitoring of chronic diseases*. Washington, DC: IBM Center for the Business of Government.

Institute of Medicine. (2001). *Crossing the chasm-a new health system for the 21st century*. Washington, DC: National Academy Press, Committee on Quality of Health Care in America.

Rachlis, M. (2006). Key to sustainable healthcare system. http://www.improvingchroniccare.org.

Ramani, V., Mavalankar, D., & Govil, D. (2008). *Strategic issues and challenges in health management*. Thousand Oaks: Sage.

Wickramasinghe, N., & Geisler, E., (Eds.). (2008). *Encyclopedia of healthcare information systems*. Hershey: IGI Global Publishers.

Wickramasinghe, N., Bali, R., Kirin, S., & Sumoi, R. (2011). *E-health*. New York: Springer. (forthcoming).

Windrum, P. (2008). *Innovation in public sector services*. New York: Edward Elgar.

Zimmet, P. (2000). 21st century review: Globalization, coca-colonization, and the chronic disease epidemic: Can the doomsday scenario be averted? *Journal of Internal Medicine, 247*(3), 301–310.

Zuvekas, S., & Cohen, J. (2007). Prescription drugs and the changing concentration of healthcare expenditures. *Health Affairs, 26*(1), 249–257.

Chapter 13
A Pervasive Technology Solution for Supporting Diabetes Self-Care

Nilmini Wickramasinghe, Indrit Troshani and Steve Goldberg

Abstract To date, the adoption and diffusion of technology-enabled solutions to deliver better healthcare has been slow. There are many reasons for this. One of the most significant is that existing methodologies that are normally used in general for information communication technology (ICT) implementations tend to be less successful in a healthcare context. This chapter describes a knowledge-based adaptive mapping to realization methodology that provides a means to traverse from idea to realization rapidly and yet without compromising rigor so that success ensues. It is discussed in connection with trying to implement superior ICT-enabled approaches for facilitating superior chronic disease management.

Keywords Chronic disease management · Diabetes · ICT · Healthcare knowledge-based methodology · E-healthcare

13.1 Chronic Disease Management

Containment of cost and yet offering the highest quality healthcare has become a global priority for healthcare delivery. In such an environment, prevention and/or early detection becomes critical since initiatives that prevent the occurrence of a disease help to circumvent costly healthcare interventions while, initiatives that detect the occurrence of a disease early usually enable better control of this disease and thereby less costly healthcare interventions. Moreover, in both instances quality is high since the patient is subjected to less invasive healthcare interventions and can

N. Wickramasinghe (✉)
Epworth Chair Health Information Management, School of Business Information Technology and Logistics, RMIT University, Melbourne VIC 3001, Australia,
e-mail: nilmini.wickramasinghe@rmit.edu.au

I. Troshani
University of Adelaide Business School, The University of Adelaide, 10 Pulteney Street, Adelaide, SA 5005, Australia
e-mail: indrit.troshani@adelaide.edu.au

S. Goldberg
131 Glen Crescent, L4J 4W4, Ontario, Canada
e-mail: sgoldberg@inet-international.com

R. K. Bali et al. (eds.), *Pervasive Health Knowledge Management*, Healthcare Delivery in the Information Age,
DOI 10.1007/978-1-4614-4514-2_13, © Springer Science+Business Media New York 2013

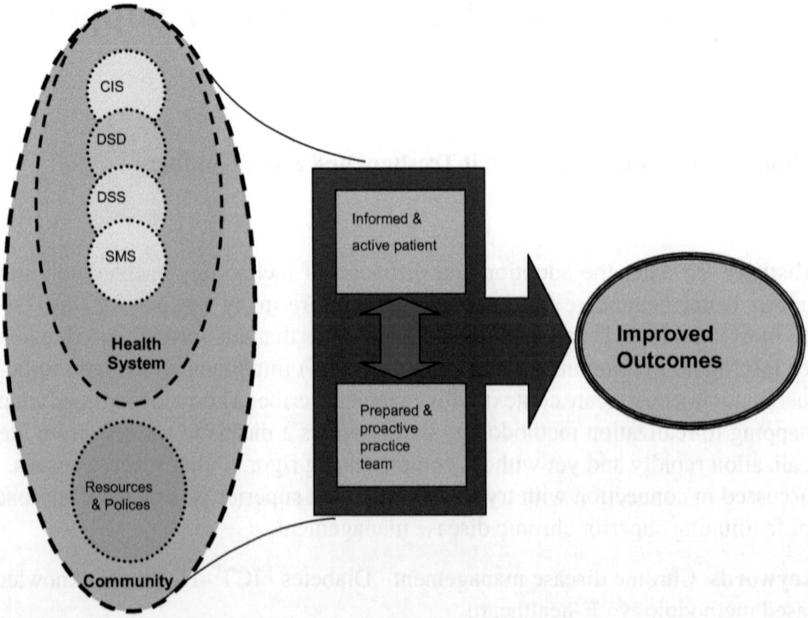

Fig. 13.1 Chronic care model. (Adapted from Rachlis 2006)

enjoy a higher quality of life. In such an environment, the effective management of chronic disease becomes particularly important.

Chronic diseases such as diabetes, asthma, or hypertension if detected early can be contained and the sufferers from these diseases can continue to lead fully and high-quality lives. Conversely, if these diseases are not well managed, they can develop into more complicated healthcare problems and life for such patients becomes less than satisfactory. Critical to effective chronic disease management is regular monitoring and an informed patient who takes responsibility for managing his/her wellness. As identified by Rachlis (2006), a chronic care model requires the interaction and coordination of numerous areas (Fig. 13.1). In particular, it requires the interaction of four key components of the healthcare system, including self-management support, delivery support, decision support and clinical information systems, and support from the community at large (Table 13.1). Taken together, this provides a conducive environment to have productive interactions between an informed and activated patient and a prepared and proactive healthcare team.

Diabetes, one important chronic disease, is increasing in its prevalence throughout not only North America but also the world (Fig. 13.2). Given the cost of treatment of increasing amount of the population, coupled with the fact of increased nonworking hours due to the need to treat the chronic disease, increases in the prevalence of diabetes, as is projected, is indeed alarming to any healthcare system.

Table 13.1 Components of chronic care model. (Rachlis 2006)

Component	Description
Organization of health system	Leadership in chronic disease management (CDM) Goals for CDM Improvement strategy for CDM Incentives and regulations for CDM Benefits
Self-management support	Assessment and documentation of needs and activities Addressing concerns of patients Effective behavior change interventions
Decision support	Evidence-based guidelines Involvement of specialists in improving primary care Providing education for CDM Informing patients about guidelines
Delivery system design	Practice team functioning Practice team leadership Appointment system Follow-up Planned visits for CDM Continuity of care
Clinical information systems	Registry Reminders to providers Feedback Information about relevant subgroups of patients needing services Patient treatment plans
Community	Linkages for patients to resources Partnerships with community organizations Policy and plan development

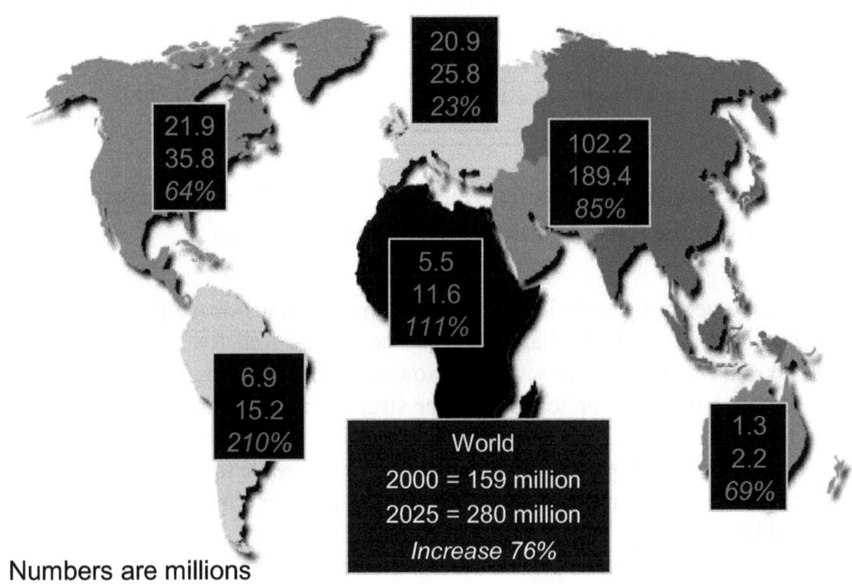

Fig. 13.2 Number of diabetics: 2000–2025

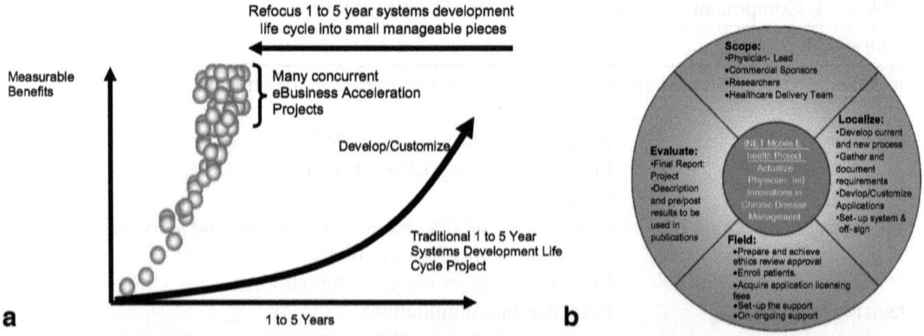

Fig. 13.3 **a** Refocusing the SDLC. **b** Components of the delivery framework. (Adapted from Wickramasinghe et al. 2009)

Regular monitoring of diabetes is a necessary part to controlling this particular chronic disease and keeping it from evolving into more complicated healthcare problems. To do this efficiently and effectively, we believe information communication technologies (ICT) can play a critical role by providing a means to enable superior monitoring anywhere anytime and thereby also allowing the patient to enjoy a high-quality lifestyle. However, technology initiatives in healthcare to date have had mixed results at best (Kulkarni and Nathanson 2005; Lacroix 1999; Frost and Sullivan 2004; Wickramasinghe and Goldberg 2004; Wickramasinghe and Mills 2001; Wickramasinghe and Silvers 2003). We believe this is connected with the failure of current information systems (IS) methodologies to correctly capture the richness and complexities of a modern healthcare environment. To address this issue, and in so doing, we provide an environment enabled by ICT that facilitates superior chronic disease management. We describe the results from a 7-year longitudinal study conducted between INET and CMMT (Goldberg et al. 2002a, b, c, d, e; Wickramasinghe and Goldberg 2003, 2004; Wickramasinghe et al. 2007).

13.2 Developing an Appropriate ICT-Enabling Environment to Facilitate Chronic Disease Management

The journey began by realizing that the tradition systems development life cycle (SDLC) was fundamentally flawed for any healthcare initiative (Wickramasinghe et al. 2009). This was due to several reasons including the length of time it would take to realize the final application and the structures and inflexible stages that had to be traversed. Thus, INET developed a refocused SDLC model (Fig. 13.3a) and delivery framework (Fig. 13.3b). In this way, it was possible to keep the strengths of the traditional SDLC and yet move from start to finish in a much compressed time frame (ibid).

Simply stated, the research goal is to use a standardized mobile Internet (wireless) environment to improve patient outcomes with immediate access to patient data and provide the best available clinical evidence at the point of care. To do this, INET

International Inc.'s research (Goldberg et al. 2002a, b, c, d, e; Wickramasinghe and Goldberg 2003, 2004) starts with a 30-day e-business acceleration project in collaboration with many key actors in hospitals such as clinicians, medical units, administration, and IT departments. Together they follow a rigorous procedure that refocuses the traditional 1–5-year systems development cycle into concurrent, 30-day projects to accelerate healthcare delivery improvements. The completion of an e-business acceleration project delivers a scope document to develop a handheld technology application (HTA) proof-of-concept-specific to the unique needs of the particular environment. The proof-of-concept is a virtual lab case scenario. A virtual Lab operates within a mobile Internet (wireless) environment by working with hospitals and technology vendors. The final step is the collection of additional data with clinical HTA trials consisting of 2-week hospital evaluations.

From the refocused SDLC model, it was then possible to design a robust and rigorous web-based business model, the INET web-based business model (Fig. 13.4). The business model then provides the necessary components to enable the delivery framework to be positioned in the best possible manner so it can indeed facilitate the key components of the chronic disease model being successfully enacted.

Successful web-based projects in healthcare require a consideration of many components (Wickramasinghe et al. 2009). Figure 13.4 provides an integrative model for all key success factors that we have identified through our research (Wickramasinghe et al. 2005; Wickramasinghe and Misra 2004; Goldberg et al. 2002a, b, c, d, e; Wickramasinghe and Goldberg 2004). What makes this model unique and most beneficial is its focus on enabling and supporting all areas necessary for the actualization of Information and Communication Technology initiatives in healthcare. By design, the model identifies the inputs necessary to bring an innovative chronic disease management solution to market. These solutions are developed and implemented through a physician-led mobile e-health project. This project is the heart of the model to bridge the needs and requirements of many different players into a final (output) deliverable a "Wireless Healthcare Program. " To accomplish this, the model is continually updated to identify, select, and prioritize the ICT project inputs that will:

1. Accelerate healthcare system enhancements and achieve rapid healthcare benefits. The model identifies the key healthcare system inputs with the four Ps:
   a. People that deliver healthcare.
   b. Process to define the current healthcare delivery tasks.
   c. Platform used in the healthcare technology infrastructure.
   d. Protection of patient data.
2. Close the timing gaps between information research studies and its application in healthcare operational settings.
3. Shorten the time cycle to fund an ICT project and receive a return on the investment.

In order to successfully implement the business model described above, it was, however, necessary to have an appropriate methodology. Based on this need, the adaptive mapping to realization (AMR) methodology was developed (Fig. 13.5).

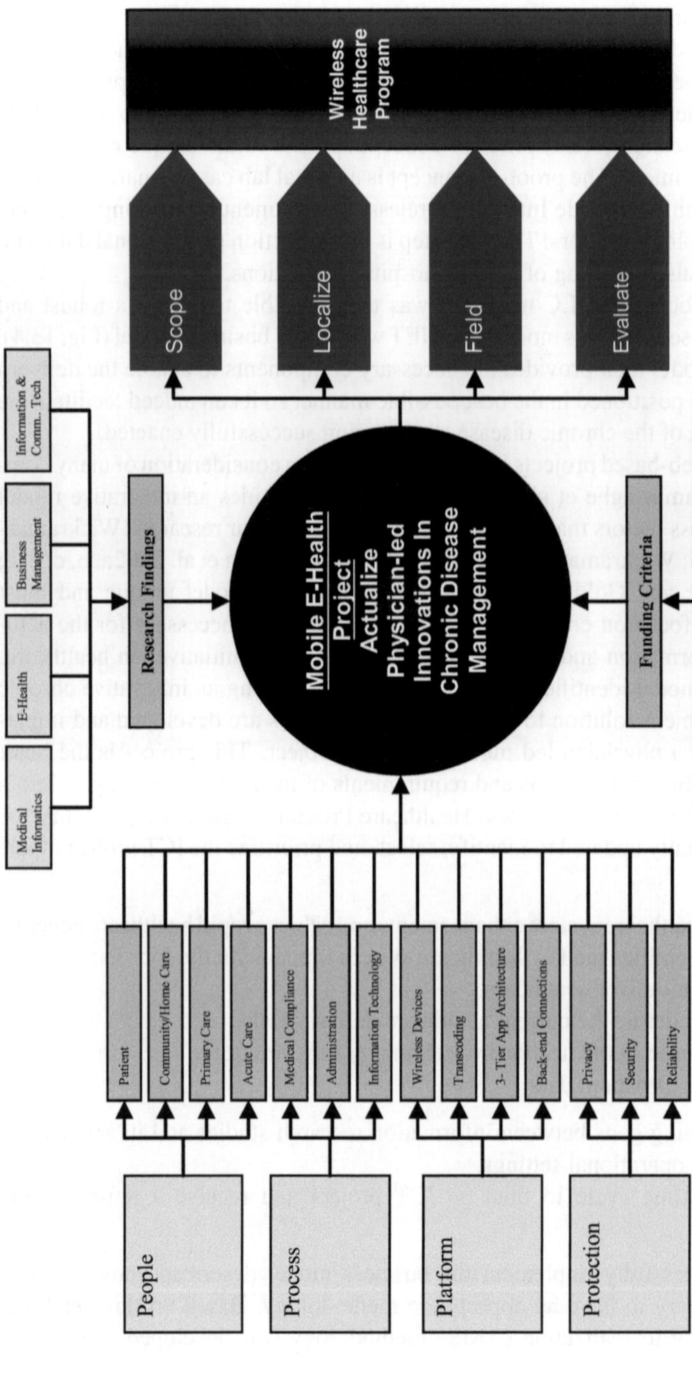

Fig. 13.4 INET web-based business model. (Adapted from Wickramasinghe et al. 2009)

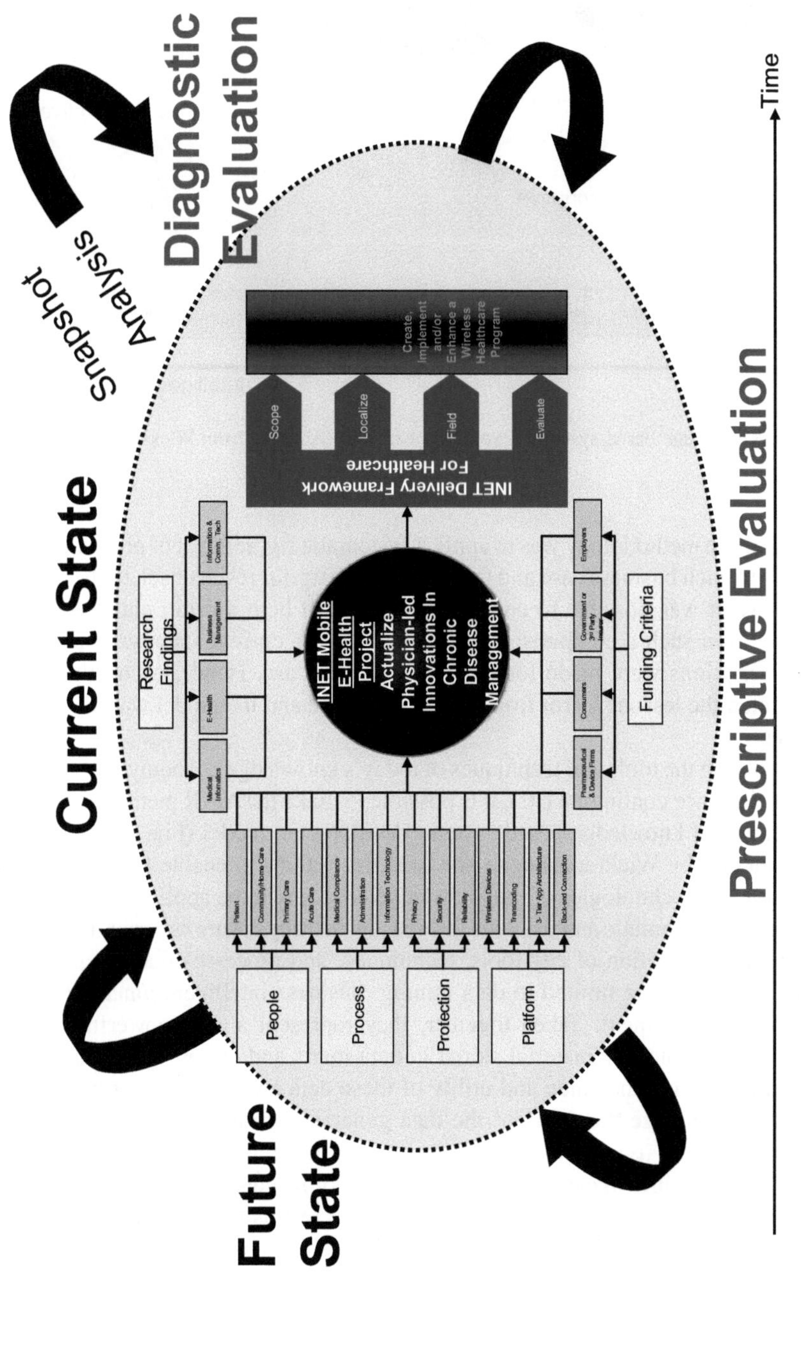

Fig. 13.5 AMR methodology. (Adapted from Wickramasinghe et al. 2009)

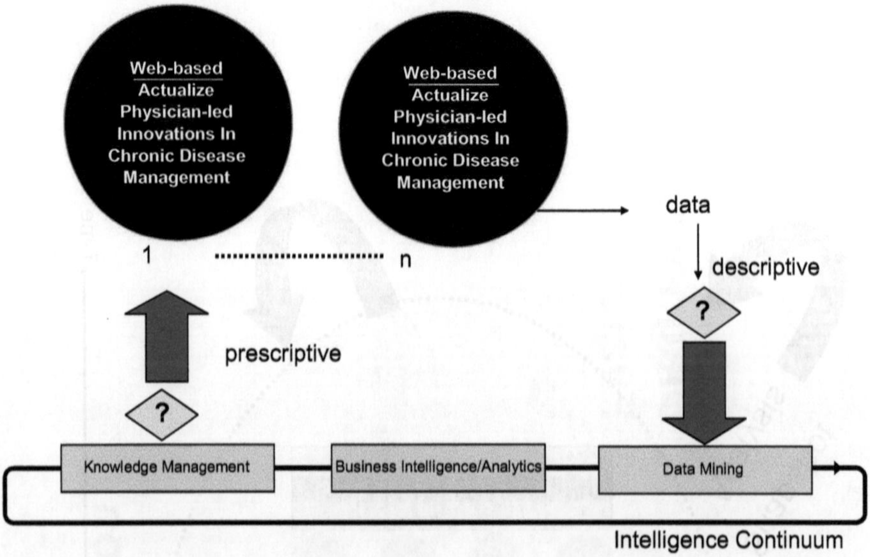

Fig. 13.6 Knowledge-based systems development model. (Adapted from Wickramasinghe et al. 2009)

The idea of the methodology was to apply a systematic rigorous set of predetermined protocols to each business case and then map the postprior results back to the model. In this way, it was possible to compare and contrast both a priori and post priori findings. From such a comparison, a diagnosis of the current state was made and then prescriptions were made for the next business case. Hence, each pilot study incorporated the lessons learnt from the previous one and the model was adapted in real time.

By applying the tools and techniques of today's knowledge economy as presented in the intelligence continuum (IC), it is possible to make the AMR methodology into a very powerful knowledge-based systems development model (Fig. 13.6). The IC was developed by Wickramasinghe and Schaffer (2006) to enable the application of the tools and technologies of the knowledge economy to be applied to healthcare processes in a systematic and rigorous fashion and thereby ensure superior healthcare delivery. The collection of key tools, techniques, and processes that make up the IC include but are not limited to data mining, business intelligence/analytics, and knowledge management. Taken together, they represent a very powerful system for refining the data raw material stored in data marts and/or data warehouses and thereby maximizing the value and utility of these data assets for any organization. In order to maximize the value of the data generated through specific healthcare processes and then use this to improve processes, the techniques and tools of data mining, business intelligence and analytics, and knowledge management must be applied in a systematic manner. Once applied, the results become part of the data set that are reintroduced into the system and combined with the other inputs of

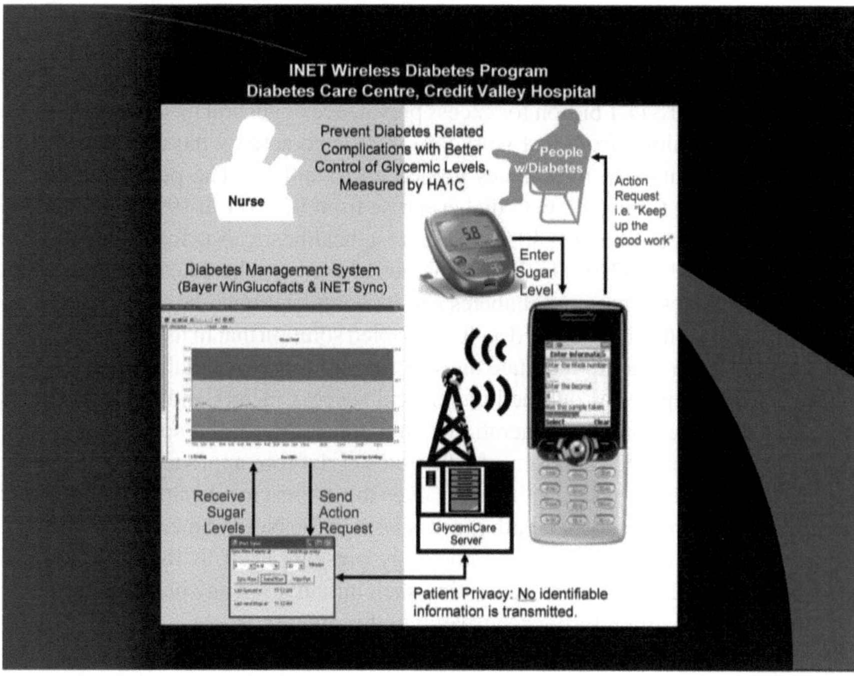

Fig. 13.7 ICT support for diabetes

people, processes, and technology to develop an improvement continuum. Thus, the intelligence continuum includes the generation of data, the analysis of these data to provide a "diagnosis," and the reintroduction into the cycle as a "prescriptive" solution. In this way, the IC is well suited to the dynamic and complex nature of healthcare environments and ensures that the future state is always built upon the extant knowledge base of the preceding current state. Through the incorporation of the IC with the AMR methodology, we then have a knowledge-based systems development model that can be applied to any setting not necessarily chronic disease management. The power of this model is that it brings best practices and the best available germane knowledge to each iteration and is both flexible and robust.

13.3 Discussion and Conclusions

In the current context, healthcare delivery especially in the United States is in need of fundamental redesign (Porter and Tiesberg 2006). The focus on cost containment also necessitates a shift to prevention rather than cure. This is particularly important in the case of chronic diseases such as diabetes.

Diabetes is the fifth deadliest disease in the United States. Since 1987, the death rate due to diabetes has increased by 45 %, while the death rates due to heart disease, stroke, and cancer have declined. The total annual economic cost of diabetes in 2002 was estimated to be $132 billion. Direct medical expenditures totaled $92 billion and comprised $23.2 billion for diabetes care, $24.6 billion for chronic diabetes-related complications, and $44.1 billion for excess prevalence of general medical conditions. Indirect costs resulting from lost workdays, restricted activity days, mortality, and permanent disability due to diabetes totaled $40.8 billion. The per capita annual costs of healthcare for people with diabetes rose from $10,071 in 1997 to $13,243 in 2002, an increase of more than 30 %. In contrast, healthcare costs for people without diabetes amounted to $2,560 in 2002. One out of every ten healthcare dollars spent in the United States is spent on diabetes and its complications.

The preceding then has outlined an ICT-enabled solution that in itself is not exorbitantly expensive in order to facilitate the superior monitoring of diabetes (Fig. 13.7). Moreover, the chapter has outlined the critical success factors and necessary steps required to traverse from idea generation to implementation of this solution. In so doing, we have also outlined a most useful flexible yet rigorous approach that is suitable to all ICT implementations in healthcare. Given the interest in e-health, computerized medical records and personal health records both in the North America and Europe. We are confident that the AMR methodology presents itself as the most suitable methodology to adopt when implementing such initiatives in any healthcare context and thus close by calling for more research in this area.

References

Frost & Sullivan. (2004). Country Industry Forecast—European Union Healthcare Industry, May 11, 2004. http://www.news-medical.net/print_article.asp?id=1405.

Goldberg, S., et al. (2002a). Building the Evidence For A Standardized Mobile Internet (wireless) Environment In Ontario, Canada. January Update. Internal INET documentation.

Goldberg, S., et al. (2002b). HTA Presentational Selection and Aggregation Component Summary. Internal documentation.

Goldberg, S., et al. (2002c). Wireless POC Device Component Summary. Internal INET documentation.

Goldberg, S., et al. (2002d). HTA Presentation Rendering Component Summary. Internal INET documentation.

Goldberg, S., et al. (2002e). HTA Quality Assurance Component Summary. Internal INET documentation.

Kulkarni, R., & Nathanson, L. A. (2005). Medical Informatics in medicine. E-Medicine. http://www.emedicine.com/emerg/topic879.htm.

Lacroix, A. (1999). International concerted action on collaboration in telemedicine: G8 sub-project 4. *Studies in Health Technology and Informatics, 64,* 12–19.

Porter, M., & Tiesberg, E. (2006). *Re-defining health care delivery.* Boston: Harvard Business Press.

Rachlis, M. (2006). Key to sustainable healthcare system. http://www.improveingchroniccare.org.

Wickramasinghe, N., & Goldberg, S. (2003). *The wireless Panacea for healthcare.* Proceedings of the 36th Hawaii International Conference on System Sciences (HICSS-35) January 6–10, 2003, Hawaii (CD-ROM), Copyright 2002 by the Institute of Electrical & Electronic Engineers, Inc (IEEE).

Wickramasinghe, N., & Goldberg, S. (2004). How M = EC2 in healthcare. *International Journal of Mobile Communications, 2*(2), 140–156.

Wickramasinghe, N., & Mills, G. (2001). MARS: The electronic medical record system. The core of the Kaiser galaxy. *International Journal Healthcare Technology Management, 3*(5/6), 406–423.

Wickramasinghe, N., & Misra, S. (2004). A wireless trust model for healthcare. *International Journal of Electronic Healthcare (IJEH), 1*(1), 60–77.

Wickramasinghe, N., & Schaffer, J. (2006). Creating knowledge driven healthcare processes with the intelligence continuum. *International Journal of Electronic Healthcare (IJEH), 2*(2), 164–174.

Wickramasinghe, N., & Silvers, J. B. (2003). IS/IT the prescription to enable medical group practices to manage managed care. *Health Care Management Science, 6*, 75–86.

Wickramasinghe, N., Schaffer, J., & Geisler, E. (2005). "Assessing e-health" forthcoming. In T. Spil & R. Schuring (Eds.), *E-health systems diffusion and use: The innovation*. Heresy: The User and the User IT Model, Idea Group Publishing.

Wickramasinghe, N., Goldberg, S., & Bali, R. (2007). Enabling superior m-health project success: A tri-country validation. *International Journal of Services and Standards*. (in press).

Wickramasinghe, N., Troshani, I., & Goldberg, S. (2009). Supporting diabetes self-management with pervasive technology solutions. *International Journal of Healthcare Delivery Reform Initiatives, 1*(4), 17–31.

Chapter 14
Achieving m-health Excellence

Nilmini Wickramasinghe and Steve Goldberg

Abstract Medical science has made revolutionary changes in the past decades. Contemporaneously, however, healthcare has made incremental changes at best. The growing discrepancy between the revolutionary changes in medicine and the minimal changes in healthcare processes is leading to inefficient and ineffective healthcare delivery and one if not the significant contributor to the exponentially increasing costs plaguing healthcare globally. Healthcare organizations can respond to these challenges by focusing on three key solution strategies; namely: (1) access—caring for anyone, anytime, anywhere; (2) quality—offering world-class care and establishing integrated information repositories; and (3) value—providing effective and efficient healthcare delivery. These three components are interconnected such that they continually impact on the other and all are necessary to meet the key challenges facing healthcare organizations today.

The application of mobile commerce to healthcare; namely, m-health appears to offer a way for healthcare delivery to revolutionize itself and simultaneously address the critical areas of access, quality and value. Integral to such an approach is the need for a robust wireless model. We propose the Wi-INET (wireless internet, intranet, extranet) model as the way to deliver m-health excellence.

Keywords Mobile commerce · m-health · Wireless healthcare program · Business model · IT architecture · Standard mobile environment

---

Some of the material in this paper has been presented previously in earlier versions of various aspects of this on going project:
Wickramasinghe, N., S. Misra & S. Goldberg 2004 "Security Challenge in a Mobile Healthcare Setting", The 5th Annual Conference of the National Business and Economics Society, Hawaii, March 10–13, 2004.
Wickramasinghe, N., and S. Goldberg 2005 "Delivering M-health Excellence: The Wi-INET Model" in Ed Encyclopaedia on wireless and Mobile Commerce Idea Group, Hershey.

N. Wickramasinghe (✉)
Epworth Chair Health Information Management,
School of Business Information Technology and Logistics, RMIT University,
Melbourne VIC 3001, Australia
e-mail: nilmini.wickramasinghe@rmit.edu.au

S. Goldberg
131 Glen Crescent, L4J 4W4 Ontario, Canada
e-mail: sgoldberg@inet-international.com

R. K. Bali et al. (eds.), Pervasive Health Knowledge Management,
Healthcare Delivery in the Information Age,
DOI 10.1007/978-1-4614-4514-2_14,

14.1 Background

Currently, the healthcare industry in the United States as well as globally is contending with relentless pressures to lower costs while maintaining and increasing the quality of service in a challenging environment (National Coalition on Healthcare 2004; Pallarito 1996; European Institute of Medicine 2001; World Health Organization Report 2000; World Health Organization Report 2004; Kyprianou and Commissioner, E.U. Health and Consumer Protection 2005; Frost and Sullivan 2004; Plunkett's Health Care Industry Almanac 2004; OECD 2004; National Center for Health Statistics 2002; Russo 2000; Lacroix 1999; Lee et al. 2003; Blair 2004; Kulkarni and Nathanson 2005; Wickramasinghe and Silvers 2003). It is useful to think of the major challenges facing today's healthcare organizations in terms of the categories of demographics, technology, and finance. Demographic challenges are reflected by longer life expectancy and an aging population; technology challenges include incorporating advances that keep people younger and healthier; and finance challenges are exacerbated by the escalating costs of treating everyone with the latest technologies. Healthcare organizations can respond to these challenges by focusing on three key solution strategies; namely: (1) access—caring for anyone, anytime, anywhere; (2) quality—offering world-class care and establishing integrated information repositories; and (3) value—providing effective and efficient healthcare delivery. These three components are interconnected such that they continually impact on the other and all are necessary to meet the key challenges facing healthcare organizations today.

In short then, the healthcare industry is finding itself in a state of turbulence and flux (National Coalition on Healthcare 2004; Pallarito 1996; European Institute of Medicine 2003; World Health Organization Report 2000; World Health Organization Report 2004; Wickramasinghe and Mills 2001). Such an environment is definitely well-suited for a paradigm shift with respect to healthcare delivery (von Lubitz and Wickramasinghe 2005). Many experts within the healthcare field area agree that m-health appears to offer solutions for healthcare delivery and management that serve to maximize the value proposition for healthcare. However, to date, little, if anything, has been written regarding how to achieve excellence in m-health, nor does there exist any useful model for framing m-health delivery.

14.2 Integrative Model for m-Health

Successful m-health projects require a consideration of many components. Figure 14.1 provides an integrative model for all key factors that we have identified through our research that are necessary in order to achieve m-health excellence (Wickramasinghe et al. 2005; Goldberg et al. 2002a–e; Wickramasinghe and Goldberg 2004). What makes this model unique and most beneficial is its focus on enabling and supporting all areas necessary for the actualization of Information and Communication Technology (ICT) initiatives in healthcare. By design, the model identifies

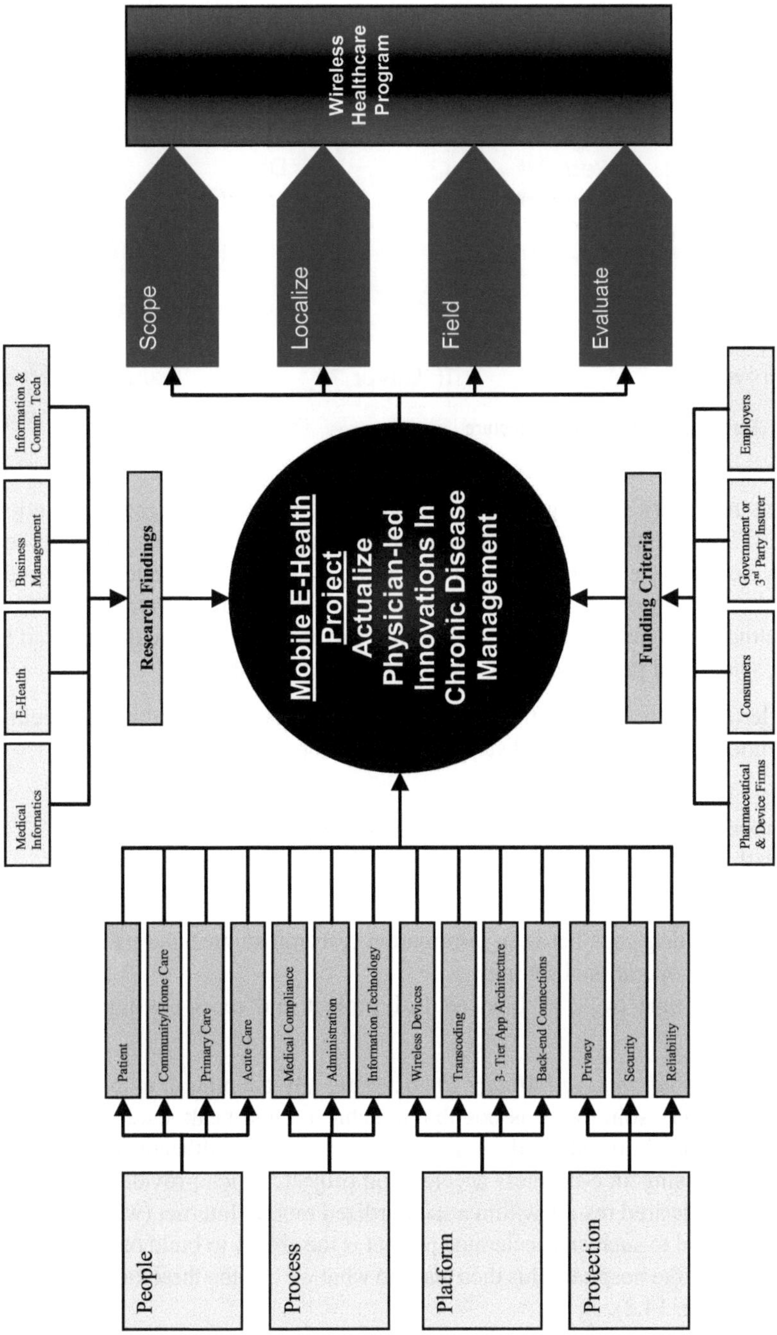

Fig. 14.1 Wi-INET business model. (Adapted from Wickramasinghe et al. 2009)

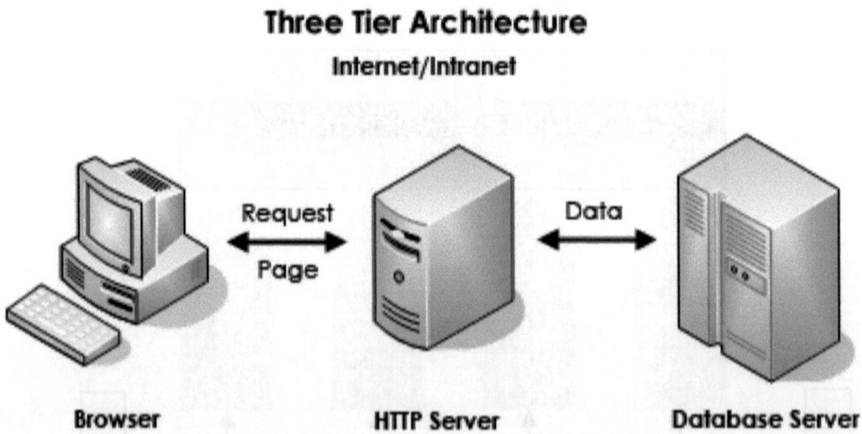

Fig. 14.2 Three-tier web-based architecture

the inputs necessary to bring an innovative chronic disease management solution to market. These solutions are developed and implemented through a physician-led mobile e-health project. This project is the heart of the model to bridge the needs and requirements of many different players into a final (output) deliverable a "Wireless Healthcare Program". To accomplish this, the model is continually updated to identify, select, and prioritize the ICT project inputs that will:

1. Accelerate healthcare system enhancements and achieve rapid healthcare benefits. The model identifies the key healthcare system inputs with the four Ps:
   a. People that deliver healthcare.
   b. Process to define the current healthcare delivery tasks.
   c. Platform used in the healthcare technology infrastructure.
   d. Protection of patient data.
2. Close the timing gaps between information research studies and its application in healthcare operational settings.
3. Shorten the time cycle to fund an ICT project and receive a return on the investment.

IT Architecture and Standard Mobile Environment By adopting a mobile/wireless healthcare delivery solution, it is possible to achieve rapid healthcare delivery improvements, which impact both the costs and the quality of healthcare delivery. This is achieved by using an e-business acceleration project, which provides hospitals a way to achieve desired results within a standardized mobile Internet (wireless) environment. Integral to such an accelerated project is the ability to build on the existing infrastructure of the hospital. This then leads to what we call the three-tier web-based architecture (Fig. 14.2).

In such an environment, tier 1 is essentially the presentation layer; which contains the *web browser* but no patient data are stored within this layer, and thereby ensuring compliance with international security standards/policies like the Health Insurance, Portability, and Accountability Act (HIPAA). Tier 2, shown as the *HTTP Server*, provides the business logic including but not limited to Lab, Radiology and clinical transcription applications, Messaging of HL7, XML, DICOM and other data protocols, and interface engines to a Hospital Information Systems (HIS), Lab Information Systems (LIS), Radiology Information Systems (RIS), as well as external messaging systems such as Smart Systems for Health (an Ontario Healthcare IT infrastructure project). This latter messaging feature may also be included in third tier, which consists of the back-end *database servers* like, Oracle, MySQL, or Sybase.

14.3 Mapping Case Study to Model

During the past 6 years, INET has used an e-business acceleration project to increase ICT project successes (Goldberg et al. 2002a–e; Wickramasinghe and Goldberg 2004). Today, INET is repurposing the e-business Acceleration project into a mobile e-health project to apply, enhance, and validate the mobile e-health project delivery model. Such a model provides a robust structure and in turn serves to ensure excellence in the m-health initiative. INETs data provide the perfect opportunity to examine the components of our model (Fig. 14.1) as it is both rich and longitudinal in nature. In mapping the data and specific business case, we have drawn upon many well-recognized qualitative techniques including conducting both structured and unstructured interviews, in-depth archival analysis, and numerous site visits (Goldberg et al. 2002a–e and Wickramasinghe and Goldberg 2004 capture and substantiate the findings discussed while Kavale 1996, Boyatzis 1998, and Einhardt 1989 detail the importance and richness of the methodologies we have adopted in presenting the following findings, and key criteria were established from Standish Group International Inc. 1994, Crossing the Quality Chasm 2001, and Canadian Healthcare Technology magazine 2005).

The INET Mobile e-Health project objectives include:

1. Accelerate consensus building with an e-health solution that is focused on a disease state and driven by the medical model. With the primary objective to streamline communications and information exchange between patients, and providers of community/home care, primary care, and acute care.
2. Acquire commercial funding early with a compelling business case. For instance, enhancing therapeutic compliance can improve patient quality of life with significant healthcare cost savings. It is well documented that in Diabetes this will have immediate and high-impact benefits for healthcare consumers, pharmaceutical firms, governments, insurers, and employers.
3. Avoid risk by reengineering large-scale healthcare delivery processes in small manageable pieces. Today, organizations can harness a rigorous method to incrementally enhance a process one step at time. A way to achieve quick wins early and frequently.

4. Rapid development of simple-to-use, low-cost, and private/secure ICT solutions. Achieve these benefits through a wireless Application Service Providers (ASPs). In addition to rapid development, a wireless ASP can easily connect and bring together many independent healthcare information systems and technology projects.

To actualize the mobile e-health project, INET is looking to the Wi-INET model as a framework. For INET, this will support an INET Mobile e-Health Project Management Office (PMO) to manage the costs, quality, and deliver many small projects and replicate projects for local and international distribution. As a first case scenario for the model, INET is proposing an INET Wireless Diabetes Program with the leadership from a Family Physician. The INET PMO is provisioning a project manager to support this physician-led project to meet both research and commercial sponsor's interests and objectives in diabetes. A detailed description of the key attributes of INET Wireless Diabetes Program includes:

- *Problem statement*: There are many communication and information exchange bottlenecks between Patients and their Family Physicians that prevent the effective treatment of diabetes. As background, a fundamental problem today is the ability to have a private and secure way to manage, search, and retrieve information at the point-of-care. In Diabetes, physicians cannot quickly and easily respond to patients with high glucose levels. They need to wait for people to: come to the office, respond to phone calls, reply using traditional mail delivery, or never receive the patient information.
- *Solution mandate*: Implement a diabetes monitoring program to enhance therapeutic compliance, such as release a program to enhance the usage of oral hypoglycemic agents (drugs), and/or the usage of blood sugar monitoring devices. As background, everyone wins when enhancing patients' ability to follow instructions in taking prescribed medication. The patient's health, safety, and quality of life improve with significant healthcare cost savings. However, it is well documented that many patients do not stay on treatments prescribed by physicians.[1] This is where wireless technology may have the greatest impact to enhance compliance. One solution may be as simple as using a cell phone and installing a secure wireless application for patients to monitor glucose levels, and provisioning a physician to use a PDA (connected to a wireless network) to confidentially access, evaluate, and act on the patient's data.
- *Business case*: In Ontario, the cost savings may represent almost \$1 billion over 3 years. INET uses a simple calculation to determine the \$1 billion savings. This can be found at http://www.inet-international.com and please select the INET mobile e-health project section to review the calculations. The business case can be backed with additional data on how the cost of prevention (drugs) is far less than the cost savings of reducing the risk of complications associated with Diabetes.

[1] Fourteen percent to 21 % of patients never fill their original prescription and 30 to 50 % of patients ignore or otherwise compromise their medication instructions (Source: http://www.managedhealthcareexecutive.com/mhe/article/articleDetail.jsp?id=105388).

For instance, the impact of a 1 % decrease in A1C is significant. More data are available to support the business case for the prevention of type 2 diabetes, such as lowering the incidence of End-Stage Renal Disease (ESRD). In summary, there are plenty of data today to quickly build consensus, fund and implement a national and international wireless diabetes program to enhance patients' quality of life with significant healthcare cost reductions; i.e., meet the objectives of access, quality, and value.

- *Systems development life cycle project delivery*: Use an INET Mobile e-Health project to scope, localize, field, and evaluate an INET Wireless Diabetes program led by a physician. Each project can easily and simply customize a program to quickly meet the unique needs of a rural and urban healthcare delivery setting, age, ethnicity, income, language, and culture. These are small manageable projects. Each project collects data on patient/healthcare provider relationships, wireless medical informatics, therapeutic compliance business case, and ICT usability to accelerate acceptance of a wireless diabetes program using wireless technology. The program may include cellular network and application usage, support, healthcare provider PDA, consulting fees for family physician and other healthcare providers. However, it is expected that the costs may not include items, such as consumer cell phone, medication, or blood sugar monitoring devices/supplies. It is recommended that commercial and/or research sponsor(s) pay for an INET project and help subsidize the user costs.

In June 2005, INET applied the Wi-INET model to pilot a Wireless Diabetes Program with the objective to decrease diabetes-related complications with better control of glycemic levels, measured by HA1C.

The core component of the program is the relationship between family physicians and patients supported by a wireless diabetes management protocol.[2] This protocol describes how a patient can enter their glucose readings into their cell phone and transmit the results to their family physician. The protocol further details how the physician, in turn, is able to monitor any number of patients on his PDA, such as a Palm Treo or RIM Blackberry device. A physician, if required, can take immediate action with a message electronically sent to the patient's cell phone. The program was tested through a pilot project with four patients, led by Dr. Sheldon Silver and was completed in July 2005. The pilot project lasted approximately 3 months. The preliminary results are significant as shown in Table 14.1.

In summary, INET's research data indicate that using the Wi-INET model will increase ICT project success in healthcare. To realize and test this, INET continues to map the player's form an INET Wireless Diabetes Program (use case scenario) to the model. To show how this works, please review the mapping exercise below. The bold text in black is a project player and the color text in [] parenthesis relates to the sections of the model presented in Fig. 14.1:

- **Physician Mobile e-Health Project Lead** ["Mobile e-Health Project" in Fig. 14.1]. Physicians provide the linkage to the medical model to enhance disease management programs to enhance patient care and safety, improve research and

[2] Wireless Diabetes Management Protocol © Dr. Sheldon Silver, MD 2005.

Table 14.1 INET wireless diabetes program results

INET wireless diabetes program			
Patient	Change in HAIC levels		% reduction in HAIC (%)
	Prepilot	Postpilot	
1	0.082	0.069	−16
2	0.090	0.071	−21
3	0.108	0.050	−54
4	0.113	0.084	−26

education, increase healthcare quality, and reduce healthcare costs. For INET's use case scenario, the final outcome is a Wireless Diabetes Program ["Wireless Healthcare Program" in Fig. 14.1]. And, the Mobile e-health projects are led by Dr. Sheldon Silver, MD, Staff Physician, Credit Valley Hospital.

- Commercial Sponsor(s) ["Funding Criteria" in Fig. 14.1]. The project delivers information and communication solutions for:
  - Consumers wishing to improve their quality of life with an enhanced relationship with their healthcare provider's, i.e., family physicians.
  - Pharmaceutical firms looking to increase revenues with e-Compliance programs.
  - Government/insurers investigating ways to significantly reduce administration and healthcare costs, and shorten healthcare delivery time cycles (wait times).
  - Employers wanting to increase productivity and avoid absenteeism with a healthier workforce.
- Research Sponsor(s) ["Research Findings" in Fig. 14.1]. The project develops intellectual property for researchers in the fields of:
  - Patient and Healthcare Provider Relationships.
  - Wireless Medical Informatics.
  - Therapeutic Compliance Business Case.
  - Wireless Information Technology Usability.
  - An INET Mobile e-Health Project Delivery Team.
- **Healthcare Delivery Team** ["People" in Fig. 14.1]. For a wireless diabetes program, the players may include:
  - Healthcare Consumer: People with Diabetes.
  - Community Care: Nurse Specializing in Diabetes.
  - Primary Care: Family Physician.
  - Acute Care: Endocrinologist and Diabetes Education/Management Centers.
- **Business Process Analyst** ["Process" in Fig. 14.1].
- Privacy and Security Consultant ["Protection" in Fig. 14.1].
- Programmer using a wireless ASP ["Platform" in Fig. 14.1].
  - Wireless Network and Devices.
  - Device and Application Transcoding.
  - Application Service Provider.
  - Back-end connection.

In conclusion, INET is looking forward to further advancements in the mobile e-health project delivery model to:

- Achieve rapid advancements in healthcare delivery.
- Improve diabetes management.
- Enhance therapeutic compliance.
- Realize significant healthcare care cost savings.[3]

INET is planning to continue its role as a sources of use case scenarios for the model with the delivery of Mobile e-Health Projects.

The preceding has served to outline all the critical aspects that must be considered when trying to actualize a mobile health initiative. Clearly, Mobile e-health or m-health projects are complex and require much planning and coordination within and between the web of healthcare players. Success is never guaranteed in any large initiative, however, in order to realize the four major healthcare deliverables depicted in Fig. 14.1 (enhance patient care and safety, improve research and education, increase healthcare quality, and reduce healthcare costs), it is vital that any m-health initiative to focus on the key success factors of people process and technology. Specifically, the technology must be correct and functioning as desired. Furthermore, it must integrate seamlessly with existing ICT infrastructure and enable the processes. The processes must be well-defined and at all times ensure that they are of a high quality and error free.

The Institute of Medicine in America (Bluetooth Security Solutions o. J.) identified medical errors as the fourth leading cause of many deaths. In trying to prevent such errors, it has identified six key quality aims; namely: (1) healthcare should be safe—avoiding injuries to patients from the care that is intended to help them, (2) effective—providing services based on scientific knowledge to all who could benefit and refraining from providing services to those who will not benefit (i.e., avoiding underuse and overuse), (3) patient-centered—providing care that is respectful of and responsive to individual patient preferences, needs, and values and ensuring that patient values guide all clinical decisions, (4) timely—reducing waiting and sometimes harmful delays for both those receiving care and those who give care, (5) efficient—avoiding waste, and (6) equitable—providing care that doesn't vary in quality based on personal characteristics. Finally, a key critical success factor pertains to security, which we now discuss in detail.

14.4 A Generic Mobile Healthcare Delivery System

In order to understand the important security considerations, it is first useful to present a generic mobile healthcare delivery system. The mobile healthcare delivery system can be defined as the carrying out of healthcare-related activities using mobile

---

[3] In Ontario, this may save $1 billion over 3 years: INET Talk "Enhance Therapeutic Compliance Using Wireless Technology," WNY Technology & Biomedical Informatics Forum Oct 14, 2004. Niagara Falls Conference, NY.

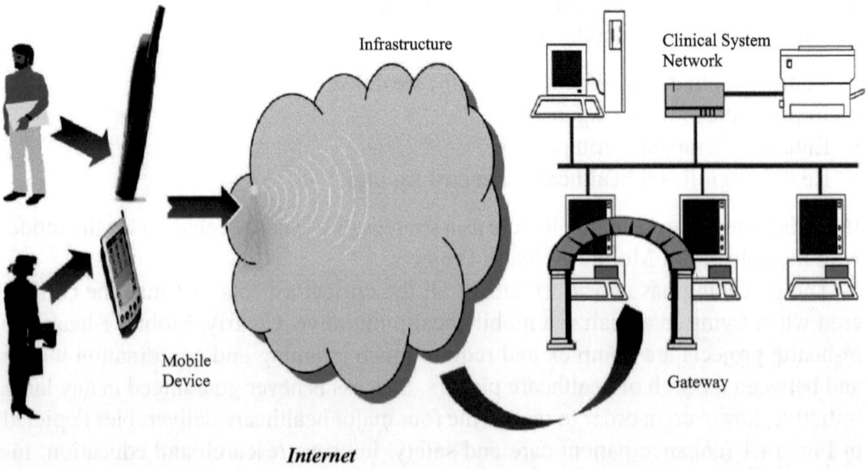

Fig. 14.3 Generic mobile healthcare delivery system. (Adapted from Wickramasinghe and Misra 2004)

devices such as a wireless phone, Personal Digital Assistant (PDA), or a wireless-enabled computer. A mobile activity occurs when an authorized healthcare provider (provider for short) accesses the clinical system of a hospital (or similar provider institutions) using a mobile device. The access is deemed to be complete when the provider, after necessary electronic negotiations with the hospital system, decides to access a patient record to either browse or make a change to the chart. The provider may be a physician interested in reviewing a patient's electronic medical record, or a nursing assistant recording medication administered, or a specialist prescribing new medication for a patient, or any other medically authorized provider viewing or changing a patient's medical record. In this generic mobile environment, the clinical system is viewed as one or more servers hosting medical applications and healthcare databases. If there is more than one server in the clinical system (typically true even for small healthcare institutions), these servers may be networked using a commercial networking protocol such as TCP/IP.

In the generic mobile healthcare delivery system (Fig. 14.3), a provider initiates a session using his or her mobile device. A communication channel is established between the device and a base wireless station automatically using a certain radio frequency (RF). The communication from the base station then travels through the Internet infrastructure to the wireless application gateway of the hospital (used hereafter as a generic substitute for healthcare institutions). There are many valid reasons, including standards prescribed by HIPAA (2002), why all concerned parties, the patient, hospital, and physician, to name a few, should expect the information exchanged during such a mobile transaction process to be secure. Specifically, parties should expect the data associated with a transaction to be confidential and delivered without violation of integrity or authenticity. All parties should expect nonrepudiability; neither the client nor the institution should be able to deny the completion of the transaction if such a transaction, in fact, occurred. For example, if a physician prescribed a medication using the mobile structure, the transaction should have the same legal force as if handwritten by the physician.

The underlying assumption in the generic model is one of access from outside the hospital. The provider, in this model, is somewhere outside the boundary of the hospital and accesses the public telecommunication infrastructure to reach the patient record. There is a significant variation to this scenario in healthcare: providers access the clinical system from anywhere within the geographical boundary of the hospital. In this model (Fig. 14.3), the wireless transmission originates from a mobile device but directly reaches the intranet of the hospital using short-range wireless technologies such as Bluetooth (Bluetooth Security Solutions o. J.; Muller 1999; Jakobsson and Wetzel 2001; o. A. 2002; Borisov et al. 2001) or IEEE 802.11 (o. A. 2002; Borisov et al. 2001). In this model, a physician typically initiates a medical transaction that must ultimately connect his/her wireless device to the hospital's medical applications and databases. The connection uses both wireless and wired channels. The wireless transmission from the mobile device is received by a nearby Access Point and then on proceeds using the wired intranet infrastructure of the hospital. A hospital may locate a number of Access Points within its premises to enable mobility of the user.

14.5 Importance of Security

Most of the poor quality connected with healthcare is related to a highly fragmented delivery system that lacks even rudimentary clinical information capabilities resulting in poorly designed care processes characterized by unnecessary duplication of services and long waiting times and delays (Canadian Healthcare Technology magazine 2005). The development and application of sophisticated information systems is essential to address these quality issues and improve efficiency yet healthcare delivery has been relatively untouched by the revolution of information technology that has transformed so many areas of business today (Wickramasinghe and Silvers 2002; Sorby et al. 2002). This then certainly justifies the need for e-business solutions for healthcare delivery. Experience from INET's research (Goldberg et al. 2002f–j) suggests that we can use mobile solutions to improve overall efficiency of service delivery with the added advantage of significant cost savings (as much as 80 % on infrastructure alone in some instances) and increased functionality compared to wired counterparts. Physicians themselves are excited by the possibilities offered by mobile solutions (Goldberg and Wickramasinghe 2002; Wickramasinghe et al. 2009).

A mobile solution is indeed very attractive but brings challenges of its own, the most critical being security. Given the nature of the information, namely patient data, to be transferred and accessed using this technology, security, privacy, and even ethical issues become key considerations in any wireless solution. Currently, many countries in Europe as well as Australia, Canada, New Zealand, and the United

Table 14.2 HIPPA requirements

Extracts from HIPAA security requirements
Establishment of trust partnership agreements with all business partners
Formal mechanisms for accessing electronic health records
Procedures and policies to control access of information
Maintaining records of authorizing access to the system
Assuring that system users receive security awareness training and the training procedures are periodically reviewed and updated
Maintaining security configuration including complete documentation of security plans and procedures, security incident reporting procedure
Communication and network control including maintaining message integrity, authenticity, and privacy. Encryption of messages is also advocated for the open network transmission portion of the message
Data authentication to ensure that data are not altered or destroyed in an unauthorized manner

Kingdom are wrestling with the development of appropriate and robust security policies. In the United States, HIPAA was enacted to establish a national standard for transactions security and privacy (HIPAA 2002; Moore and Wesson 2002). According to HIPAA, a number of security criteria must be met by all electronic healthcare transactions. Some of these criteria directly affect how healthcare systems can be accessed as well as define appropriate ways in which to interact with these technologies. Table 14.2 details the relevant extracts of the HIPAA requirements; readers interested in the complete HIPPA security requirements are referred to (HIPAA 2002).

It is difficult to argue with the security goals of HIPAA. Mobile healthcare systems, therefore, must strive to achieve these goals not only to provide a secure healthcare transaction environment but also to deliver high-quality healthcare through the mediation of wireless technologies.

14.6 Wired Equivalent Security

Wired Equivalent Security (WES) may be defined as a standard that makes a mobile transaction as secure as an equivalent "wired" transaction. In other words, if the wired version of a transaction requires the exchange of digital certificates between the customer and the merchant, the wireless transaction should also insist on the digital certificate; if the wired version of a transaction requires the transaction content to be encrypted using a, say, 128 bit key, the wireless transaction should also insist on the same 128 bit key; and so on. Unfortunately the infrastructure, both hardware and software, capable of supporting a mobile transaction is not exactly the same for that of the wired counterpart. Ideally, it would be desirable to build a common security framework that can support both fixed and mobile transactions. The basis of the common security framework would be a security model that assures authenticity, confidentiality, integrity, availability, and nonrepudiability for any transaction whether wired or wireless.

The advantage of a common security framework is straight forward. An organization can build a business model to support all of its business activities. This business model would use the unified security model to assure security of data and transactions. Such a unified security model would also enable a healthcare organization to leverage its existing security infrastructure and move rapidly into the support of wireless initiatives. As the diffusion and adoption of wireless throughout healthcare organizations increases, the need for such a wired equivalent security structure becomes increasingly important and significant.

14.7 Elements of a Security Model

Security of a computing system and associated data is multifaceted. Dutta and McCrohan (2002) view security problems of electronic businesses as that of a "blended threat" where the threat may originate from multiple sources, propagate without human intervention, and have different points of attack. Dutta and McCrohan (2002) go on to propose a balanced approach to security that takes into account four major sets of factors: Organizational Structures and Procedures, Critical Infrastructure Protection, Technological Solutions, and Management Actions. Even within these four factors, security issues can be easily categorized into several dimensions. Security threats may originate from a source external to the organization or may have internal origins. Management of security-related problems may be preventive as well as restorative. Preventive actions, as the name implies, are deployed before a security breach occurs. Use of firewalls, proxy servers, and encryption of data are examples of common preventive actions. Restorative actions occur after the fact of a breach. These actions may include reconstruction of a data set, changes into authentication procedures, and upgrades to access control procedures. Both preventive and restorative actions may be managerial and technical.

What are then the activities associated with maintaining the security of a computer system? Table 14.3 shows a list of activities that may be used by any healthcare organization interested in a secure operating environment. While this list is by no means exhaustive, it serves to highlight the multidimensional problem of maintaining security in any healthcare setting.

14.8 Security Issues in Wireless

The introduction of wireless does not change the set of required security activities rather it increases the level of vulnerabilities by introducing additional problems as follows:

- *Between the provider and the mobile device*: This is the initial point in the process of a transaction. This stage implicitly assumes that the person originating a transaction is the mobile device owner and is an authorized provider. Unfortunately,

Table 14.3 Key security activities

Activity type	Activities
Primarily managerial	Identifying sensitivity level of data Defining community of users and their access levels and privileges Identifying allowable information services over a network Preparing incidence reports and response procedures Preparing contingency plans for recovery from security and other disasters Preparing security training and awareness plans Defining security roles of various individuals associated with the system
Primarily technical	Defining levels and methods of interconnection among subsystems Defining the security infrastructure and isolation levels of sensitive segments Defining backup and recovery procedures Defining change management procedures
Primarily security-related	Deploying preventive measures such as Firewalls, Proxy servers, and Intrusion detection systems Deploying routing measures for scanning for virus Implementing physical and environmental controls for security of physical assets such as computer hardware, network routers Maintaining audit trails for all successful and unsuccessful access to the system Encrypting sensitive data both in storage and in transmission
Recovery from an attack	Restoration of data and programs within a predefined time constraint Use of alternative services during recovery Modification to the plans and procedures related to security awareness Modification to the system configuration

this leads to an uncomfortable assumption that the possessor of the mobile device is indeed an authorized healthcare provider and the owner of the device. To ensure end-to-end security, a number of issues must be resolved: can a transaction be prevented if an unauthorized person tries to masquerade as a provider and engages in a transaction assuming the identity of a provider? If an unauthorized transaction occurs, is the provider who has the true ownership of the device liable? Also, what is the liability of the hospital if an unauthorized person successfully completes a healthcare transaction leading to undesirable consequences for one or more patients? Conversely, if the mobile device is unwillingly compromised (e.g., stolen), can a transaction be prevented?

- *Between the mobile device and the mobile infrastructure operator*: This stage of a transaction occurs over the open air. Typically, the provider's directive is transmitted from his mobile device to a base station. In the generic view (Fig. 14.2), the base station is some kind of transmission tower operated by a service operator and not within the business model of the hospital. On the other hand, if the provider is originating a transaction within the hospital's intranet (Fig. 14.3), the base station is likely to be a mobile communication access point (hot spot) and within the control of the hospital. In either case, the data transmission is wireless and there is a possibility of interception of the radio transmission. If a masquerader can intercept a transmission, not only is there the loss of confidentiality but also other potential consequences. For example, the masquerader may be able to gain access to confidential information about a patient and maliciously change medical directive leading to severe damage or even loss of life.

- *Between the mobile infrastructure operator and the wireless application gateway of the merchant*: This third stage of a transaction occurs in the network of the service operator and is not a factor in the model of Fig. 14.3. Neither the hospital nor the provider has any control over the network or the manner in which data are transmitted over the network. In this respect, this third stage of a mobile transaction is no different than its wired counterpart: a hospital using the Internet. Infrastructure operators do not guarantee security of data transmitted through their network. It is the responsibility of hospitals and the providers to protect their information assets.
- *Between the wireless application gateway and the web services of the merchant*: This stage of a mobile transaction is likely to be under the control of the hospital supporting wireless access. Issues of security for this stage are no different than would be expected in any operating environment.

There are similarities and differences between a mobile and a fixed (those not using a mobile device) transaction. As in the case of a fixed transaction, content of a mobile transaction must be protected from unauthorized access and alteration whether it is in storage or being transmitted. However, protecting data that move is a bit more difficult than data that do not move since one has to worry about additional issues such as the mobility and location of the user as well as type of wireless technologies used. With this goal in mind, we analyze security issues using several factors: User-Centric, Content-Centric, Access pathways, and Policy goals. These factors are presented in Table 14.4.

14.9 WES in a Healthcare Setting

Let us now briefly return to the INET scenario to understand the key considerations and implications when incorporating wired equivalent security into a healthcare setting and how in fact this might be actualized.

INET typically begins with a hospital's current wired implementations of security and electronic authorization practices as defined by the Canadian College of Health Record Administrators.[4,5] An example of a wired implementation of these guidelines is Meditech's electronic signature capabilities for Imaging and Therapeutic services[6] where, for instance, a physician enters his/her userID and password as a means

---

[4] Security of Computerized Health Information, Canadian College of Health Record Administrators (CHRA), Don Mills, Ontario, Canada, CHRA 1989, Reprinted June 1990.

[5] Electronic Authentication, Canadian College of Health Record Administrators (CHRA), Don Mills, Ontario, Canada, CHRA 1990, Revised 1997.

[6] Imaging and Therapeutic Services (ITS), Electronic Signature, User Guide, Meditech Client Server, Hamilton Health Sciences, March 3, 2002.

Table 14.4 Key factors to analyze security issues

Factor	Key issues
User-centric (primarily a physician)	These strategies must address the major issue of user identification irrespective of the location and mode of access • Decision regarding the person or persons authorized to use Wireless LAN technology • Conditions under which wireless devices can be used • Training of these authorized individuals in security procedures including the use of built-in encryption in the wireless devices • Policies and guidelines on reporting losses of wireless devices and security incidents The basic issue is very clear—only a trusted user is allowed to access the resources of an organization. If a customer is not trusted, a trust relationship must be established before any access is possible
Content-centric	In a Wired equivalent model, both wired and wireless clients should be able to access the same set of contents and carry out the same set of transactions. This is at the moment difficult as the processing capacity of devices used for these transactions differs significantly. The solution to this is to use specialized application development languages such as Wireless Application Protocol (WAP) and Compact HTML. This also may require the establishment of separate wireless application gateways. The industry solution to this mismatch is to translate a WAP request to standard HTML and vice versa. Unfortunately, this translation introduces a source of security breach since any encrypted message will have to be converted to plain text before translation. Since there is no immediate solution to this issue, the best approach is to make the translation seamless for a client. We suggest that type of contents that can be accessed through a wireless link should be a business decision and should be based on the ability to maintain the necessary security
Access pathways	Access into the wired services typically has multiple pathways. Wired equivalent security requires that these pathways should not impact the overall security of the system. The concept of demilitarized zone (DMZ) can be used for this purpose. The suggested approach is to isolate the publicly visible servers from the sensitive corporate data
Policy goals	Any client, whether wired or wireless, can come into the web servers or WAP servers subject to normal authentication procedures. However, access to sensitive data should be limited to trusted transactions that have to satisfy the necessary intrusion detection rules. The healthcare organization also must define security standards and policies for all accesses that need to be updated on a regular basis

to select and sign-off the appropriate digital (electronic) reports. INET findings demonstrate (Goldberg et al. 2002f–j; Goldberg and Wickramasinghe 2002) that wireless technology can meet these wired electronic authentication criteria. The usual wireless IT Infrastructure uses handheld devices (PDAs, Tablets, and phones), wireless Mobile IP networks, and Transcoding technology as an extension of existing wired IT infrastructure tier 1 presentation layer. This enables wireless access to portal technologies userID and password screen.

Additional risk or threat to patient data is protected using wired technology. The Ontario Human Resources Cluster of the Ministry of Health and Long-Term Care[7] provide the security plans, guidelines, and analyses to confirm these wired security measures and policies. INET had discovered (Goldberg et al. 2002f–j; Goldberg and Wickramasinghe 2002) that a wireless IT infrastructure can meet the same rigor as wired technology as long as it can be proven that there is no additional risk or threat to patent data. One way is to demonstrate that a wireless IT infrastructure will not store patient data outside a wired clinical management system. This mandates that a wireless IT infrastructure must be an "ultra" thin client with no caching of data, no printing of data, and no storage of patient data along the pathway between a wired infrastructure and the wireless device, and in the wireless device.

Finally, using the approach identified in Table 14.4 is extremely helpful as a way for hospitals and other healthcare stakeholders to meet a wired equivalent security model. Table 14.5 provides specific detailed scenarios from INET's experiences to illustrate these key factors and how they can be addressed.

14.10 Discussion and Conclusions

Healthcare in the United States and globally is at the cross-roads. It is facing numerous challenges in terms of demographics, technology, and finance. The healthcare industry is responding by trying to address the key areas of access, quality, and value. m-health, or mobile e-health, provides a tremendous opportunity for healthcare to make the necessary evolutionary steps in order to realize its goals and truly achieve its value proposition. What is important is to ensure m-health excellence. This requires not only detailed theoretical studies but ultimately the need to turn theory into practice. By an in-depth analysis of the rich and longitudinal data of INET, we have presented the Wi-INET model to facilitate the achievement of m-health excellence. Systematic and detailed analysis and integration of all the key drivers and implication of healthcare delivery have enabled the development of the Wi-INET model. Moreover, its structure facilitates rapid development and actualization of m-health solutions. To the best of our knowledge, it is the first such model and while it is certainly not a panacea it does help to set the stage and outline the key issues that must be addressed for a successful m-health initiative and enables healthcare to reap the benefits of wireless. We are confident that through the adoption of the Wi-INET model, healthcare delivery too can make revolutionary changes and we can all enjoy superior healthcare delivery.

[7] Security Plans Guidelines, IT Security Policy, Human Services I&IT Cluster, Ontario Management Board Cabinet, Ontario Government of Canada, March 27, 2001.

Table 14.5 Wireless IT infrastructure in healthcare

Factor	Mandatory Requirements Defined By The INET 2002 Study[a] at Hamilton Health Sciences http://www.hamiltonhealthsciences.ca/ and INET's more recent wireless technology application findings at Universal Health Services[b] http://www.uhsinc.com/, Queens University Anesthesiology Informatics Laboratory[c] http://www.portablehealth.com/quail/, and University of Toronto Incubator[d] http://www.excelerator.ca/	Commercialized Technology Product Examples (Related To INET Study and Findings)
User-centric (primarily a physician)	Wireless handheld devices must address the major issue of user identification irrespective of the location and mode of access. A wireless technology infrastructure should be equivalent to a wire network infrastructure. To achieve this, handheld devices are ultrathin clients using wireless mobile IP networks to access centralized clinical and diseases management systems. The physician follows the same security policies as wireless, i.e., electronic authentications currently used to digitally sign-off a report	Palm http://Palm.com HP http://h18000.www1.hp.com/products/tabletpc/ http://welcome.hp.com/country/us/eng/prodserv/handheld.html
	Handheld Device • Browser is used on the Handheld Device and restricted to postportal Transcoding server. Please refer to Content-Centric factor • Store No Cache On The Device when user turns off wireless handheld device and automatically clears cache after inactive use within a predetermined timeframe • No Printing allowed from the device	
	Wireless Mobile IP Networks • IP-based networks access to the Internet • Packet Data • Private Network Gateway (ATM Standard) • Wireless IP Data Network Security • Automatic Transition to form cellular to 802.11b networks for moving from outside to inside the hospital	Motorola (iDEN) http://idenphones.motorola.com/iden/what_is_iden.jsp Avaya http://www.avaya.com/ac/common/index.jhtml?location=M1H1005G1015F2063
Content-centric	In a wired equivalent model, both wired and wireless clients should be able to access the same set of contents and carry out the same set of transactions. This is now difficult as the processing capacity of devices used for these transactions differs significantly. The solution to this is to use a pre- and post-Transcoding server. This Transcoding technology works at a tier 1 presentation layer to navigate, aggregate, and adapt to many deferent types of wireless and wired devices without storing patient data outside the centralized systems	

Table 14.5 (continued)

	Postportal Transcoding • Automatic identification of a device type, i.e., PDA, Phone, Tablet and rendering it the specific device • Proxy Server Restricts Browser Access to only one URL (Hospital). No Access to unauthorized URLS (No Splitting) • Browser capability to render a web page to a PDA device based on HTML protocols. A Browser and a Proxy Service achieve this process • The server renders an Internet web page • The browser renderings are Handheld technology applications • No Patient Data can be stored outside the hospital	PumaTech http://www.pumatech.com/tl_browseit.html Voyage Data http://www.voyagedata.com/ Odyssey Software http://www.odysseysoftware.com/apifusion_main.html
	Preportal Transcoding • Create Handheld Technology Application (HTTP, HTML Protocols) by selecting and aggregating single or multiple web or Host applications to fit within the footprint of wireless or wired device displays without storing Patient data records • Hospital Host Connections • Handheld Technology Applications Template Development Tool. This tool uses drag-and-drop and graphical whiteboard methodologies • Server Operations. Handheld Technology Application Template navigates Web Page(s) or Host Application content to publish a new web page for HTA presentation rendering. No Patient Data are stored during these transformations • Portal Management to select Handheld Technology Applications Templates by users or groups for authorized access only	Voyage Data http://www.voyagedata.com/ NetManage http://www.netmanage.com/products/onweb/index.asp Odyssey Software http://www.odysseysoftware.com/apifusion_main.html
	Preportal Transcoding Quality Assurance • A service to release and maintain a Hospital Wireless Health Care Information Portal. Testing web (HTTP, HTML) Pages on a secure web site • Scalability Testing • Integrity testing routinely and automatically scans a portal for potential areas of user dissatisfaction • Handheld technology application functionality testing • Performance Testing	Compuware http://www.compuware.com/products/pointforward/

Table 14.5 (continued)

Access pathways	The wired security is unchanged for tier 1, tier 2, and tier 3 Layers. These infrastructures are inside the firewall. The handheld devices, wireless mobile IP networks, and Transcoding technologies extend the tier 1 presentation layer (portal) to accommodate for decentralized access of centralized systems Tier-1: Portal and directory and security services Tier-2: Application Server and Messaging Services • Application Components to digitize missing process not found in existing Clinical or disease management systems, i.e., Ontario Management Board Secretariat—e-Form initiative • Minimize coding requirements, i.e., no programming • Interfaces with HIS, RIS, LIS, PACS, and Clinical Management System—i.e., HL7 XML Interfaces Tier-3: Back-end data • Fill in electronic health (medical) record gaps with new normalized databases • Create mapping solutions to provide a transition into unique patient identifiers (UPI)—Map one system to the next until a consensus is formed on the UPI	Computer Associates http://www3.ca.com/Solutions/Solution.asp?ID=271 Digital Speed http://www.digitalspeed.net/products/automation/
Policy goals	Conduct risk/threat assessment on incremental component of a wireless infrastructure to set policies—HIPAA Security-Compliant Wireless Extension of a tier 1 Wired IT Infrastructure • Handheld Devices • Wireless Mobile IP Network • Pre- and postportal transcoding server • Preportal Transcoding Quality Assurance Unchanged wired Infrastructure tier 1 Portal, tier 2 Application Server and Messaging Services, and tier 3 Back-End Database security policies and practices	Computer Associates http://www3.ca.com/Solutions/Collateral.asp?CID=33058ID=271

[a]Please refer to the current references listed in this chapter.

[b]http://www3.ca.com/press/PressRelease.asp?CID=36481.

[c]Goldstein, D. H. MD BCH MSC FRCPC, VanDenKerkhof, E. G. RN DRPH, and Rimmer, M. J., New Media: A Model for Real Time Information at the Patient's Side Using Portable Computers on an Acute Pain Service. Can J Anaesth 2002; 49(7):749–754.

[d]http://www.excelerator.ca/pages/exceleratees/index.html and click on "Digital Speed" Logo for details.

References

Blair, J. (2004). Assessing the value of the internet in health improvement. *Nursing Times, 100,* 28–30.

Bluetooth Security Solutions. (o. J.). Resolution to the Technical Security Complexities of the wirelessly connected. San Diego: WIDCOMM Inc. http://www.widcomm.com/bluetooth/pdfs/BluetoothSecurityWP.pdf.

Borisov, N., et al. (2001). Intercepting Mobile Communications: The Insecurity of 802.11. 7th Annual International Conference Mobile Computing and Networking 2001. 16–21 July, 2001, Rome, Italy. http://www.acm.org/sigmobile.

Boyatzis, R. (1998). *Transforming qualitative information thematic analysis and code development.* Thousand Oaks: Sage.

Canadian Healthcare Technology magazine. (2005). *Wireless reporting for diabetes patients offers up dramatic results* (September ed., p. 4). http://www.inet-international.com/INET/Update/PressCoverage2005.htm.

Crossing the Quality Chasm. (2001). *A new health system for the 21st century*. Washington, DC: Committee on Quality of Healthcare in America Institute of Medicine, National Academy Press.

Dutta, A., & McCrohan, K. (2002). Management's role in information security in a cyber economy. *California Management Review, 45*(1), 67–87.

Eisenhardt, K. (1989). Building theories from case study research. *Academy of Management Review, 14,* 532–550.

European Institute of Medicine. (2003). *Health is wealth: Strategic vision for European healthcare at the beginning of the 21st century*. Salzburg: European Academy of Arts and Sciences.

Frost & Sullivan. (2004). Country Industry Forecast—European Union Healthcare Industry, May 11, 2004. http://www.news-medical.net/print_article.asp?id=1405.

Goldberg, S., et al. (2002a). Building the evidence for a standardized mobile internet (wireless) environment in Ontario, Canada. January Update, internal INET documentation.

Goldberg, S., et al. (2002b). HTA Presentational Selection and Aggregation Component Summary. Internal documentation.

Goldberg, S., et al. (2002c). Wireless POC Device Component Summary. Internal INET documentation.

Goldberg, S., et al. (2002d). HTA Presentation Rendering Component Summary. Internal INET documentation.

Goldberg, S., et al. (2002e). HTA Quality Assurance Component Summary. Internal INET documentation.

Goldberg, S., et al. (2002f). Building the Evidence For A Standardized Mobile Internet (wireless) Environment In Ontario, Canada. January 2002 Update. unpublished data.

Goldberg, S., et al. (2002g). HTA Presentation Rendering Component Summary. unpublished data.

Goldberg, S., et al. (2002h). HTA Presentational Selection and Aggregation Component Summary. unpublished data.

Goldberg, S., et al. (2002i). HTA Quality Assurance Component Summary. unpublished data.

Goldberg, S., et al. (2002j). Wireless POC Device Component Summary. unpublished data.

Goldberg, S., & Wickramasinghe, N. (2002). Mobilizing healthcare. Proceedings of the 5th ICECR conference, Montreal.

HIPAA Security requirement Matrix. (2002). http://www.hipaa.org.

Jakobsson, M., & Wetzel, S. (2001). Security Weaknesses in Bluetooth. RSA Conference '01, 8–12 Apr. 2001.

Kavale, S. (1996). *Interviews an introduction to qualitative research interviewing*. Thousand Oaks: Sage.

Kulkarni, R., & Nathanson, L. A. (2005). Medical Informatics in medicine, E-Medicine. http://www.emedicine.com/emerg/topic879.htm.

Kyprianou, M., & Commissioner, E.U. Health and Consumer Protection. (2005). The new European Healthcare Agenda—The European Voice conference "Healthcare: Is Europe getting better?". http://www.noticias.info/asp/aspcommunicados.asp?nid=45584.

Lacroix, A. (1999). International concerted action on collaboration in telemedicine: G8 sub-project 4. *Studies in Health Technology and Informatics, 64,* 12–19.

Lee, M. Y., Albright, S. A., Alkasab, T., Damassa, D. A., Wang, P. J., & Eaton, E. K. (2003). Tufts health sciences database: Lessons, issues, and opportunities. *Academic Medicine, 78,* 254–264.

Moore, T., & Wesson, R. (2002). Issues regarding wireless patient monitoring within and outside the hospital. 2nd Hospital of the Future Conference Proceedings, Chicago, USA.

Muller, T. (1999). Bluetooth Security Architecture Version 1.0. BSIG White Paper, p. 8, 15 July 1999. http://citeseer.nj.nec.com/context/1083381/0.

National Center for Health Statistics. (2002). *Health expenditures*. Hyatsville: CDC, NCHS. http://www.cdc.gov/nchs/fastats/hexpense.htm.

National Coalition on Healthcare. (2004). *Building a better health: Specifications for reform.* Washington, DC: National Coalition on Healthcare.

Organisation for Economic Co-operation and Development (OECD). (2004). OECD Health Data 2004, CD-ROM. http://www.oecd.org/health/healthdata.

Pallarito, K. (1996, March). Virtual Healthcare. *Modern Healthcare,* 42–44.

Plunkett's Health Care Industry Almanac. (2004). 2005 Edition. Houston: Plunkett Research. ISBN 1593920180.

Russo, H. E. (2000). The Internet: Bulding knowledge & offering integrated solutions to health care. *Caring 19,* 18–20, 22–24, 28–31.

Sorby, I., et al. (2002). *Characterising cooperation in the Ward—a framework for producing requirements to mobile electronic healthcare records.* Proceedings of the 2nd Hospital of the Future conference, Chicago.

Standish Group International Inc. (1994). The CHAOS Report. http://www.standishgroup.com/sample_research/chaos_1994_1.php.

Lubitz, D. von, & Wickramasinghe, N. (2005). Healthcare and technology: The doctrine of networkcentric healthcare. (in press Health Affairs).

(o. A.). (2002). Wi-Fi: It's Fast, It's Here—and It Works, Special Report: The Wireless Net. *Business Week.* http://www.businessweek.com/technology/content/apr2002/tc2002041_1823.htm.

Wickramasinghe, N., & Goldberg, S. (2004). How M = EC2 in healthcare. *International Journal of Mobile Communications, 2*(2), 140–156.

Wickramasinghe, N., & Mills, G. (2001). MARS: The electronic medical record system the core of the Kaiser galaxy. *International Journal Healthcare Technology Management, 3*(5/6), 406–423.

Wickramasinghe, N., & Misra, S. (2004). A wireless trust model for healthcare. *International Journal of Electronic Healthcare, 1*(1), 60–77.

Wickramasinghe, N., & Silvers, J. B. (2002). IS/IT The Prescription To Enable Medical Group Practices Attain Their Goals. (forthcoming in Healthcare Management Science).

Wickramasinghe, N., & Silvers, J. B. (2003). IS/IT the prescription to enable medical group practices to manage managed care. *Health Care Management Science, 6*(2), 75–86.

Wickramasinghe, N., et al. (2005). Assessing e-health forthcoming. In T. Spil & R. Schuring (Eds.), *E-health systems diffusion and use: The innovation.* Heresy: The User and the User IT Model, Idea Group Publishing.

Wickramasinghe, N., Troshani, I., & Goldberg, S. (2009). Supporting diabetes self-management with pervasive technology solutions. *International Journal of Healthcare Delivery Reform Initiatives, 1*(4), 17–31.

World Health Organization Report. (2000). *Health systems: Improving performance* (pp. 1–215). Geneva: World Health Organization.

World Health Organization Report. (2004). *Changing history* (pp. 1–167). Geneva: World Health Organization.

Chapter 15
Using Wireless to Monitor Chronic Disease Patients in Urban Poor Regions

Nilmini Wickramasinghe and Steve Goldberg

Abstract The healthcare delivery system in the United States is in crisis. Runaway expenditures and problems with access and affordability of care are plaguing the industry. Several chronic diseases, such as diabetes and hypertension, consume a disproportionate slice of healthcare services. By some estimates, chronic diseases account for over 70–75 % of direct healthcare costs.

Diabetes is one of the five major chronic diseases. It afflicts over 20 million people in the United States and accounts for almost $100 billion in medical costs. The prevalence of diabetes in the United States and worldwide is on the rise.

It has long been established that technology may play a role in contributing to a more efficient delivery of care that may also assist in controlling costs. Of particular interest is the potential use of wireless technology in the monitoring of diabetic patients that would contribute to more efficient management of the disease.

This chapter presents a discussion of an experiential study in which the use of cellular telephones was applied in the monitoring of blood glucose levels by diabetic patients in their homes and the transfer of this information to a central unit in the hospital. The diabetic patients were accustomed to daily measuring their blood glucose and recording the measures in a logbook; hence this technology intervention represented a significant change to their normal care path and pattern. They would bring the logbook to their regular visits to the hospital and also when any emergency occurred. This system of record keeping was flawed, as patients would neglect to record all entries, record wrong readings, and commit similar errors.

As the chapter discusses, with the application of wireless technology, the patient enters the blood glucose reading into his cell phone and the information is transmitted to the hospital. The medical staff then follows up and monitors the patient's progress.

Much of the data used in this chapter came from a larger scale project funded by an IBM grant awarded to N. Wickramasinghe and E. Geisler from the IBM Center for the Business of Government.

N. Wickramasinghe (✉)
Epworth Chair Health Information Management, School of Business Information Technology and Logistics, RMIT University, Melbourne VIC 3001, Australia,
e-mail: nilmini.wickramasinghe@rmit.edu.au

S. Goldberg
131 Glen Crescent, L4J 4W4, Ontario, Canada
e-mail: sgoldberg@inet-international.com

R. K. Bali et al. (eds.), *Pervasive Health Knowledge Management*, Healthcare Delivery in the Information Age,
DOI 10.1007/978-1-4614-4514-2_15,

This improved monitoring process engenders positive outcomes such as savings in time and cost and better management of the disease.

Keywords Diabetes · Chronic diseases · Type 1 diabetes · Type 2 diabetes · Gestational diabetes

15.1 Healthcare Delivery in Crisis

The US healthcare delivery industry is in crisis. Spending over 16 % of the Gross National Product (GNP), the US healthcare system is nearly three times as costly as almost any other health system in the world. It would therefore be logical to expect that such an expensive system would be delivering consistently high quality of care to the country's population. However, the reality is painfully different. Expenditures are increasing on a yearly basis, as are medical errors and the numbers of the underinsured, uninsured, and underserved in the American population (Institute of Medicine 2001).

Table 15.1 shows some statistic of the runaway costs of health care. Whereas the population has grown by 29 % in the period 1980–2005, the cost of health care in that period increased by almost sevenfold. Since 2000, health costs have risen by over 9 % per year, three times the rate of inflation in that period (CMS 2007).

A broad coalition of scholars, politicians, healthcare providers, insurers, and regulators, as well as patients and many citizen groups have recognized this crisis. There is a consensus in the country that reducing the level of expenditures and offering quality health care to as many people as possible is a high priority. As a possible solution, technology and automation in health care have the potential to help reduce costs and to improve the quality of care with a patient-centric focus.

Recognizing this, the US government has affirmed the intention of the current administration to emphasize the role of technology in the administration and delivery of health services (Bush 2004). The focus on technology in health care will undoubtedly continue to occupy a key role in future administrations, since the crisis in health care continues unabated.

Table 15.1 US National health expenditures. (Source: CMS at http://www.cms.hhs.gov/nationalhealthexpenddata/)

	2005	2000	1990	1980
Total in millions	$1,987,689	$1,353,256	$714,019	$253,916
Percent of gross domestic product (GDP)	16 %	13.8 %	12.3 %	9.1 %
US population (in millions)	29.68	282.5	253.8	230.4
Increase in expenditures:			% of GDP	
1980–2005 = 680 %			75.8 %	
2000–2005 = 47 %			15.9 %	
Population growth:				
1980–2005 = 29 %				
2000–2005 = 5.3 %				

The crisis in healthcare delivery in the United States is also manifested in its shortcomings in providing accessible and affordable care to disadvantaged populations. When medical care is delivered, it is often inadequate to meet the complex health, social, economic, educational, and environmental needs of the disadvantaged and underserved, particularly inner-city urban residents. This creates a situation in which state and federal governments are facing a growing challenge: inner-city individuals suffering from various chronic diseases are uninsured or underinsured and have no choice but to rush to emergency rooms of local hospitals when their illness has escalated into more complicated and costly medical conditions (Geisler et al. 2003; Rachlis 2006).

15.2 The Purpose of This Study

Recognizing the crisis in health care and the role that technology may play in providing some attractive solutions, the study focuses on the possibilities of applying wireless technology to facilitate the monitoring of patients with the chronic disease of diabetes within an inner-city population. Details are reported on the complex effort of bringing together three crucial components: (1) technology application, (2) urban population of underserved individuals, and (3) patients with diabetes.

The following then provides a discussion of an exploratory study that demonstrated the feasibility of a technological solution (namely, a wireless application) that provided noted improvements in the monitoring of patients with diabetes. The chapter describes the tremendous impacts of chronic diseases in general and diabetes in particular on the crisis in the healthcare system. Lessons learned from this study are described and recommendations are offered to local, state, and federal governments that are struggling with the runaway costs and challenges of the delivery of health care to the population (Geisler and Wickramasinghe 2009; Geisler and Heller 1998; Wickramasinghe and Goldberg 2004).

15.3 Chronic Diseases and the Case of Diabetes

The crisis in health care is even more ominous when we consider the impacts of chronic diseases (CDC&P 2006). Chronic diseases are incurable diseases, said to be the greatest threat to the nation's health and to its health delivery system. There are five major chronic diseases: *cardiovascular diseases* (hypertension, heart disease, congestive heart disease), *strokes*, *asthma*, *cancer*, and *diabetes* (some add a sixth chronic disease, *arthritis*). These chronic diseases account for 83 % of healthcare expenditures in the general population (CDC&P 2006). The numbers vary, but all are in the 70–85 % range. Thrall (2005), for example, estimates chronic diseases to account for over 75 % of direct healthcare cost. These diseases also account for 70 % of morbidity and mortality in the population due to medical reasons (Zuvekas and Cohen 2007). Table 15.2 shows the prevalence and costs of these diseases.

Table 15.2 Prevalence and medical costs of chronic diseases. (Source: CDC&P 2006)

Prevalence in the United States
Cardiovascular disease: 65 million
Diabetes: 20.8 million
Cancer: 10–15 million
Stroke: 5.5 million
Asthma: 30.8 million
(Arthritis: 60 million)
Medical Costs
Cardiovascular disease: 256 billions (including stroke)
Diabetes: 92 billion
Cancer: 72 billion
Asthma: 130 billion

Note: The medical costs for these diseases account for 35 % of total healthcare expenditures. Indirect costs account for at least 30–35 % additional expenses.

Thrall (2005) commented that in addition to the direct costs of chronic diseases, the indirect costs in lost productivity and nonreimbursed costs to patients and their families are in the order of hundreds of billions of dollars. Also, since chronic diseases are more prevalent with age, this phenomenon is bound to be much more severe as the US population, especially the "baby boomers," continue to age.

These numbers are a genuine cause for alarm and a continuing challenge to governments at all levels. These government institutions pay for at least half of all healthcare expenditures. As the prevalence and impacts of chronic diseases continue to rise, any attempt to better manage these diseases—however, minor in its contributions—should be considered by health policy makers as an attempt to cope with such a runaway crisis (Hrejsa et al. 2006; Wickramasinghe et al. 2005).

15.4 The Case of Diabetes

In this chapter, the focus is on the chronic disease of diabetes. The statistics are indeed alarming. Diabetes is a group of diseases characterized by high levels of blood glucose, resulting from defects in the production of insulin. There are three generally accepted major types of diabetes. *Type* 1 diabetes, also called juvenile-onset diabetes, develops usually in children and young adults when the body's own immune system destroys the pancreatic cells that produce the hormone insulin.

Type 2 diabetes, also known as adult-onset diabetes, generally starts as insulin resistance and, as the need for insulin increases in the body, the pancreas tends to lose its capability to produce the hormone. Type 2 diabetes accounts for over 90 % of all diagnosed cases and is generally associated with old age, family history, obesity, physical inactivity, and race or ethnicity. High-risk populations in the United States are African Americans, Hispanic Americans, and Native Americans—all with high representation in the disadvantaged and underserved segments of the US population (Barcelo 2001).

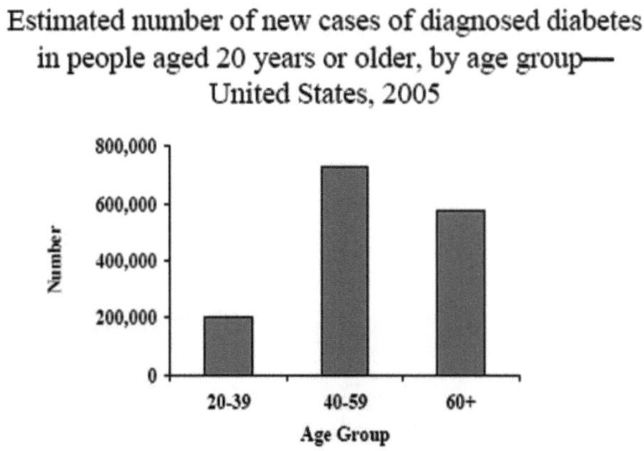

Fig. 15.1 Estimated number of new cases of diagnosed diabetes in people aged 20 years or older, by age group—United States, 2005. (Source: 2001–2003 National Health Interview Survey estimates projected to year 2005)

Gestational diabetes afflicts women during pregnancy and is characterized by glucose intolerance. Following pregnancy, almost 10 % of women with gestational diabetes are diagnosed with type 2 of the disease, whereas women who have suffered from gestational diabetes are prone to developing the disease. About 20–50 % of these women develop type 2 diabetes in the 5–10 years after pregnancy, and almost 70 % of women previously diagnosed with gestational diabetes will develop type 2 diabetes during their lifetime (National Institute of Diabetes and Digestive and Kidney Diseases 2005).

The projections for a worldwide rise in the numbers of people with diabetes are alarming. It is estimated that by 2010 there will be 220 million people with the disease, and by 2025 the number increases to 280 million (compared with 110 million in 2000: Zimmet 2000).

Figure 15.1 shows the estimated number of new cases of diagnosed diabetes in adult patients. For people in the age range of 20 years or older, almost one in ten have diabetes whereas people in the age range of 60 years or older, one in five have the disease. Figure 15.2 shows the projected increases globally for diabetes.

The distribution of people diagnosed with diabetes by race or ethnicity are even more revealing. In the African-American group, 13.5 % of those over 20 years of age have diabetes. Almost 10 % of Hispanic Americans over the age of 20 have diabetes, and almost 13 % of Native Americans (American Diabetes Association 2004).

15.5 Social–Economic Factors in Managing Diabetes

Diabetes is clearly identified as a chronic disease on the rise, consuming a growing portion of healthcare expenditures and afflicting more intensely the segments in the US population of African Americans, Hispanic Americans, and Native Americans. Moreover, diabetes is also prevalent in these segments in the urban, inner-city population who tend to be on the lower portion of the socioeconomic scale. Research into the management of diabetes has shown that poor and less literate patients are

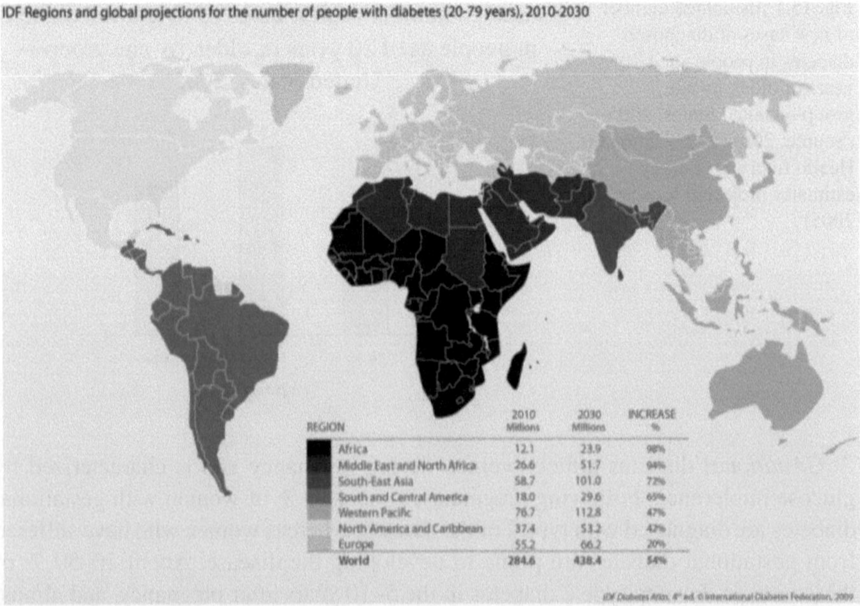

Fig. 15.2 Increase in diabetes throughout the world. (Source IDF http://www.idf.org)

underserved with respect to diabetic care. McCall et al. (2004) have found that low-income, elderly patients received less diabetic care than other segments in the patient population. They also found that minority patients and the use of emergency departments in hospitals received less diabetic care.

Similarly, Schillinger et al. (2002) concluded that inadequate health literacy (ability to read, comprehend, and act upon medical instructions) that is prevalent in ethnic and older minorities is "associated with worse glycemic control and higher rates of retinopathy." They also concluded that low health literacy "may contribute to the disproportionate burden of diabetes-related problems among disadvantaged populations."

A disturbing finding by Suwattee et al. (2003) showed that diabetes management in a large public urban hospital was lacking throughout the institution, including the diabetes clinic. This and other similar studies paint a worrisome picture of large segments of the population who are disadvantaged, who have diabetes, and who lack adequate care for their disease (Smith and Maynard 2004).

15.6 Defining the Problem

In the current healthcare environment in the world and particularly in the United States, there is a crisis of several chronic diseases that consume a disproportionate slice of healthcare expenditures and are constantly on the rise. Diabetes is one of the chronic diseases, afflicting over 20 million Americans, with urban disadvantaged populations bearing the brunt of the disease.

The central research questions then include: What is the role that technology can play in contributing to a potential solution to this problem? How can technology help us to better manage diabetes among the urban disadvantaged people diagnosed with diabetes? We are certainly not aiming to offer a radical solution to the problem—but rather a small, yet measurable contribution that would help to improve the management of the disease in the urban setting.

15.7 How Can Wireless Help?

Chronic diseases such as diabetes, if detected early, can be contained and patients can continue to lead full and high-quality lives. If the disease is not well managed, patients may develop more complicated health problems (Wickramasinghe and Mills 2001). Critical to effective management of a chronic disease is regular monitoring and an informed patient who takes responsibility for managing his wellness.

Regular monitoring of diabetes is a necessary part to controlling the disease and keeping it from becoming life threatening. To effectively and efficiently monitor diabetic patients, there is a role for wireless technologies. They can provide the means to enable affordable superior monitoring anywhere and anytime, thereby allowing the patient to enjoy a quality lifestyle (Rachlis 2006).

15.8 Use of Wireless Technology in Health Care

Medical science has made revolutionary changes in the past few decades. However, healthcare delivery organizations have made, at best, incremental changes. The growing discrepancy between the revolution in medicine and the minimal changes in healthcare processes is leading to inefficient delivery and is one, if not the significant, contributor to the exponentially increasing costs. Thus, the application of mobile technologies to health care ("m-health") appears to have the potential to affect substantial changes in the efficiency of healthcare delivery.

The use of m-health solutions includes the application of wireless technology by providing hospitals with ways to achieve efficient monitoring and control of patients within a standardized mobile Internet (wireless) environment. Integral to this successful application is the ability of the hospital to build on its existing infrastructure. In Fig. 15.3, we show a standardized wireless environment. This model is the framework used by the Canadian company INET, which played a key role in the study (Goldberg et al. 2002).

Wireless technology has the ability to connect healthcare providers (physicians and nurses) with each other, with hospital administrators, and with patients. The technology is part of the much-publicized electronic health environment (e-health),

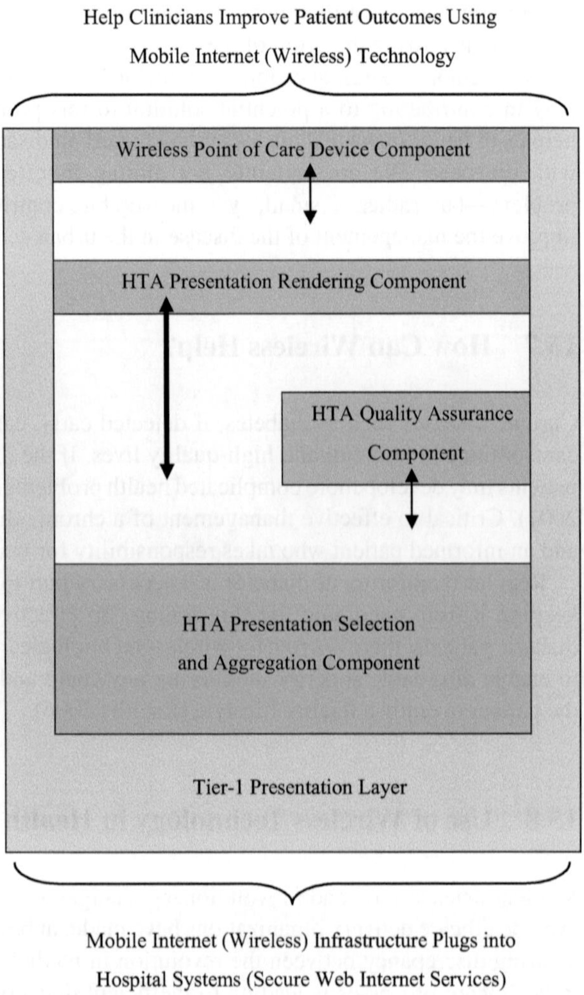

Fig. 15.3 A standardized mobile internet (wireless) application. (Adapted from Wickramasinghe and Goldberg 2004)

also known as telemedicine and telehealth (Fraunholz and Unnithan 2007). The application of communication via handheld devices, cellular technology, and the Internet endows healthcare providers with outstanding capabilities to monitor and to interface across distances, all with clarity and at a very affordable cost (Dougherty et al. 1999; Moore and Wesson 2002).

In monitoring diabetic patients, wireless technology provides the benefits of telemedicine by which patients can be monitored and observed, and their medical condition managed anytime and anyplace. This means that patients can be monitored from the hospital whether they are at home, at work, or anywhere else outside the hospital.

15.9 The INET Solution

INET is a technology company from Ontario, Canada. The company has developed a workable system, which connects handheld devices to a stationary center, and which allows for the transfer of medical data. This system provides the medical provider with the capability to interface with patients by their use of a cellular telephone.

The technology proved to be very useful in the distance monitoring of diabetes. There are many communication and information exchange bottlenecks between patients and their physicians that prevent the effective treatment of the disease. The fundamental problem seems to be the ability to have a private and secure way to manage, search, and retrieve information at the point-of-care. In the case of diabetes, providers cannot quickly and easily respond to patients with high glucose levels when these patients are out of the hospital and out of reach of traditional methods of contact between them and their care providers (Montori et al. 2004). The care providers need to wait for patients to come to their office or hospital, respond to phone calls, reply using mail delivery, or never receive the information.

The INET solution is anchored in the use of a specially equipped cell phone and the installation of a secure wireless application that allows patients to monitor glucose levels and to immediately transfer the data to their care provider. The physician or nurse uses a handheld device such as a Personal Digital Assistant (PDA), which is connected to a wireless network to confidentially access, evaluate, and act on the patient's data.

The INET solution calls for the patient (or family member) to enter the reading from the glucose monitor into the special cell phone. This requires the ability to read the data from the monitor and to input the numbers into the cell phone. In the past, INET considered the possibility of the direct reading of the glucose monitor into the special cell phone by utilizing Bluetooth technology. However, the company soon discovered that this significantly limited the pervasiveness of the technology.

For example, there are very few glucose monitors with embedded Bluetooth technology and the Java implementation software on the cell phone varies widely among manufacturers. Thus, the likelihood of having a patient with a cell phone that has the right Java implementation with Bluetooth technology and a glucose monitor with Bluetooth capability is very unlikely. A study was conducted in Canada by a medical research organization to test this possibility of direct transfer from the glucose monitor to the special cell phone. The results show that this approach is very expensive and has limited success. The technology cost was about $2,000 per patient. In addition, there was a need to conduct individual training sessions with a high level of ongoing support. In another study of monitoring hypertension, the Bluetooth approach was also considered infeasible and expensive, in favor of the INET-type approach. The important issue to remember is that the INET approach is based on using cell phone technology that the patient is already using and is quite familiar with its features. The only change is adding a bookmark to the cell phone at no additional cost (except for the small fee per month for data transmission of about $5 per cell phone). There is also no need for additional training. The patient uses a simple to follow

Table 15.3 Wireless diabetes management protocol

Patient's phone loaded with program and ID#
Enter blood sugar readings
Data sent back electronically and wirelessly to physician/nurse
Data consist of only ID#, blood sugar reading, date and time of reading
No other identifying data: privacy protected
Physician/nurse monitor data on PDA
Action plan sent back to patient
Data entered in patient's hospital record

step-by-step instruction sheet. After installation, the patients typically need no, or very little, ongoing technical support. The INET experience in Canada with pilot projects of 45 patients has shown that there were only four calls for support in the entire set of projects, which necessitated only about 5 minutes each to complete to the satisfaction of the patient.

In the population we are targeting in our study in the urban setting of Chicago, the underserved patients are literate in terms of reading their blood levels and inserting them into the cell phone. Previous pilot studies have shown that there are very few mistakes in entering the readings into the phones and that there is a good likelihood that the medical staff at the hospital will spot these errors and act on them.

A technology similar to that of INET in the monitoring of diabetes is used in the Netherlands to monitor newborn babies. Ronald Spanjers and Anne Rutkowski of Tilburg University have reported the pilot practices of such telehealth/telecare in the Netherlands. Cameras monitor newborn babies at the hospital and send the pictures to the parents' cell phone. This Baby Mobile technology is the transmission of what is called Virtual Baby Visit. Parents can monitor and see their newborn babies anytime and anywhere by wireless and with the use of their cell phones.

15.10 INET's Pilot Study

INET conducted a pilot study in Canada to prove the applicability of its wireless system with a sample of 25 patients with diabetes who received treatment in a local hospital. The hospital had 365 beds and its diabetes care center receives about 2,700 new referrals per year, including adults and children.

This pilot study was conducted in 2006 with a grant from Bayer Diabetes Care Division. Table 15.3 outlines the key steps in the protocol used in the study. These steps allow for a seamless communication flow between patient and provider. There are several advantages to this system:

1. Easy to use.
2. Motivates patients to take responsibility for their care.
3. Inexpensive, with significant cost savings.
4. Improved provider–patient therapeutic relationships.
5. Efficient use of provider's time.

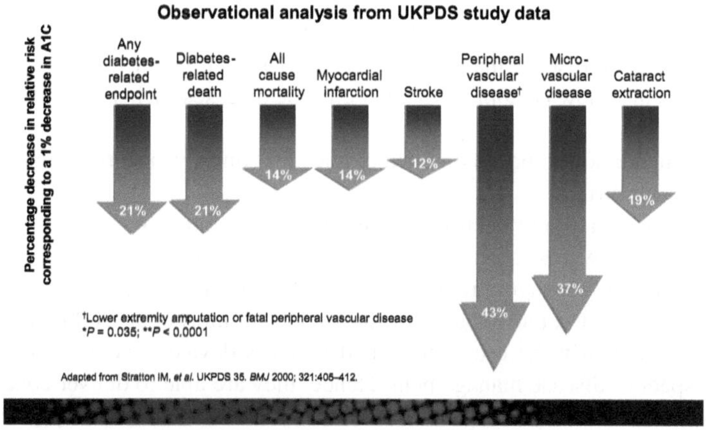

Fig. 15.4 UKPDS: decreased risk of diabetes-related complications associated with a 1 % decrease in A1C. (Adapted from Chalasani et al. 2011)

But, perhaps the most salient benefit from the INET system is the decreased risk of diabetes-related complications that are associated with lower levels of glycosylated hemoglobin (A1C) in the blood of diabetic patients. Figure 15.4 shows the various complications, as observed in the United Kingdom Prospective Diabetes Study (UKPDS).

The UKPDS was a 20-year study of over 5,000 patients with type 2 diabetes in 23 clinical centers in the United Kingdom (Stratton et al. 2000). This major study concluded that better blood glucose control reduces risks of: (1) major diabetic eye disease by 25 % and (2) early kidney damage by 30 %.

This comprehensive study has made it abundantly clear that better monitoring of blood levels in diabetic patients reduces the severe complications that arise from the disease. This means that any improvement in monitoring and control of blood glucose levels will pay off in fewer complications, better care, and ultimately in substantial reduction in the cost of health care (Wendling 2006). It is therefore also safe to conclude that even small improvements in monitoring diabetic patients may result in saving lives, limbs, and improving the quality of life of patients.

The pilot study conducted by INET was a success. Patients were very satisfied with the program. They found the wireless method to be far superior to the logbook method of keeping records of their daily blood sugar. The results of the pilot study are good news and indeed provide directional data that support the role for pervasive technologies in aiding the superior management and care for diabetic patients.

15.11 Using Wireless to Monitor Chronic Patients: Recommendations

From the lessons learned from this pilot project, it is possible to provide the following recommendations for hospitals and caregivers as well as for government leaders and decision-making in the areas of healthcare policy. These recommendations are relevant for all chronic diseases where monitoring the condition of the patient is essential for good disease management. What has been learnt from our project on diabetes can also now be applied to other chronic diseases such as hypertension and asthma.

Recommendation 1: Focus on technologies that improve information collection, transfer, and control.

Healthcare policy and decision makers should seriously consider technologies that are geared towards information collection, communication, transfer, and control. In the battle to manage chronic disease and keep costs under control, information technologies offer the most "bang for the buck" (Montori et al. 2006). These technologies, particularly the use of handheld wireless devices, focus on a single yet crucial aspect of disease management. Hence, they are able to deliver concentrated benefits. With relatively inexpensive investments, hospitals, aided by government agencies, can implement these technologies and not only gain benefits from them, but also in this manner contribute to alleviating the national crisis in health care.

Recommendation 2: Focus on disadvantaged populations because even small improvements in managing their chronic diseases will produce higher levels of positive outcomes.

Government health policy makers can make a contribution to holding back healthcare expenditures by focusing on disadvantaged populations for applications of technologies, such as wireless monitoring of diabetes. Since these patients have not been the targets of medical advances, even small improvements in monitoring their chronic diseases will potentially produce extraordinary benefits.

Recommendation 3: Develop plan for implementation of technological solutions.

Hospital administrators and government policy makers should develop plans for the implementation of technological solutions to chronic disease management. The concise plans should take into account the complexity of hospitals and the healthcare delivery system. Simply instructing hospitals to adopt these technologies will result in resistance to the change and internal dissatisfaction in the hospital. The various constituencies in the hospital environment should be on board and support the application for it to have a chance of success.

Recommendation 4: Develop a system for justification of the application.

Any planned implementation of a new technology system requires ample justification of costs and benefits. In the case of application of wireless technology to chronic diseases management, there is also a need to offer justification to why we need the technology, the costs associated with its implementation, and the potential benefits and value to be derived from the technology. Government and hospital constituents who support the application need to develop a system that will justify its implementation to other stakeholders in the healthcare industry.

Recommendation 5: Install monitoring software as original equipment in all cellular telephones.

This is a far-reaching recommendation that has the flavor of a long-term "dream." We recommend that all cellular telephones be equipped—during their manufacture—with the software necessary to conduct wireless monitoring of chronic diseases. This will be another "feature" of the telephones, with healthcare implications. With current technological achievements of miniaturization, the installation of such software is a relatively simple production procedure. In addition, adding a very small amount to the price of the device will pay the cost of installing this proprietary program. The marketing effort would be similar to the sponsoring of environmentally safe ("green") devices. Customers who purchase cellular telephones would welcome the extra cost, knowing that the device can easily and seamlessly be used by a patient with a chronic disease to monitor his condition (Japsen 2007; Parker 2006).

15.12 Conclusion

Pervasive wireless technology provides an inexpensive form of system to monitor patients with diabetes. It allows them to take daily measurements of their glucose levels and electronically transmit them to their hospital. This simple procedure engenders several benefits, both economic and clinical outcomes. The pilot project described in this chapter is an empirical testing of such technology. We are confident in its far-reaching benefits and recommend that all handheld wireless devices be henceforth equipped with software that allows for monitoring of patients with diabetes and other debilitating chronic diseases—all of which are one of the key factors responsible for the runaway costs and the crisis in our system of healthcare delivery. In particular, we believe that this pervasive wireless solution can help to address healthcare delivery disparity in the Urban poor regions and close by calling for further research in this important area.

Acknowledgment Some of the literature cited in this chapter was gathered as part of a larger funded project by The IBM Center for the Business of Government, awarded in part to one of the coauthors of this chapter.

References

American Diabetes Association. (2004). *Medical management of Type-2 diabetes* (5th ed.). Alexandria: ADA.

Barcelo, A. (June, 2001). Diabetes in the Americas. *Epidemiological Bulletin, 22*(2), 15–23.

Bush, G. W. (2004). State of the union address. http://whitehouse.gov/news/release/2004/01/20040120-7.html. Accessed Dec 2009.

Centers for Disease Control and Prevention (CDC&P). (2006). *Estimating the cost of chronic diseases*. Washington, DC. (In cooperation with the National Center for Chronic Disease Prevention and Health Promotion, and the Agency for Healthcare Research and Quality).

Centers for Medicare & Medicaid Services (CMS). (2007). National health expenditing data. http://www.cms.hhs.gov/nationalhealthexpendata/.diabetes.niddk.nih.gov/. . . /statistics/index.htm.

Chalasani, S., Wickramasinghe, N., et al. (2011). *Business and IT aspects of wireless enabled healthcare solutions*. Proceedings of the 17th Americas Conference on Information Systems Detroit, 4–7 Aug 2011.

Dougherty, G., et al. (1999). Home-based management can achieve intensification cost-effectively in type I diabetes. *Pediatrics, 103*(1), 122–128.

Fraunholz, B., & Unnithan, C. (2007). Potential of telemedicine: A preliminary evaluation through the innovation diffusion lens. *International Journal of Healthcare Technology & Management, 8*(3/4), 315–332.

Geisler, E., & Heller, O. (1998). *Management of medical technology: Theory, practice, and cases.* Boston: Kluwer.

Geisler, E., & Wickramasinghe, N. (2009). *The role and use of wireless technology in the management and monitoring of chronic diseases*. Report prepared for the IBM Center for the Business of Government.

Geisler, E., Krabbendam, K., & Schuring, R. (2003). *Technology, healthcare and management in the hospital of the future*. Westport: Praeger.

Goldberg, S., et al. (2002). Wireless POC Device Component Summary. Internal INET documentation.

Hrejsa, R., Sauve, S., Stella, P., & Geisler, E. (2006). Vaccine crisis: Some issues in technology and national healthcare policy. *International Journal of Healthcare Technology & Management, 7*(6), 453–462.

Institute of Medicine. (2001). *Crossing the quality chasm: A new health system for the 21st century.* Washington: National Academy Press, Committee on Quality of Health Care in America.

Japsen, B. (2007, April 8). Firms gang up on diabetes. *Chicago Tribune*.

McCall, D., et al. (2004). Are low-income elderly patients at risk for poor diabetes care? *Diabetes Care, 27*(3), 1060–1065.

Montori, V., et al. (2004). Telecare for patients with type I diabetes and inadequate glycemic control: A randomized controlled trial and meta-analysis. *Diabetes Care, 27*(4), 1088–1094.

Montori, V., Gafni, A., & Charles, C. (2006). A shared treatment decision-making approach between patients with chronic conditions and their clinicians: The case of diabetes. *Health Expectations, 9*(1), 25–36.

Moore, T., & Wesson, R. (2002). *Issues regarding wireless patient monitoring within and outside the hospital.* Paper presented at the Proceedings of the 2nd Hospital of the Future Conference, Chicago, IL.

National Institute of Diabetes and Digestive and Kidney Diseases. (2005). *National diabetes statistics fact sheet: General information and national estimates on diabetes in the United States.* Bethesda: U.S. Department of Health and Human Services, National Institute of Health.

Parker, P. (2006). *The 2007–2012 outlook for diabetes monitoring devices in the United States*. San Diego: Icon Group International.

Rachlis, M. (2006). Key to sustainable healthcare system. http://www.improvingchroniccare.org. Accessed Jan 2011.

Schillinger, D., et al. (2002). Association of health literacy with diabetes outcome. *Journal of the American Medical Association, 288*(4), 475–482.

Smith, N., & Maynard, C. (2004). The burden of diabetes-associated cardiovascular hospitalizaitons in VA and non-VA medical facilities. *Diabetes Care, 27*(3), B27–B32.

Stratton, I., et al. (2000). UKPDS 35. *British Medical Journal, 321,* 405–412.

Suwattee, P., Lynch, C., & Pendergrass, M. (2003). Quality of care for diabetes patients in a large urban public hospital. *Diabetes Care, 26*(3), 563–568.

Thrall, J. (2005). Prevalence and cost of chronic diseases in a healthcare system structured for treatment of acute illnesses. *Radiology, 235*(1), 9–12.

Wendling, P. (2006). Home blood pressure monitoring redirects diabetes patients. *Family Practice News, 36*(23), 21–23.

Wickramasinghe, N., Geisler, E., et al. (2005). A framework for assessing e-health preparedness. *International Journal of Electronic Healthcare, 1*(3), 316–334.

Wickramasinghe, N., & Goldberg, S. (2004). How M= EC2 in Healthcare. *International J. Mobile Communications, 2*(2), 140–156.

Wickramasinghe, N., & Mills, G. (2001). MARS: The electronic medical record system: The core of the Kaiser galaxy. *International Journal of Healthcare Technology and Management, 3*(5/6), 406–423.

Zimmet, P. (2000). 21st century review: Globalization, coca-colonization, and the chronic disease epidemic: Can the doomsday scenario be averted? *Journal of Internal Medicine, 247*(3), 301–310.

Zuvekas, S., & Cohen, J. (2007). Prescription drugs and the changing concentration of healthcare expenditures. *Health Affairs, 26*(1), 249–257.

Chapter 16
An Examination of the Business and IT Aspects of Wireless-Enabled Healthcare Solutions

Suresh Chalasani, Steve Goldberg and Nilmini Wickramasinghe

Abstract Healthcare is an industry that touches us all. Currently, healthcare systems in all OEDC countries are being confronted with escalating costs and major concerns pertaining to access, quality, and value of service. Such a situation appears to be untenable and most governments are turning to information communication technologies (ICT) as a possible panacea. Globally then, both wired and wireless technologies are now being used for healthcare delivery. However, in the frenzy to secure the best solutions and applications, few have delved deeper into the key issues of how to successfully assimilate these new technologies into the whole healthcare delivery process as well as the ramifications and implications to other systems already in place. In this chapter, we consider wireless healthcare solutions to monitor chronic diseases and suggest that a key barrier for preventing the full realization of the true potential of wireless solutions lies in the enabling of information and necessary data to pass seamlessly form one platform to another. We suggest ways to integrate data from wireless healthcare solutions with the existing electronic health records (EHR) systems, and discuss the impact of wireless-enabled solutions on the meaningful use of EHRs.

Keywords Pervasive technology · m-health · Diabetes · Knowledge management · e-health · Electronic health records

---

An earlier version of this chapter was first presented at the 17th Americas Conference on Information Systems, Detroit Michigan Aug 4th-7th 2011.

S. Chalasani (✉)
Department of Business, UW-Parkside, 900 Wood Road,
53141-2000 Kenosha, Wisconsin, USA
e-mail: chalasan@uwp.edu

S. Goldberg
131 Glen Crescent, L4J 4W4, Ontario, Canada
e-mail: sgoldberg@inet-international.com

N. Wickramasinghe
Epworth Chair Health Information Management,
School of Business Information Technology and Logistics,
RMIT University, Melbourne VIC 3001, Australia

R. K. Bali et al. (eds.), *Pervasive Health Knowledge Management,*
Healthcare Delivery in the Information Age,
DOI 10.1007/978-1-4614-4514-2_16,

16.1 Introduction

Globally, healthcare expenditure as a percentage of Gross Domestic Product (GDP) by 29 members of the Organization for Economic Cooperation and Development (OECD) rose from 5.0 % to 8.1 % between 1970 and 1997 (Huber 1999). Moreover, since 2000, total spending on healthcare in these countries has been rising even faster than economic growth (OECD 2010a, b). To address this significant problem and thereby provide value-driven superior healthcare, most, if not all, countries within the OECD are investigating possibilities for a variety of e-health implementations. Such e-health solutions include various wired and wireless solutions including electronic medical records, e-prescription systems, PACS and other lab/radiology systems as well as various billing and practice management type systems. Given this influx of technology into healthcare delivery, the most recent Obama healthcare reform identifies that a key consideration of the use of technology in healthcare delivery should be concerned with meaningful use. It is the contention of this chapter that meaningful use of the technology as well as its full potential can only be realized when the specific solution is assimilated and integrated into the context so that data and information can pass seamlessly from one platform to another. Thus, this chapter describes a specific case study of diabetes monitoring device (DiaMonD) and then discusses how it is easier for clinics and hospitals to achieve meaningful use with wireless technologies. This chapter concludes with business models for revenue generation using wireless monitoring solutions.

16.2 Chronic Disease Management

Many have noted that the United States has an unparalleled capacity to treat, especially in the context of trauma and infectious diseases (Gibbons et al. 2010; Porter and Tiesberg 2006). However, and sadly, the US healthcare system too often fails to provide appropriate and adequate healthcare delivery for patients with chronic diseases such as diabetes and hypertension. Chronic diseases such as diabetes, asthma, or hypertension if detected early can be contained and the sufferers from these diseases can continue to lead high-quality lives. Conversely, if these diseases are not well managed, they can develop into more complicated healthcare problems and life for such patients becomes less than satisfactory. Critical to effective chronic disease management is regular monitoring and an informed patient who takes responsibility for managing his/her wellness. As identified by Rachlis (2006), a chronic care model requires the interaction and coordination of numerous areas. In particular, it requires the interaction of four key components of the healthcare system including self-management support, delivery support, decision support, and clinical information systems and support from the community at large. These support mechanisms provide a conducive environment for productive interactions between an informed and activated patient and a prepared and proactive healthcare team.

Diabetes, one important chronic disease, is increasing in its prevalence throughout not only North America but also the world. The world diabetes population is expected to increase by 76 % from 159 million in 2000 to 236 million in 2025, and thus diabetes has been called a silent epidemic by the World Health Organization. The cost of treatment of an increasing number of diabetics is indeed alarming to any healthcare system.

Regular monitoring of diabetes is a necessary part to controlling this particular chronic disease and keeping it from evolving into more complicated healthcare problems. To do this efficiently and effectively, we believe information communication technologies (ICT) can play a critical role by providing a means to enable superior monitoring anywhere anytime and thereby also allowing the patient to enjoy a high-quality lifestyle. However, technology initiatives in healthcare to date have had mixed results at best (Wickramasinghe and Goldberg 2007, 2009). We believe this is connected with the failure of current information systems (IS) methodologies to correctly capture the richness and complexities of a modern healthcare environment. To address this issue and in so doing provide an environment enabled by ICT that facilitates superior chronic disease management, we describe the idea behind wireless monitoring of diabetes.

16.3 DiaMonD: A Pervasive Wireless Solution

DiaMonD—diabetes monitoring device—is a pervasive technology solution to provide superior healthcare for sufferers of diabetes. The solution incorporates software that facilitates the ubiquitous monitoring of an individual's diabetes, thereby, contributing to diabetes self-management. The solution is grounded in trying to support key components of a chronic disease care model (Table 16.1). INET International Inc.'s research (Goldberg 2002a–e) starts with a 30-day e-business acceleration project in collaboration with many key players in hospitals, such as clinicians, medical units, administration, and IT departments. Together, they follow a rigorous procedure that refocuses the traditional 1–5-year SDLC into concurrent 30-day projects to accelerate healthcare delivery improvements. At completion, an e-business acceleration project delivers a scope document to develop a handheld technology application (HTA) proof-of-concept specific to the unique needs of a particular environment. The proof-of-concept is a virtual lab case scenario, which operates within a mobile Internet (wireless) environment by working with hospitals and technology vendors. The final step is the collection of additional data with clinical HTA trials consisting of 2-week hospital evaluations.

The INET web-based model provides the necessary components to enable the delivery framework to be positioned in the best possible manner so it can indeed facilitate enacting the key components of the chronic disease model successfully (Table 16.1). The model is positioned to suit the complex nature of healthcare environments by iteratively, systematically, and rigorously incorporating lessons learnt data to healthcare processes for ensuring superior healthcare delivery. This manner not only maximizes the value of past data and organizational learning, but it also makes processes amendable as complex needs and requirements evolve.

Table 16.1 Components of chronic care model. (Rachlis 2006)

Component	Description
Organization of health system	Leadership in chronic disease management (CDM) Goals for CDM Improvement strategy for CDM Incentives and regulations for CDM Benefits
Self-management support (SMS)	Assessment and documentation of needs and activities Addressing concerns of patients Effective behavior change interventions
Decision support system (DSS)	Evidence-based guidelines Involvement of specialists in improving primary care Providing education for CDM Informing patients about guidelines
Delivery system design (DSD)	Practice team functioning Practice team leadership Appointment system Follow-up Planned visits for CDM Continuity of care
Clinical information systems (CIS)	Registry Reminders to providers Feedback Information about relevant subgroups of patients needing services Patient treatment plans
Community	Linkages for patients to resources Partnerships with community organizations Policy and plan development

It is important to note that in the INET web-based model the three key areas of risk, namely, people, processes, and technology, are minimized through the use of pervasive technology, which we believe is a unique benefit of the INET solution. Specifically, since the proposed solution is an application that is compatible with any mobile phone or wireless device (e.g., a PDA), data transfers occur between patients and providers on a well-vetted model. Therefore, the learning curve for patients is minimal as they are likely to be in possession of mobile devices.

What makes this model unique and most beneficial is its focus on enabling and supporting all areas necessary for the actualization of ICT initiatives in healthcare. By design, the model identifies the inputs necessary to bring an innovative chronic disease management solution to market. These solutions are developed and implemented through a physician-led mobile e-health project. This project is the heart of the model that bridges the needs and requirements of many different players into a final (output) deliverable, a "Wireless Healthcare Program. " To accomplish this, the model is continually updated to identify, select, and prioritize the ICT project inputs that will:

- Accelerate healthcare system enhancements and achieve rapid healthcare benefits.
- Close the timing gaps between information research studies and their application in healthcare operational settings.
- Shorten the time cycle to fund an ICT project and receive an adequate return on the investment.

The model identifies key healthcare system inputs with four Ps, namely: (1) People that deliver healthcare, (2) Process to define the current healthcare delivery tasks, (3) Platform used in the healthcare technology infrastructure, and (4) Protection of patient data. These four Ps were chosen after discussions with various healthcare professionals as to the areas they believed were critical inputs for any model. These categories are mutually exclusive and collectively exhaustive based on the views of experts consulted. In applying the DiaMonD solution to any particular context of diabetes sufferers, it is necessary to consider the scope or extent of the diabetes problems in this context, the specific contextual features such as demographics as well as current processes in place to treat patients so that the application will be tailored to this population hence "localize" is an important aspect in the delivery framework. Thus, the delivery framework helps to make the solution applicable to any context of diabetes patients, which is an essential consideration given that diabetes cuts across all areas of the community. Together the components of the model will help in actualizing physician-led solution for the management of chronic diseases in general and of diabetes in particular. To successfully implement the INET web-based model described above, it was necessary to have an appropriate methodology. Based on this need, the adaptive mapping to realization (AMR) methodology was developed (Wickramasinghe and Goldberg 2007). The idea of the methodology was to apply a systematic rigorous set of predetermined protocols to each business case and then to map the postprior results back to the model. In this way, it was possible to compare and contrast both a priori and post priori findings. From such a comparison, first a diagnosis of the current state was made, and then prescriptions were derived for the next business case. Hence, each pilot study incorporated the lessons learnt from the previous one and the model was adapted in real time.

By applying the tools and techniques of today's knowledge economy as presented in the intelligence continuum (IC), it is possible to make the AMR methodology into a very powerful knowledge-based systems development model. The IC was developed by Wickramasinghe and Schaffer (2006) to enable the application of tools and technologies of the knowledge economy to be applied to healthcare processes in a systematic and rigorous fashion, thereby ensuring superior healthcare delivery. The collection of key tools, techniques, and processes that make up the IC include, but are not limited to, data mining, business intelligence/analytics, and knowledge management (Wickramasinghe and Goldberg 2007). Together, they represent a very powerful system for refining the raw data stored in data marts and/or data warehouses, thereby maximizing the value and utility of these data assets for any organization. To maximize the value of the data generated through specific healthcare processes and then to use this to improve processes, IC techniques and tools must be applied in a systematic manner. Once applied, the results become part of the data set that are subsequently reintroduced into the system and combined with other inputs of people, processes, and technology to develop an improvement continuum.

Thus, the IC includes the generation of data, the analysis of these data to provide a "diagnosis," and their reintroduction into the cycle as a "prescriptive" solution. In this way, the IC is well suited to the dynamic and complex nature of healthcare environments and ensures that the future state is always built upon the extant knowledge base of the preceding state. Through the incorporation of the IC with the AMR methodology, we then have a knowledge-based systems development model that can be applied to any setting, not necessarily to chronic disease management. The power of this model is that it brings best practices and the best available germane knowledge to each iteration, and is both flexible and robust.

Given the uniqueness of this approach, it was necessary to develop this model from the beginning rather than look at other existing models. This was done by trying to understand key criteria from various stakeholders such as patients, healthcare professionals, and hospital personnel and sort this information into a coherent whole. This was an iterative process, which involved many and multiple discussions with the various stakeholders until all parties were agreed the model captured the essential elements as discussed in details in Goldberg (2002a–e).

To date, directional data have already shown the benefits of this solution in various pilot studies in Canada (Wickramasinghe and Goldberg 2009). We believe that DiaMonD is a most beneficial solution given the huge and growing impact of diabetes. In particular, it is very cost effective for both patients and healthcare providers. We believe that as more pilot studies are conducted in different settings, this will add data that will show the full and far-reaching benefits of the proposed solution. What is certain is that current methods for treating patients with diabetes are unwieldy, generating significant costs, not especially patient-centric, and doing little to stem the development of secondary complications, thus a better solution is required.

Thus, DiaMonD represents a pervasive technology- enabled solution, which, while not exorbitantly expensive, can facilitate the superior monitoring of diabetes. The proposed solution enables patient empowerment by way of enhancing self-management. This is a desirable objective because it allows patients to become more like partners with their clinicians in the management of their own healthcare (Radin 2006; Mirza et al. 2008) by enhancing the traditional clinical–patient interactions (Opie 1998). The process steps in monitoring diabetes using the DiaMonD approach are outlined below.

1. Each patient receives a blood glucose measurement unit.
2. Patient conducts the blood glucose test and enters the blood glucose information into a handheld wireless device.
3. The blood glucose information is transmitted to specialized database servers that store patient data. Patient's handheld device uniquely identifies the patient for recording the blood glucose data. Thus, no patient information such as the name, ethnicity, or date of birth is transmitted to the clinic.
4. The patient's blood glucose data are then stored/integrated with the clinic's electronic medical record (EMR) system.
5. An alert is generated for the clinical staff with the patient's blood glucose information.

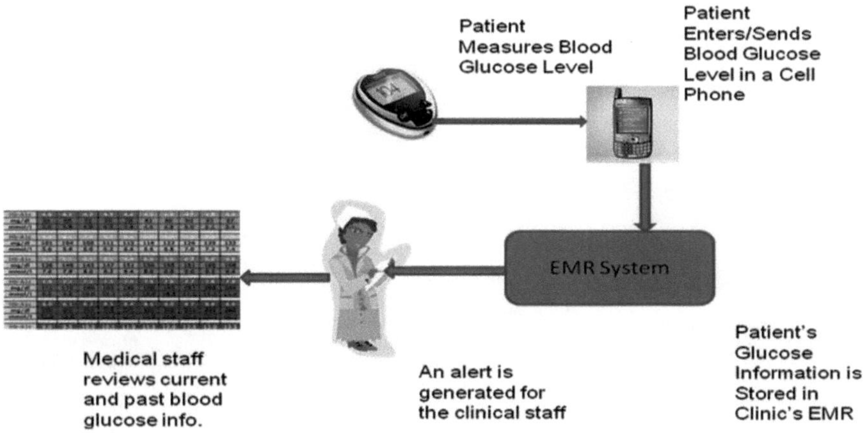

Fig. 16.1 Flow of blood glucose information from the patient to clinical staff via EHR

6. The blood glucose information of the patient is reviewed by the clinical staff (physician/nurse).
7. Feedback on glucose levels is transmitted back to the patient's handheld device. Feedback examples include complimenting the patient when glucose levels are normal or asking the patient to come for a follow-up appointment when the levels are out of norm.
8. Monitor trends in diabetes management for patients over a period of time.

This process is illustrated in Figs. 16.1 and 16.2. The iterative nature of the DiaMonD approach is consistent with the AMR methodology, and hence the solution continuously diagnoses, evaluates, and prescribes so that the future course of patient management and self-care is built on the current readings and medical advice.

16.4 Integration of Wireless Monitoring with Existing Electronic Health Records

Electronic health record (EHR) is the most commonly used term for storing accessing patient medical information electronically (Wickramasinghe and Schaffer 2010). EHR systems provide significant functionality that enable entering and accessing patient demographic data, patient charts, medical history, progress notes, medications, immunizations, past medical history, vital signs, laboratory data, transcription, and e-prescriptions. Computerized physician order entry (CPOE) systems can capture the physicians' orders with respect to patient care. CPOE is often a component of the EHRs and enables physicians to enter orders and disseminate those orders to the labs, radiology department, pharmacy, and other healthcare providers such as specialists. Personal health record (PHR) systems enable patients to access their personal medical information via the Internet. PHR systems allow patient access to their medical records, prescriptions, laboratory data, appointments, and other pertinent

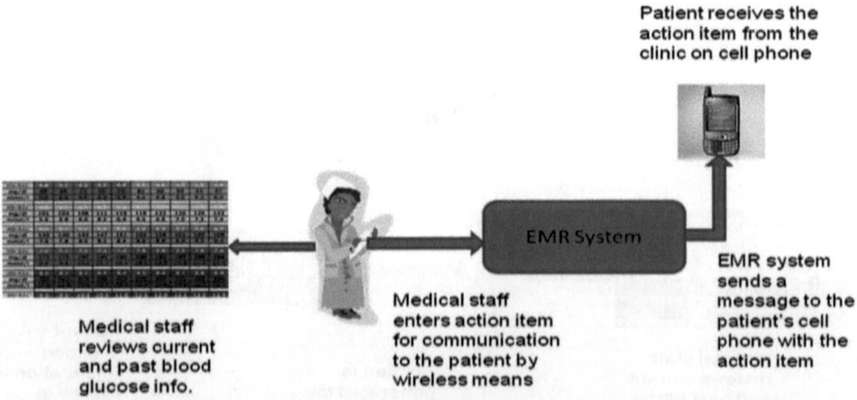

Fig. 16.2 Flow of messages from the clinical staff to the patient via EHR

medical information. Google Health is a PHR system that allows patients to upload their medical data from selected clinics into Google Health.

To integrate data from wireless monitoring devices into existing EHR/PHR infrastructure, the software modules outlined below play a key role.

- *Software module 1—wireless devices to EHR interface*: Accepts patient blood glucose readings from wireless devices and stores the data into electronic medical records systems.
- *Software module 2—health data analyzer*: Analyzes patient blood glucose data over time and provides summary data and suggested next steps. Automatically generates alert messages for patients and clinical staff to follow-up.
- *Software module 3—PHR data extractor*: Exports blood glucose data for patients and enables patients to store their data into their PHR systems.

The three software modules will utilize a back-end database that stores the patient data and blood glucose readings. The interaction of these three software modules and the other software components with the external environment is depicted in Fig. 16.3.

The current processes for monitoring chronic diseases are based on manual intervention. Patients often record their blood glucose and blood pressure information using hand-written notes or in spreadsheets and the clinical staff look for such data in the patient charts and/or EHR systems that they may have. The software technologies discussed in this section have the ability to automatically integrate data from wireless monitoring with the EHR/PHR infrastructure.

16.5 Impact of Wireless Technologies on Meaningful Usage of EHRs

In 2010, the US federal government defined 25 objectives that healthcare providers need to meet to demonstrate the meaningful use of EHRs. If the providers are able to demonstrate meaningful use of EHRs, they stand to gain tens of thousands of dollars

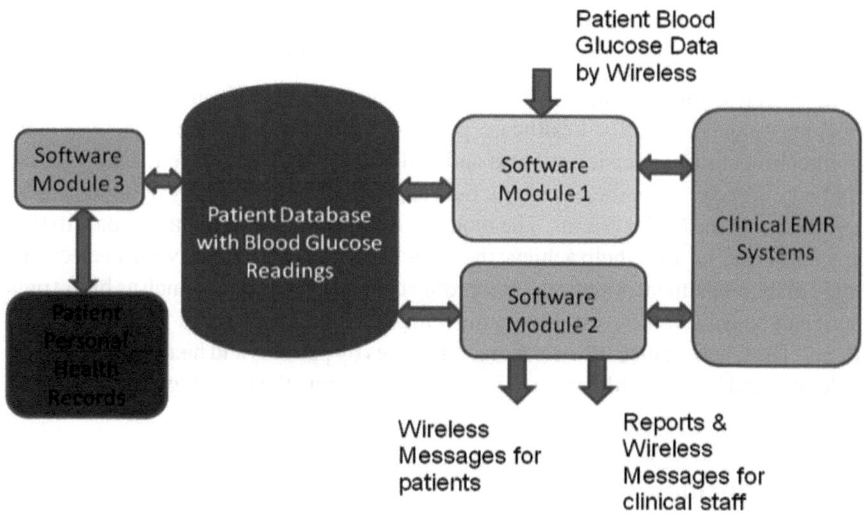

Fig. 16.3 The relationship between the proposed software modules and the PHR, EHR systems

in incentives for the adoption of EHRs. Out of the 25 objectives, 15 objectives are deemed core objectives and are outlined below (Federal Register 2010).

- Use CPOE for medication orders directly entered by any licensed healthcare professional who can enter orders into the medical record per state, local, and professional guidelines.
- Implement drug/drug and drug/allergy interaction checks.
- Maintain an up-to-date problem list of current and active diagnoses.
- Maintain active medication list.
- Maintain active medication allergy list.
- Record and chart changes in vital signs, including: height, weight, blood pressure, calculate and display BMI, plot and display growth charts for children 2–20 years, including BMI.
- Record smoking status for patients 13 years old or older.
- Provide patients with an electronic copy of their health information (including diagnostic test results, problem list, medication lists, medication allergies) upon request.
- Capability to exchange key clinical information (e.g., problem list, medication list, medication allergies, and diagnostic test results) among providers of care and patient-authorized entities electronically.
- Protect electronic health information created or maintained by the certified EHR technology through the implementation of appropriate technical capabilities.
- Generate and transmit permissible prescriptions electronically (eRx).
- Record demographics, including: preferred language, gender, race, ethnicity, date of birth.
- Implement one clinical decision support rule relevant to specialty or high clinical priority, along with the ability to track compliance that rules.

- Report ambulatory clinical quality measures to CMS or states.
- Provide clinical summaries for patients for each office visit.

With wireless monitoring for chronic diseases, demonstrating meaningful use becomes much easier for healthcare providers. For example, the objective of implementing clinical decision support and ability to track compliance for diseases like diabetes is easier since the blood glucose readings are automatically obtained and integrated with the EHR systems. The modules that enable export of patient data to PHR systems (see Fig. 16.3) help achieve the objective "Provide patients with an electronic copy of their health information." Recording changes in vital signs such as blood pressure can be achieved by wireless monitoring of blood pressure for hypertensive patients. Thus, acceptance of wireless technologies by patients and healthcare teams accelerates and helps healthcare providers to demonstrate the meaningful use of EHRs.

16.6 Concluding Remarks

Two distinct business models can be used for companies to become commercially viable with wireless monitoring of patients with chronic diseases. Companies can provide one or both of the following services: (1) chronic disease data service to patients and (2) chronic disease data service to the clinics. The business models for these two services are briefly described below. The description below assumes a fictitious company by name "ChronicCare" and is limited to patients with diabetes.

1. ChronicCare Data Service to Patients Patients subscribe to ChronicCare by paying an annual subscription fee. The subscription fee varies depending on the services that the patient chooses (see below). In return, ChronicCare provides the following services to each patient:

- Collect and store patient blood glucose data.
- Send blood glucose data for storage in the patient's primary care physician (PCP) clinical EHR system.
- Analyze blood glucose data and send messages to patient's (PCP) and other clinical staff.
- Enable patients to view and export blood glucose information (over years or months or for any selected period of time) to a preferred format including the patient's personal health records.
- Provide services that automatically send all patient blood glucose data to a new clinic when the patient changes PCP.

2. ChronicCare Data Service to Clinics Clinics subscribe to ChronicCare by paying an annual subscription fee that varies based on the patient volume and the services they need. In return, ChronicCare provides the following services to the clinic:

- Integrate the blood glucose data from the clinic's patients with the EHR system.
- Enable PCPs and other clinical staff to view the patient blood glucose data and generate myriad reports.

- Enable PCPs and clinical staff to send messages seamlessly to patients by wireless means (e.g., clinical staff may enter a plan of action for the patient in the EHR system, which could be automatically sent to the patient's wireless device using ChronicCare services).
- Provide research services to clinics on the effectiveness of drug 1 (e.g., metformin) versus drug 2 (e.g., onglyza) by age group, ethnicity, etc.
- Synchronize the EHR systems with blood glucose readings of new patients.

There is an estimated number of 23.6 million diabetes patients in the United States (2007 data) and an estimated 57 million patients in the United States who are deemed prediabetic. A large majority of these patients may be willing to pay a small fee per year to have their blood glucose readings stored with time that they can access anytime and anywhere. An alternative business model is to provide free access to patients to store their blood glucose data, while the main revenue generation occurs via online advertising. Google Health PHR allows patients free access, with the online advertising providing the main source of revenue.

While wireless technologies for monitoring chronic diseases have not been very prevalent, they are expected to increase significantly in the coming years. This chapter outlined the technical aspects of wireless monitoring for chronic diseases. It also discussed how data from wireless monitoring can be integrated into the existing EHR/PHR infrastructure. This chapter indicated the impact of wireless technologies on the meaningful use of EHRs. In future, discussing the meaningful use criteria in the context of wireless technologies and expanding on the business models for wireless monitoring of chronic diseases are good directions for further research.

References

Federal Register. (2010). 28 July 2010, pp. 44370–44374. http://www.archives.gov/press/press-releases/2010/nr10-22.html. Accessed Dec 2011

Gibbons, M., Bali, R., & Wickramasinghe, N. (2010). *Perspectives of knowledge management in urban healthcare*. New York: Springer.

Goldberg, S. (2002a). Building the Evidence for a standardized Mobile Internet (wireless) Environment in Ontario, Canada. January Update, Internal INET Documentation, Ontario, Canada, INET.

Goldberg, S. (2002b). HTA Presentation Rendering Component Summary. Internal INET documentation, Ontario, Canada, INET.

Goldberg, S. (2002c). HTA Presentational Selection and Aggregation Component Summary. Internal INET Documentation, Ontario, Canada, INET.

Goldberg, S. (2002d). HTA Quality Assurance Component Summary. Internal INET documentation, Ontario, Canada, INET.

Goldberg, S. (2002e). Wireless POC Device Component Summary. Internal INET documentation, Ontario, Canada, INET.

Huber, M. (1999). Health expenditure trends in OECD countries 1970–1997. *Health Care Financing Review, 21*(2), 45–60.

Mirza, F., Norris, T., & Stockdale, R. (2008). Mobile technologies and the holistic management of chronic diseases. *Health Informatics Journal, 14*(4), 309–321.

OECD. (2010a). Growing health spending puts pressure on government budgets. http://www.oecd.org/document/11/0,3343,en_2649_34631_45549771_1_1_1_37407,00.html. Accessed 27 Feb 2011.

OECD. (2010b). OECD health data 2010. http://stats.oecd.org/Index.aspx?DatasetCode=HEALTH. Accessed 27 Feb 2011.

Opie, A. (1998). Nobody's asked me for my view: Users' empowerment by multidisciplinary health teams. *Qualitative Health Research, 18,* 188–206.

Porter, M., & Tiesberg, E. (2006). *Re-defining health care delivery.* Boston: Harvard Business Press.

Rachlis, M. (2006). Key to sustainable healthcare system. http://www.improveingchroniccare.org. Accessed Dec 2011.

Radin, P. (2006). To me, it's my life: Medical communication, trust, and activism in cyberspace. *Social Science & Medicine, 6,* 591–601.

Wickramasinghe, N., & Goldberg, S. (2003). *The wireless panacea for healthcare.* Proceedings of 36th Hawaii International Conference on System Sciences, Hawaii, 6–10 January, IEEE.

Wickramasinghe, N., & Goldberg, S. (2007). Adaptive mapping to realization methodology (AMR) to facilitate mobile initiatives in healthcare. *International Journal of Mobile Communications, 5*(3), 300–318.

Wickramasinghe, N., & Goldberg, S. (2009). The S'ANT approach to facilitate a superior chronic disease self-management model. *IJANTTI, 1*(4), 21–34.

Wickramasinghe, N., & Schaffer, J. (2006). Creating knowledge driven healthcare processes with the intelligence continuum. *International Journal of Electronic Healthcare,* 2(2), 164–174.

Wickramasinghe, N., & Schaffer, J. (2010). *Realizing v driven e-health solutions.* Washington, DC: IBM Center for The Business of Government.

Chapter 17
Applying the IPM Framework to Improve Remote Performance Management in the Contexts of Chronic Disease Care

Fatemeh Hoda Moghimi, Steve Goldberg and Nilmini Wickramasinghe

Abstract The exponential growth of data coupled with a rapid increase of service demands in healthcare contexts requires a robust framework, which can support IT intelligent solutions as well as web-based service handling. We proffer the Intelligent Performance Management (IPM) framework as such an Internet based model that can enable greater access to clinical components by providing collaborative layers for service offerings on the web using Business Intelligence techniques. Thus, this chapter examines the technical and conceptual layers of the IPM framework and also defines some of the associated knowledge driven healthcare services by the IPM model in order to enhance healthcare performance management. To illustrate the benefits of the IPM framework to improve web-based performance management in healthcare contexts, we focus on chronic disease care in the case of improving a new wireless monitoring solution, an area, which requires high-quality performance management to facilitate development of appropriate remote care and management.

Keywords Intelligent performance management · Web services · Business intelligence · Knowledge management · Chronic disease care

17.1 Introduction

Healthcare organizations today are increasingly under pressure to make performance management a part of their culture (Adler et al. 2003). The popularity of the web has made it a prime vehicle of disseminating information (Vaughan-Nichols 2002). The relevance of increasing performance management in the healthcare area using intelligent tools and web-based services has led to a significant body of

F. H. Moghimi · N. Wickramasinghe (✉)
Epworth Chair Health Information Management, School of Business Information Technology and Logistics, RMIT University, Melbourne VIC 3001, Australia
e-mail: moghimi87@gmail.com

N. Wickramasinghe
e-mail: nilmini.wickramasinghe@rmit.edu.au

S. Goldberg
131 Glen Crescent, L4J 4W4, Ontario, Canada
e-mail: sgoldberg@inet-international.com

R. K. Bali et al. (eds.), *Pervasive Health Knowledge Management*, Healthcare Delivery in the Information Age,
DOI 10.1007/978-1-4614-4514-2_17,

recent research addressing some issues related to performance management efficiency (Spil et al. 2002). In this chapter, we attempt to review key issues regarding current performance management systems and suggest a web-based model using business intelligence to introduce needed e-service into the healthcare context.

Specifically, in this chapter, we only focus on identifying the role of business intelligence tools and techniques to enhance online and real-time performance management efficiency; however, we envisage that in the future it will also be possible to find some more services and tools to improve performance management. When healthcare organizations look at making investments to improve patient care, they tend to look at funding staff or equipment—an MRI machine, for example—rather than IT (Cognos 2008). However, performance management solutions include activities to ensure that goals are consistently being met in an effective and efficient manner. Performance management can focus on performance of the organization, a department, procedure to build a process or service, employees, etc. Information in this topic will give some sense of the overall activities involved in performance management.

In this research, we try to answer the research question how can e-performance management be incorporated into healthcare. We do this by giving an introduction on business intelligence and its importance to improve performance management. Then, after defining healthcare performance management and reviewing current performance management issues, the role of an online and real-time solution is presented and a technical framework to design an intelligence e-performance management is demonstrated.

17.2 Background

Although performance management applications are found in widely divergent functional areas, in healthcare contexts considering the importance of real-time outcomes, they all require the following key features:

- Intelligent timing.
- Multidimensional views of data.
- Calculation-intensive capabilities.

Regarding the identification of these requirements, through this research an online intelligent performance management framework is proposed to enhance healthcare real-time performance management.

17.2.1 Healthcare Information Treatment

The proliferation of databases in every quadrant of healthcare practice and research is evident in the large number of claims databases, registries, electronic medical record (EMR) data warehouses, disease surveillance systems, and ad hoc research database systems (Wickramasinghe et al. 2008a). Pattern-identification tasks such

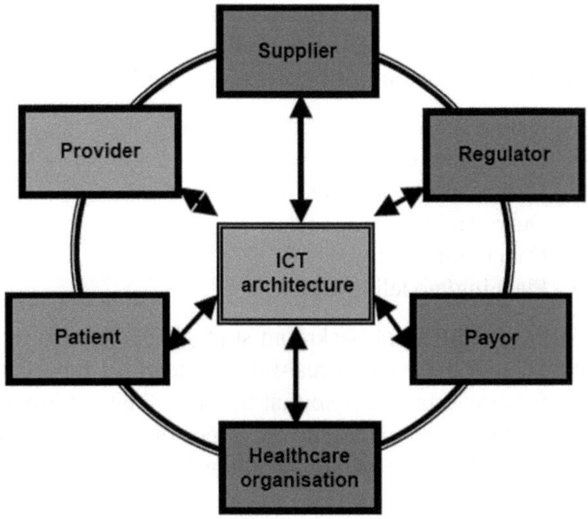

Fig. 17.1 The web of primary healthcare information flows. (Source: Wickramasinghe et al. 2008b)

as detecting associations between certain risk factors and outcomes, ascertaining trends in healthcare utilization, or discovering new models of disease in populations of individuals rapidly become daunting even to the most experienced healthcare researcher or manager (Holmes et al. 2002).

Figure 17.1 presents the central role of the information communication technologies (ICT) architecture as well as the far-reaching implications of data and information flows throughout this web; and thus, the importance of such data and information for the various key players. Maximizing these data and information assets then becomes a key need for healthcare organizations in order to realize their value proposition. This then is where the techniques of knowledge management, data mining, and business intelligence become strategic necessities for healthcare (Wickramasinghe et al. 2008b).

17.2.2 Business Intelligence

Perhaps the biggest single evolutionary driver in the expansion of modern data warehouse management is the democratization of Business Intelligence (BI; Kalakota and Robinson 2001). BI can mean different things to different groups of people (Fayyad et al. 2008). For the purposes of this research, we subscribe to the comprehensive definition by Cindi Howson and Wayne Eckerson who state that "BI is an umbrella term that encompasses the processes, tools, and technologies required to turn data into information, and information into knowledge and plans that drive effective business activity. BI encompasses data warehousing technologies and processes on the back end, and query, reporting, analysis, and information delivery tools and processes on the front end" (Eckerson et al. 2007). Also of relevance is that "BI encompasses data warehousing, data integration, reporting, analysis and data mining technologies" (Eckerson 2006). The proliferations of BI tools, which are of importance in this research, include the six main categories as follows (TDWI 2010):

- Online analytical processing (OLAP).
- Production reporting.
- Dashboards/scorecards.
- Query and reporting tools.
- Data mining tools.
- Planning/modeling tools.

With the shift from backroom strategic application to essential daily management tool comes the need for real-time, or near real-time, data collection (Gartner 2006).

It is important to note that true real-time, or instantaneous, data availability is oftentimes more an ideal driven by perceived competitive pressures, than a necessary or even a desirable goal (Scheduling 2010). While many enterprises report that users are demanding data refresh rates down to the millisecond, only those individuals who depend on "business-aware" applications, in fields like performance management or transactional processing, are likely to need such immediate and fluid information (Adler et al. 2003). Most operational applications, and nearly all BI tools, can fulfill their tasks with periodic or near real-time data (Howson 2007). Based on an extensive review of the literature, it appears that the best solution to increase the efficiency of web services is a comprehensive business intelligence solution in the back end and also front end.

17.2.3 Web-Based Service Management Systems

Given the high rate of growth of the volume of data available on the WWW, locating information of interest in such an anarchic setting becomes a more difficult process every day (Sanjay and Wee 2004). Thus, there is the recognition of the immediate need for effective and efficient tools for information consumers, who must be able to easily locate disparate information on the web, ranging from unstructured documents and pictures to structured, record-oriented data (Bhowmick et al. 2004).

Web services are at a higher level of abstraction with respect to conventional middleware services, and therefore directly impact business-level metrics and need to be guided by them (Alonso et al. 2003). Management of web services can be classified based on its scope; it is distinguished between infrastructure-, application-, and business-level (or business-oriented) management. Infrastructure-level management focuses on the web services platform (Casati et al. 2003). Thus, to analyze web services from an Infrastructure-level management in a business perspective it is important to define and correlate metrics through interfaces, conversations, and compositions (Sanjay and Wee 2004). The other important thing is that simplicity and flexibility in managing the manager are crucial. In fact, metrics and reports are not "static," and there is the frequent need to modify them to perfect the analysis and cope with changes (Casati et al. 2003).

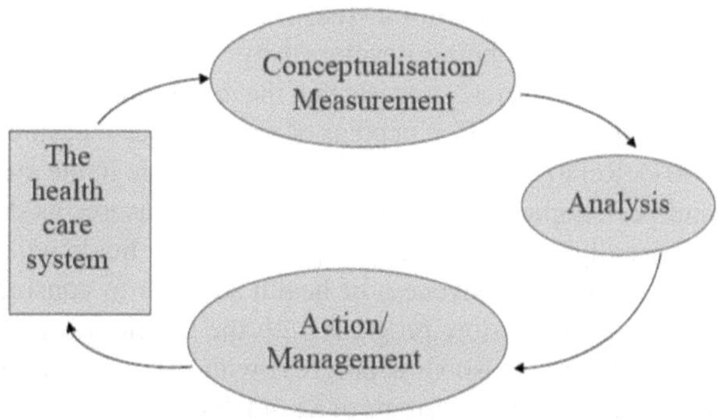

Fig. 17.2 The performance measurement and management. (Adapted from Nutley and Smith 1998)

17.2.4 Healthcare Performance Management

There are similarities and differences across many countries in performance management institutions, using "performance management" in a broad sense (Hurst and Jee-Hughes 2001). All countries rely heavily on professional licensure, self-regulation and peer review for controlling the quality of medical and nursing care. That is not surprising in view of the asymmetry of knowledge referred to above. Apart from that, the institutions of "external" performance management differ widely between countries (Hurst and Jee-Hughes 2001). The optimal role for external scrutiny is not yet well defined (Hurst and Jee-Hughes 2001). Questions remain about who should be the recipients of performance indicators and what incentives there should be to act upon them (Hurst and Jee-Hughes 2001). Figure 17.2 depicts these key aspects.

There are signs that providers may be more responsive than other actors in the healthcare system are to such publication (Spil et al. 2002). However, publication can also have unintended and unwanted side effects. That is probably an inevitable consequence of the fact that the available measures of health outcomes and responsiveness are frail and incomplete (Spil et al. 2002). A possible implication is that "external" review and peer review should be seen as complementary and used in a climate of co-operation (Cognos 2008). Meanwhile, it is clear that the searches both for better indicators of the "quality" of healthcare, and for a better understanding of what determines the behavior of the key actors in health systems, should go on.

17.3 Challenges Currently Facing Performance Management in the Healthcare Area

Based on an extensive literature review, although some countries are trying to apply performance management, they are faced with some limitations and challenges with online and real-time access usually being the most important of them.

Performance Indicators/Measures A selective review of the performance indicators/measures being developed by WHO, OECD, and each of the four OECD Member[1] countries, suggests that the development of indicators is proceeding at different speeds, in different areas of performance measurement (Hurst and Jee-Hughes 2001). Relatively slow progress is being made in the area of health outcomes (Hurst and Jee-Hughes 2001). Moreover, such measures as do exist at a population level are usually proxies. Faster progress is being made with the development of indicators of the responsiveness of health services to consumers (Hurst and Jee-Hughes 2001). There is slow progress with the development of equity indicators (Cognos 2008). There is also slow progress with the compilation of overall measures of the efficiency of health systems of a kind that command widespread confidence (Cognos 2008). The asymmetry of knowledge between healthcare professionals, on the one hand, and healthcare consumers and lay managers, on the other, is likely to stay for some time to come. Nevertheless, given the effort now being put into collecting performance indicators in many OECD member countries, there seems to be good prospects for improving coverage of such indicators in OECD Health Data within the next few years (Hurst and Jee-Hughes 2001). However, there may be a need for international harmonization of measures if comparative work is to proceed at an international level (Hurst and Jee-Hughes 2001).

Controllable and Uncontrollable Variations A key issue is how to discriminate between controllable and uncontrollable variations in performance (Hurst and Jee-Hughes 2001). As we have seen, that arises particularly in the area of health outcome measures, when health status measures are used as proxies for health outcomes (Gold et al. 2002). There is likely to be less of a problem with process "measures" of outcomes or with measures of responsiveness. However, even here it may require investigation and analysis to identify what levers must be pulled to improve performance (Gold et al. 2002). For example, poor quality in the service provided by a department in a globally budgeted public hospital may be due to inefficient working practices (which are the responsibility of local management), shortages of resources (which are the responsibility of the relevant funding body) or inappropriate national wage scales (which are likely to be the responsibility of central government; Gold et al. 2002).

Aggregate the Indicators Another issue, which faces all who devise sets of performance indicators, is whether or not to aggregate the indicators to provide composite or summary measures (Hurst and Jee-Hughes 2001). The main argument in favor of aggregation is that without it, those trying to monitor performance may drown in a sea of detail. The main argument against aggregation is that to the extent indicators reflect performance against different goals; aggregation requires adding "apples" and "pears" (Marsden et al. 2006). Value judgments are required to weight different objectives, unless market prices or average unit costs can be used as weights. Moreover, if only summary indicators are published, the origin of variations in

[1] United States, United kingdom, Canada, and Australia.

performance tends to be concealed. However, it is possible to publish both summary measures and their components.

Setting Standards or Benchmarks for Performance The other issue is how to set standards or benchmarks for performance. One possibility—adopted recently by the United Kingdom—is to adopt certain ambitious but achievable targets for key areas of care, combined with a "traffic light" system (Hurst and Jee-Hughes 2001). The national standards will be included targets for key conditions and diseases, waiting times, the quality of care, and efficiency (Hurst and Jee-Hughes 2001). All NHS organizations will be classified as "green," "yellow," or "red" on the basis of their performance. Red organization will be those failing to meet a number of the core national targets. "Yellow" organizations will be those meeting all or most national core targets but would not be in the top 25 % of performance (Hurst and Jee-Hughes 2001). Green organization will be those meeting all targets and scoring in the top 25 % of organizations on performance, taking account of "value added." The benchmarks will be reviewed periodically (Hurst and Jee-Hughes 2001).

17.4 Business Intelligence as a Solution

There are three critical concepts of performance management: monitoring, analytics, and planning. With BI, all three are brought together to help give everyone in the health organization the information they need to make informed decisions.

Monitoring Quickly and easily enables the creation of dashboards and scorecards with its functional soft wares, so that everyone can align with departmental and organizational goals. In addition, other aspects include: enabling automating the supporting processes, displaying process metrics, and KPIs in Office Performance Point Server business intelligence software, and managing the workflow with Office SharePoint Server. Office SharePoint Server also lets the hospital share reports and analysis and collaborate with colleagues.

Reporting and Analysis This involves equipping people with reporting and analysis tools and technologies that will help capture the structured and unstructured information they use to make decisions. In addition, easy creation of reports and performing of analysis with BI Reporting Services is supported. Moreover, a pivot functionality and slice and dice technique enables hospitals to look at data in different ways and drill down to explore trends (Spil et al. 2002). Of course, users can always count on Office Excel to manipulate data and create reports. However, BI reporting services are more functional.

Data Warehouse Features within the data warehouse support the obtaining of insights into the data needed through an integrated, centrally managed, and trusted data source. Many healthcare organizations are using data warehouses for data and records management, and so are already familiar with how easy it is to manage data in such a setting. In addition, it is possible to combine data from multiple sources into one location and provide access to information, and even create an integrated database.

17.5 Proposed Intelligent e-Performance Management Framework

Today, we are seeing the emergence of a powerful distributed computing paradigm, broadly called web services (Vaughan-Nichols 2001). In the healthcare domain, using web services will play a key role in dynamic performance management.

17.5.1 Technical Aspects of an Intelligent e-Performance Management Framework

The intelligent e-performance management framework (Fig. 17.3), technically, will have three main components as follows:

- Information system infrastructure.
- A service-based framework.
- Online data access.

Furthermore, Data staging area, Data presentation area, web-based protocols and e-services are four different layer of the second component. Through the intelligence e-performance application, data will be sent electronically from each GP's (or primary care physician's) local systems to data warehouse. It will integrate with information from the both administrative and clinical sides, and arranged using online analytical processing cubes for rapid analysis. The results are then presented as a series of scorecards and key performance indicators on the authority's intranet by some dashboards, SharePoint, or office performance points.

In the web-based layer, gateways are used to control the amount of server resources allocated to each traffic class. By dynamically changing the amount of resources it can control the response time experienced by each traffic class (Pacifici et al. 2003).

In such an environment, a web service provider may provide multiple web services, each in multiple grades, and each of those to multiple customers. The provider will thus have multiple classes of web service traffic, each with its own characteristics and requirements.

17.5.2 A Set of e-Services Recommended by the Proposed Framework

There are many ways BI can help clinical organizations manage their performance. Whether it is early detection of illness trends, understanding lab turnaround times, or

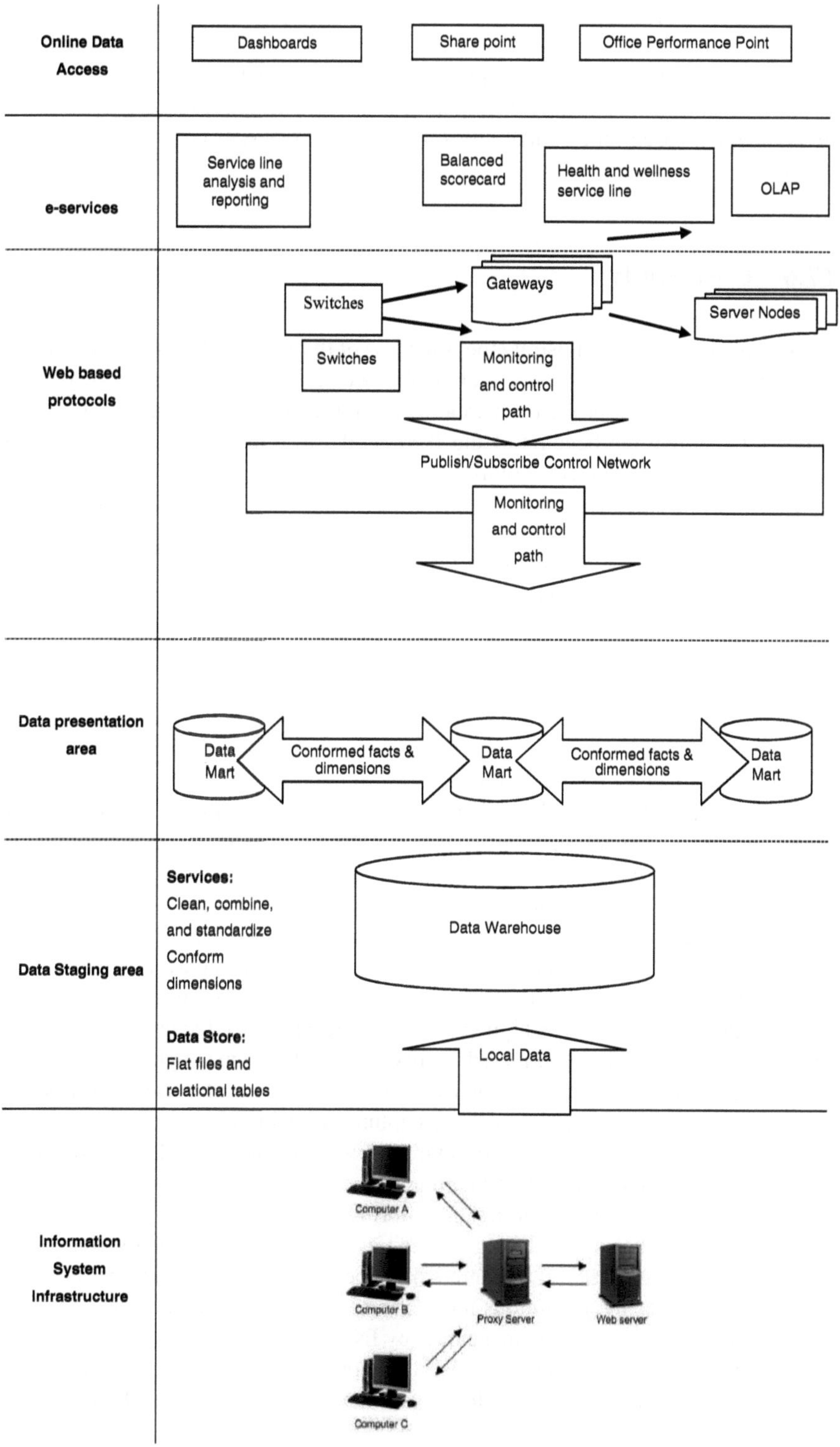

Fig. 17.3 The intelligent e-performance management framework

meeting compliance and accreditation standards, having easy access to real-time information can help the organization take their progress to the next level. As presented in Table 17.1, some specific examples are described how healthcare organizations can use BI to better manage their organization's performance. (These services are recommended based on BI capabilities justified by Microsoft business intelligence group).

17.6 Case Study

In this case vignette, we illustrate the functions of the Intelligent Performance Management (IPM) framework across a clinical process; the case of chronic disease care has been chosen to improve the wireless solution outcomes. The aim of this case study is to outline the benefits of the IPM Model to improve outcomes of a new wireless "diabetes monitoring solution."

The case of "diabetes monitoring solution" demonstrates the IPM framework's effectiveness in chronic disease management. Chronic diseases such as diabetes, asthma, or hypertension if detected early can be contained and the sufferers from these diseases can continue to lead high-quality lives. Conversely, if these diseases are not well managed, they can develop into more complicated healthcare problems and life for such patients becomes less than satisfactory. Critical to effective chronic disease management is regular monitoring and an informed patient who takes responsibility for managing his/her wellness. Diabetes, one important chronic disease is increasing in its prevalence throughout not only North America but also the world.

The world diabetes population is expected to increase by 76 % from 159 million in 2000 to 236 million in 2025, and thus diabetes has been called a silent epidemic by the World Health Organization. The cost of treatment of an increasing number of diabetics is indeed alarming to any healthcare system.

Regular monitoring of diabetes is a necessary part to controlling this particular chronic disease and keeping it from evolving into more complicated healthcare problems. To do this efficiently and effectively, we believe ICT can play a critical role by providing a means to enable superior monitoring anywhere anytime and thereby also allowing the patient to enjoy a high quality lifestyle. However, technology initiatives in healthcare to date have had mixed results at best (Wickramasinghe and Goldberg 2007, 2009). We believe this is connected with the failure of current information systems (IS) methodologies to correctly capture the richness and complexities of a modern healthcare environment. To address this issue and in so doing provide an environment enabled by ICT that facilitates superior chronic disease management, we describe the idea behind wireless monitoring of diabetes.

DiaMonD—diabetes monitoring device—is a pervasive technology solution to provide superior healthcare for sufferers of diabetes. The solution incorporates software that facilitates the ubiquitous monitoring of an individual's diabetes, thereby, contributing to diabetes self-management by INET international Canada.

The INET web-based solution (Fig. 17.4) provides the necessary components to enable the delivery framework to be positioned in the best possible manner so

Table 17.1 Some specific examples that show how healthcare organizations can use BI

IPM capabilities	Description
Service line analysis and reporting	Healthcare organizations can use BI tools to conduct service line analysis and reporting. Analyzing and reporting on service lines allows the organization to accurately—and in real-time—understand service inefficiencies, and improve the coordination of services, patient satisfaction, and the quality of care. Health organizations typically track and analyze performance metrics for health and wellness service lines (e.g., weight management and nutrition), women and infant services, traditional lines of service (e.g., musculoskeletal, orthopedic, and emergency), and chronic disease lines (e.g., cancer, heart, and diabetes).By using BI, organizations can analyze and report on service lines to help improve the quality and efficiency of medical service delivery, align with organizational goals, reduce costs, and improve margins
Health and wellness service line management	BI can help healthcare organizations manage performance at all levels of operation, including the health and wellness service line. This service line includes wide-ranging programs such as those that build awareness about disease prevention and healthy lifestyles or that help individuals cope with specific health and well-being issues. Within the health and wellness service line, organizations look to improve disease prevention testing and adherence, analyze demographic information and trends to align service offerings, analyze recurring episodes of illness, and track immunization rates and disease outbreaks. Effective tracking and analysis of these indicators can help healthcare organizations reduce episodes of illness, improve outcomes, reduce costs, and improve patient satisfaction. BI can help organizations better understand and track trends in health issues and health programs with easy access to real-time information. Healthcare professionals can drill down into the data to explore details behind the trends, allowing them to quickly respond and to adjust efforts
Balanced scorecard	BI tools help healthcare organizations use the Balanced Scorecard as a strategic management system to track organizational performance across financial, clinical, business process, and learning and growth measures. Once performance metrics are set, organizations identify the key drivers, or desired outcomes, and then define indicators to gauge progress. By using BI to manage to key indicators, healthcare organizations can achieve consistent strategy execution and monitor performance. By tracking patient satisfaction, quality of care, financial performance, and enhanced learning and growth metrics, the Balanced Scorecard can provide a complete view of the organization. BI enables organizations to link together all the key elements of the Balanced Scorecard with easy-to-use templates and a single interface for viewing KPIs. Decision makers can track operational performance drivers and analyze financial, operational, and clinical KPIs across the organization with customizable scorecards for groups and individuals

Table 17.1 (Continued)

IPM capabilities	Description
On-Line Analytical Processing (OLAP)	Typical manufacturing OLAP applications as a part of a Business Intelligence solution include production planning and defect analysis. Important to all of the mentioned tasks is the ability to provide managers with the information they need to make effective decisions about an organization's strategic directions (Howson 2007). The key indicator of a successful OLAP application is its ability to provide information as needed, that is, its ability to provide "just-in-time" information for effective decision making. This requires more than a base level of detailed data (Baragoin et al. 2001). Just-in-time information is computed data that usually reflects complex relationships and is often calculated on the fly (Baragoin et al. 2001). Analyzing and modeling complex relationships are practical only if response times are consistently short (Baragoin et al. 2001). In addition, because the nature of data relationships may not be known in advance, the data model must be flexible (Baragoin et al. 2001). A truly flexible data model ensures that OLAP systems can respond to changing business requirements as needed for effective decision making (Baragoin et al. 2001)

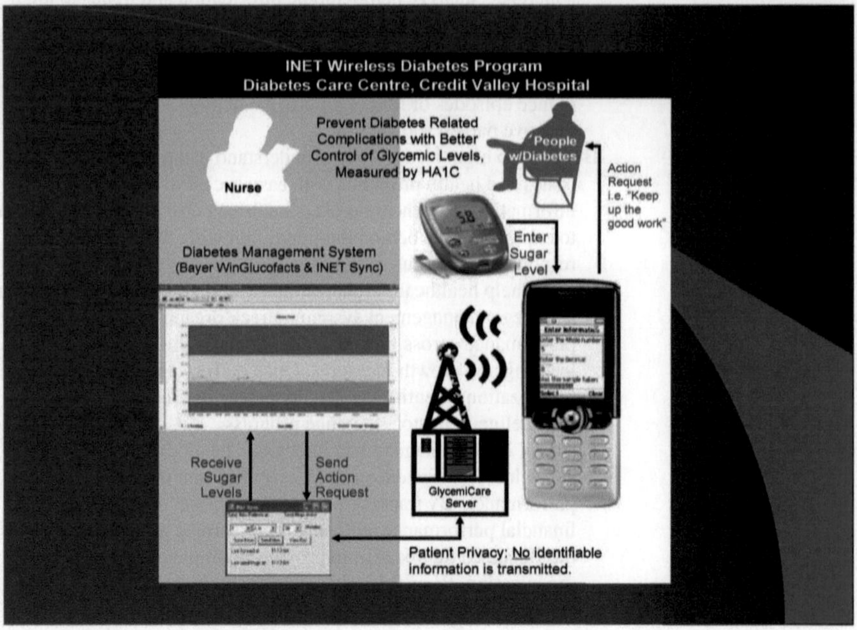

Fig. 17.4 The INET web-based solution

it can indeed facilitate enacting the key components of the chronic disease model successfully.

The process steps in monitoring diabetes using the DiaMonD approach are outlined below (Chalasani et al. 2011):

1. Each patient receives a blood glucose measurement unit.
2. Patient conducts the blood glucose test and enters the blood glucose information into a hand-held wireless device.
3. The blood glucose information is transmitted to specialized database servers that store patient data. Patient's hand-held device uniquely identifies the patient for recording the blood glucose data. Thus, no patient information such as the name, ethnicity, or date of birth is transmitted to the clinic.
4. The patient's blood glucose data are then stored/integrated with the clinic's EMR system.
5. An alert is generated for the clinical staff with the patient's blood glucose information.
6. The blood glucose information of the patient is reviewed by the clinical staff (physician/nurse).
7. Feedback on glucose levels is transmitted back to the patient's hand-held device. Feedback examples include complimenting the patient when glucose levels are normal or asking the patient to come for a follow-up appointment when the levels are out of norm.
8. Monitor trends in diabetes management for patients over a period of time.

The INET solution is developed based on two distinct business models:

a. Chronic care data service to patients.
b. Chronic care data service to clinics.

Based on an analytical literature review and observation, it is found that second part is more analytical. Therefore, performance management is a key and critical component through this part; however, the first part is more hardware-oriented, depending on the DiaMonD device and patients' ability to use it.

To demonstrate the benefits of IPM model in part B, three key clinical steps are defined (Fig. 17.5):

Step 1: Reading the patient blood glucose from wireless devices and storing the data into electronic medical records systems.
Step 2: Accessing and analyzing the patient blood glucose data over time and providing summary data and suggesting next steps.
Step 3: Making suitable structured, semistructured, and ad hoc decisions for patients and providing them with quick recommendations.

To evaluate this new solution and also improve the outcomes, the IPM model is applied in this case. To prove the importance of the IPM model to improve the outcomes of the INET solution, a cross-functional analysis developed by an IT expert group must occur. Through this analytical research, first of all the critical issues of the INET solution were extracted. Then IPM functions/services reviewed to find the best

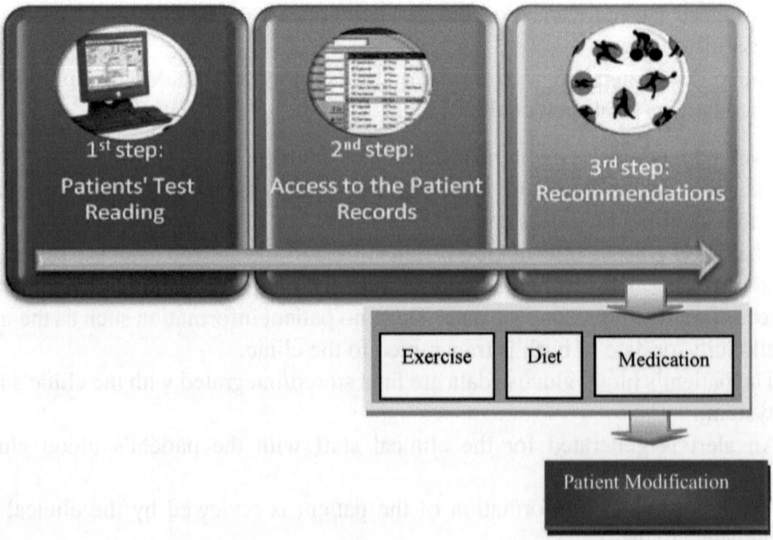

Fig. 17.5 Three key steps to chronic care data service

technical function to improve the issues. The cross-functional analysis is presented by Table 17.2:

17.7 Research Design and Methodology

This research is being conducted using a mix method of standard qualitative and quantitative techniques. To justify the proposed framework content analysis followed by semistructured interviews with an expert group of chronic care practitioners is used. Techniques for conducting appropriate case study research as outlined by Yin have been followed at all times (Yin 1994).

To incorporate the intelligent solutions and services into the proposed IPM Model, business intelligence solution followed by data warehousing technique will be developed.

The research steps are:

Step 1. Understand clinical requirements, dataset structure by an analytical literature review, observation, and review of the relevant documents from INET.

Step 2. Qualitative data collection to extract a set of performance metrics and KPI(s) by domain experts.

Step 3. Data validation and data analysis using Nvivo software.

Step 4. Develop and test the IPM Model by preparing target datasets: select and transform relevant features; data cleaning; data integration; and applying the defined e-services and develop front page.

Table 17.2 The cross-functional analysis to present IPM services and functions to improve INET solution issues

INET solution issues	1st step	2nd step		3rd step	
IPM functions/ services	Real-time respond to requests	Extraction of data from databases, reports, etc.	Analysis of a large volume of information for decision making	Ability to make ad hoc decisions	Evaluate the outcomes
On-Line Analytical Processing (OLAP)	A wide variety of possible views or a multidimensional conceptual view of the data by supporting a dimensional aggregation path or hierarchies and/or multiple hierarchies	–	This service is usually implemented in a multiuser client/server mode and offers consistently rapid responses to queries, regardless of database size and complexity	OLAP helps the user synthesize business information through comparative, personalized viewing, as well as thorough analysis of historical and projected data in various "what-if" data model scenarios. The users are allowed to define new ad hoc calculations as part of the analysis and can report on the data in any desired way	Providing real-time and analytical reports to evaluate the outcomes
Health and wellness service line management	Online data access by share point, office performance care, and dashboards	–	Analyze demographic information and trends to align service offerings Analyze recurring episodes of illness Track immunization rates and disease outbreaks Effective tracking and analysis of these indicators Improve patient satisfaction	Easy access to real-time information to make ad hoc and complex decisions	–

Table 17.2 (continued)

INET solution issues	1st step	2nd step		3rd step	
IPM functions/ services	Real-time respond to requests	Extraction of data from databases, reports, etc.	Analysis of a large volume of information for decision making	Ability to make ad hoc decisions	Evaluate the outcomes
Balanced scorecard	–	–	–	–	Develop a measurement system to evaluate the solution performance Extracting the gaps through the solution performance
Service line analysis and reporting	Online data access by share point, office performance care, and dashboards	–	Analyzing and modeling complex relationships to make analytical reports	Providing "just-in-time" information for effective decision making	–
Data warehousing/data marts	–	Removing informational processing load from transaction-oriented databases Integrating data from multiple sources Sharing data and allowing others to easily access data Reducing cost to access historical data	–	Supporting ad hoc reporting and inquiry	–

Step 5. Quantitative data collection to justify the IPM outcomes.
Step 6. Data validation and data analysis using SPSS software.

Input to the system will be a dataset of Diabetes patients who are using the INET solution, and the outcomes will be decision functions results of performance metrics.

17.8 Research Issues

The research issues raised by the literature review and initial modeling are summarized.

First of all, we know that data in the web are typically semistructural (Wickramasinghe and Goldberg 2007). So, this nature of data may introduce serious challenges to reiterative data through a real-time and online data warehouse. The other important issue is the difference between type and efficiency of such intelligence services in order to their solution providers. This means choosing a vendor is very important as well as choosing a solution. Designing appropriate security levels and permissions through this application is the other significant issue in this research.

Moreover, although participants believe that the Internet could and should play an important role in the delivery of health services, there was a concern about the lack of evidence about the effectiveness of Internet delivered services. Our own review of the literature and research on e-health and e-mental health sites largely supports these concerns. One of the steps that include the theoretical framework developed, needs to be tested in the research. However, empirical testing of the framework is likely to face a number of challenges such as identifying common metrics for measuring the performance indicators. Furthermore, regarding the case study, this research will be faced with other issues. For example, the performance of a wireless monitoring solution has many dimensions and detecting the main performance factors in all of these dimensions is not easy but with the contribution of the relevant expert group, this research will be able to cover these main dimensions.

17.9 Conclusions and Future Research

This study has outlined a research in progress to examine the key role of web-based performance management in healthcare contexts. In an attempt to answer the research questions "how can e-performance management be incorporated into healthcare contexts?" Our discussion of these intelligent solutions serves to demonstrate that an intelligence e-performance application enables the realization of the performance management.

Hence, we believe that if healthcare organizations apply some e-services through data mining and business intelligence as well as some techniques, strategies, and protocols, it will be possible for healthcare delivery to realize its value proposition of superior access, quality, and value.

In future work, we will focus on justifying the proposed framework by conducting pilot tests. This will also involve developing an algorithm and model for online and real-time mining useful information for patients as well as clinical staff from the proposed application with respect to knowledge discovery to improve web-based healthcare performance management. We contend that trying to incorporate the tools, techniques, and strategies of e-performance information into healthcare contexts is critical in order to truly deliver superior healthcare and thus close by calling for more research in this area.

References

Adler, P., et al. (2003). Performance improvement capability: Keys to accelerating performance improvement in hospitals. *California Management Review, 45*(2), 12–33.

Alonso, G., et al. (2003). *Web services: Concepts, architectures, and applications*. Heidelberg: Springer.

Baragoin, C., Andersen, C., Bayerl, S., Bent, G., Lee, J., & Schommer, C. (2001). *Business intelligence architecture: Mining your own business in telecoms using DB2 intelligent miner for data* (1st ed., Chapter 2, p. 17). California: IBM Corp.

Bhowmick, S. S., Madria, S. K., & Keong Ng, W. (2004). *Web data management* (ed.). New York: Springer.

Casati, F., et al. (2003). Business-oriented management of web services. *Communications of the ACM, 46*(10), 115–134.

Chalasani, S., Wickramasinghe, N., Goldberg, S., & Koritala, S. (2011). *Business and IT aspects of wireless enabled healthcare solutions*. AMCIS 2011 Proceedings—All Submissions. Paper 422. http://aisel.aisnet.org/amcis2011_submissions/422.

Cognos, I. (2008). Performance management in healthcare. White paper.

Eckerson, W. W. (2006). Deploying dashboards and scorecards. TDWI report. *TDWI*, 5.

Eckerson, W. W., & Howson, C. (2007). Enterprise BI: Strategies and technologies for deploying BI on an enterprise scale. Report Excerpt. http://www.tdan.com/view-articles/4739. Accessed 08 Feb 2011.

Fayyad, U., Piatetsky-Shapiro, G., & Smyth, P. (2008). *From data mining to knowledge discovery in databases* (pp. 12–17).

Gartner Study. (2006). *Data Integration Identifies Key Usage Trends* (pp. 3–6).

Gold, R., Stevenson, D., & Fryback, G. (2002). Halys and Aalys and Dalys, oh my: Similarities and differences in summary measures of population health. *Annual Review of Public Health, 23*, 115–134.

Holmes, J., et al. (2002). Clinical data mining: Who does it, and what do they do? *AMIA, 9*(13), 32–53.

Howson, C. (2007). *Success business intelligence* (2nd ed.). New York: McGraw Hill.

Hurst, J., & Jee-Hughes, M. (2001). Performance measurement and performance management in OECD health systems. *OECD Labour Market and Social Policy Occasional, 47*.

Kalakota, R., & Robinson, M. (2001). *e-business 2.0: Roadmap for success* (2nd ed.). Boston: Wesley.

Marsden, G., Kelly, C., & Snell, C. (2006). Selecting indicators for strategic performance management transportation research record. *Journal of the Transportation Research Board, 1956*, 67–82.

Nutley, S., & Smith, P. C. (1998). League tables for performance improvement in health care. *Journal of Health Services Research & Policy, 31*(1), 50–57.

Pacifici, G., et al. (2003). *Performance management for cluster based web services*. Hawthorne: IBM TJ Watson Research Center.

Sanjay, S., & Wee, K. (2004). *Web data management*. New York: Springer.
Scheduling, A. E. J. (2010). A strategic pathway for improved data warehouse/business intelligence performance. Advanced System Concepts, Inc., http://whitepapers.technologyevaluation.com/view_document/21262/job-scheduling-a-strategicpathway-for-improved-data-warehouse-business-intelligence-performance.html. Accessed Feb 2011.
Spil, T., Stegwee, R., & Teitink, C. (2002). *Business intelligence in healthcare organizations*. Proceedings of the 35th Hawaii International Conference on System Sciences. Hawaii: Computer Society.
TDWI. (2010). TDWI survey 2010. http://www.tdwi.org. Accessed 02 Feb 2011.
Vaughan-Nichols, S. (2001). Web services: Beyond the hype. *IEEE Computer, 35*, 18–21.
Vaughan-Nichols, S. (2002). Web services: Beyond the hype. *IEEE Computer, 35*, 18–21.
Wickramasinghe, N., & Goldberg, S. (2007). Adaptive mapping to realization methodology (AMR) to facilitate mobile initiatives in healthcare. *International Journal of Mobile Communications, 5*(3), 300–318.
Wickramasinghe, N., & S. Goldberg. (2009). The S'ANT approach to facilitate a superior chronic disease self-management model. *IJANTTI, 1*(4), 21–34.
Wickramasinghe, N., Bali, R. K., & Schaffer, J. L. (2008a). The healthcare intelligence continuum: Key model for enabling KM initiatives and realising the full potential of SMT in healthcare delivery. *Biomedical Engineering and Technology, 1*(4), 415–426.
Wickramasinghe, N., Geisler, E., & Schaffer, J. L. (2008b). Realising the value proposition for healthcare by incorporating KM strategies and data mining techniques with the use of information and communication technologies. *International Journal of Healthcare Technology and Management, 7*(3/4), 303–318.
Yin, R. K. (1994). *Case study research: Design and methods* (2nd ed.). Thousand Oaks: Sage.

Part IV
Various Global Initiatives

Chapter 18
The Possibilities Are Only Limited by Our Imaginations

Nilmini Wickramasinghe

Abstract Moore's law describes a long-term trend in the history of computing hardware (Wikipedia 2011). Specifically, it discusses the fact that the number of transistors that can be placed inexpensively on an integrated circuit doubles approximately every 2 years and that this trend has continued for more than half a century and is expected to continue until at least 2015 or 2020. In the last few years, let alone decades, we have seen a huge increase in the variety, style, type and functionality of technology solutions permeate all areas of our environment. Hence, we should not be surprised at the possible technology solutions that are waiting just around the corner; truly our imaginations are the only limitations to the possible solutions. An important question then becomes what does this mean for healthcare organisations and healthcare delivery globally? How choices should be made between the different solutions and options. These questions are not easy and to help them address this final section of the book serves to provide a miscellany of chapters that discuss important aspects regarding developments and possibilities in the area of pervasive technologies and knowledge management in healthcare contexts.

18.1 Introduction

Moore's law describes a long-term trend in the history of computing hardware (Wikipedia 2011). Specifically, it discusses the fact that the number of transistors that can be placed inexpensively on an integrated circuit doubles approximately every 2 years and that this trend has continued for more than half a century and is expected to continue until at least 2015 or 2020. In the last few years, let alone decades, we have seen a huge increase in the variety, style, type and functionality of technology solutions permeate all areas of our environment. Hence, we should not be surprised at the possible technology solutions that are waiting just around the corner; truly our imaginations are the only limitations to the possible solutions. An important question then becomes what does this mean for healthcare organisations and healthcare delivery globally? How choices should be made between the different solutions and

N. Wickramasinghe (✉)
Epworth Chair Health Information Management, School of Business
Information Technology and Logistics,
RMIT University, 3001 Melbourne VIC, Australia
e-mail: nilmini.wickramasinghe@rmit.edu.au

R. K. Bali et al. (eds.), *Pervasive Health Knowledge Management*,
Healthcare Delivery in the Information Age,
DOI 10.1007/978-1-4614-4514-2_18,

options. These questions are not easy and to help them address this final section of the book serves to provide a miscellany of chapters that discuss important aspects regarding developments and possibilities in the area of pervasive technologies and knowledge management in healthcare contexts.

18.2 Chapters in this Section

Chapter 19 "Online Health Information For Chronic Disease: Diabetes" N. Hassan, K. Win and P. Hyland discusses the possibilities of having healthcare information online to facilitate better patient care in the context of diabetes.

Chapter 20 "Development of an Internet-Based Chronic Disease Self-Management System" A. Sunyaev and D. Chornyi discusses the role of Internet-based solutions for supporting and enabling self-management for patients suffering from chronic diseases.

Chapter 21 "Enablers of Implementing Knowledge Management Systems for Better Organisational Outcomes: An Indian Study" R. Gururajan and H. Tsai discusses findings from India, one of the emerging economies of today that is also growing with regard to IT use and mobile phone penetration.

Chapter 22 "Expectations, Usability and Job Satisfaction, as Determinants for the Perceived Benefits for the Use of Wireless Technology in Healthcare" A. Baig et al. presents findings from a study that examines physicians perspectives on the potential and perceived benefits of pervasive solutions to support healthcare delivery.

Chapter 23 "Web 2.0 Panacea or Placebo for Superior Healthcare Delivery" N. Wickramasinghe, B. Davey and A. Tatnall provides a discussion of the role of Web 2.0 and some of the possibilities it affords to healthcare delivery.

Chapter 24 "e-Health Readiness assessment from HER Perspective" J. Li, discusses the issue of readiness.

Chapter 25 "Identifying the Taiwanese Electronic Health Record Systems Evaluation Framework and Instrument by Implementing the Modified Delphi Method" S. Yu, K. Win and T. Chung. This is the final chapter in this section and provides an example from Taiwan of how to develop an appropriate evaluation system.

References

http://en.wikipedia.org/wiki/Moore's_law.

Chapter 19
Online Health Information for Chronic Disease: Diabetes

Naffisah Mohd Hassan, Khin Than Win and Peter Hyland

Abstract The focus of healthcare has changed from healthcare provider paternalistic approach to consumer-focused approach. The aim of this study is to implement an online health information site for patient education of Diabetes. To achieve this, design criteria for effective patient education were considered and diabetes patients' information site was implemented, which includes patient information access, diabetes challenge, administrator module, and the scheduler module. Implementing patients' access for their health information with providing patients tailored health information according to their needs to enhance patient education is important. This project contributes vastly in consumer health informatics as it develops the system that will enhance consumer involvement in their own healthcare.

Keywords Diabetes · Chronic disease · Chronic disease management · Online patient education · Online health information

19.1 Introduction

The American Academy of Family Physicians defines patient education as the process of influencing patient behavior and producing changes in knowledge, attitudes, and skills needed to maintain or improve health. Patient education can also be described as passing on knowledge that will bring benefit to the patients (Andrews 2007). Encyclopedia of Nursing and Allied Health (2002) defines Patient education involves helping patients become better informed about their condition, medical procedures, and choices they have regarding treatment. The National Standards for Diabetes Self-Management Education defines patient education as "an exchange of knowledge, tools, and practices that will address the client's ... needs" (Ellis et al. 2004).

N. M. Hassan (✉) · K. T. Win · P. Hyland
School of Information Systems and Technology,
University of Wollongong, Notrhfields Avenue, 2500 Wollongong NSW, Australia
e-mail: nmh876@uowmail.edu.au

K. T. Win
e-mail: win@uow.edu.au

P. Hyland
e-mail: phyland@uow.edu.au

R. K. Bali et al. (eds.), *Pervasive Health Knowledge Management*,
Healthcare Delivery in the Information Age,
DOI 10.1007/978-1-4614-4514-2_19,

Purposefully, this definition is nonspecific and inclusive, encouraging educational processes that are adaptable and individualized. Patient education is very important for all individuals especially those who suffer chronic disease, e.g., Diabetes mellitus (DeLeo et al. 2002; Timpka et al. 2008). These patients tend to engage emotionally (Cousineau and Domar 2007; Holley 2007) with their disease and are always keen to learn something new about their disease, compared to those without a chronic disease. Educating and supporting patients in managing their daily care and routine is crucial to achieve the treatment goals (Thakurdesai et al. 2004). There are several ways to educate a patient and mostly it is done by healthcare workers (Sciamanna et al. 2004) like doctors and nurses. However, many patients like to gather health information elsewhere, for example, via the Web.

19.2 The Concept of Online Health Information

It is noted that reliability, credibility, accessibility, and readability of information are main concerns from consumers for health information websites (Mitchell et al. 2004). Several researchers have identified evaluation tools for quality of health information online. It was noted that the Health on the Net (HON) Foundation code of principles are widely used from many health information websites to demonstrate the credibility of their site. HON code of principles include following attributes: authoritive, complementarity, privacy, attribution, justifiability, transparency, financial disclosure, and advertising policy (HON code). Health Summit Working Group (HSWG) also has established evaluation criteria for health information site, which includes credibility, content, disclosure, links, design, interactivity, and caveats (Thakurdesai et al. 2004). Online health information is used to fill an information void, which can enhance coping and self-efficacy, affect health-related decisions and behavior of users and their friends and family, and is often discussed with healthcare providers (Cline and Haynes 2001).

A variety of mediums exist through which individuals can access health information online. These include websites, listservs, online support groups, chat rooms, instant messaging, and email. More than 70,000 websites contain health information (Grandinetti 2000) and the number of health websites is rapidly increasing (Nielsen//NetRatings 2002). In addition to website utilization and Internet consultation with medical professionals, online support communities have been identified as one of the primary methods of online health information seeking for both consumers and members of their social networks (Cline and Haynes 2001). In this chapter, two methods of online health information that is Online Patient Education and online patient information system will be covered.

People have become more informed as a result of online health information and, for patients with a chronic illness, the Web allows them to access information to better manage their condition (Hill and Weinert 2004). One concern that is widely expressed about online health information is that patients can freely access information about their disease from either reliable or unreliable sources (Runge et al. 2006; Washington et al. 2008) and can easily mislead readers due to several factors, especially the existence of outdated and inaccurate information (Washington et al. 2008), coming from invalid sources (Bull et al. 2005; Kerr et al. 2006). Doctors are concerned about their patients who seek medical information through the Web, which they have found can leave their patients more confused (Thakurdesai et al. 2004). The doctors often need to set the facts straight again so that it will not interfere with the patient's treatment goal. Despite this drawback, it cannot be denied that there are benefits of having Online Patient Education for those who suffer with chronic disease. The drawbacks can be reduced by help from the patient's doctor who can show the most accurate information for the patients to learn about their disease (Kim et al. 2004), thus reducing the risk of misleading information and wasting patients' time reading unnecessary material.

19.2.1 Patient Health Education

Patients acquire information about their condition in a variety of ways: by discussing their condition with health professionals; by reading written materials or watching films made available in hospitals or doctors' offices; through specific healthcare organizations, such as the American Cancer Association; and through drug advertisements on television and in popular magazines. With the explosion of information on the World Wide Web, patients can access a wide range of medical information from professional medical journals to online support and chat groups with a health focus.

Most common way of patient's education is face-to-face; however, in many circumstances patients have expressed inadequacy of patient education in face-to-face communication (Koivunen et al. 2008). These could be related to staff workload, communication skills (Koivunen et al. 2008), and presenting a lot of information to patient in a short period of time (Thakurdesai et al. 2004). When patients understand their disease status, complications and their management, they would be more involved in their healthcare and obtain better health outcome as it would create increasing patient knowledge and experience (Mollaoğlu and Beyazit 2009). Computer-assisted education will aid patients' education as patients would visualize the importance of their disease management. Effective patients education would help to reduce diabetes complications, improve health service utilization and reduce healthcare costs, improve quality of life, and reduce psychological problems (Duke et al. 2009a). Providing tailored information to patients will assist in patient education as patients would not need to browse through all information, which they might encounter on a nontailored website. It is well documented that users of websites are swamped by the vast amount of material available on the Web (Tang and Newcomb 2004). Therefore, it is important to individualize information according to patient's needs.

19.2.2 Online Patient Education

Nowadays, with one click on the Web, patients can get millions of "hits" on the disease that they need to research. The Web has become a valuable resource for people seeking health information; however, the quality of this information has the potential to critically affect health outcomes for many users (Boyer et al. 1998). The high usage of Web search for health information has led to much research about the benefits and problems of web-based information for Online Patient Education. According to a survey done by Fox et al. (2007) on behalf of Pew Internet, about a fifth of American adults say that a disability, handicap, or chronic disease keeps them from participating fully in work, school, housework, or other activities. Only about 50 % of patients with a disability or chronic disease use the Web at all, compared to 74 % of people who do not have a chronic condition. Of those patients with a chronic condition who do use the Internet, 86 % have used it for information about at least one of 17 health topics, compared with 79 % of Internet users with no chronic condition. This has led to the new phenomenon, "Online Patient Education (OPE)," which is still poorly understood.

Online Patient Education refers to online material that is specifically tailored to the needs of patients who suffered from a specific disease (Casebeer et al. 2002). However, online health information varies significantly in quality and some of it might not be suitable for the needs of a patient with a specific disease. A patient may have to read all the available material in order to find the right information about his/her disease, which can be overwhelming and result in information overload. Although online health information can help patient education, it does not always provide interactivity of information exchange for the patient regarding his/her disease.

It is noted that reliability, credibility, accessibility, and readability of information are main concerns from consumers for health information websites (Mitchell et al. 2004). Several researchers have identified evaluation tools for quality of health information online. It was noted that the HON Foundation code of principles are widely used from many health information websites to demonstrate the credibility of their site. HON code of principles include following attributes: authoritive, complementarity, privacy, attribution, justifiability, transparency, financial disclosure, and advertising policy (HON code). HSWG also has established evaluation criteria for health information site, which includes credibility, content, disclosure, links, design, interactivity, and caveats (Thakurdesai et al. 2004).

19.2.3 Benefits of Online Patient Education

By reviewing 47 sources of literature review including journals articles, a set of benefits were found. The most frequently cited benefits in the literature are described below and shown on the horizontal axis of Table 19.1 and Fig. 19.1, which further breaks the OPE benefits into two major themes.

19.2.3.1 Theme 1: Improved Health Outcomes

Online Patient Education aims to improve health literacy, which is one of the most important elements in improving health outcomes (Nutbeam 2000), which include

Table 19.1 Benefits of online patient education for chronic disease (Hassan et al. 2011)

Chronic disease	Advantages of online patient education											
	Improved health outcomes	Improved patient emotional state and satisfaction	Improved health education and knowledge acquisition	Adherence to treatment	Improved self-care behavior and self-care management	Improved social support	Increased patient confidence towards treatment	Time and cost effectiveness	Easy access educational material	Improved patient awareness	Reduced hospitalizations	Improved quality of interaction with physician
Chronic asthma (3)	√		√	√	√			√			√	√
Cancer (5)	√	√	√	√		√	√					
Chronic bowel disease (2)		√	√	√	√			√	√			
Diabetes mellitus (6)	√		√	√	√	√		√				√
Cardiovascular disease (3)	√	√	√	√	√		√	√			√	√
Chronic kidney disease (2)	√				√							
Epilepsy and seizures (2)	√	√	√		√	√						
Obesity (4)	√	√	√		√	√		√		√		√
Lower back pain (2)		√		√	√							
Anxiety, depression, and mental illness (3)	√	√	√	√			√		√	√		√
Others chronic diseases (17)	√	√	√		√		√	√	√	√	√	√
Total paper	9	8	9	7	9	4	4	6	3	3	3	6

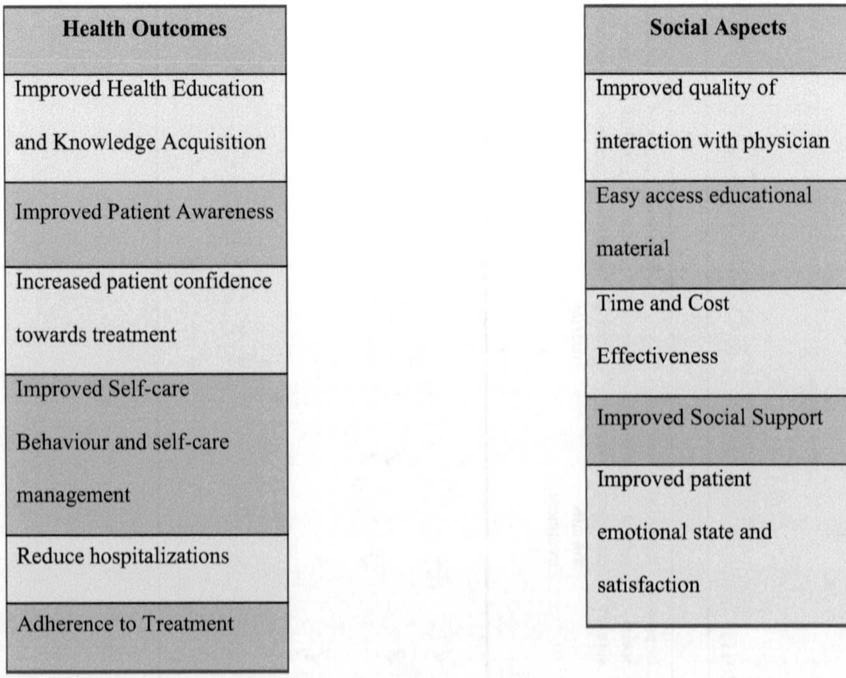

Fig. 19.1 Benefits according to themes

reduced morbidity, reduced disability, and avoidable morbidity. Several researchers found that patients who received effective Online Patient Education regarding their disease tended to improve their health outcomes (Ellis et al. 2004; Singh et al. 2005). Positive effects were found among patients undergoing Online Patient Education on diabetes (Ellis et al. 2004). Studies that used a randomized controlled trial showed that diabetes Online Patient Education improved glycemic control among adults with diabetes (Ellis et al. 2004; Singh et al. 2005). Another 13 studies concluded that Online Patient Education does improve overall patient health outcomes. Continuing care and Online Patient Education help maintain good control of the disease and prevent complications. Online Patient Education can continually provide "active health" since it can deliver educational messages to patients at the time of their choice without waiting to be informed. In the United States, those who suffer from chronic illnesses make up 70 % of medical costs and 80 % of deaths; improving the way their conditions are managed holds great potential for cost savings and reduced mortality rates (Ball and Lillis 2001). Many randomized controlled trials have shown great potential for the Internet to deliver effective weight loss programs (Norman et al. 2007; Booth et al. 2008; Robinson-O'Brien et al. 2009). However, Online Patient Education is not always effective, e.g., patients suffering from obesity show no improvement in health outcomes due to Online Patient Education (van Dam et al. 2005).

Improved Health Education and Knowledge Acquisition

Earlier reviews have reported that Online Patient Education had positive effects on patient knowledge and health education (Ellis et al. 2004). About 15 studies that used randomized controlled trials, three studies that used quasi-experimental methods, and three studies that used cross-sectional methods found that Online Patient Education offered better health education and improved patient's knowledge of their disease. The right education materials produce well-educated and knowledgeable patients, which can lead to better health outcomes. Homer (2000) found that in a study that involved two groups of asthmatic patients, the computer-based and online educational program group had significantly better results than the group receiving no computerized education. Reliable online patient information websites offer up-to-date information and cutting edge knowledge for various diseases (Ybarra and Suman 2006). It helps patients to understand what they are dealing with and to reduce the possibility of harmful or ineffective self-treatment.

Improved Patient Awareness

A great numbers of studies found that Online Patient Education can help in increasing patients' awareness of their disease (Gomella 2000; Jones et al. 2001; Mangunkusumo et al. 2007; Cothran et al. 2009; O'Connor et al. 2009). According to (Ball and Lillis 2001), helping patients get the right educational material and information about their disease from the Web improved patients' awareness of their disease. Chronic diseases, like obesity, anxiety, and depression, show the highest level of improvement in patient awareness after involvement with Online Patient Education. By reading the tailored information, patients tend to be more aware of their medical condition and this can contribute to the positive benefits in improving their health.

Increased Patient Confidence Towards Treatment

Patients who are newly diagnosed with cancer perceive the Web as a powerful tool, both for acquiring information and for enhancing confidence to make informed decisions (Bass et al. 2006). Another study showed that persons with coronary artery disease reported an increased confidence in their choice of treatment after viewing an interactive educational video online (Nahm et al. 2008). Two studies by Gustafson et al. (2002) reported that computer-based and Online Patient Education improved comfort with care and confidence in the medical doctor. Online Patient Education makes it easier for healthcare workers to instill confidence in patients about the treatments that were designed for them. Patients with high levels of confidence towards their treatment also show positive attitudes towards treatment (Potts and Wyatt 2002).

Improved Self-Care Behaviors and Management

According to the American Diabetes Associations, diabetes patients need to be educated in nutrition, physical activity, self-monitoring of blood and urine, and taking medications. Educating patients in managing their daily life with a chronic disease, such as heart disease or diabetes, is an important goal of therapy today (Allen et al. 2007), and good self-care behavior is an essential clinical outcome. The aims of chronic disease Online Patient Education are to make patients knowledgeable about the disease, build positive attitudes, and make them active partners in therapy or treatment. This can be achieved through a holistic approach to the patient augmented by Online Patient Education. In Australia, more than eight diabetes websites regarding diabetes are available to the general public and serve to educate diabetes patients with state-of-the-art knowledge in order to promote self-care behavior among patients. Through the Web, those with chronic disease are learning how to manage their conditions correctly. For instance, after seeking information from disease-specific websites, one-third of chronic disease sufferers reported taking their medications more regularly (Ball and Lillis 2001).

Reduced Hospitalization

Kashem et al. (2008) found that frequent monitoring and communication through a secure Internet communication system reduced hospitalizations and emergency department visits in a cohort of patients with advanced HF (Kashem et al. 2008). By having the right information in the time of emergency or when patients in need of medical information regarding their disease can help reducing unnecessary visit to the hospital. Goessens et al. (2008) found that asthmatics in both groups of his experiment needed little hospital and emergency department services, only four patients, one twice, visited the emergency department. Asthma, cardiovascular, and diabetes patients show lower rates of hospitalization after undergoing Online Patient Education (Malasanos et al. 2005; Heart Failure Society Of 2006; Bussey-Smith and Rossen 2007). This was shown that by having the right information online patients become more alert to their medical condition and this can lead to decreasing numbers of emergency cases and hospitalization.

Adherence to Treatment

It is believed that a patient, who is educated about his or her health-related problem, will have better adherence to treatment (Thakurdesai et al. 2004; Mosca et al. 2005; Dolor et al. 2009). This can be achieved if the patient has access to tailored online patient educational material at anytime and anywhere. From the patients' point of view, by knowing what they are going to go through helps them to prepare themselves for their treatment. Without knowing what they are going to face, patients might be reluctant to cooperate in their treatment, which could make it more difficult to cure or improve their medical conditions. Nonetheless, some chronic disease patients refused to undergo treatment after finding out what they were going to face during treatment (Viele 2003). For example, a number of cancer patients refused treatment after viewing an online multimedia video explaining about their treatment.

19.2.3.2 Theme 2: Social Aspects

Online Patient Education can also be viewed as improving social aspect among patients. This can be shown with a set of benefits that can be categorized into the same theme such as improved quality interaction between patient and physician, easy-access educational material, time and cost effectiveness for patients and healthcare providers, improved social support, and improved patient emotional state and satisfaction.

Improved Quality of Interaction with Physician

A number of studies agreed that Online Patient Education can improve the quality of communication between patients and their doctors (Jeste et al. 2008; Leveille et al. 2009; Street et al. 2009). Patients who use Online Patient Education tend to have quality interactions and communications with their doctors. The knowledge that the patients get from health websites, in turn, helps them to direct the right question to their doctors. And, this helps to reduce unnecessary and meaningless discussion between doctors and patients.

Easy-Access Educational Material

Casebeer et al. (2002) say that Online Patient Education material can be easily accessed by patients at any time and from anywhere. The patients can access educational material using their own time arrangement and can do it repeatedly to improve their understanding of the education material.

Time and Cost Effectiveness

Using OHI proved to be more time and cost effective for both patients and healthcare provider. Online Patient Education has been shown (Levin-Zamir and Peterburg 2001) to be more cost effective as it reduces patients' expenses to travel to the hospital or medical center. It also saves patients' time by reducing travel time, especially during peak time (Azar and Gabbay 2009). As for the healthcare, the Web offers new, inexpensive, and rapid methods to provide and enhance patients' asthma education (Cabana and Le 2005). In the United States, those who suffer from chronic illnesses make up 70 % of medical costs and 80 % of deaths; improving the way their conditions are managed holds great potential for cost savings and reduced mortality rates (Ball and Lillis 2001).

Improved Social Support

Online Patient Education has been shown to improve social support among patients who suffer from chronic diseases. Two studies by Gustafson et al. (2002) reported that computer-based and Online Patient Education increased social support. Full support from support groups or others patients who share the same disease helps patients to be more comfortable to deal with their disease. Social support is very important for chronic disease patients because they need all the support they can get to cope with their illness (Weinert et al. 2008).

Improved Patient Emotional State and Satisfaction

Online Patient Education can improve a patient's emotional state and satisfaction. Wilken (1994) observed that learning is a way for patients to gain some control of the situation and, thus, decrease anxiety. Eleven studies that used randomized controlled groups and three studies that used cross-sectional surveys report that Online Patient Education offered patients a better emotional state and improved their satisfaction. Through increased knowledge, patients develop a healthier lifestyle. Usually, patients with chronic diabetes suffer depression and anxiety as they are worried about their medical condition. Educating the patients can help to stabilize their emotional state but from the patients' perspective, diabetes education consists of an overwhelming amount of new information, which is often presented on only one occasion. The patients want their education to be a continuous process (Thakurdesai et al. 2004), which means patients preferred to undergo a continuous education regarding their disease and the Web seems to be an effective medium in this respect because patients can access information anytime, anywhere, over and over again.

Patients who use the Web spend less time asking about things that are unrelated or untrue about their disease and also less time is needed to explain about misleading medical recommendations and theories that frustrate both patients and their physicians. By using Online Patient Education, time spent with patients discussing treatment can be saved, compared to those seeking information solely from their physician. This leads to higher patient satisfaction (Abbott 1998; Ullrich and Vaccaro 2002) because patients usually value their physician's advice and guidance. Patients who get reliable medical information are more likely to make better use of the healthcare system because they know when they are in need or not in need of medical treatment. Well-educated patients make better patients because they tend to be more realistic and they also become more proactive in managing their disease (Ullrich and Vaccaro 2002).

19.2.3.3 Other Benefits and Advantages

Online Patient Education offers benefits for almost all parties. For example, Thakurdesai et al. (2003) found that online diabetes education can accelerate the education process for those who suffer chronic disease and have little time to waste. Online Patient Education offers significant benefits to those who suffer from chronic disease if the development process follows the right design. The right design will contribute to better quality of health websites, health education, and successful implementation of health information website

It is noteworthy that almost all chronic diseases use Online Patient Education to educate patients. There is strong support in the literature for the existence of benefits such as improved health outcomes, improved health education and knowledge acquisition, improved self-care behavior and management, and also improved patient emotional state and satisfaction. Other benefits are also reported less frequently, so it is difficult to tell if these are applicable only to specific chronic diseases. OPE is not without its critics as we shall see in the next section while discussing the limitations of OPE.

19.2.4 Disadvantages and Limitations of Online Patient Education

However, one cannot deny that there are a few disadvantages of using Online Patient Education compared with other types of patient education. For example, videos were more effective than the Web in educating participants about relevant health issues (Ahern et al. 2006; Booth et al. 2008). A few researchers even argue that by having Online Patient Education, the patient is less active physically especially for patients with obesity. Saperstein et al. (2007) admit that sitting at the computer encourages inactivity, but they observe that patients reading text-based information in brochures or sitting in a support group are also inactive. Thus, using the Web is no more inactive than traditional methods of patient education. Conversely, many randomized controlled trials have shown great potential for the Internet to deliver effective weight loss programs (Norman et al. 2007; Booth et al. 2008; Robinson-O'Brien et al. 2009), so the disadvantages described above may not apply.

Another major concern about Online Patient Education was the high variability in content quality. Misleading or inaccurate information on the Web can confuse patients but quality monitored Online Patient Education can reduce this issue. If doctors can help in leading patients to the right online material, patients will more exposed to better quality material from the Web, which can reduce the risk of misleading and inaccurate information. There are a few studies, which reflect concern on the accessibility of Online Patient Education material. According to Rezailashkajani et al. (2008), there is an increasing trend of Web use in Iran, however, not all chronic bowel disease patients have access to the Web, and many patients may not even have basic computer skills to use the Web. These can decrease efficiency of an Online Patient Education system or restrict its use to more affluent groups of the society.

Barriers to using Online Patient Education include low patient computer skills, unwillingness to use the technology, and poor architectural and technical design of the OPE site. Without appropriate information technology skills, patients cannot connect to the Internet let alone access education material from the Web. Therefore,

Online Patient Education might not be a universal type of patient education due to these limitations. Other concerns on using Online Patient Education are not being cost effective due to rapid changes in technology and ethical and security issues of using the Web. Cabana and Le (2005) state that a comprehensive survey of Asthma websites by Croft and Peterson (2002) noted that Online Patient Education material makes little innovative use of technology as compared to other types of patient education. However, this finding cannot be generalized to all Online Patient Education because the survey only focused on websites of asthma according to other researchers, Online Patient Education is one of the effective methods of patient education (Elliott et al. 2007; Booth et al. 2008).

19.2.5 Reflection

Online Patient Education is worth exploring and researchers were encouraged to continuing research on these fascinating issues. Due to the fact that Online Patient Education offers greater benefits, it is worth developing online patient information systems in order to help the healthcare in educating patients with chronic diseases especially diabetes. Therefore, it is important for the health organization to take several considerations before designing OPE site for chronic disease patients.

19.2.6 Design Consideration

It is very important for any Online Patient Education site to follow a specific set of criteria to make sure that patients get benefits from using the site. Published literatures were reviewed and identified for design consideration for Online Patient Education.

19.2.6.1 Patient-Tailored Information

To ensure that information in the OPE site is beneficial to users, tailored information is needed in order to cater to the need of the patient itself. For example, according to (Griffiths and Christensen 2007), consideration should be given to developing programs tailored to rural users. O'Connor et al. (2009) also agreed by highlighting in their finding the importance of tailoring health communication messages to individual characteristics in order to maximize OPE effectiveness. Schulz et al. (2009) believe that any failure to address consumers' needs at one of the three levels of health literacy can become an obstacle for the development of modification of health-related behaviors and self-management procedures. For the above reason, they designed a system called ONESELF following main asset: a policy of tailoring information resulting, in the outcome, in the selection of technological options that favor the growth of declarative and procedural knowledge and support its integration towards a behavioral response (Schulz et al. 2009). It is clear that tailored information is most important consideration that needs to be taken seriously when designing an OPE.

19.2.6.2 Interactivity

Any well-designed website contains some sort of interactivity function. This is supported by Schulz et al. (2004) when they said that a well-designed OPE allows users to ask for further information on declarative and procedural levels, as well as discuss any information in synchronous (via the chat room) or asynchronous (via the forum) ways. Leveille et al. (2009) used interventions that relied on tip sheets and downloadable visit preparation forms, in addition to motivational messages from the e-coach, to help patients in educating them about their disease. In his research, the intervention included 22 weeks of participation in an online, asynchronous, peer-led support group, and health teaching units. Unlike traditional patient handouts, the OPE should offer patients interactivity and engagement, which can enhance their learning and understanding. Therefore, it can be concluded that interactivity is one of the important consideration in designing OPE.

19.2.6.3 User-Friendly Design

Patients usually have several medical issues such as low hearing, poor eyesight, and sometimes disability to use their hand due to swelling or gangrenes, especially diabetes patients. Therefore, it is important for an OPE site to allow users to adjust several visibility functions of the screen in order to enhance the readability and usability of the site (Ream et al. 2009). Having several links related to their disease will also add to the usability of an OPE site. For example, patients can keep track of their sugar level if they can access the lab results via the Diabetes OPE site.

19.2.6.4 Offer Other Internet Activities

According to Rice (2006), Patient is more pleased if the OPE offer other Internet activities such as email, weather check, and other interesting stuff. For example, Hill et al. (2006) found that the e-mail function ("Mailbox") gave the women private access to each other and to the research team. This will enhance the usage of OPE among patients, which can added net benefit of using OPE effectively.

19.2.6.5 Accessibility

OPE should be available for patients at anytime and anywhere. In order to have that, sites need to be easily searched form various search engine such as Google, Crawlers, or other popular engines (Cothran et al. 2009).

19.2.6.6 Interpretability

Most individuals only understand a few medical terms as compared to those who are directly involved in healthcare business (Rezailashkajani et al. 2008). Therefore, by providing a set of glossary, explaining specific medical terms used in the OPE site, will ensure that the patients who use the site will have better understanding of the information related to the OPE site.

19.2.6.7 Content

In order to ensure that patients get the right information related to their disease, all information on the site must follow specific guidelines according to the type of diseases. For example, Schulz et al. (2009) designed a section of the website—called "Library" (Biblioteca)—where they initially inserted a series of texts selected by the health professionals involved in the project. In particular, they reached a consensus on some key information on low back pain that they normally delivered to patients during face-to-face interaction, e.g., the nature of back pain, its etiology, the vertebral column and the importance of postures and physical activity, and this content strictly follows certified health professional's advice. Healthcare professionals and institutions need to ensure that the information provided in the context of Online Patient Education is not harmful, inaccurate, or misleading. (Bohacek et al. 2003).

19.2.6.8 Privacy

Privacy issues are also important even though all information displayed in an OPE site is for patient education purposes (Doupi and van der Lei 2005). Considerations regarding the patients' rights to privacy and confidentiality, as well as aspects of medical data ownership and use, should be taken care in any OPE site to avoid any issues. By enhancing the security of the OPE site, as well as patients' interest in their healthcare and usefulness of the system can be monitored and patients also can see their health information securely.

19.2.7 Patients' Change Factors: The Patient Motivation to Change

In order for the patients to achieve greater benefits from OPE, they need to be motivated in changing their lifestyles to healthier ways. HeartCare, a US Internet-based program for patients recovering from coronary artery bypass graft surgery, provides individual-tailored education, support, and ongoing patient–clinician communication. HeartCare was in part designed for patients who had attended a cardiac rehabilitation program to encourage continued patient lifestyle modification (Thomson and Micevski 2005).

A well-known theory in health promotion research and practice (Bunton et al. 2000), the transtheoretical model (TTM), has become one of the most dominant models used to explain and predict health behavior change. TTM proposed that people evolution is through five distinct stages of behavior change: precontemplation, contemplation, preparation, action, and maintenance. These stages describe how people move from being unaware, unwilling, or too discouraged to change, to considering the possibility of change, then to becoming committed and prepared to make the change, and finally taking action and sustaining the change in the long run (Liang et al. 2006). Willey et al. (2000) agreed that the TTM has been successfully applied in a wide range of health-related behaviors including: reduction of dietary fat consumption, smoking cessation, participation in mammography screening, adoption of exercise, sun protection, condom use, and diabetes self-management. As for Diabetes patient, medication persistency is very crucial and self-motivation to become healthier can be regarded as a long-term behavioral change.

In order for the patients to use OPE effectively, a well-designed Online Health Information System needs to be available for them to access at anytime and anywhere. Online Health Information Systems that provide access to patients' medical records or lab results, for example, can help patients to be engaged in changing their behavior and lifestyle. If patients can access their own medical information, patients become more motivated and determined to change and be consistent in improving their condition. Therefore, we develop online health information system specifically for Diabetes patients called Online Patient Information Systems (OPIS) as an example of tailored OPE for chronic disease patients.

19.3 Accessible Online Patient Information Systems

Several online patient information systems have been developed in the world to enhance patients' involvement in their own healthcare, such as a web-based self-monitoring system for people living with HIV/AIDS (Gómez et al. 2002), Structured Evaluated Personalized Support (STEPPS) for Burn care (Doupi and Lei 2005), POEM System (Lee et al. 2007), and Dias Net (Plougmann et al. 2001) for Diabetes. It has been noted that these systems enhance patient–provider communication, better healthcare outcome and patient empowerment, and effective patient education. It is also recommended that these sites should ensure patient empowerment, (Plougmann et al. 2001) include easily locatable information (Rea et al. 2008), link to related information (Rezailashkajani et al. 2008), and integrate with patient record (Doupi and Lei 2005) having reminders (Lee et al. 2007) and glossary (Rezailashkajani et al. 2008).

19.3.1 Patient Accessible Diabetes Information Systems

The development process involved understanding stakeholders' requirement of the system. It is important that healthcare providers are involved in the decision making process of the system implemented as the information provided will be patients' health information. Therefore, various stakeholders such as the Local Division of General Practice (LDGP), Diabetes Physician, General Practitioners, Exercise Physician, Diabetes Educator, and the technical staff from the LDGP were consulted to gather requirements of the system. Development team and the various stakeholders met fortnightly to implement the system proposed. Moreover, patient's opinions related to willingness to use online health information material was surveyed at the local community and 82.3 % of respondents believed that it would be beneficial for them to have their health information accessible. The design consideration was considered through understanding the requirements of online health information, criteria for effective patient education, stake holders' interviews, and user surveys.

Iterative development process was followed and evolutionary prototypes were developed and demonstrated to stakeholders and users regularly during the development process. The application-developed Online Patient Education is web-based, add-on module for the Diabetes Patients currently residing in the local community. However, Online Patient Education material will be available for anyone else as well.

19.3.1.1 Design Consideration

It is essential that the diabetes health information site for patients follows the established criteria to ensure maximum effectiveness for users. Published literatures were reviewed and identified design consideration for the website (Table 19.2). After analyzing previous patient education website, the following were considered for this project.

Content

To ensure the credibility of information, the information provided on the web follows the Diabetes Management Guidelines from the Royal Australian College of General Practitioner. Diabetes Management guidelines are a consolidated source of healthcare knowledge from best clinical practices and integrating guidelines into health records that would improve patients' health outcome. Using the standard management guideline will ensure the accuracy and completeness of information provided to users, which could ensure the information quality.

User-Friendly Design

As patients with Diabetes could include elderly or patients with poor eyesight, the users are allowed to adjust the font sizes on the screen. Link to site map is included and all the lab results, blood pressure, and Body Mass Index (BMI) are displayed both in text form and graphical displays. That will enhance the readability and understandability as users can visualize their results compared against the normal range or the targeted results.

Table 19.2 Examples of OPIS design consideration

Disease/condition	Study	Design consideration
Diabetes	Plougmann et al. (2001), Dias Net online patient diary	Reminder, better patient education, learning mode, prediction mode
	Thakurdesai et al. (2004), Evaluation of health information website	Follow HSWG criteria
Inflammatory bowel disease	Rezailashkajani et al. (2008), Persian web-based patient education system	Weblink, glossary, forum, communicate, exchange material
Breast cancer	Clayman et al. (2008), Interview providers and patients for developing patient education	Addressing patient information need, easy to understand patient information
Cardiovascular	Goessens et al. (2008), Internet-based coaching	A tailored treatment plan
Psychiatry	Koivunen et al. (2008), evaluates effect of IT use in psychiatric ward, $N=89$	Patient-centered tailored information, peered support for patient and counseling
Burn care	Doupi and Lei (2005), Design STEPPS	Integrate with electronic patient record, user friendliness, online material
HIV	DeGuzman and Ross (1999), interview results of HIV-related health professionals, $N=16$	Confidentiality, privacy, interactive counseling, multimedia, individualized, support group, interactivity

Interpretability

Medical terms in the site will be explained in the Glossary so that healthcare consumers will understand information related to diabetes.

Patient-Tailored Information

The information provided in the site will be according to patients needs. According to patients' information, they will lead to the relevant pages. Recommendations are tailored according to the diabetes guidelines.

Interactivity

Users can input data in diabetes challenge, weight management module, and eye and feet examination recommendations in patient's forum. Decision support systems related to weight loss management and examination are in place to deliver patient-tailored information. The system will send email reminders if users are involved in the diabetes challenge for regular activities.

Accessibility

To ensure the site can be easily searched from crawlers and web searches, metadata were included in every page. Site map is provided for users to navigate easily within the site. The site also allows information search for users.

Privacy

Every usage of system will be logged with the activity log. That will enhance security of the system as well as patients' interest in their healthcare and usefulness of the system can be monitored. Local diabetes patients will be able to see their health information securely. The privacy policy will be displayed on the homepage.

The site follows the HON code of principles and fulfils the HSWG evaluation criteria for health information website.

19.4 System Description

19.4.1 Project Scope

The system will allow diabetic patients whose records are in the system to have secured access to all their data. Other patients and public users will be able to participate in the diabetes challenge, which is a guided weight-loss system. Participants enter their height and weight over a user-defined period of time and the system.

19.4.2 Environment Scope

The application has been written using Java and its dynamic web pages technology, servlets and Java Server Pages (JSP). The servlet container used is Apache's Tomcat 5.5. The database used is Microsoft SQL Server 2000, because Microsoft SQL Server 2000 was used. The client-side pages are HTML with JavaScripts and Cascading Style Sheets (CSS). It is recommended that the site be viewed using Microsoft Internet Explorer 6 or higher.

19.4.3 Application Scope

19.4.3.1 Patient Module

This module allows only those diabetic patients who have an account in the system to view their diabetes-related test results. Patients can access their results of

HbA1c (Hemoglobin A1c), total Cholesterol, triglycerides, High-Density Lipoprotein (HDL), Low-Density Lipoprotein (LDL), Microalbuminuria, and blood pressure. These results are presented to patients both in text format and in the graphical presentation. Presenting the lab results in the graphical format allows patients to visualize their data more and allowed them to compare against the normal range, historical data, and recommended range for them. It also provides information regarding eyes and feet examination. Diabetes patients should attend regular check according to the diabetes guidelines. The system will inform them when they will need to have the next follow-up visit. Apart from telling the user how often they should go for their checkups, these sections include small JavaScript-based calculators so that users can enter related data and let the system calculate their check-up frequency for them.

19.4.3.2 Sign Up Module

This module takes care of all new users sign up and the information is stored separately from the patient health information database. The information includes email (primary key), password, password challenge question, first name, last name, date of birth, and gender.

19.4.3.3 Diabetes Challenge Module

The Lifestyle modifications play a significant role in the diabetes management. Patient will need to target their BMI to be in the healthy range. Lifestyle modifications such as exercise and diet modification will assist in reaching the target BMI. Therefore, motivating patients to be actively participating in the lifestyle modification is important. Moreover, if patients could see their pathology results, they would be more involved in their healthcare management as they could see the outcome of the lifestyle changes and the diabetic control.

Patients often felt that they are not the principal decision makers for their healthcare and healthcare providers arranged and decided their health plan (Lorence et al. 2005, p. 354). As the site will allow the patients to target their weight loss, it is empowering patients in their healthcare decision making and patients will be more active in participating.

The website allows visitors who have diabetes but are not registered there to attempt losing their weight. They can create an account from which a weight loss challenge can be managed by themselves to monitor their own progress, with options to update their weight at specific intervals. Users can then see for themselves how they are doing for the progress of their weight loss. Information is also provided to suggest ways for the user to continue improving their health by weight loss. If the consumers set the unrealistic goals, the site will inform them and suggest on targeting the appropriate weight loss range. Self-management support is integral to improving care, outcomes, collaborative care, and patient education (Bodenheimer et al. 2002) and the site assists these by having diabetes challenge module.

Information related to dietary advice and nutrition is displayed on the website in "Did you know" section and the Diabetes challenge module. They are displayed together with motivational messages randomly.

19.4.3.4 Administrator Module

The module allows management of the Challenger accounts, allows updating of Medical Guidelines. The Medical Guidelines are presented as a static set of values (which are stored by the system in an XML file) and the administrator can change the values and implement the changes system-wide, allows management of the Patient forum, "Did you know" entries, and site glossary section. The site glossary is an informative implementation. The administrator can add terms into the site glossary, where medical terms are provided with definitions to enhance consumer understandability. These terms are underlined with dotted lines on the site and definitions of the terms are presented when the user pass the mouse on the word.

It allows management of "Weight loss tips." Weight loss tips are randomly shown to the user in the Diabetes challenge module, this section will allow adding and maintaining of tips. Healthcare providers will need to monitor and control efficiently and conveniently. Hence, the control panel allows them to manage users and update the health guidelines for diabetes in general.

Links to other diabetes-related information such as Diabetes Australia and consumer health information website such as Better Health websites links will be provided and the administrator will be able to manipulate links easily.

19.4.3.5 Scheduler Module

The scheduler module is responsible for sending out reminder emails to the account holders and system maintenance, sending reminders to Challenge users to update their BMI, also check through the database and terminate challenges that are due for termination, the scheduler runs on Tomcat and is started up when the application starts up. It is programmed to run daily.

There will be a patient forum where they can login and post messages, which will be moderated by the administrator. This will enhance interactivity among patients and support. Secure email reminders will be sent to anyone participating in the Diabetes challenge.

19.5 Discussion

The system developed attempts to reach the patients and consumers through the Internet and assist in patient education and enhanced patients to be involved in their own healthcare. OPE is an effective strategy for presenting information and improving knowledge outcomes among patients. Health outcomes have improved significantly as a result of OPE. Patient emotional state and patient satisfaction are improved for persons with chronic disease. Social support can be provided effectively using online computer support groups. Patient confidence and adherence to treatment are also beneficial for patients who effectively use online patient education. Findings have shown that health education and knowledge acquisition can be improved through Online Patient Education with chronic disease. Aside from all the benefits of online patient education, one cannot ignore the importance of getting the right material for patient education in providing accurate health information to the public, especially those who suffer from chronic disease such as Diabetes. The system provides the users (Diabetes patients from the local community), a secured access to their personal health information. This promotes patients to review their health and lab results. Implementing patients' access for their health information and providing patients tailored health information according to their needs to enhance patient education is innovative. Although many health information systems are currently available in Australia, patient access to health record could not be seen in most places as online personal health record systems are not widely available in Australia.

Using diabetes management guideline as the source of information satisfies using the information according to the principle of evidence-based medicine. The diabetes challenge modules targeted the lifestyle modifications through weight loss challenges and dietary information, which also assist in reducing the alarming increase of obesity in the world, which has not been decreased by new treatment regimens (Noël and Pugh 2005). Having discussion forum in the site assists patients by having Internet-based support interventions and helping them in managing diabetes.

This project contributes towards effective diabetes healthcare management as it has assisted in patients' involvement in their healthcare. Diabetes challenge module motivates patients to be involved in active lifestyle management. Patients can decide their target and set goals according to their preferences and involved them in decision making processes in healthcare. The system promotes consumer involvement in healthcare, and empowered patients in their healthcare. The system will not replace the healthcare providers in patient care, but it will assist to have a better patient–provider relationship as patients will become active partners in their healthcare for diabetes management. The system will complement health education for patients as discussed in Sect. 19.2.1. This will strengthen the patient–provider relationship as patients will be more informed and have a proactive role in their healthcare.

19.6 Conclusion

This project contributes vastly in consumer health informatics as it develops the system that will enhance consumer involvement in their own healthcare. It considers the information quality of health websites, health education, and successful implementation of health information website through stakeholders' involvement. Future work will be to analyze improvement in health outcome for those involved in patient accessible diabetes information system.

References

Abbott, S. A. (1998). The benefits of patient education. *Gastroenterology Nursing, 21*(5), 207–209.

Ahern, D. K., Kreslake, J. M., & Phalen, J. M. (2006). What is eHealth (6): Perspectives on the evolution of eHealth research. *Journal of Medical Internet Research 8*(1), e4.

Allen, M., Iezzoni, L. I., Huang, A., Huang, L., & Leveille, S. G. (2007). *Internet-based coaching to improve patient-clinician communication in primary care.* AMIA, Annual Symposium Proceedings/AMIA Symposium, 861.

Andrews, G. (2007). ClimateGP—web based patient education. *Australian Family Physician, 36*(5), 371–372.

Azar, M., & Gabbay, R. (2009). Web-based management of diabetes through glucose uploads: Has the time come for telemedicine? *Diabetes Research and Clinical Practice, 83*(1), 9–17.

Ball, M. J., & Lillis, J. (2001). E-health: Transforming the physician/patient relationship. *International Journal of Medical Informatics, 61*(1), 1–10.

Bass, S. B., Ruzek, S. B., Gordon, T. F., Fleisher, L., McKeown-Conn, N., & Moore, D. (2006). Relationship of internet health information use with patient behavior and self-efficacy: Experiences of newly diagnosed cancer patients who contact the National Cancer Institute's Cancer Information Service. *Journal of Health Communication, 11*(2), 219–236.

Bodenheimer, T., Lorig, K., Holman, H., & Grumbach, K. (2002, November 20). Patient self-management of chronic disease in primary care. JAMA, *288*(19), 2469–2475.

Bohacek, L., Gomez, M., & Fish, J.S. (2003). An evaluation of internet sites for burn scar management. *Journal of Burn Care and Rehabilitation, 24*(4), 246–251.

Booth, A. O., Nowson, C. A., & Matters, H. (2008). Evaluation of an interactive, internet-based weight loss program: A pilot study. *Health Education Research, 23*(3), 371–381.

Boyer, C., Selby, M., Scherrer, J. R., & Appel, R. D. (1998). The health on the net code of conduct for medical and health Websites. *Computers in Biology and Medicine, 28*(5), 603–610.

Bull, S. S., Gaglio, B., McKay, H. G., & Glasgow, R. E. (2005). Harnessing the potential of the internet to promote chronic illness self-management: Diabetes as an example of how well we are doing. *Chronic Illness, 1*(2), 143–155.

Bunton, R., Baldwin, S., Flynn, D., & Whitelaw, S. (2000). The 'stages of change' model in health promotion: Science and ideology. *Critical Public Health, 10*(1), 55–71.

Bussey-Smith, K. L., & Rossen, R. D. (2007). A systematic review of randomized control trials evaluating the effectiveness of interactive computerized asthma patient education programs. *Annals of Allergy, Asthma & Immunology, 98*(6), 507–516.

Cabana, M. D., & Le, T. T. (2005). Challenges in asthma patient education. *Journal of Allergy and Clinical Immunology, 115*(6), 1225–1227.

Casebeer, L., Allison, J., & Spettell, C. M. (2002). Designing tailored Web-based instruction to improve practicing physicians' chlamydial screening rates. *Academic Medicine, 77*(9), 929.

Clayman, M.L., Boberg, E. W., & Makoul, G. (2008). The use of patient and provider perspectives to develop a patient-oriented website for women diagnosed with breast cancer. *Patient Education and Counseling, 72*, 429–435.

Cline, R. J. W., & Haynes, K. M. (2001). Consumer health information seeking on the Internet: The state of the art. *Health Education Research, 16*(6), 671–692.

Cothran, M. M., Sereika, S. M., Fischl, A. R., Schmitt, P. L., & Charron-Prochownik, D. (2009). A self-instructional program for diabetes educators on preconception counseling for women with diabetes. *Diabetes Educator, 35*(4), 652–656.

Cousineau, T. M., & Domar, A. D. (2007). Psychological impact of infertility. *Best Practice & Research Clinical Obstetrics & Gynaecology, 21*(2), 293–308.

Croft, D. R., & Peterson, M. W. (2002). An evaluation of the quality and contents of asthma education on the world wide web. *Chest, 121*(4), 1301–1307.

Dam, H. A. van, Horst, F. G. van der, Knoops, L., Ryckman, R. M., Crebolder, H. F. J. M., & Borne, B. H. W. van den. (2005). Social support in diabetes: A systematic review of controlled intervention studies. *Patient Education and Counseling, 59*(1), 1–12.

DeGuzman M. A., & Ross, M. (1999). Assessing the application of HIV and AIDS related education and counselling on the internet. *Patient Education and Counseling, 36,* 209–228.

DeLeo, G., Krishna, S., Balas, E. A., Maglaveras, N., Boren, S. A., Beltrame, F., & Fato, M. (2002). *WEB-WAP based telecare.* Proceedings/AMIA, Annual Symposium, 200–204.

Dolor, R. J., Yancy, W. S. Jr., Owen, W. F., Matchar, D. B., Samsa, G. P., Pollak, K. I., Lin, P.-H., Ard, J. D., Prempeh, M., McGuire, H. L., Batch, B. C., Fan, W., & Svetkey, L. P. (2009). Hypertension Improvement Project (HIP): Study protocol and implementation challenges. *Trials, [Electronic Resource] 10,* 13.

Doupi, P., & Lei, J. van der. (2005). Design and implementation considerations for a personalized patient education system in burn care. *International Journal of Medical Informatics, 74*(2–4), 151–157.

Duke, S. A. S., Colagiuri, S., & Colagiuri, R. (2009a). *Individual patient education for people with type 2 diabetes mellitus* (review), Cochrane collaboration, is. 2. Chichester: Wiley.

Duke, S.-A. S., Colagiuri, S., & Colagiuri, R. (2009b). Individual patient education for people with type 2 diabetes mellitus. *Cochrane Database of Systematic Reviews,* (1), CD005268.

Elliott, J. O., Charyton, C., & Long, L. (2007). A health literacy assessment of the National Epilepsy Foundation Web site. *Epilepsy & Behavior, 11*(4), 525–532.

Ellis, S. E., Speroff, T., Dittus, R. S., Brown, A., Pichert, J. W., & Elasy, T. A. (2004). Diabetes patient education: A meta-analysis and meta-regression. *Patient Education and Counseling, 52*(1), 97–105.

Fox, K. M., Gandhi, S. K., Ohsfeldt, R. L., Blasetto, J. W., & Davidson, M. H. (2007). Effectiveness of statins in medicare-eligible patients and patients > 65 years using clinical practice data. *International Journal of Clinical Practice, 61*(10), 1634–1642.

Goessens, B. M. B., Visseren, F. L. J., Nooijer, J. de, Borne, H. W. van den, Algra, A., Wierdsma, J., & Graaf, Y. van der. (2008). A pilot-study to identify the feasibility of an Internet-based coaching programme for changing the vascular risk profile of high-risk patients. *Patient Education and Counseling, 73,* 67–72.

Gomella, L. G. (2000). The wild, wild web: Resources for counseling patients with prostate cancer in the information age. *Seminars in Urologic Oncology, 18*(3), 167–171.

Gómez, E. J., Cáceres, C., López, D., & Del Pozo, F. (2002). A web-based self-monitoring system for people living with HIV/AIDS. *Computer Methods and Programs in Biomedicine, 69*(1), 75–86.

Grandinetti, D. A. (2000). Doctors and the web: Help your patients surf the Net safely. *Medical Economics, 63*(8), 28–34.

Griffiths, K. M., & Christensen, H. (2007). Internet-based mental health programs: A powerful tool in the rural medical kit. *Australian Journal of Rural Health, 15*(2), 81–87.

Gustafson, D. H., Hawkins, R. P., Boberg, E. W., McTavish, F., Owens, B., Wise, M., Berhe, H., & Pingree, S. (2002). CHESS: 10 years of research and development in consumer health informatics for broad populations, including the underserved. *International Journal of Medical Informatics, 65*(3), 169–177.

Hassan, N. M., Win, K. T., & Hyland, P. (2011). *Benefits of Online Patient Education (OPE) for Chronic Disease.* Paper presented at the Fourth International Conference on Internet Technologies and Applications (ITA11), UK: Glyndŵr University.

Heart Failure Society Of, A. (2006). Executive summary: HFSA 2006 comprehensive heart failure practice guideline. *Journal of Cardiac Failure, 12*(1), 10–38.

Hill, W. G., & Weinert, C. (2004). An evaluation of an online intervention to provide social support and health education. *CIN: Computers, Informatics, Nursing, 22*(5), 282–288.

Hill, W., Weinert, C., & Cudney, S. (2006). Influence of a computer intervention on the psychological status of chronically ill rural women: Preliminary results. *Nursing Research, 55*(1), 34–42.

Holley, U. A. (2007). Social isolation: A practical guide for nurses assisting clients with chronic illness. *Rehabilitation Nursing, 32*(2), 51–56.

Homer, C., Susskind, O., Alpert, H. R., Owusu, M. P. M., Celestina, Schneider, L., et al. (2000). An evaluation of an innovative multimedia educational software program for asthma management: Report of a randomized, controlled trial. *Pediatrics, 106*(1), 210–215.

Jeste, D. V., Dunn, L. B., Folsom, D. P., & Zisook, D. (2008). Multimedia educational aids for improving consumer knowledge about illness management and treatment decisions: A review of randomized controlled trials. *Journal of Psychiatric Research, 42*(1), 1–21.

Jones, J. M., Nyhof-Young, J., Friedman, A., & Catton, P. (2001). More than just a pamphlet: Development of an innovative computer-based education program for cancer patients. *Patient Education and Counseling, 44*(3), 271–281.

Kashem, A., Droogan, M. T., Santamore, W. P., Wald, J. W., & Bove, A. A. (2008). Managing heart failure care using an internet-based telemedicine system. *Journal of Cardiac Failure, 14*(2), 121–126.

Kerr, C., Murray, E., Stevenson, F., Gore, C., & Nazareth, I. (2006). Internet interventions for long-term conditions: Patient and caregiver quality criteria. *Journal of Medical Internet Research, 8*(3), e13.

Kim, H. A., Bae, Y. D., & Seo, Y. I. (2004). Arthritis information on the Web and its influence on patients and physicians: A Korean study. *Clinical & Experimental Rheumatology, 22*(1), 49–54.

Koivunen, M., Hätönen, H., & Välimäki, M. (2008). Barriers and facilitators influencing the implementation of an interactive Internet-portal application for patient education in psychiatric hospitals. *Patient Education and Counseling, 70*, 412–419.

Lee, T., Yeh, Y., Liu, C., & Chen, P. (2007). Development and evaluation of a patient-oriented education system for diabetes management. *International Journal of Medical Informatics, 76*(9), 655–663.

Leveille, S. G., Huang, A., Tsai, S. B., Allen, M., Weingart, S. N., & Iezzoni, L. I. (2009). Health coaching via an internet portal for primary care patients with chronic conditions: A randomized controlled trial. *Medical Care, 47*(1), 41–47.

Levin-Zamir, D., & Peterburg, Y. (2001). Health literacy in health systems: Perspectives on patient self-management in Israel. *Health Promotion International, 16*(1), 87–94.

Liang, H., Xue, Y., & Berger, B. A. (2006). Web-based intervention support system for health promotion. *Decision Support Systems, 42*(1), 435–449.

Lorence, D., Monatesti, S., Margenthaler, R., & Hoadley, E. (2005). Toward a patient-centric medical information model: Issues and challenges for US adoption. *International Journal of Electronic Healthcare, 1*(4), 349–364.

Malasanos, T. H., Burlingame, J. B., Youngblade, L., Patel, B. D., & Muir, A. B. (2005). Improved access to subspecialist diabetes care by telemedicine: Cost savings and care measures in the first 2 years of the FITE diabetes project. *Journal of Telemedicine & Telecare, 11*(Suppl. 1), 74–76.

Mangunkusumo, R. T., Brug, J., De Koning, H. J., Der Lei, J., & Raat, H. (2007). School-based internet-tailored fruit and vegetable education combined with brief counselling increases children's awareness of intake levels. *Public Health Nutrition, 10*(3), 273–279.

Mitchell, J. A., Fun, J., & McCray, A. T. (2004). Design of genetics home reference: A new NLM consumer health resource. *JAMIA, 11*(6), 439–447.

Mollaoğlu, M., & Beyzit, E. (2009). Influence of diabetic education on patient metabolic control. *Applied Nursing Research, 22*, 183–190.

Mosca, L., Linfante, A. H., Benjamin, E. J., Berra, K., Hayes, S. N., Walsh, B. W., Fabunmi, R. P., Kwan, J., Mills, T., & Simpson, S. L. (2005). National study of physician awareness and adherence to cardiovascular disease prevention guidelines. *Circulation, 111*(4), 499–510.

Nahm, E.-S., Blum, K., Scharf, B., Friedmann, E., Thomas, S., Jones, D., & Gottlieb, S. S. (2008). Exploration of patients' readiness for an eHealth management program for chronic heart failure: A preliminary study. *Journal of Cardiovascular Nursing, 23*(6), 463–471.

Nielsen//NetRatings. (2002). Health and finance sites capture fastest growing rankings in January. http://www.nielsen-netratings.com/pr/pr_020203.pdf. Accessed 01 Mar 2010.

Noël, P. H., & Pugh, J. A. (2005). Management of overweight and obese adults. *British Medical Journal, 325*, 757–761.

Norman, G. J., Zabinski, M. F., Adams, M. A., Rosenberg, D. E., Yaroch, A. L., & Atienza, A. A. (2007). A review of eHealth interventions for physical activity and dietary behavior change. *American Journal of Preventive Medicine, 33*(4), 336.e16–345.e16.

Nutbeam, D. (2000). Health literacy as a public health goal: A challenge for contemporary health education and communication strategies into the 21st century. *Health Promotion International, 15*(3), 259–267.

O'Connor, D. B., Warttig, S., Conner, M., & Lawton, R. (2009). Raising awareness of hypertension risk through a web-based framing intervention: Does consideration of future consequences make a difference? *Psychology, Health & Medicine, 14*(2), 213–219.

Plougmann, S., Hejlesen, O., & Cavan, D. A. (2001). DiasNet-a diabetes advisory system for communication and education via the internet. *International Journal of Medical Informatics, 64*(2–3), 319–330.

Potts, H. W. W., & Wyatt, J. C. (2002). Survey of doctors' experience of patients using the Internet. *Journal of Medical Internet Research 4*(1), e5.

Rea, S., Lim, J., Falder, S., & Wood, F. (2008). Use of the Internet by burns patients, their families and friends. *Burns, 34*(3), 345–349.

Ream, E., Blows, E., Scanlon, K., & Richardson, A. (2009). An investigation of the quality of breast cancer information provided on the internet by voluntary organisations in Great Britain. *Patient Education and Counseling, 76*(1), 10–15.

Rezailashkajani, M., Roshandel, D., Ansari, S., & Zali, M. R. (2008). A web-based patient education system and self-help group in Persian language for inflammatory bowel disease patients. *International Journal of Medical Informatics, 77*(2), 122–128.

Rice, R. E. (2006). Influences, usage, and outcomes of Internet health information searching: Multivariate results from the pew surveys. *International Journal of Medical Informatics, 75*(1), 8–28.

Robinson-O'Brien, R., Perry, C. L., Wall, M. M., Story, M., & Neumark-Sztainer, D. (2009). Adolescent and young adult vegetarianism: Better dietary intake and weight outcomes but increased risk of disordered eating behaviors. *Journal of the American Dietetic Association, 109*(4), 648–655.

Runge, C., Lecheler, J., Horn, M., Tews, J.-T., & Schaefer, M. (2006). Outcomes of a web-based patient education program for asthmatic children and adolescents. *Chest, 129*(3), 581–593.

Saperstein, S. L., Atkinson, N. L., & Gold, R. S. (2007). The impact of Internet use for weight loss. *Obesity Reviews, 8*(5), 459–465.

Schulz, P. J., Rubinelli, S., Mariotti, G., & Keller, N. (2009). Meeting the ranging of informational needs of chronic low back pain sufferers: Conceptual design and rationale of the interactive website ONESELF. *Disability & Rehabilitation, 31*(25), 2118–2124.

Sciamanna, C. N., Novak, S. P., Houston, T. K., Gramling, R., & Marcus, B. H. (2004). Visit satisfaction and tailored health behavior communications in primary care. *American Journal of Preventive Medicine, 26*(5), 426–430.

Singh, N., Armstrong, D. G., & Lipsky, B. A. (2005). Preventing foot ulcers in patients with diabetes. *JAMA, 293*(2), 217–228.

Street, R. L. Jr., Makoul, G., Arora, N. K., & Epstein, R. M. (2009). How does communication heal? Pathways linking clinician-patient communication to health outcomes. *Patient Education and Counseling, 74*(3), 295–301.

Tang, P., & Newcomb, C. (2004). Informing patients: A guide for providing patient health information. *JAMIA, 5,* 563–570.

Thakurdesai, P. A., Kole, P. L., & Pareek, R. P. (2004). Evaluation of the quality and contents of diabetes mellitus patient education on internet. *Patient Education & Counseling, 53*(3), 309–313.

Thomson, N. R., & Micevski, V. (2005). A descriptive project evaluation to determine Internet access and the feasibility of using the Internet for cardiac education. *Heart and Lung: Journal of Acute and Critical Care, 34*(3), 194–200.

Timpka, T., Eriksson, H., Ludvigsson, J., Ekberg, J., Nordfeldt, S., & Hanberger, L. (2008). Web 2.0 systems supporting childhood chronic disease management: A pattern language representation of a general architecture. *BMC Medical Informatics & Decision Making, 8,* 54.

Ullrich, P. F. J. M. D. a., & Vaccaro, A. R. M. D. (2002). Patient education on the internet: Opportunities and pitfalls. *Spine, 27*(7), E185–E188.

Viele, C. S. (2003). Diagnosis, treatment, and nursing care of acute leukemia. *Seminars in Oncology Nursing, 19*(2), 98–108.

Washington, T. A., Fanciullo, G. J., Sorensen, J. A., & Baird, J. C. (2008). Quality of chronic pain websites. *Pain Medicine, 9*(8), 994–1000.

Weinert, C., Cudney, S., & Hill, W. (2008). Retention in a computer-based outreach intervention for chronically ill rural women. *Applied Nursing Research, 21*(1), 23–29.

Willey, C., et al. (2000). Stages of change for adherence with medication regimens for chronic disease: Development and validation of a measure. *Clinical Therapeutics, 22*(7), 858–871.

Wilken, D. (1994). *Challenge for the 1990s: Patient education.* Paper presented at the Enhancing Teaching Skills workshop.

Wofford, J. L., Currin, D., Michielutte, R., & Wofford, M. M. (2001). The multimedia computer for low-literacy patient education: a pilot project of cancer risk perceptions. *Med Gen Med, 3*(2):23

Ybarra, M. L., & Suman, M. (2006). Help seeking behavior and the internet: A national survey. *International Journal of Medical Informatics, 75*(1), 29–41.

Chapter 20
Development of an Internet-Based Chronic Disease Self-Management System

Ali Sunyaev and Dmitry Chornyi

Abstract Patient self-management programs and information systems that support them can improve the quality of healthcare. Flaws in user experience reduce the willingness of patients to adopt such systems. To explore how emerging technology such as rich Internet applications can be used to address the usability issues of personal health information systems, we developed a health self-management application that is based on an open-source framework. In this work, we present the architecture of the system, discuss the issues we faced and lessons we learned while developing it. This work can help researchers and practitioners in evaluating approaches towards developing new generation of personal health solutions. Furthermore, this work serves as a basis for implementing a feature-rich system that can improve chronic disease self-management.

Keywords Chronic disease · Self-management · Health management system · Health self-management system · IT architecture

20.1 Introduction

Chronic medical conditions take a huge toll on the lives (Undem 2009) of a growing number of people (Heisler 2006) and are a major contributor to the rising costs of healthcare (Kanaan 2008; Hoffman et al. 1996). As public attitudes towards roles in healthcare change, the evidence is growing that chronic patients need more comprehensive treatment than they can receive at their doctor's office (Holman and Lorig 2000). Instead of being passive recipients of care, patients recognize their responsibility in managing their condition through day-to-day decisions about diet, self-measurement, medications, and exercise. A new trend is emerging: people with chronic conditions become their own principal caregivers, with healthcare professionals acting as consultants supporting them in this role (Holman and Lorig

A. Sunyaev (✉)
University of Cologne, Pohligstr. 1, 50969 Cologne, Germany
e-mail: sunyaev@wiso.uni-koeln.de

D. Chornyi
Technische Universität München, Arcisstraße 21, 80333 Munich, Germany
e-mail: chornyi@cs.tum.edu

R. K. Bali et al. (eds.), *Pervasive Health Knowledge Management*, Healthcare Delivery in the Information Age,
DOI 10.1007/978-1-4614-4514-2_20, © Springer Science+Business Media New York 2013

2000). By encouraging patients to participate actively in determining the course of their diseases and ensuring they have the skills, knowledge, and confidence to manage their health, patient self-management programs can improve health outcomes (Bodenheimer et al. 2002), increase treatment satisfaction (Sawicki 1999) and safety (Koutkias and Malousi 2010), as well as reduce healthcare costs (Lahdensuo et al. 1998).

Some patient self-management programs rely on recording patient data over extended periods of time, analyzing these, and encouraging patients to make daily healthcare decisions based on these data (Von Korff et al. 1997). Information technology represents a key tool in supporting such scenarios (Bu et al. 2007). Designers of information systems for patient self-management face a new set of challenges.

Maintaining motivation to support long-term user commitment was shown to be a problem that can be solved through increased personalization, interactivity, and social support through data sharing (Mattila et al. 2010). In this regard, seamless integration with the existing healthcare IT ecosystem is beneficial, as a system that can collaborate with existing Personal Health Record (PHR) providers can take advantage of their infrastructure and data to deliver additional value to the user. Finally, usability is important, as it was shown that flaws in user experience reduce the willingness of patients to adopt personal health information systems (Peters et al. 2009).

To explore how these issues can be addressed in practice, in this chapter we described the development of a prototype of a distributed health self-management service that can support patients with diabetes at tracking their blood glucose levels. Our design efforts were guided by the goals of usability, security, extensibility, and interoperability with third-party healthcare information systems.

The rest of this chapter is organized as follows. Section 20.2 discusses different types of web clients in the context of their suitability for our project. Section 20.3 looks at the system we developed. Section 20.4 presents the evaluation of the system, while Sect. 20.5 discusses the lessons learned in the course of the project. Section 20.6 summarizes our work.

20.2 Web Clients

20.2.1 Traditional Web Applications

In the past few years, the World Wide Web has become the de facto deployment environment for new software systems (Mikkonen and Taivalsaari 2008). Since the 1990s, web-based applications have been used to accomplish an increasing range of tasks including purchasing goods, bidding on auctions, booking tickets, trading stocks, and since recently, managing personal health records (Sunyaev et al. 2010a). Compared to desktop applications, web applications are characterized by reduced deployment and maintenance costs, simple architectures, intrinsic multiplatform availability, and broader user appeal. As network and hardware capabilities expanded, web applications evolved from simple web sites to robust multitier systems that are aimed at replacing complex desktop applications. These developments amplified two serious shortcomings of traditional web applications in the areas of software engineering and usability, as illustrated in the following paragraphs.

The principle technologies that browsers use to display web pages—HTML markup language, CSS style sheet language and JavaScript scripting language—do not introduce a coherent foundation for real applications on the web. They rather reflect the historical evolution of the web, where new features have been added on top of existing features in a mostly ad hoc fashion (Mikkonen and Taivalsaari 2008). Moreover, the methods and tools that are currently used for web application development often overlook the principles of sound software engineering, such as modularity, consistency, simplicity, reusability, and portability (Mikkonen and Taivalsaari 2008). As Mikkonen and Taivalsaari put it, "The use of the web as an application platform undermines the work that has been done in the software engineering area in the past thirty years or so" (Mikkonen and Taivalsaari 2008).

Web applications have also undone decades in usability advances. The proliferation of the Internet has created a void in terms of acceptable user experiences for desktop and Internet applications (Farrell and Nezlek 2007). For instance, the page-based display update model of the web browser that requires a complete page refresh for every user action is outright antiquated and is reminiscent of the I/O model of the IBM 3270 series terminals from the 1970s (Mikkonen and Taivalsaari 2008). So far, many users and developers were willing to give up the user interface improvements brought by desktop computers in return for immediate access to new data and applications (O'Rourke 2004). However, as web applications are expanded to the new areas of use, with online competition and user expectations rising, developers are increasingly pushed to bring web experience closer to that of a desktop. To do this, several usability problems of web applications need to be addressed (Preciado et al. 2005):

- *Process problems*: Complex web applications often force a user to navigate through a series of pages to complete a single task.
- *Data problems*: Web applications do not support interactive explorations of the data. Usually, user has to search data through the use of input forms and then to navigate the hypertext in order to be able to see the desired data.
- *Configuration problems*: Many web applications require the configuration of a product/system from multicriteria choices, but are, in general, unable to present a customized product/system to users in an intuitive way and in a single step.
- *Feedback problems*: Web applications do not allow a continued and ordered interaction without page refreshments, so the user interaction with traditional web pages is limited.

20.2.2 Rich Internet Applications

Rich Internet Applications (RIAs) can solve both the usability- and software engineering-related problems of traditional web clients. In particular, RIAs can offer sophisticated user interfaces with rich interaction possibilities that are close to those of desktop applications. RIAs also rely on different development methods than traditional web applications. In this regard, RIAs can be organized into three distinct types (Farrell and Nezlek 2007):

1. *Plug-in-based*: Involve creating the application for a dedicated platform and then deploying this application as an embedded solution or a standalone application launched from the browser. Examples are Adobe Flash/Adobe Flex/AIR, Java/JavaFX, and Microsoft Silverlight.
2. *Script-based*: Employ a combination of technologies to achieve their results, typically including XHTML/HTML, CSS, DOM, and JavaScript. They are characterized by revised use of JavaScript to load data asynchronously, modify static content, and interact with page elements. To simplify development, a variety of frameworks exist, including Prototype, Dojo, Google Web Toolkit, and Eclipse RAP.
3. *Browser-based*: Use browser facilities and a user interface language to define an application. An example is XUL developed by the Mozilla Project.

We consider script-based RIAs to be particularly promising for shaping the future web landscape, because unlike the other two categories, RIAs are not confined to any single plug-in or browser, have small footprint, and are fast to download and to launch (Noda and Helwig 2005). Furthermore, the functionality gap between script-based and other types of RIAs can be expected to narrow as the HTML 5 standard is adopted and implemented. Although script-based RIAs internally still use HTML, CSS, and JavaScript to control the browser, manually writing markup and scripts is no longer the main method of developing RIAs. Instead, developers use frameworks that allow writing RIAs in conventional programming languages, thus bringing the web software engineering process closer to that of the desktop.

20.2.3 Eclipse RAP

Eclipse Rich Ajax Platform (RAP) [1] is a script-based RIA framework that brings the Eclipse Rich Client Platform (RCP)[2] to the web. It allows a developer to build a rich web client almost just as if it were a regular desktop Java application. This includes access to all Java APIs, UI design using the RWT widget toolkit, and access to the standard services that Eclipse workbench offers (e.g., JFace viewers and data binding, job scheduling). In fact, RCP and RAP frameworks are so similar that applications can be developed from the same code base in the strategy of single-sourcing (Lange 2008). Also, Eclipse RAP can make use of OSGi inside the web container, enabling the full usage of the Eclipse plug-in model (Eclipse Foundation 2006).

[1] http://www.eclipse.org/rap/.

[2] http://www.eclipse.org/home/categories/rcp.php.

20.3 Design and Implementation

20.3.1 Architecture

In the course of this project, we developed a health self-management system (*Health Management System* or *HMS*) that is oriented towards patients with diabetes and is based on the Eclipse RAP platform. The goals of the project were to test how RIAs can be used to improve usability and acceptance of the system and to create a robust architecture that can serve as a base for more complex and feature-rich systems. We identified the following key usage scenarios that drove the discovery and the design of the architecture:

- *Measurement management*: The system can be used to keep track of blood glucose test results that record the blood sugar levels. Measurements can be created, viewed, and grouped by various criteria.
- *Interoperability*: User should be able to import measurements from Microsoft HealthVault and Google Health—the two major PHR platforms.
- *Data visualization*: User can view a graph of blood sugar levels over a period of time or compare several periods.

All of the aforementioned functions are only to be available after the proper authentication and authorization. Due to sensitivity of the medical data, it should be stored and accessed on the per-user basis.

The derived design resulted in a multilayer architecture, as presented in Fig. 20.1. The decision was made to use Java-based products in the overall architecture as these mapped to our existing experience and skills best.

On the back-end side, the system is implemented using Enterprise JavaBeans 3 and Java Persistence API ORM framework. These components are deployed to a Sun GlassFish Application Server v2.1 that provides a number of services through the EJB container. Particularly, the *HMS* takes advantage of the EJB 3 declarative security to restrict access to certain functions only for registered users, as well as declarative transaction management. User data are stored in the Oracle Database 10 *g*. The database also serves as an Authentication Provider through the Glassfish *JDBCRealm* (Chan 2006). This ensures end-to-end industry-strength system security, as no security code was required to be written manually. In addition, the security of the *HMS* can be strengthened by enabling the transparent database encryption that is offered by the selected database (Nanda 2005). The system uses JAXB (Sun Microsystems 2008) to process data imported from external systems and Apache log4j (Gulcu 2002) for the technical and audit logging.

The client is implemented as an Eclipse RAP application. It declares a single *perspective* with two *views* (Clayberg and Rubel 2008): *History and Overview* (Fig. 20.2). The *History* view displays blood glucose measurements, grouped by years and months as a tree. The tree nodes are loaded lazily; they can be expanded, collapsed, and selected arbitrarily. The tree is implemented as a JFace TreeViewer and has a context menu accessible through a right mouse click with menu items depending

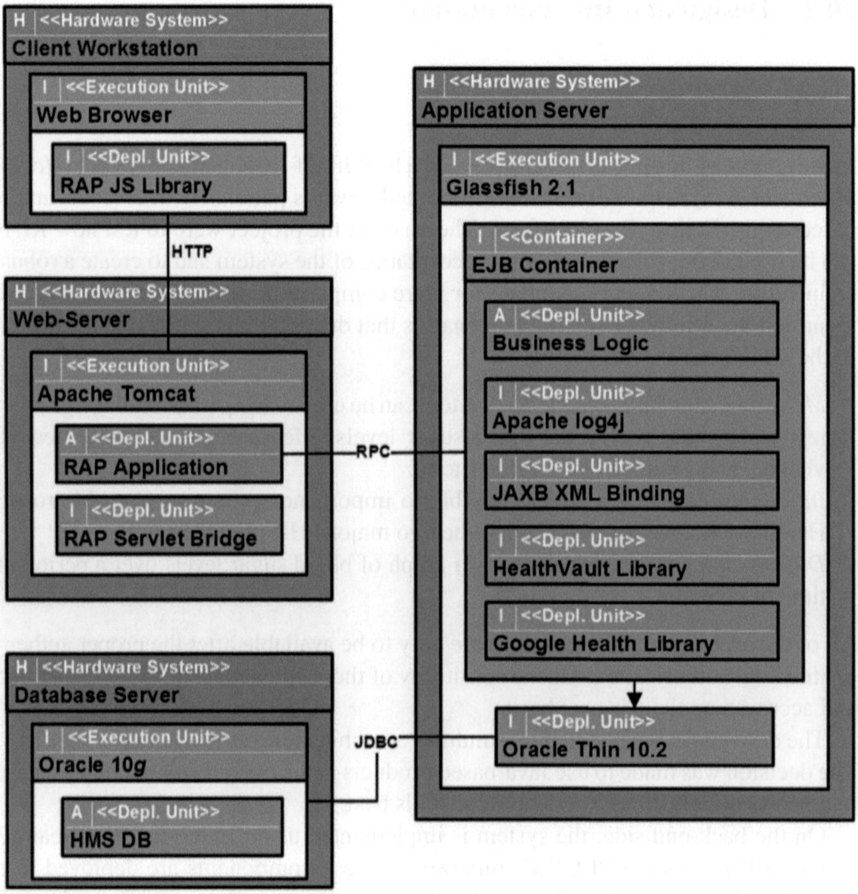

Fig. 20.1 Execution view of the architecture

on the current selection. Using this menu and the toolbar menu that is defined for the view, measurements can be created, updated, viewed, and deleted. The *Overview* view uses the Annotated Time Line component from the Google Visualization API to draw graphs of blood sugar levels according to the user selection. It can also be used to compare these levels over several months or years. The global application menu provides access to additional functions like account management and data import.

20.3.2 PHR Interoperability

Integration with third-party PHR providers is crucial to making a personal health information system useful to a wide circle of people. It enables users to take advantage of the existing PHR ecosystem instead of being locked-in to a single provider. To

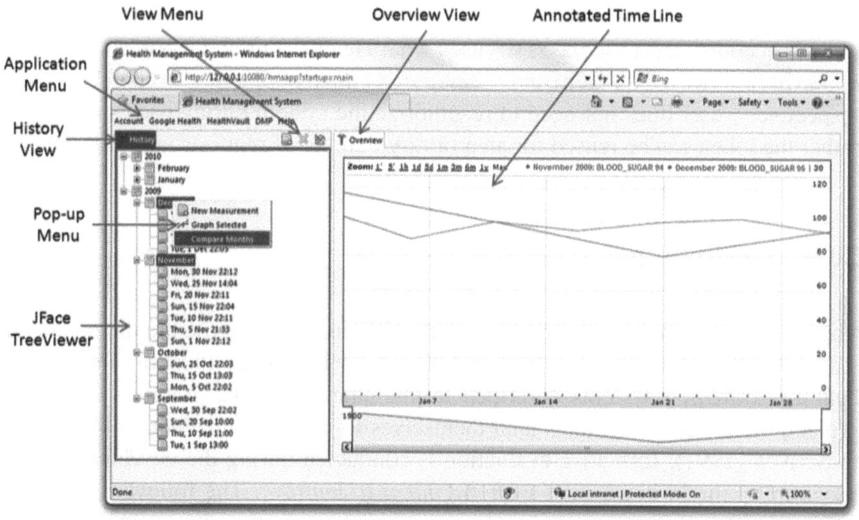

Fig. 20.2 User interface

this end, the *HMS* supports importing blood glucose measurements directly from a linked Google Health or Microsoft HealthVault user account.

Both Microsoft and Google offer extensive support for developers, who are willing to integrate with their PHR platforms. This includes protocol and development documentation, tutorials, support forums, libraries for several programming languages and even a full development SDK, a Device Development Kit, and an application configuration program in the case of Microsoft (Sunyaev et al. 2010b). These resources were used to implement seamless integration with each of the presented PHR platforms. At current project stage, only a one-way import function was implemented; however, data export can also be added with little incremental effort as soon as a data reconciliation strategy is established.

Experience proved the integration with both PHR platforms to be fairly similar, both in development effort and in the inner mechanisms. In both cases, a third-party application needs first to be registered with the PHR provider. In case of Google, this is done through registering a domain and getting a manual approval from the Google Health team. With Microsoft, registration is automated and is done by the means of generating a certificate in the HealthVault Application Manager and uploading it to the HealthVault Application Center.

After the application is approved, it can request a custom authentication URL to direct the user to a special login page where he can authorize this application to access his data. In case a user grants his permission for data access, the *HMS* acquires and stores the authorization token for this user in the database. This token can then be used to sign SOAP requests to the PHR platform that issued it. Both Microsoft HealthVault and Google Health respond with an XML string that contains the requested data. The *HMS* uses JAXB to construct Java objects from the received XML and present them to the user. Users then select the measurements they want to be persisted to their account. Because the *HMS* uses what HealthVault and Google Health call *offline access* (MSDN 2009b) and *access for installed applications* (Google 2009b), respectively, user does not need to reauthorize the system during each session, but rather the token can be reused for an arbitrary number of requests until it is deleted.

20.4 Evaluation

The presented software architecture and the developed prototype are the main constituents of the effort to explore the feasibility of rich Internet applications for personal health information systems described in this chapter. At the present stage of the project, the produced artifacts lend themselves to *formative evaluation*. According to Scriven (1991), formative evaluation is conducted during the development of a program by the in-house staff *with the intent to improve*. The following two subsections present a brief general architectural evaluation as well as a more detailed usability evaluation of the prototype.

20.4.1 Architecture Evaluation

Software architecture evaluation encompasses assessing to which extent the architecture fulfills the quality criteria that are derived from system requirements. Table 20.1 summarizes the relevant criteria for the HMS and their embodiment in the architecture of the system.

20.4.2 Usability Evaluation

Two popular approaches to evaluating the usability of user interfaces are user testing and usability inspection (Nielsen 1994). While user testing is the most commonly applied method, it requires recruiting a sufficient number of users to test all the versions of an evolving design, which may be problematic given the temporal and budgetary constraints. Informal methods like inspection on the other hand are more cost-effective and are also capable to find problems overlooked by user testing. Hence, the two methods can be complimentary (Nielsen 1994) and can be used as building blocks for constructing an evaluation method that is appropriate to a particular situation (see e.g., Sunyaev et al. 2009).

Cognitive walkthrough has been suggested as a usability inspection method that can be used early in the development cycle and can be conducted by developers alone (Wharton et al. 1994). Its essence is the description and evaluation of a hypothetical process—a conjecture about the steps user takes when faced with certain problems and situations, with the focus on the interplay between user's intentions on the one

Table 20.1 Architecture evaluation summary

Criterion	Concretization in the architecture
Interoperability	Support for SOAP communication protocol, data exchange in the ASTM Continuity of Care Record format
Extensibility	Flexibility through the Eclipse RAP plug-in model, loose coupling in the multilayer architecture, clear separation of concerns
Security	Industry-strength authentication and authorization through the EJB security, transport layer security through SSL, database encryption
Ubiquity	Web application available on all PC platforms. Since application logic APIs can be exposed as web services, thin clients can be developed for mobile platforms with little effort
Scalability	Enterprise JavaBeans and the Oracle database are highly scalable. In Eclipse RAP, clustering with load balancing can be used to scale horizontally

hand, and cues and feedback provided by the interface on the other (Wharton et al. 1994).

The cognitive walkthrough was selected as an appropriate evaluation method due to the early project stage and the volatility of requirements. One of the goals of this scientific project was to explore the general suitability of Eclipse RAP to data-intensive personal health information systems, particularly in comparison to competing technology.

When viewed from the user's point of view, our experience with Eclipse RAP was largely positive. This framework allows creating web applications with much richer and smoother interactions than those possible with JavaServer Faces.[3] Particularly, Eclipse RAP offers a basis to solve process problems, data problems, and feedback problems in user interaction (Preciado et al. 2005). For instance, the HMS RIA client allows completing a multistep processes—editing account details on several screens—without refreshing the page. The developed solution also enables interactive data explorations, where user can select a number of measurements in the history view, graph them, and then pan and zoom to examine details without any interruptions. Finally, RAP can provide immediate feedback for data validation, or even more sophisticated elements like progress bars and background tasks with notifications. However, Eclipse RAP creates usability problems of its own. As Lange points out, users associate appearance with certain behavior, and vice versa (Lange 2008). Here, the challenges are twofold. On the one hand, Eclipse RAP looks more like a desktop application, so users may expect it to behave exactly like one. For instance, they may press Ctrl + S on their keyboard, expecting the document to be saved, but instead will be presented with a browser "Save As ..." dialog. On the other hand, while Eclipse RAP runs in a browser, it does not behave like a web page, in a way users are accustomed to. For instance, an RAP application cannot be scrolled in a browser, the "Back" button cannot be used, and text cannot always be selected, or images saved. Also, users do not usually expect a web application to provide functions through a right-click menu, as it is normally reserved to the web browser.

[3] http://java.sun.com/javaee/javaserverfaces/.

There are several possible solutions to usability problems. Over time, users will recognize rich Internet applications as a distinct type of web applications and will learn to attach certain kind of expectations to them. This, along with the further evolution of RIA technologies, will narrow the expectation gap. User acceptance will also depend on the ability of developers to acknowledge both the strong and weak sides of RIA frameworks and use them only where they are appropriate.

20.5 Lessons Learned

Compared to technologies like JavaServer Pages and JavaServer Faces, Eclipse RAP requires some additional configuration and integration work. In the case of *HMS*, it took us some time to integrate the RAP client with the rest of the JavaEE architecture. This included performing the *programmatic login* (Sun Microsystems 2008) with the application server, as well as manually resolving the remote Enterprise JavaBeans through the Java Naming and Directory Interface. Also, the development environment, including an RAP runtime needed to be properly set up prior to development. This, however, is fairly simple in case the application is deployed into a Jetty Web server running in Equinox, as it is suggested in (Lange 2008).

Nevertheless, after the initial learning curve was overcome, our development experience with RAP was positive and we managed to achieve high productivity. Particularly beneficial was the possibility to leverage our existing Eclipse RCP skills to build web clients with RAP. In the course of the project, we did not write a single line of HTML, CSS, or JavaScript—all development was done in Java, which allowed us to focus on a sound object-oriented design. Some functions, like validations were significantly easier to implement in Eclipse RAP, than it would have been with JavaServer Faces. The platform proved to be stable, which was quiet unexpected, given the relative youth of the project and the nontrivial browser interoperability problems Eclipse RAP has to solve. We tested our RIA client in major browsers and had no issues to report. Sometimes the side-effects of the aforementioned advantages start to present unique development challenges. For instance, script-based RIAs, and Eclipse RAP in particular, suffer from what Lange calls "No Web in Web" (Lange 2008). In this case, the reliance on the framework to handle sessions, generate markup code and scripts backfires when custom behaviors need to be implemented for integration with third-party systems. RIAs often try to work around this limitation using IFrames, complex JavaScript, and custom widgets. When developing the *HMS*, we experienced this deficiency as we implemented integration with external PHR platforms. Both Microsoft HealthVault and Google Health recommend an "online" approach to data access, where the application is reauthorized during each session, because it is more secure (MSDN 2009a; Google 2009a). This scenario requires redirecting the browser to the authorization page of the PHR provider and then back to the third-party system—a behavior that cannot be easily implemented with RAP. For this reason, as described previously, the *HMS* uses other type of access, where it stores an access token between sessions, but which is also less secure.

For developers, it is important to recognize that RIAs are not always the best choice for web clients and not to resolve to "design-by-buzzword." The main consideration in choosing between an ordinary web application and a rich Internet application is whether the system being developed is actually an application (Lange 2008). Despite their advantages with regard to user interaction, RIA frameworks are not an optimal choice for creating regular web sites that primarily display static or dynamic content and need to adhere to a very specific design (Lange 2008). Because the *HMS* is clearly an application, our choice to implement it as an RIA was justified.

20.6 Conclusion

This chapter established that patient self-management programs and the information systems that support them can provide a number of benefits to the patients. Recognizing that flaws in user experience can reduce the willingness of patients to adopt such systems, and that traditional web applications often fall short of user expectations in usability, rich Internet applications were explored as a possible alternative. It was further verified that Eclipse RAP can serve as a basis for building a user-friendly health self-management system that integrates with leading PHR platforms. While employing Eclipse RAP in a real-world development project, we found out that it is a mature platform that can be productively used by developers to build an RIA front-end for a Java EE system. Moreover, applications that are based on Eclipse RAP do not suffer from some of the architectural and usability drawbacks that traditional web applications have. This chapter provided a technology-oriented view on the project conducted. We analyze implications for data quality elsewhere (Sunyaev and Chornyi 2012). In the next project phase, further input from medical professionals and patients will be gathered with an aim to expand the functions of the system and subsequently evaluate its performance with regard to various stakeholders (e.g., as proposed by Carson et al. 1998). As the next step in our research, we are conducting a real-world evaluation with ten type 1 diabetes patients. This will result in detailed usage profiles for our disease self-management application, which can lead to refined patient workflow support and new functions.

References

Bodenheimer, T., Lorig, K., & Holman, H. (2002). Patient self-management of chronic disease in primary care. *Journal of the American Medical Association* (*JAMA*), *288*(19), 2469–2475.

Bu, D., Pan, E., Walker, J., Adler-Milstein, J., Kendrick, D., Hook, J. M., Cusack, C. M., Bates, D. W., & Middleton, B. (2007). Benefits of information technology–enabled diabetes management. *Diabetes Care, 30*(5), 1137–1142.

Carson, E. R., Cramp, D. G., Morgan, A., & Roudsari, A. V. (1998). Clinical decision support, systems methodology, and telemedicine: Their role in the management of chronic disease. *IEEE Transactions on Information Technology in Biomedicine, 2*(2), 80–88.

Chan, S. W. (2006). JDBCRealm in GlassFish. http://blogs.sun.com/swchan/entry/jdbcrealm_in_glassfish. Accessed 01 Nov 2009.

Clayberg, E., & Rubel, D. (2008). *Eclipse Plug-ins*. Addison-Wesley Professional.

Eclipse Foundation. (2006). Proposal for Rich AJAX Platform (RAP). http://www.eclipse.org/proposals/rap/. Accessed 01 Nov 2009.

Farrell, J., & Nezlek, G. S. (2007). *Rich internet applications the next stage of application development*. Paper presented at the International Conference on Information Technology Interfaces, Cavtat.

Google. (2009a). Getting started with account authorization. http://code.google.com/apis/accounts/docs/GettingStarted.html.

Google. (2009b). OAuth for installed applications. http://code.google.com/apis/accounts/docs/OAuthForInstalledApps.html. Accessed 01 Dec 2009.

Gulcu, C. (2002). *The complete Log4j manual: The reliable, fast and flexible logging framework for Java* (1st ed.). QOS.ch.

Heisler, M. (2006). *Building peer support programs to manage chronic disease: Seven models for success*. Oakland: California HealthCare Foundation.

Hoffman, C., Rice, D., & Sung, H. Y. (1996). Persons with chronic conditions. Their prevalence and costs. *Journal of the American Medical Association* (*JAMA*), *276*(18), 1473–1479.

Holman, H., & Lorig, K. (2000). Patients as partners in managing chronic disease. Partnership is a prerequisite for effective and efficient health care. *BMJ, 320*(7234), 526–527.

Kanaan, S. B. (2008). *Promoting effective self-management approaches to improve chronic disease care: Lessons learned*. Oakland: California HealthCare Foundation.

Koutkias, V. G., & Malousi, A. (2010). A personalized framework for medication treatment management in chronic care. *IEEE Transactions on Information Technology in Biomedicine, 14*(2), 464–472.

Lahdensuo, A., Haahtela, T., Herrala, J., Kava, T., Kiviranta, K., Kuusisto, P., Pekurinen, M., Perämäki, E., Saarelainen, S., Svahn, T., & Liljas, B. (1998). Randomised comparison of cost effectiveness of guided self management and traditional treatment of asthma in Finland. *BMJ, 316,* 1138–1139.

Lange, F. (2008). *Eclipse rich Ajax platform: Bringing rich client to the web*. Berkeley: Apress.

Mattila, E., Korhonen, I., Salminen, J., Ahtinen, A., Koskinen, E., Sarela, A., Parkka, J., Lappalainen, R. (2010). Empowering citizens for wellbeing and chronic disease management with wellness diary. *IEEE Transactions on Information Technology in Biomedicine, 14*(2), 456–463.

Mikkonen, T., & Taivalsaari, A. (2008). *Web applications—Spaghetti code for the 21st century*. Paper presented at the Proceedings of the 2008 Sixth International Conference on Software Engineering Research, Management and Application.

MSDN. (2009a). Choosing a healthVault application architecture. http://msdn.microsoft.com/en-us/healthvault/cc296309.aspx. Accessed 01 Nov 2009.

MSDN. (2009b). Offline access. http://msdn.microsoft.com/en-us/healthvault/bb871490.aspx. Accessed 01 Nov 2009.

Nanda, A. (2005, September-October). Transparent data encryption. *Oracle Magazine*.

Nielsen, J. (1994). *Usability inspection methods*. Paper presented at the Conference on Human Factors in Computing Systems, Boston, Massachusetts, United States.

Noda, T., & Helwig, S. (2005). *Rich internet applications*. Technical Comparison and Case Studies of AJAX, Flash, and Java based RIA. UW E-Business-Consortium Opinion Papers.

O'Rourke, C. (2004, July/August). A look at rich internet applications. *Oracle Magazine*.

Peters, K., Niebling, M., Slimmer, C., Green, T., Webb, J. M., & Schumacher, R. (2009). *Usability guidance for improving the user interface and adoption of online personal health records*. Oakbrook Terrace: User Centric, Inc.

Preciado, J. C., Linaje, M., Sanchez, F., & Comai, S. (2005). *Necessity of methodologies to model rich internet applications*. Paper presented at the Seventh IEEE International Symposium on Web Site Evolution, 2005, (WSE 2005).

Sawicki, P. T. (1999). A structured teaching and self-management program for patients receiving oral anticoagulation. A Randomized Controlled Trial. *Journal of the American Medical Association (JAMA), 281,* 145–150.

Scriven, M. (1991). *Evaluation thesaurus* (4th ed.). Newbury Park: Sage.

Sun Microsystems. (2008). *The Java EE 5 tutorial. For sun Java system application server 9.1.* Santa Clara: SunMicrosystems, Inc.

Sunyaev, A., & Chornyi, D. (2012). Supporting chronic disease care quality: Design and implementation of a health service and its integration with electronic health records. *ACM Journal of Data and Information Quality (JDIQ), 3.*

Sunyaev, A., Hansen, M., & Krcmar, H. (2009). *Method engineering: A formal description. Information systems development—towards a service provision society* (pp. 645–654). US: Springer.

Sunyaev, A., Chornyi, D., Mauro, C., & Krcmar, H. (2010a). *Evaluation framework for personal health records: Microsoft healthVault vs. google health.* Paper presented at the Proceedings of the Hawaii International Conference on System Sciences (HICSS 43), Kauai, Hawaii, 5–8 Jan 2010.

Sunyaev, A., Kaletsch, A., & Krcmar, H. (2010b). *Comparative evaluation of google health API vs. Microsoft healthvault API.* Paper presented at the Proceedings of the Third International Conference on Health Informatics, Valencia, Spain, 20–23 Jan 2010.

Undem, T. (2009). *Gaps in the system: Californians struggle with caring for their chronic conditions.* Washington, DC: Lake Research Partners.

Von Korff, M., Gruman, J., Schaefer, J., Curry, S. J., & Wagner, E. H. (1997). Collaborative management of chronic illness. *Annals of Internal Medicine, 127*(12), 1097–1102.

Wharton, C., Rieman, J., Lewis, C., & Polson, P. (1994). *The cognitive walkthrough method: A practitioner's guide. Usability inspection methods* (pp. 105–140). New York: Wiley.

Chapter 21
Enablers of Implementing Knowledge Management Systems for Better Organisational Outcomes: An Indian Study

Raj Gururajan and Heng-Sheng Tsai

Abstract In the era of knowledge economy, how to exploit knowledge assets is essential for businesses to improve their competitive advantage. Issues such as how to enable or facilitate knowledge management systems (KMS) in an organisation have proven to be important for academia and industry. For the reason that sharing and managing knowledge involves a series of activities that are related to culture, the findings in a geographic area or a certain industry may not necessarily be applicable to other areas or industries with different cultural backgrounds. Research issues such as what are the enablers for organisations in implementing their knowledge management systems with a focus on reaching better organisational outcomes have been discussed and highlighted in literature. However, a more comprehensive investigation, with an effort on gathering all the enablers and examining them altogether in a certain context, has not been completed. Therefore, this study is motivated to investigate the research issue 'What are the enablers for implementing knowledge management systems in India?' by using both qualitative and quantitative approaches. Firstly, the authors used a multiple case study method to examine whether the enablers identified in the literature still influence the implementation of KMS in India. Secondly, the results were further tested with a larger sample (400 organisations in four Indian cities) to confirm and consolidate the findings. These findings indicate that all the enabling factors of KMS identified in the literature are applicable in the Indian context. However, there exists a significant difference between metropolitan and regional cities. The findings of this study depict a more complete blueprint for researchers and practitioners in understanding the enabling factors for Indian businesses and organisations in implementing knowledge management systems.

Keywords Knowledge management · KMS · Enabler · Organisational outcome · India

---

R. Gururajan (✉)
School of Information Systems, Faculty of Business and Law,
University of Southern Queensland, Queensland, 4352, Australia
e-mail: Raj.Gururajan@usq.edu.au

H.-S. Tsai
Office of Research Operations, University of Southern Queensland, Queensland, Australia

R. K. Bali et al. (eds.), *Pervasive Health Knowledge Management*,
Healthcare Delivery in the Information Age,
DOI 10.1007/978-1-4614-4514-2_21,

21.1 Introduction

Knowledge management (KM) plays an important role for organisations. It involves activities such as the process of creating, acquiring, sharing and managing knowledge at individual and organisational level (Alavi and Leidner 2001). Knowledge and knowledge management are both multi-faceted concepts and activities, and strongly related to cultural background (Bock et al. 2005). In this context, Srinivas (2009) indicates that the theories of knowledge management generated—based on western cultural background—are not necessarily applicable to eastern cultures such as India.

Currently, KM is providing a better understanding of its success factors and KM approaches are more focused to address particular challenges such as securing knowledge from experts leaving an organisation (Heisig 2009). However, issues and factors that enable or facilitate an organisation to further enhance its knowledge management are essential elements in the decision-making process of managers and executives (Emelo 2009; Gan 2006; Khalifa and Liu 2003; Lee and Choi 2003). The enablers for organisations in implementing their knowledge management systems (KMS) were proposed and discussed in the literature (Lee and Choi 2003; Robbins et al. 2001; Yu et al. 2004). However, most of the studies focused on only few factors. Therefore, building a theoretical framework to understand these factors and their influences is necessary to form a new starting point for comprehensive understanding (Heisig 2009). In addition, researchers indicated that a majority of these factors/enablers were based on western countries and this western environment is different from the Asian context (Chaudry 2005; Srinivas 2009). In a rapidly developing country such as India, where the management system in organisations is markedly different to that of western styles, the question of 'whether the enablers still influence the implementation of knowledge management systems in the same way?' is still under debate. This research issue is significant because cultural issues appear to influence aspects of management decision making. Our review of the literature also indicated there is very limited information regarding KM in the Indian context.

As the seventh largest country and the second most populous country in the world, economic reforms since 1991 have transformed India into one of the fastest growing economies (ERS 2009). The Indian subcontinent is identified with its commercial and cultural wealth in much of its long history (Oldenburg 2007). Four major religions, Hinduism, Buddhism, Jainism and Sikhism originated here, whilst Zoroastrianism, Judaism, Christianity and Islam arrived in the first millennium CE and shaped the region's diverse culture. India is a republic consisting of 28 states and seven union territories, with a parliamentary system of democracy. It has the world's 12th largest economy at market exchange rates and the fourth largest in purchasing power (India 2009). Long traditions, combined with an advanced educated pool of managers and strong yet conservative management practices, indicate that KM enablers might be different for India. Thus, this study posted the question, 'What are the enablers for implementing knowledge management systems in India?'

In this study, a theoretical model for KM enablers was constructed in order to reach a more comprehensive understanding of the research issue. This model is based on a review of the literature and a multiple case study with 80 organisations in four Indian cities. These cities are located in metropolitan and regional areas with various population sizes, social structures and history. Subsequently, the initial model developed was examined by a survey in the same cities with larger samples. This is explained further in the following sections.

21.2 Literature Review

The literature review of this study consists of three sections. In the first section, the basic concepts and definitions of knowledge, knowledge management and knowledge management systems are provided. In the second section, the organisational outcomes that may be influenced by implementing knowledge management systems are presented. Subsequent to this, the enablers of knowledge management systems are gathered and discussed as the foundation for the theoretical model proposed in this study.

21.2.1 Knowledge Management and Knowledge Management Systems

Although knowledge and knowledge management are complex and multi-faceted concepts (Alavi and Leidner 2001), knowledge management has become increasingly important in today's highly competitive business environment. For example, knowledge assets of organisations have played a crucial role in this shift and are becoming increasingly important (Yelden and Albers 2004). Furthermore, in the knowledge-based view of the firm, knowledge is the foundation of a firm's competitive advantage and, ultimately, the primary driver of a firm's value (Bock et al. 2005; Gan 2006).

Researchers have provided definitions to better understand the concepts of knowledge and knowledge management. For example, knowledge management has been defined as the process of capturing, storing, sharing and using knowledge (Davenport and Prusak 1998). KM is also the systematic and explicit management of knowledge-related activities, practices, programs and policies within the enterprise (KM 1997) or the art of creating value to organisations by leveraging intangible assets (Sveiby 1997). Accordingly, knowledge is defined as a justified belief that increases an entity's capacity for effective action (Alavi and Leidner 2001; Huber 2001). Knowledge can be further viewed as a state of: mind; an object; a process; a condition of having access to information or a capability (Alavi and Leidner 2001).

To manage knowledge assets more effectively, knowledge management systems are the IT-based platform designed for facilitating KM by providing larger databases, more powerful computation ability, higher performance data structures and smarter query techniques (Weber et al. 2001). KMS refer to a class of information systems applied to managing organisational knowledge. It is defined as IT-based systems developed to support and enhance the organisational processes of knowledge creation, storage/retrieval, transfer and application (Alavi and Leidner 2001; Li and Tsai 2009). The main function of KMS is to guide employees in obtaining helpful knowledge from knowledge bases and make existing experiences freely available to other employees of an organisation (Abdullah et al. 2005). The final goals of KMS are to employ many different techniques to represent knowledge, with the aim of enhancing the decision-making capability of human decision-makers (Cowie et al. 2009). According to recent studies (e.g. Li and Tsai 2009), KMS have proven to be efficient and effective in organising knowledge of high complexity and in large amounts.

Some studies have explored the various aspects of KMS. For example, several aspects of KMS should be taken into consideration in implementation of KM in an organisation (Li and Tsai 2009): (1) how to transfer tacit knowledge to explicit knowledge; (2) how to retrieve desired knowledge from knowledge bases; (3) how to visualise knowledge and (4) how to create more valuable knowledge by reuse. Furthermore, with the rapid development of wireless technologies, new research issues are gaining prominence. For example, in a mobile and networked environment, the solutions of how to provide up-to-date, context-specific information to whom and where, is appropriate (Cowie et al. 2009). Another example is how to use mobile clinical support systems to address different intelligent decision support such as knowledge delivery on demand, medication advice, therapy reminders, preliminary clinical assessment for classifying treatment categories and providing alerts of potential drugs interactions and active linking to relevant medical conditions (Cowie et al. 2009). These requirements, raised from new technological developments, have fostered the studies of KMS to a new stage. One important research issue is how knowledge management systems influence the outcomes of organisations.

21.2.2 KM and Organisational Outcomes

Knowledge management promotes efficiency and optimal use of resources to achieve organisational goals. This awareness is creating new interest in KM solutions that have the potential to improve business performance (Lamont 2009). For example, there are numerous cases of international companies that have demonstrated that by successfully applying KM it will improve organisational competitiveness and performance (Wong and Aspirwall 2006). In a fast-changing environment, knowledge processes are the most precious resources to sustain and enhance long-term organisational competitiveness (Song 2002).

Determining key outcomes of implementing KMS in organisations appears to be difficult. These outcomes include achieving organisational efficiency, competitive advantage, maximising organisational potential and better management of knowledge assets (Gan 2006). The first organisational outcome can be enhanced by implementing KMS is competitive advantage. A firm's competitive advantage depends more than anything on its knowledge: on what it knows, how it uses what it knows and how fast it can know something new (Prusak 1997). For example, to ensure continued competitive advantage, organisations need to fully understand both their customers and competitors (Al-Hawamdeh 2002; North et al. 2004). Customers are an integral component of the organisation's intellectual capital and it is the reason for the organisation's existence (Stewart 1997). To ensure that an organisation effectively leverages this intellectual capital with regard to their customers, information technology solutions such as customer relationship management (CRM) are useful to manage whatever knowledge of customers the organisation possesses (Probst et al. 2000).

Another organisational outcome that can be enhanced is to maximise organisational potential by implementing KMS. For knowledge-intensive organisations, the main driver in maximising the value of its research and development endeavours and investments is through recycling and reusing experiments and results obtained (Al-Hawamdeh 2002). Companies such as 3M and BP maximised organisational potential from effective knowledge management to achieve successes in the competitive industries that they are in (Cortada and Woods 1999).

A KMS also assists an organisation to manage knowledge assets in a comprehensive way. Knowledge has become a central focus of most organisations these days. As a result, managing knowledge assets—finding, cultivating, storing, disseminating and sharing them—has become the most important economic task of employees in any organisation (Stewart et al. 2000). Notwithstanding the above outcomes, studies increasingly indicate that organisational outcomes could be enhanced by implementing knowledge management systems (Lamont 2009). Therefore, an understanding of the obstacles and enablers of implementing KMS may be helpful as the starting point in order to further understand this issue.

21.2.3 Obstacles and Enablers of Implementing KMS

Previous studies have indicated that when organisations implement their knowledge management systems, some obstacles and enablers exist in the process. For example, many firms actively limit knowledge sharing because of the threats associated with industrial espionage, as well as concerns about diverting or overloading employees' work-related attention (Constant et al. 1996). Once knowledge sharing is limited across an organisation, the likelihood increases that knowledge gaps will arise, and these gaps are likely to produce less-than-desirable work outcomes (Bock et al. 2005).

Despite the fact that organisations may reward their own employees for effective knowledge management practices, this may create obstacles for knowledge management. One example is that some organisations provide pay-for-performance compensation schemes, plus it can also serve to discourage knowledge sharing if employees believe that knowledge sharing will hinder their personal efforts to distinguish themselves relative to their co-workers (Huber 2001). Furthermore, there are major challenges in promoting the transfer and integration of explicit and tacit knowledge between channel members, including: lack of recipient's cognitive capacity; lack of the sender's credibility; lack of motivation of the sender or the recipient; the existence of an arduous relationship between the sender and recipient and causal ambiguity due to the complexity of knowledge (Frazier 2009; Szulanski and Jensen 2006).

Recent studies have attempted to provide guidelines and successful experiences to reduce obstacles. For instance, there are four areas that need to be focused on when implementing knowledge management systems. These areas include (Emelo 2009): understanding who the knowledge sources are: measuring where and how knowledge flows; getting knowledge to flow more rapidly and freely and reinforcing knowledge with supportive relationships. In addition, a review of the literature reveals that there are many enablers that are known to influence knowledge management practices (Gan 2006). These enablers can be broadly classified into either a social or technical perspective. The social perspective of knowledge management enablers plays an important role and has been widely acknowledged (Smith 2004). These enablers are further discussed below.

One of the enablers is collaboration. Collaboration is an important feature in knowledge management adoption. It is defined as the degree to which people in a group actively assist one another in their tasks (Lee and Choi 2003). A collaborative culture in the workplace influences knowledge management as it allows for increased levels of knowledge exchange—a prerequisite for knowledge creation. This is made possible because collaborative culture eliminates common barriers to knowledge exchange by reducing fear and increasing openness in teams (Gan 2006).

Another enabler is mutual trust. It exists in an organisation when its members believe in the integrity, character and ability of each other (Robbins et al. 2001). Trust has been an important factor in high-performance teams as explained in organisational behaviour literature. The existence of mutual trust in an organisation facilitates open, substantive and influential knowledge exchange. When team relationships have a high level of mutual trust, members are more willing to engage in knowledge exchange.

A further important enabler is learning. It is defined as any relatively permanent change in behaviour that occurs as a result of experience (Robbins et al. 2001). In organisations, learning involves the dynamics and processes of collective learning that occur both naturally and in a planned manner within the organisation (Gan 2006).

In addition to the above, leadership is often stated to be a driver for effective knowledge management in organisations (Khalifa and Liu 2003). Leadership is defined as the ability to influence and develop individuals and teams to achieve goals that have been set by the organisation (Robbins et al. 2001). Adequate leadership can exert substantial influence on organisational members' knowledge creation activities. The presence of a management champion for the knowledge management initiative in order to set the overall direction for knowledge management programmes—and who can assume accountability for them—is crucial to effective knowledge management (Yu et al. 2004).

Organisational incentives and rewards that encourage knowledge management activities amongst employees play an important role as an enabler (Yu et al. 2004). Incentives are something that have the ability to incite determination or action in employees within an organisation (Robbins et al. 2001). Rewards, on the other hand, can be broadly categorised as being either extrinsic or intrinsic. Extrinsic rewards are positively valued work outcomes that are given to the employee in the work setting, whilst intrinsic rewards are positively valued work outcomes that are received by the employee directly as a result of task performance (Wood et al. 1998). Research supports the view that both intrinsic and extrinsic rewards have a positive influence on knowledge management performance in organisations (Yu et al. 2004).

Organisational structure plays an important role as it may either encourage or inhibit knowledge management. The structure of the organisation impacts the way in which organisations conduct their operations and, in doing so, affects how knowledge is created and shared amongst employees (Lee and Choi 2003). One enabler to KM is the level of non-centralisation. This refers to the degree to which decision making is non-concentrated at a single point, normally at higher levels of management in the organisation (Robbins et al. 2001; Wood et al. 1998). The concept of centralisation includes only formal authority—that is, rights inherent in one's position. An organisation is said to be highly centralised if the top management makes the organisation's key decisions with little or no input from lower-level employees (Robbins et al. 2001).

Another structural enabler is the level of non-formalisation. It refers to the written documentation of rules, procedures and policies to guide behaviour and decision making in organisations (Wood et al. 1998). When an organisation is highly formalised, employees would then have little discretion over what is to be done, when it is to be done and how they should do it, resulting in consistent and uniform output (Robbins et al. 2001). However, formalisation impedes knowledge management activities. This is because knowledge creation requires creativity and less emphasis on work rules, thus, the range of new ideas that emerge from a highly formalised structure is limited.

Most teams are composed of individuals who operate from a base of deeply specialised knowledge (Davvy 2006). These individuals need mechanisms to translate across the different 'languages' that exist in organisations (Ford and Staples 2006). This brings rise to the need for employees with T-shaped skills—that is, skills that are both deep and broad (Leonard-Barton 1995). Employees who possess T-shaped skills not only have a deep knowledge of a particular discipline (e.g. financial auditing), but also about how their discipline interacts with other disciplines (e.g. risk analysis, investment analysis and derivatives). Iansiti (1993) states that the deep knowledge in a particular discipline is aptly represented by the vertical stroke of the 'T', whilst knowledge of how this discipline interacts with other disciplines is represented by the horizontal top stroke of the 'T' (Iansiti 1993).

Lastly, but no less important an enabler, is IT infrastructure. It plays an important role in knowledge management. Technology infrastructure includes information technology and its capabilities, which are considered to assist organisations to get work done, and to effectively manage knowledge that the organisation possesses (Holsapple 2005). The information technology infrastructure within an organisation can be broadly categorised into hardware technologies and software systems. It has been found that information technology infrastructure plays a crucial role in knowledge management as it allows for easy knowledge acquisition and facilitates

Table 21.1 Job position of the interviewees

Job position of interviewee	Frequency	Percentage (%)
Proprietors, partners and executives	24	30.00
Middle managers and professionals	39	48.75
Operational staff	17	21.25
Total	*80*	*100*

Table 21.2 Seniority of the interviewees

Seniority	Frequency	Percentage (%)
2 years or under	5	6.25
Over 2 and under 5 years	22	27.50
Over 5 and under 10 years	16	20
Over 10 years	36	45
N/A	1	1.25
Total	*80*	*100*

timely communication amongst employees. Information technology infrastructure also speeds up the pace of knowledge creation and assists in the process of building organisational memory (Okunoye and Karsten 2002). These aspects were investigated in this study for their applicability in the Indian context.

21.3 Qualitative Data Collection and Analysis

A multiple case study was conducted to identify the possible enablers for organisations when implementing their KMS. Twenty organisations were chosen in each of the Indian cities: Chennai; Coimbatore; Madurai and Villupuram. A total number of 80 local and international organisations were interviewed with focus given to the exploration of factors that influence KMS implementation. Hence, the unit of analysis is 'organisation'.

For better understanding of the background of the interviewees, the organisations and the cities, some background information is provided in this section. Basic information of the interviewees is summarised in Tables 21.1 and 21.2. Table 21.1 indicates that the interviewees cover three main job levels: senior executives; middle managers and operational staff. Table 21.2 summarises the seniority of interviewees. The percentage of interviewees who worked in the organisations for more than 2 years is over 90 %. This assists the interviewers in better understanding the organisational environment and its working culture.

Subsequent to the above, Table 21.3 depicts the distribution of industry for the 80 organisations that the interviewees worked at. The classification scheme of industries is adopted from the Australian Bureau of Statistics (ABS 1993). The dominating industries included manufacturing (22.50 %), finance and insurance (20 %) and information technology (10 %). The frequency of distribution represents the economic and social structure of the four Indian cities. The following paragraphs provide some background information related to these Indian cities.

Table 21.3 Frequency of distribution by industry

Industry	Frequency	Percentage (%)
Agriculture, forestry and fishing	0	0.00
Mining	1	1.25
Manufacturing	18	22.50
Electricity, gas and water supply	1	1.25
Construction and design	6	7.50
Transport and storage	2	2.50
Accommodation, cafe and restaurant	0	0.00
Retail trade	6	7.50
Wholesale trade	3	3.75
Government administration and defence	1	1.25
Education, training and research	2	2.50
Communication	4	5.00
Property and business services	3	3.75
Finance and insurance	16	20.00
Health and community services	1	1.25
Cultural and recreational services	1	1.25
Personal and other services	0	0.00
Information technology	8	10.00
Other	7	8.75
Total	*80*	*100*

The first city is Chennai. It is the capital city of the Indian state of Tamil Nadu. Chennai is the fifth most populous city in India, with a population of 4.34 million in the 2001 census. Chennai's economy has a broad industrial base in the automobile, technology, hardware manufacturing and healthcare industries. The city is India's second largest exporter of software, information technology and information technology-enabled services. A major portion of India's automobile manufacturing industry is based in and around the city. Chennai Zone contributes 39 % of the State's GDP. Chennai accounts for 60 % of the country's automotive exports and is referred to as the Detroit of South Asia (Chennai 2009; Muthiah 2004). The cases interviewed in Chennai include the industries of education, IT, finance/insurance, manufacturing, transport, health and construction. The enablers identified from the cases of Chennai cover the widest range from collaboration to IT infrastructure.

The next city is Coimbatore. It is the administrative headquarters and a major textile and engineering hub of (Southern) India. Coimbatore is also known as Manchester of South India. More recent estimates peg the population of Coimbatore at 1.5 million people. Coimbatore is known for its textile mills, factories, engineering firms, automobile parts manufacturers, health care facilities, educational institutions, pleasant weather and hospitality. The Coimbatore city is a traditional, multi-cultural inclusive society. The city's primary industries are engineering and textiles. The district also houses the country's largest number of hosiery and poultry industries (Coimbatore 2009). The cases of Coimbatore include the industries of communication, manufacturing, finance/insurance, government sector, IT, construction and retail trade. Although the enablers of KMS implementation vary significantly from one industry to another, in the case of Coimbatore, there is still a wide coverage of the enablers.

The third city is Madurai. It is the oldest inhabited city in the Indian peninsula. The city is widely known as the Temple City, City of Culture, City of Jasmine or Athens of the East. With a population of 1,374,838 according to the 2001 Census, Madurai was the capital city of ancient Southern civilisation. Madurai's cultural heritage goes back 2,500 years, and the city has been an important commercial centre and has conducted trade as far as Rome and Greece since as early as 550 BCE. Madurai district houses reputable organisations in the private sector, which are engaged in the production of a variety of goods such as tyres, industrial rubber products, machinery, textiles, conveyor belts, chemicals, etc. (Madurai 2009). The industries for cases in Madurai include construction, mining, property and business services, IT, finance/insurance, manufacturing, wholesale/retail trade and education. Even the coverage of industry is wider compared to other cities, however, only seven of the nine enablers were identified from the cases in Madurai. Structural factors such as non-centralisation and non-formalisation were not mentioned by any interviewees, and the factors of collaboration, leadership and IT infrastructure were only mentioned once by the interviewees. The tendency of centralisation on enablers of KMS becomes more obvious: the size and structure of organisations may be the reason for this difference.

The last city is Villupuram. This country city is a municipality in Villupuram District, in the Indian state of Tamil Nadu. It serves as the headquarters of Villupuram District, the second largest district in the State. Villupuram also has a major train station. The town's main source of income is agriculture. Villupuram District lies in the north-east of Tamil Nadu. Its literacy rate was low until the early 1980s, but has since improved constantly and is currently about 75 %. As of the 2001 India census, Villupuram's population was 960,373 (Villupuram 2009). The industries of cases in Villupuram include wholesale and retail trade, communication, finance/insurance, construction, gas, electricity, and water supply and others. Due to the structure of industry and organisations in Villupuram, the tendency of centralisation on the enablers identified is more obvious than Madurai. Only five of the nine factors were identified, hence, another four factors—collaboration, mutual trust, leadership and non-centralisation—were not mentioned by any interviewees. In addition, the factors of non-formalisation, T-shaped skills and IT infrastructure were only brought to the conversations once in different cases. The differences between cities are evident.

The first two Indian cities (Chennai and Coimbatore) are distinguished as metropolitan and industrial cities. They are grouped as the first team. The structure of society and the level of commercial and industrial developments discriminate the first group from the other cities, including Madurai and Villupuram. These cities are grouped as the second team in this study for their cultural and agricultural characteristics. The different characteristics of the cities were also founded on data collection for this study. For example, public awareness in the related field for the first team is more prominent than the other.

Furthermore, the regional cities (team 2) house less government offices and more small businesses compared to the metropolitan cities (team 1). The willingness of the interviewees to allow recording of their conversations varied between these two teams. For instance, in team 1, 30 % of interviewees cancelled their meetings for this reason; and 83 % of interviewees turned down the appointments in team 2.

Table 21.4 Distribution of the enablers for KMS implementation

Enabler identified	Distributions (ranked)	Percentage (%)
Learning	49	61.25
Incentives and rewards	42	52.50
Information technology infrastructure	19	23.75
T-shaped skills	12	15.00
Non-formalisation	11	13.75
Mutual trust	9	11.25
Non-centralisation	7	8.75
Leadership	5	6.25
Collaboration	3	3.75

Moreover, in team 1 the executives of the selected case have a general phobia that their conversations would be exposed to competitors. Another difference exists in the background of the interviewees: a certain number of cases in team 2 are dealers for household products such as products in steel and wood or selling paints, cell phones, stationery, garments and cookware, etc. This industrial structure may influence the results to some extent.

Based on the statistics and introduction, it is understandable that each of the Indian cities has its unique economic structure, population, history and culture. They cover different economic and geographic areas of India. The four cities can then be grouped into two main categories for further analysis: metropolitan and regional cities. The metropolitan group includes Chennai and Coimbatore, and the regional group includes Madurai and Villupuram. In later sections of this study, it is found that even in the same nation, the results of data analysis can significantly vary from one group to another.

Table 21.4 builds the linkages between the body of literature and the case study. The enablers of KMS that have been discussed in previous literature are summarised in this table. The enablers were all identified throughout the multiple case study. The results are illustrated in Table 21.4.

21.4 The Proposed Theoretical Model

Based on the literature review and the results of the Indian case study, the following theoretical model was constructed in Fig. 21.1 for further investigation. The concepts of these factors have been discussed in Sect. 21.2.3.

In order to further examine whether these KMS enablers can be confirmed in a bigger Indian sample, nine hypotheses were formulated based on the theoretical model. Each of the hypotheses seeks to identify whether it is a significant factor (enabler) for Indian organisations. These potential factors/enablers include collaboration, mutual trust, learning, leadership, incentives and rewards, non-centralisation, non-formalisation, T-shaped skills and information technology infrastructure. The

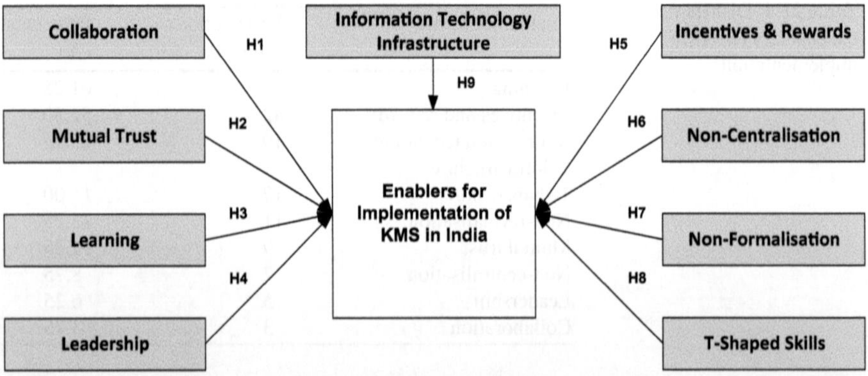

Fig. 21.1 Proposed theoretical model for the enablers of KMS in India

Table 21.5 Hypotheses setup for further testing

Hypothesis	Content of hypothesis
H1	'Collaboration' is an enabler for implementing KMS in Indian organisations
H2	'Mutual Trust' is an enabler for implementing KMS in Indian organisations
H3	'Learning' is an enabler for implementing KMS in Indian organisations
H4	'Leadership' is an enabler for implementing KMS in Indian organisations
H5	'Incentives and Rewards' is an enabler for implementing KMS in Indian organisations
H6	'Non-Centralisation' is an enabler for implementing KMS in Indian organisations
H7	'Non-Formalisation' is an enabler for implementing KMS in Indian organisations
H8	'T-Shaped Skills' is an enabler for implementing KMS in Indian organisations
H9	'Information Technology Infrastructure' is an enabler for implementing KMS in Indian organisations

hypotheses are summarised in Table 21.5, and have been tested through a survey study, which is discussed in the following section.

21.5 Quantitative Data Collection and Analysis

Subsequent to the multiple case study and model building, a survey was administered in the same Indian cities to further examine and confirm the results of the case study. The survey either adapted measures that had been validated by other researchers or converted the definitions of constructs into a questionnaire format. A five-point Likert scale was used to measure the extent that each factor influences the respondent's organisation. Opinions from 400 respondents (100 in each city) in the domain of KMS implementation, with a focus on what are the enablers of KMS, were collected and analysed. The results of the survey study and hypothesis testing are presented in this section. Table 21.6 illustrates the demographic information of the survey respondents.

Table 21.6 Frequency distribution of survey

	Frequency	Percentage (%)	Age group	Frequency	Percentage (%)
Gender					
Male	342	85.50	Under 26	39	9.75
Female	58	14.50	26–30	92	23.00
Total	*400*	*100*	31–35	102	25.50
Seniority			36–40	86	21.50
2 years or under	96	24.00	41–45	40	10.00
Over 2 and under 5 years	149	37.25	46–50	25	6.25
Over 5 and under 10 years	76	19.00	51–55	12	3.00
Over 10 years	79	19.75	56–60	4	1.00
Total	*400*	*100*	*Total*	*400*	*100*

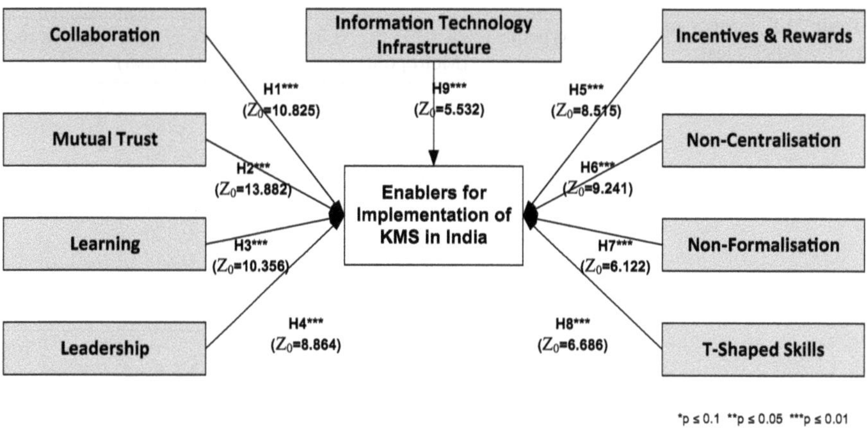

Fig. 21.2 The results of hypothesis test (whole dataset)

In addition, the data were analysed with SPSS v.17.0. The statistical method of comparing mean is appropriate to measure the factors in this study (Garvin 2000; Tsai 2007). The significance of Hypothesis 1 to 9 was tested at $\alpha = 0.05$ with 2-tailed Z-tests. The results of hypothesis test are illustrated in Fig. 21.2. The composite reliability was tested with Cronbach's alpha value by SPSS. The results of reliability analysis are shown in Table 21.7. All of the test values are higher than 0.9, therefore, a high internal consistency was demonstrated (Coakes and Steed 2003; Hair et al. 2006).

All the factors were found to be significant as enablers of KMS implementation in India. That is, the enablers identified from the multiple case study and literature were all supported in the survey data. These factors include: collaboration; mutual trust; learning; leadership; incentives and rewards; non-centralisation; non-formalisation; T-shaped skills and information technology infrastructure. The results of Z-tests are illustrated in Fig. 21.2. The results of hypothesis tests are also summarised in Table 21.9.

Subsequent to the results of hypothesis tests on the whole dataset, an analysis down to 'level of city group' was conducted. The team of metropolitan cities include Chennai and Coimbatore and the team of regional cities include Madurai and

Table 21.7 Reliability statistics

Measures	Cronbach's alpha	Cronbach's alpha based on standardised items	No. of items
Collaboration	0.939	0.943	4
Mutual trust	0.905	0.919	4
Learning	0.957	0.960	4
Leadership	0.980	0.983	4
Incentives and rewards	0.972	0.973	4
Non-centralisation	0.963	0.963	4
Non-formalisation	0.975	0.976	4
T-shaped skills	0.955	0.962	4
IT infrastructure	0.951	0.958	4

Table 21.8 Further analysis for hypothesis test

Hypothesis	Z_0 (Metropolitan)	Significance	Z_0 (Regional)	Significance
H1	14.693	*	2.918	*
H2	21.632	*	3.289	*
H3	14.377	*	2.354	*
H4	15.311	*	−0.476	
H5	15.314	*	−0.851	
H6	14.908	*	0.326	
H7	10.848	*	−0.844	
H8	13.095	*	−0.749	
H9	13.975	*	−2.525	

*In opposite direction.

Villupuram. The second-level data analysis divided the whole dataset into two subgroups accordingly. The nine hypotheses were further tested with the two separate datasets. The results of analysis are listed in Table 21.8.

The results of second-level data analysis indicate that there is a significant difference between the two groups. In the metropolitan city group, each of the nine enablers is tested significant. On the other hand, in the second group, only the factors of collaboration, mutual trust and learning are tested significant. In addition, the factor 'Information Technology Infrastructure' was significant in the opposite direction. The differences between the groups are significant. To summarise, results of the hypothesis tests are listed in Table 21.9. The implications, discussions and limitations of data analysis are discussed in the last section.

21.6 Discussions and Conclusions

Having a more comprehensive understanding of what factors can facilitate the implementation of KMS for an organisation is essential and fundamental for executives and managers in order to best exploit their knowledge assets. This study summarised the enabling factors previously discovered and discussed in the literature for further identifying and confirming outcomes in the Indian context with a rigorous two-stage

Table 21.9 Summary of hypothesis tests

Hypothesis	Whole dataset	Metropolitan dataset	Regional dataset
H1	Supported	Supported	Supported
H2	Supported	Supported	Supported
H3	Supported	Supported	Supported
H4	Supported	Supported	Not supported
H5	Supported	Supported	Not supported
H6	Supported	Supported	Not supported
H7	Supported	Supported	Not supported
H8	Supported	Supported	Not supported
H9	Supported	Supported	Not supported

data collection process and analysis. The process included using a multiple case study to explore and identify these factors in Indian organisations, then to further form the proposed model and test it by a broader survey study. A total number of 80 local and international organisations located in four Indian cities were interviewed in the case study, and another 400 organisations were investigated in the survey. The implications and limitations are discussed in this section.

The three most significant organisational culture-related factors—collaboration, mutual trust and learning—are fully supported throughout the whole Indian dataset as well as in metropolitan and regional city datasets. That is, the results are consistent in having the three abovementioned factors accepted as enablers in KMS implementation in India. This finding is also endorsed by the previous literature. For instance, collaboration is suggested as an important enabler in knowledge management, which leads to increased levels of knowledge exchange and knowledge creation (Gan 2006; Lee and Choi 2003). In addition, mutual trust and learning were also found in the literature to be the enablers of knowledge management (Lee and Choi 2003; Nonaka and Takeuchi 1995; Robertson and Hammersley 2000; Takeuchi and Nonaka 2004).

Notwithstanding the above three enablers, other enablers including leadership, incentives and rewards, non-centralisation, non-formalisation, T-shaped skills and information technology infrastructure are all supported by the whole Indian dataset in the hypotheses tests. This indicates that these factors are generally enabling factors for KMS implementation in India. The result is also confirmative with previous literature (Akhavan et al. 2005; Bock et al. 2005; Holsapple 2005; Yu et al. 2004). However, after classifying the whole dataset into metropolitan and regional city subgroups, the results are contrary. The metropolitan dataset indicates that these six factors are all accepted as enablers of KMS implementation in India. On the other hand, the regional dataset reveals that all the factors are not supported as enabling factors. The factor of information technology infrastructure is significantly negative. The result indicates that there exists a substantial difference between these city groups, even though they are all in the same nation.

The first implication for the result is that previous studies have indicated the findings of KM studies may be bound by cultural background. However, in this study, all the enabling factors of KMS identified from different contexts were significantly supported by the whole Indian dataset. This may indicate that these factors are actually effective across different cultural backgrounds and nations. Based on the analysis of case study, a logical inference is that every nation has its unique culture, however, there are still similarities in the areas of business operation, knowledge management and KMS implementation. This is especially true for large or international organisations. Even with the cultural differences, findings in KM studies may still be useful for a multi-national or multi-cultural context if the findings are built on the basis of a wide range of cases.

A further implication is that dimensions other than cultural background may play an important role in generalising the findings of KM studies. In this study, the dissimilarities between cities are more significant than between nations, even though these cities share the same language and culture. The main contrasts between the cities are the economic and industrial structure, as well as the organisational style and size. Based on the analysis of this study, when these dimensions change, recognition of the interviewees towards the influences of KMS-enabling factors change as well. These changes have been reported in the last section and the previous paragraphs in this section. This may explain that most culture-related factors (e.g. learning) were supportive in all cities, despite a major cultural bias between them. However, the structure-oriented factors (e.g. non-centralisation) and system-oriented factors (e.g. IT infrastructure) vary dramatically between the cities due to the diversity in industrial structure and organisational style.

Based on the above discussions, this study makes contributions in the domain of KM. Firstly, this study proposed a theoretical model illustrating the enabling factors of KMS implementation. This model allows researchers and practitioners to understand the enablers of KMS in a more comprehensive and systematic manner compared to previous studies. Secondly, in spite of many studies indicating that culture-related enablers may vary between nations with different cultural backgrounds, all of the nine enablers of KMS identified in different times and places were supported with Indian data. Lastly, the second-level data analysis indicated that various characteristics between cites may lead to substantial differences with regard to what factors actually facilitate their KM. The results would be meaningful for further studies. The limitations of this study include that the data are cross-sectional instead of longitudinal and, thus, the results of this study could only be inferred rather than proven. Furthermore, the findings should not be interpreted as necessarily applicable to organisations with different culture or other characteristics.

Acknowledgments The authors would like to thank Mr. Gerald Gan, for his previous works and contributions on part of the literature reviews and survey instruments.

References

Abdullah, R., Selamat, M. H., Sahibudin, S., & Alias, R. A. (2005). A framework for knowledge management system implementation in collaborative environment for higher learning institution. *Journal of Knowledge Management Practice, 6,* 7–11.

ABS (1993). *Australian and New Zealand standard industrial classification*. Australian Bureau of Statistics. http://www.abs.gov.au/AUSSTATS/abs@.nsf/66f306f503e529a5ca25697e0017661f/acc2f9615290d8eeca25697e0018faf6!OpenDocument. Accessed 02 Oct 2006.

Akhavan, P., Jafari, M., & Fathian, M. (2005). Exploring failure-factors of implementing knowledge management systems in organizations. *Journal of Knowledge Management Practice, 6*.

Al-Hawamdeh, S. (2002). Knowledge management: Re-thinking information management and facing the challenge of managing tacit knowledge. *Information Research, 8*(1).

Alavi, M., & Leidner, D. E. (2001). Review: Knowledge management and knowledge management systems: Conceptual foundations and research issues. *MIS Quarterly, 25*(1), 107–136.

Bock, G.-W., Zmud., R. W., & Kim, Y.-G. (2005). Behavioral intention formation in knowledge sharing: Examining the roles of extrinsic motivators, social-psychological forces, and organisational climate. *MIS Quarterly, 29*(1), 87–111.

Chaudry, A. (2005). *Knowledge sharing practices in Asian institutions: A multi-cultural perspective from Singapore*. Paper presented to World Library and Information Congress 71st IFLA General Conference and Council, Oslo, Norway.

Chennai. (2009). Wikipedia. http://en.wikipedia.org/wiki/Chennai. Accessed 02 Oct 2009.

Coakes, S. J., & Steed, L. G. (2003). *SPSS: Analysis without anguish*. Milton: Wiley.

Coimbatore. (2009). http://en.wikipedia.org/wiki/Coimbatore. Accessed 02 Oct 2009.

Constant, D., Kiesier, S., & Sproull, L. (1996). The kindness of strangers. *Organization Science, 7*(2), 119–135.

Cortada, J., & Woods, J. (1999). *The knowledge management yearbook 1999–2000*. Oxford: Butterworth-Heinemann.

Cowie, J., Cairns, D., Blunn, M., Wilson, C., Pollard, E., & Davidson, D. (2009). A mobile knowledge management and decision support tool for soil analysis. *International Journal of Information Management, 29*, 397–406.

Davenport, T. H., & Prusak, L. (1998). *Working knowledge*. Boston: Harvard Business School Press.

Davvy, C. (2006). Recipients: The key to information transfer. *Knowledge Management Research and Practice, 4*(1), 17–25.

Emelo, R. (2009, May). The future of knowledge management. *Chief Learning Officer*, pp. 44–47.

ERS. (2009). *India*. Economic Research Service, Department of Agriculture, United States. http://www.ers.usda.gov/Briefing/India/. Accessed 02 Oct 2009.

Ford, D., & Staples, D. (2006). Perceived value of knowledge: The potential informer's perception. *Knowledge Management Research and Practice, 4*(1), 3–16.

Frazier, G. L. (2009). Physical distribution and channel management: A knowledge and capabilities perspective. *Journal of Supply Chain Management, 45*(2), 23–36.

Gan, G. G. G. (2006). *Knowledge management practices in multimedia super corridor status companies in Malaysia*. Queensland: University of Southern Queensland.

Garvin, D. (2000). *Learning in action: A guide to putting the learning organization to work*. Boston: Harvard Business School Press.

Hair, J., Black, W., Babin, B., Anderson, R., & Tatham, R. (2006). *Multivariate data analysis* (6th ed.). Upper Saddle River: Pearson Prentice Hall.

Heisig, P. (2009). Harmonisation of knowledge management—comparing 160 KM frameworks around the globe. *Journal of Knowledge Management, 13*(4), 4–31.

Holsapple, C. (2005). The inseparability of modern knowledge management and computer-based technology. *Journal of Knowledge Management, 9*(1), 45–52.

Huber, G. P. (2001). Transfer of knowledge in knowledge management systems: Unexplored issues and suggested studies. *European Journal of Information Systems, 10*, 72–79.

Iansiti, M. (1993). Real-world R&D: Jumping the product generation gap. *Harvard Business Review*, 138–147.

India. (2009). http://en.wikipedia.org/wiki/India. Accessed 02 Oct 2009.

Khalifa, M., & Liu, V. (2003). Determinants of successful knowledge management programs. *Electronic Journal of Knowledge Management, 1*(2), 103–112.

KM, W. (1997). Knowledge management: An introduction and perspective. *Journal of Knowledge Management, 1*(1), 6–14.

Lamont, J. (2009, February). Knowledge management: Naturally green. *KM World*, pp. 5–6.

Lee, H., & Choi, B. (2003). Knowledge management enablers, processes and organisational knowledge: An integrative view and empirical investigation. *Journal of Management Information Systems, 20*(1), 179–228.

Leonard-Barton, D. (1995). *Wellsprings of knowledge: Building and sustaining the sources of innovation*. Boston: Harvard Business School Press.

Li, S. T., & Tsai, F. C. (2009). Concept-guided query expansion for knowledge management with semi-automatic knowledge capturing. *Journal of Computer Information Systems Summer,* 53–65.

Madurai. (2009). http://en.wikipedia.org/wiki/Madurai. Accessed 02 Oct 2009.

Muthiah, S. (2004). *Madras rediscovered*. Chennai: East West Books (Madras) Pvt Ltd.

Nonaka, I., & Takeuchi, H. (1995). *The knowledge-creating company: How Japanese companies create the dynamics of innovation*. USA: Oxford University Press.

North, K., Reinhardt, R., & Schmidt, A. (2004). *The benefits of knowledge management: Some empirical evidence*. Paper presented to The Fifth European Conference on Organisational Knowledge Learning and Capabilities, Innsbruck, Austria.

Okunoye, A., & Karsten, H. (2002). *ITI as a enabler of knowledge management: Empirical perspective from research organisations in sub-Saharan Africa*. Paper presented to 35th Hawaii International Conference on System Sciences, Hawaii, USA.

Oldenburg, P. (2007). *India history: Microsoft Encarta online encyclopedia*. Microsoft Corporation.

Probst, G., Raub, S., & Romhardt, K. (2000). *Managing knowledge—building blocks for success*. UK: Wiley.

Prusak, L. (ed.). (1997). *Knowledge in organizations*. Boston: Butterworth-Heinemann.

Robbins, S., Millett, B., & Cacioppe, R. (2001). *Organisational behaviour: Leading and managing in Australia and New Zealand* (3rd ed.). Malaysia: Prentice Hall.

Robertson, M., & Hammersley, G. (2000). Knowledge management practices within a knowledge-intensive firm: The significance of the people management dimension. *Journal of European Industrial Training, 24*(2), 241–253.

Smith, P. (2004). Knowledge management: People are important. *Journal of Knowledge Management Practice, 5(1),* 4–18.

Song, S. W. (2002). An internet knowledge sharing system. *Journal of Computer Information Systems, 42*(3), 25–30.

Srinivas, N. (2009). Mimicry and revival: The transfer and transformation of management knowledge to India 1959–1990. *International Studies of Management and Organisation, 38*(4), 38–57.

Stewart, T. (1997). *Intellectual capital*. London: Nicholas Brealey.

Stewart, K., Baskerville, R., Storey, V., Senn, J., Raven, A., & Long, C. (2000). Confronting the assumptions underlying the management of knowledge: An agenda for understanding and investigating knowledge management. *The Data Base for Advances in Information Systems, 31*(4), 41–53.

Sveiby, K. (1997). *The new organisational wealth: Managing and measuring knowledge-based assets*. San Francisco: Berret-Koehler.

Szulanski, G., & Jensen, R. (2006). Presumptive adaptation and the effectiveness of knowledge transfer. *Strategic Management Journal, 27,* 10–29.

Takeuchi, H., & Nonaka, I. (eds.). (2004). *Hitotsubashi on knowledge management*. Singapore: Wiley.

Tsai, H.-S. (2007). *A framework and successful strategies for m-business transformation*. Queensland: University of Southern Queensland.

Villupuram. (2009). http://en.wikipedia.org/wiki/Viluppuram. Accessed 02 Oct 2009.

Weber, R., Aha, D. W., & Becerra-Fernandez, I. (2001). Intelligent lessons learned systems. *Expert Systems with Applications, 20*(1), 17–34.

Wong, K. Y., & Aspirwall, E. (2006). Development of a knowledge management initiative and system: A case study. *Expert Systems with Applications, 30*(4), 633–641.

Wood, J., Wallace, J., Zeffane, R., Schermerhorn, J., Hunt, J., & Osborn, R. (1998). *Organisational behaviour: An Asia-Pacfic perspective*. Australia: Wiley.

Yelden, E., & Albers, J. (2004). The case for knowledge management. *Journal of Knowledge Management Practice*.

Yu, S.-H., Kim, Y.-G., & Kim, M.-Y. (2004). *Linking organisational knowledge management drivers to knowledge management performance: An exploratory study*. Paper presented to 37th Hawaii International Conference on System Sciences, Hawaii, USA.

Chapter 22
Expectations, Usability, and Job Satisfaction as Determinants for the Perceived Benefits for the Use of Wireless Technology in Healthcare

Abdul Hafeez-Baig and Raj Gururajan

Abstract This study was conducted to measure the perceptions of Indian healthcare professionals towards the use of wireless handheld devices in the Indian healthcare environment. The mixed mode methodology was adopted to address the research question, regarding the perceived benefits of the wireless technology by Indian healthcare professionals and their intentions to use such a technology in health-care domain. Due to the exploratory nature of the study, the focus group technique was used to identify the initial themes, and these themes were used to develop the survey instrument to further explore the perceptions of the wider healthcare community. Exploratory and confirmatory factor analysis was conducted through SPSS and AMOS, respectively, to understand the relationship of the factors to the perceived perceptions. The findings of the study provide empirical evidence that there is a strong relationship between the constructs Expectations, Usability, and Job Satisfaction and the Indian healthcare professionals' intention to adopt the wireless handheld devices in a healthcare setting. The findings of this study are limited to one of the states in India and further research is required before generalizing the findings of this study.

Keywords Adoption · Handheld devices · Healthcare · Wireless technology

22.1 Introduction

The use of wireless devices for data management is becoming increasingly common in the developed countries' healthcare system. In recent months, a variety of health-care applications have emerged as the cost of the wireless devices has decreased and their processing capabilities have improved. The use of wireless handheld devices has also become popular among end users, as such devices are considered tools that improve both efficiency and productivity (Chousiadis and Pangalos 2003). Even though the future of wireless handheld devices and their usability looks promising, due to the distinct nature of the data, information and working environment in healthcare environment, the adoption of these devices remains a complex process.

A. Hafeez-Baig (✉) · R. Gururajan
School of Information Systems, Faculty of Business and Law,
University of Southern Queensland, Queensland, 4352, Australia
e-mail: abdulhb@usq.edu.au

R. K. Bali et al. (eds.), *Pervasive Health Knowledge Management*,
Healthcare Delivery in the Information Age,
DOI 10.1007/978-1-4614-4514-2_22,

Gururajan et al. (2005) have already reported the perceived advantages of wireless technology to a healthcare setting. These were predominantly derived from existing health literature. Their study conducted in previous years (Gururajan et al. 2005) highlighted the benefits of using the wireless handheld devices and software issues associated with such devices in a healthcare setting, indicating the complexities involved in adopting the new technology at the enterprise level, specifically to the complex healthcare sector (Gururajan et al. 2005).

Subsequent to these publications, their study was conducted with Queensland nurses in 2004, clearly indicating that the drivers can be loosely grouped into four categories, namely: (1) documentation, (2) information management, (3) advantages, and (4) benefits (Gururajan 2005). The reported study established that nurses appear to have a good understanding of the advantages of the technology with comments such as *user-friendliness*, *quicker responses*, *timelier recording*, and *availability of more time* all being associated with the benefits of the devices, and mentioned in the interviews (Gururajan et al. 2007). The comments retrieved from the interviews included that healthcare professionals were aware of the reduction in documentation and the quicker responses associated with the technology. In essence, their study established that if adoption is slow, it may be more an indication of the implementation problems rather that the perceptions of the relative advantages of the technology. These findings are crucial in an Information Systems (IS) perspective, as there is a general trend to establish technology acceptance in information systems domain, based on the perceived feelings rather than the real feelings of the user. When it comes to domains such as nursing, due to the prolonged and continual use of Information and Communication Technologies (ICT), in conjunction with other medical technologies, the workforce issues associated with clinical procedures demand a higher level of comprehension on technology acceptance issues rather than testing models with students as surrogates at a one-time instance. In essence, while many behavioral models, such as Rogers' (1995) Innovation Diffusions theory and Davies et al.'s (1989) Technology Acceptance Model (TAM), portray attributes of technology diffusion, and to some extent their predecessors, technology acceptance, it is important to notice that these models may fail in specific domains such as health, as discovered by Gururajan et al. (2005).

In order to test the proposition that the current perceptions of TAM may not be adequate in identifying the adoption factors in the health domain, a research philosophy was devised to suit the study. While many of the TAM studies are based on quantitative techniques only, it was felt that it would be appropriate to follow a mixed method approach where qualitative techniques can be used to provide proper directions for a subsequent quantitative study. The rationale behind this thinking was based on indications that current TAM models may be inadequate in specific domains and hence it would be appropriate to understand the domain prior to the quantitative generalization of results. In addition to this rationale, there is ample evidence to suggest that qualitative approaches can be used to determine the research direction when the research issues are not clearly known. In the case of this study, due to the limited availability of empirical studies on wireless handheld technology adoption, it was felt that this research philosophy would provide direction to the research method utilized.

In summary, the results reported in this study were derived from adopting a different research philosophy to that of the most common IS studies in the technology adoption domain and specifically tailored to the health domain. It is believed that this approach has strengthened the findings of this research study.

22.2 Literature Review

In healthcare literature, the concept of wireless technology is discussed by many authors (Hu et al. 2002; Wisnicki 2002; Dyer 2003; Sausser 2003; Simpson 2003; Gururajan et al. 2007). For example, Gururajan et al. (2007) provides details of implementing a wireless technology for a healthcare provider in Australia and the associated issues encountered in such an implementation. Wisnicki (2002) provides details of how broadband technology, a component of wireless technology, can be used in healthcare. The discussion provided by Wisnicki (2002) involves the high cost of setting up wireless technology in a healthcare setting, improvements to patient care using this technology, and potential cost-effective quality of service to patients. Sausser (2003) provides information on how to improve clinical quality using wireless technology including challenges for maintaining security and privacy. Sausser (2003) also discusses the concept of portable devices for data collection purposes by providing an argument on the benefits that can be realized using these devices. Simpson (2003), while critiquing the nursing domain, stresses the need for the innovative use of IT to improve patient care. He points out those new IT technologies can help to address some of the chronic problems encountered, including saving nurses' time, skilled nursing care, and home health care. He also provides details on the expended time per hour of nursing care and suggests that new technologies would provide solutions to some of the acute problems of nursing due to these time constraints. Dyer (2003), on the other hand, provides details of how text messaging using wireless devices can be effectively used to remind patients of their appointments. He reports the idea behind a radically new system of managing patient care in conjunction with modern telecommunication applications using wireless devices to improve the quality of patient care. Common to all these studies is the use of emerging wireless technologies in healthcare and the potential benefits that can be achieved.

Despite these indications as to how wireless technology can help healthcare organizations to address some of their problems, there is no decisive research study to identify the factors that enable the adoption of wireless technology in healthcare. Especially in the nursing domain, wireless handheld devices play a crucial role in collecting data at the point of care. Data collection using a wireless device must be integrated properly with clinical practices to derive any benefits. Therefore, it is believed that both internal and external factors will play a crucial role in defining the adoption of wireless handheld technology in healthcare. This has resulted in the following overarching research question of this study:

Would the perceived benefits of the wireless technology lead to the adoption of wireless handheld devices in the Indian healthcare environment?

22.3 Research Methodology

The methodology adopted to address the research question was the mixed mode methodology; the qualitative technique of focus groups was adopted to explore the initial themes. The quantitative technique of a survey approach was adopted to gather the views of the wider community of healthcare professionals and to understand their views about the use of wireless handheld devices in an Indian healthcare setting. In this research study, qualitative approach is adopted due to the exploratory nature of the research. Both qualitative and quantitative approaches are not competing against each other, rather findings of qualitative research complements the finding of the quantitative research in this study.

Qualitative methods employ techniques such as interviews, field studies, observation, case studies, and phenomenological, ethnographical, and grounded theory (Tashakkori and Teddlie 1998; Nemana 2004). Due to the relative newness of this study, it was felt that this study could accommodate multiple approaches of qualitative research. While the first phase utilized a focus group discussion and in-depth interview techniques, the second phase used a quantitative study, which was based on the result of the qualitative techniques. This study derived the quantitative instrument from the qualitative data, as previous quantitative instruments were found to be unsuitable to the nursing domain in testing the technology adoption issues. We believe that this aspect is particularly favorable for this study as it can identify and then confirm known factors that would enable the adoption of technology in a given setting. Furthermore, this approach can help identify emerging factors beyond those identified in the traditional TAM studies, which can in turn lead to the refinement of what is already established in the literature.

Previous studies also indicate that qualitative methods are better positioned to identify the social construction of reality or meanings and also to explain the behavioral aspects of a particular group of people (Neuman 1997). This study differs from previous TAM studies in this specific aspect, as in this study, the factors are being extracted from real users in their own setting, and not from surrogates. Furthermore, human behavioral aspects are better captured through qualitative methods such as interviews because the behavioral patterns are defined through social interactions, and the historical and cultural perspectives that influence an individual's life.

Qualitative methods accommodate personal experiences. Due to the nature of the qualitative data, these methods are criticized for reliability issues (Neuman 1997). Studies indicate that these issues can be overcome by employing quality interpretations (Tashakkori and Teddlie 1998). Quality interpretation indicates either personal interaction with the participants or participation in the research process (Patton 1990). In techniques such as hermeneutics, personal experiences are explained and an understanding of issues is explained through participation in the research. This is done either as an observer or as a participant of the process. Thus, feelings, emotions, and related concepts are experienced and then explained. These measures are considered to be quality features of interpretation. Employing these measures in qualitative data provides an excellent understanding.

These aspects have been accommodated in the first phase, qualitative data collection, of this study where interviews were conducted. Specifically, the contents of the interview transcripts were analyzed thematically. Codes were developed, which provided the basis for cross-case analysis and helped identify and analyze emerging patterns of themes (Patton 1990; Carlson 2004).

Furthermore, in a discipline like IS, the contemporary research approach is to employ quantitative methods. Qualitative methods are not generally employed to a greater extent due to the criticism that the qualitative methods lack the rigor required to address reliability and validity issues. In this study, this claim is rejected as qualitative approaches also address issues of reliability and validity. The aspects of reliability and validity were established by demonstrating that the interview themes saturated after the 20th interview (Gururajan 2005). Furthermore, we believe that in our study, construct validity has been adequately addressed. Firstly, multiple sources of information were used (Ying 2003). While interviews constitute the primary source of information, some of the informants provided supporting secondary data, which comprised archival white papers and other resources. Secondly, the informant nurses involved in the study belonged to various categories of departments, and therefore provided different perspectives. Considering different perspectives constitutes an important type of triangulation of qualitative information sources as it prevents biased opinions (Patton 1990). Thirdly, the interviewer employed to conduct the interviews was independent of the investigators (Patton 1990; Denzin 1989). This reduces the potential bias, which is commonly cited as a limitation of the qualitative methods in general interviews (Frankfort-Nachmias 1996). Finally, the chains of evidence, tracing the conclusions to the interview summary and to the interview transcripts, were also maintained. According to Yin (1994), these enhance the construct validity as well as the reliability of the research, thereby boosting its overall quality. With this, we believe that we have adequately addressed the reliability and validity concerns that are inherent in qualitative methods.

In addition to the above, some recent studies (Gregor 2005) have argued that IS discipline should address the inclusion of more qualitative approaches, especially in studying issues relating to ICT. In the context of this study, we argue that the behavioral factors influence ICT usage as suggested by TAM models. As a consequence, the inclusion of qualitative research techniques is of paramount importance.

When the initial exploratory qualitative phase was completed, this study employed a quantitative approach to confirm the results of the exploratory study and to establish further generalizations. While this is most common in IS, what is new in this study is deriving the instrument from the interview data as current instruments used in TAM studies appeared to be restrictive. It is believed that this approach has strengthened the outcome of the study by providing consistency to the findings established through the qualitative approaches in the previous stage. It also brought out newer perspectives through quantitative data collection techniques. Specifically, factor analysis was used in this stage.

To measure the intention to use the wireless technology in a healthcare setting was further subdivided into three themes, identified through the focus group data analysis, published in our earlier research, and as outlined below (Gururajan 2007; Gururajan et al. 2008):

1. Expectations (E) of the healthcare professionals in a healthcare setting.
2. Usability (U) associated with the use of wireless handheld devices in a healthcare setting.
3. Job Satisfaction (JS) provided by wireless handheld devices in a healthcare setting.

Through data reduction techniques and confirmatory factor analysis, the associations of items measuring the intention of the Indian healthcare professional towards wireless handheld devices was further tested through exploratory and confirmatory factor analysis. Once the associations and unique contributions of the items towards the variables was confirmed, the researchers used Analysis of Moment Structures (AMOS) to develop a model to determine the causal effects of the variables, E, U, and JS, towards the intention to use wireless handheld devices in the Indian environment. The next section provides the detailed analysis of this strategy adopted in this research.

22.4 Data Analysis and Discussion

The data were initially analyzed for reliability by calculating the Cronbach's Alpha for the overall items used to measure the intention of the healthcare professionals and individual items used to measure the three themes identified through the qualitative study. A brief summary of the reliability analysis is shown in Table 22.2. The overall reliability of 0.891 for all the items used to measure the perceived intentions of the healthcare professionals for "Perceived Benefits" (PB) from the healthcare professionals towards the wireless handheld technology in the Indian healthcare environment, and subsequently the value of the Cronbach's Alpha was also calculated for the factors measuring the PB. The perceived benefits from the use of wireless handheld devices were measured by 12 items in the survey instruments developed through the findings of the qualitative study. A Pearson's correlation analysis was conducted to explore the interitem correlations of the items used to measure the perceived benefits that could be achieved through the use of wireless handheld technology in a healthcare setting.

Interitem correlation analysis provides strong evidence for the relationship of the 12 measuring items with the PB variable. For example, none of the correlation values were significantly higher either, most of the values were below 0.5 for the interitem correlation value. The actual value ranged from 0.24 to 0.51, except the item that wireless handheld devices will provide added values, which was 0.7, which is not unreasonably higher either. Furthermore, the data reduction technique that was used to see the natural groupings and associations of the items with each other was further explored. Furthermore, to ascertain that the items associated with each variable were

Table 22.1 Rotated component matrix[a] for data reduction technique

Descriptions	Expectations	Usability	Job satisfaction
Provide added value	0.864		
Peer group attitude will influence	0.822		
Healthcare will benefit from the use	0.758		
Improve patient expectation	0.707		
Will provide real-time access		0.815	
Will save time		0.807	
Will provide benefits		0.686	
Flexibility will provide added value		0.646	
Make my existing job easy			0.842
Improve my job performance			0.841
Mobility is relevant in my job			0.657

[a]Rotated factor analysis provide three factors, Expectations, Usability, and Job Satisfactions. The clearly shows high loading of these items to three constructs

Table 22.2 Summary of reliability statistics

Items	Cronbach's alpha	Cronbach's alpha based on standardized items	No. of items
PB	0.891	0.891	12
E	0.848	0.840	4
U	0.819	0.819	4
JS	0.793	0.793	3

only measuring the same variable and were associated with the item as well, the factor analysis was conducted through the SPSS data reduction technique, as shown below in Table 22.1.

The data reduction technique clearly identified three-factor solutions with high loading associated with each variable identified as E, U, and JS (loading ranges from 0.657 to 0.864). There was only one item, which did not associate with any of the variables through the factor analysis, and this item was dropped from any further higher-level statistical techniques. After the data reduction technique, a reliability analysis was conducted on the individual variables with the associated items to assure the associations of items identified through factor analysis. A summary of this reliability is provided in Table 22.2.

The three-factor solutions identified through the data reduction technique show a high level of reliability in all the three variables and their respective items from the questionnaire (Cronbach's Alpha value ranges from 0.793 to 0.848). According to Hair et al. (2006), this level of reliability is considered a high level of reliability items measuring the same variables (Hair et al. 2006). The initial correlation analysis was also studied through the statistical software package SPSS version 18 to ascertain the associations of the items and that all the correlations were statistically significant.

Reliability alpha values for the three variables, E, U, and Job JS, were also high. These values aligned with the literature on reliability and provided confidence that further higher-level statistical analysis could be performed on the data to further explore the Indian healthcare professionals' intention to use wireless handheld devices in a healthcare setting. Furthermore, AMOS 18 was used to conduct the confirmatory factor analysis and to measure the healthcare professionals' perceptions that healthcare will benefit from the use of wireless handheld devices in a healthcare setting.

Table 22.3 Summary of confirmatory factor analysis

<table>
<tr><th>No</th><th>Variable Name</th><th>Confirmatory Factor</th><th>Indices Values</th></tr>
<tr><td>1</td><td>Expectation</td><td>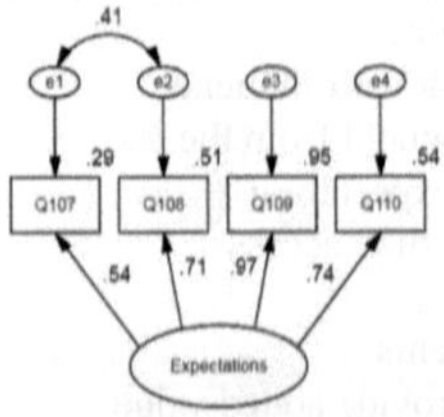
</td><td>Chi Square X^2 = 8.8
P = 0.003
X^2/df = 8.8 CMIN = 8.8
GFI = .99 AGFI = 0.94
TLI = .96 CFI = .99
RMR = .091
RMSEA = 0.10</td></tr>
<tr><td>2</td><td>Usability</td><td>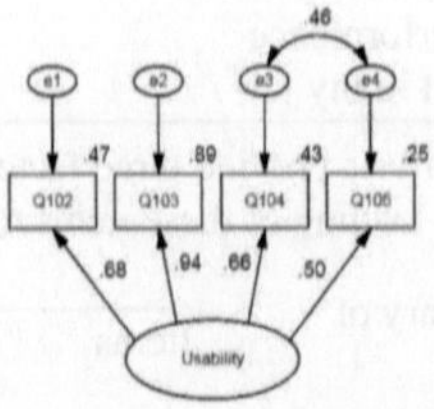
</td><td>Chi Square X^2 = 10.6
P = 0.001
X^2/df = 10.6 CMIN = 10.5
GFI = .99 AGFI = 0.93
TLI = .94 CFI = .99
RMR = .091
RMSEA = 0.12</td></tr>
<tr><td>3</td><td>Job Satisfactions</td><td>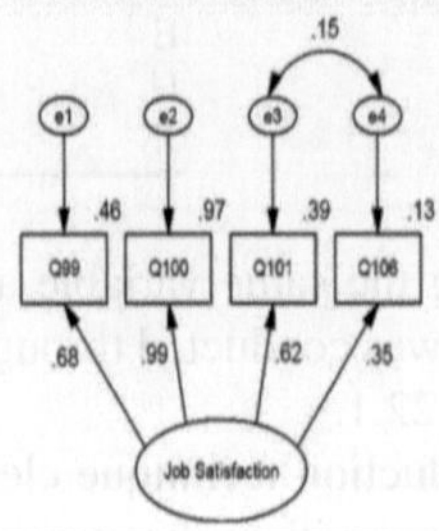
</td><td>Chi Square X^2 = 8.2
P = 0.004
X^2/df = 8.2 CMIN = 8.2
GFI = .99 AGFI = 0.94
TLI = .95 CFI = .99
RMR = .021
RMSEA = 0.10</td></tr>
</table>

The number of 'fit' statistics have been used by researchers to assess how well the model fits the data (Byrne 2001; Hair et al. 2006). The fit statistics used in this research can be summarised as follows:

1. Chi-square (for χ^2, an acceptable level of fit is $p > 0.05$; a reasonable level of fit is $p > 0.001$).
2. Normed chi-square (for χ^2/df, an acceptable level of fit is $1 < \chi^2/df < 2$; a reasonable level of fit is $\chi^2/df < 3$).
3. Goodness-of-fit index (for GFI, an acceptable level of fit is $0.95 < GFI < 1$; a reasonable fit value would be $0.90 < GFI < 0.95$).
4. Tucker-Lewis index (for TLI, an acceptable value is $TLI > 0.95$; a reasonable value of fit is $0.9 < TLI < 0.95$; a lack of model parsimony would be $TLI > 1$).
5. Root-mean-square error of approximation (for RMSEA, an acceptable fit value is $RMSEA < 0.05$; a reasonable level of fit would be $0.05 < RMSEA < 0.08$; Holmes-Smith 2000; Byrne 2001).

Table 22.3 below summarises the findings of the confirmatory factor analysis through the AMOS technique.

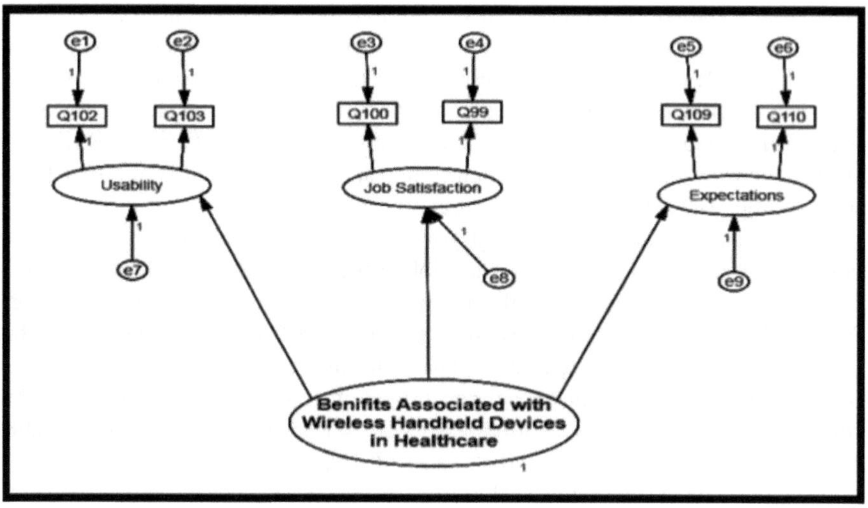

Fig. 22.1 Summary of relationship for the variables U, JS, and E to intention to use

The confirmatory factor analysis shown above reaffirms the fact that the individual items used in this research to develop and measure individual constructs uniquely contributed to measuring the same constructs. The CFC analysis also confirmed that the factors identified by data reduction techniques used through SPSS as factor analysis were correct as well. Confirmatory factor analysis techniques also identified the fact that there existed some correlations between the two items uniquely contributing to the same construct; this correlation ranges from 0.15 to 0.46 as shown above. According to Hair et al. (2006), such correlation is at an acceptable level and there are no very highly correlated items existing in any of the constructs. Therefore, at this stage of the analysis, all the items would be retained for further analysis. A further high-level multiple regression analysis was conducted to further explore the role of the variables "Job Satisfaction, Usability, and Expectations" of the healthcare professionals in the context of their perceptions that healthcare will benefit from the use of wireless handheld devices in an Indian healthcare setting. The figure below used the AMOS application to explore this relationship between the constructs.

Figure 22.1 presents fit indices for the data and shows good fit between the data and the proposed individual model for the composite variable used to predict the effect of constructs Usability, Job satisfactions, and the Expectations on the construct "Perceived Benefits" to understand the intention of healthcare professionals towards the wireless handheld technology in healthcare setting. All the prominent indices show a good fit between the data and the model for each of the composite variables. For example, the value of the Goodness-of-fit index (GFI), a measure of the relative amount of variance and covariance, for all the composite variables was well above the benchmark value ($\geq$0.9) and is considered as being a good fit (Joreskog and Sorbom 1993); the Root mean square residual (RMR) values for all the composite variables were less than the benchmark value ($\leq$0.05) as suggested by Hair et al. (2006), Wu et al. (2007), and Wu et al. (2008). This means that the model explains the correlation to be within an average error of RMR values (ranges from 0.002 to 0.011, way below 0.05; Hu and Bentler 1995). These results show that the measurement model used to calculate the composite variables has a good fit with the data based on GFI, RMSER, and AGFI. In addition to these, other indices of fit such as NFI, CFI, and RMR also support the view that the model for each composite variable fits the sample data fairly well (Bentler 1990, 1995; Hu and Bentler 1995).

This model was developed through AMOS to understand the relationship of the constructs Expectations, Usability, and Job Satisfaction identified through the exploratory factor analysis and confirmed by the confirmed factor analysis through AMOS. The measurement indices, such as GFI, RMR, RMSEA, AGFI, and chi-square, were found to be significant and within the range of acceptable values to demonstrate that data fit the model and provide the strength of relationship (chi-square $\chi^2 = 13.3$, $p = 0.038$, $\chi^2/df = 2.2$, CMIN = 13.3, GFI =0 0.99, AGFI = 0.98, TLI = 0.99, CFI = 0.99, RMR = 0.014, and RMSEA = 0.043). Therefore, one of the implications from this research can be drawn as, that individuals who are responsible for implementations of wireless handheld technology and training of the employees on the use of wireless handheld technology in healthcare environment should understand that if individuals do not see any benefits in terms of their expectations from the handheld technology and technology alignment with their existing job specification, uptake of the wireless technology may be questionable. Healthcare professionals measure the perceived benefits of using wireless technology is closely associated with "Job Satisfaction, Usability, and Expectations" of the healthcare professionals towards their intentions to use the wireless technology. All the three variables, U, JS, and E, provided a significant path, with p values statistically significant as well. The finding of this research provides initial insight for the potential use and perceived benefits associated with the use of wireless handheld devices in a healthcare environment.

22.5 Conclusion and Limitations

This research was conducted to understand the perceptions of Indian healthcare professionals towards the uses of wireless handheld technology in the healthcare environment. The findings of this study demonstrate that constructs such as Usability, Expectations, and Job Satisfaction are critical for the healthcare professionals' intention to use such a technology. The study also provides evidence that perceived benefits from the wireless handheld technology is critical for the acceptance of such technology in the Indian healthcare environment. To the researcher's best knowledge, finding of this could be of a unique nature. However, the findings of this study cannot be generalized as the data used were limited to a single state of India and further research is needed in different states of India and even in different societies to be able to generalize the findings of this research study.

References

Bentler, P. M. (1990). Comparative fit indexex in structural models. *Psychological Bulletin, 107,* 238–246.
Bentler, P. M. (1995). *EQS structural equation program manual.* Encino: Multivariate Software.
Byrne, B. M. (2001). *Structural equation modeling with AMOS.* Mahwah: Lawrence Erlbaum Associates.
Carlson, L. (2004). Health information technology widely praised, slowly adopted. *Employee Benefit News, 18*(15), 41.
Chousiadis, C., & Pangalos, G. (2003). Implementing authentication and mointoring in healthcare information sysytems. *Health Informatics Journal, 9*(2), 79–87.
Davies, F. D., Bagozzi, R. P., et al. (1989). User acceptance of computer technology: A comparison of two theoretical models. *Communications of the ACM, 35*(8), 982–1003.
Denzin, N. K. (1989). *The research act* (3rd ed.). Englewood Cliffs: Prentice Hall.
Dyer, O. (2003). Patients will be reminded of appointments by text messages. *British Medical Journal, 326*(402), 281.
Frankfort-Nachmias, C., & Nachmias, D. (1996). *Research methods in the social sciences* (5th ed.). New York: St. Martin's Press.
Gregor, S. (2005). The struggle towards an understanding of theory in information systems. In Hart D. & Gregor S. (Eds.), *Information systems foundations workshop 2004* (pp. 3–11). Canberra: ANU ePress. https://researchers.anu.edu.au/publications/10742
Gururajan, R. (2005). A study of the use of hand-held devices in an emergency department. *Journal of Telehealth, 1*(3), 31–34.
Gururajan, R. (2007). *Drivers of wireless technology in healthcare: An Indian Study.* Proceedings of the 15th European Conference on Information Systems (ECIS 2007), University of St Gallen., St Gallen, Switzerland.
Gururajan, R., Kerr, D., et al. (2005). *An investigation into the factors of adoption of wireless applications for data management by nurses.* Asic-Pacific Decision Sciences Institute, Tiwan, Asic-Pacific Decision Sciences Institute (APDSI).
Gururajan, R., McDonald, J., Gururajan, V., & Genrich, R. (2007) An exploratory qualitative study to determine factors influencing the adoption of mobile learning for tertiary education. *International Journal of Technology, Knowledge and Society, 2*(6), 33–40. ISSN 1832-3669
Gururajan, R., Hafeez-Baig, A., et al. (2008). *Clinical factors and technological barriers as determinants for the intention to use wireless handheld technology.* Healthcare Environment: An Indian Case Study. 16th European Conference on Information Systems, National University of Ireland, Galway.
Hair, J. F., Black, W. C., et al. (2006). *Multivariate data analysis.* Upper Saddle River: Pearson Education Inc.
Holmes-Smith, P. (2000). *Introduction to structural equation modeling using AMOS 4.0: Course notes.* Melbourne: SREAMS.
Hu, L., & Bentler, P. M. (1995). Evaluating model fit. In R. H. Hoyle (Ed.), *Structural equation modeling: Concepts, issues and applications.* Thousand Oaks: Sage.
Hu, P. J., Chau, P. Y. K., et al. (2002). Adoption of telemedicine technology by health care organisations: An exploratory study. *Journal of Organisational Computing and Electronic Commerce, 12*(3), 197–222.
Joreskog, K. G., & Sorbom, D. (1993). *LISREL 8: Structural equaction modeling with the SIMPLIS command language.* Chicago: Scentific Software International.
Nemana, R. (2004). *Future of wireless in healthcare.* Paper presentate to ElderTech Symposium.
Neuman, W. L. (1997). *Social Research Methods: Qualitative and Quantitative Approaches.* Boston: Allyn and Bacon.
Patton, A. Q. (1990). *Qualitative evaluation and research methods.* Newbury Park: Sage.
Rogers, E. M. (1995). *Diffusion of innovations.* New York: Free Press.

Sausser, G. D. (2003). Thin is in: Wb-based systems enhance security, clinical quality. *Healthcare Financial Management, 57,* 86–88.

Simpson, L. R. (2003). The patient point of view—IT matters. *Nurse Admin Q, Lippincott Williams & Wilkins Inc., 27,* 254–256.

Tashakkori, A., & Teddlie, C. (1998). *Mixed methodology: Combining qualitative and quantitative approaches*. Thousand Oaks: Sage.

Wisnicki, H. J. (2002). Wireless networking transforms healthcare: Physician's practices better able to handle workflow, increase productivity (The human connection). *Ophthalmology Times, 27*(21), 38–41.

Wu, J.-H., Wang, S.-C., et al. (2007). Mobile computing acceptance factors in the healthcare industry: A structural equaction model. *International Journal of Medical Informatics, 76,* 66–77.

Wu, J.-H., Shen, W.-S., et al. (2008). Testing the technology acceptance model for evaluating healthcare professionals' intention to use an adverse event reporting system. *International Journal for Quality in Health Care, 20*(2), 123–129.

Yin, R. K. (1994). *Case study research—design and methods* (2nd ed.). Thousand Oaks: Sage.

Ying, A. (2003). Mobile physician order entry. *Journal of Healthcare Information Management, 17*(1), 58–63.

Chapter 23
Web 2.0 Panacea or Placebo for Superior Healthcare Delivery?

Nilmini Wickramasinghe, Bill Davey and Arthur Tatnall

Abstract Tim Berners-Lee once said that 'Web 2.0' was 'what the Web was supposed to be all along' (Berners-Lee 1989, 2006). In 2008, Eseynbach and colleagues coined the term 'Medicine 2.0' to describe the broad adoption of Web 2.0 technologies into the healthcare context as well as the emergence of personal healthcare application platforms and personally controlled health record platforms (Eseynbach 2008). Should we then extrapolate and infer then, that this is what e-health should have been all along or will this latest development be another headache for healthcare systems globally, which are already haemorrhaging money with no sign of any solution to effect sustainable value-driven healthcare solutions. The following examines the possibilities for Web 2.0 to enable superior healthcare delivery in an attempt to shed some light on this question.

Keywords Web 2.0 · Healthcare · Social networking · Internet · Learning tools · Information

23.1 Introduction

Today, healthcare systems globally are under tremendous pressure to deliver cost-effective solutions (Wickramasinghe et al. 2011). In addition, most notably in the United States, there is also a growing pressure for healthcare organisations to justify meaningful use of technologies adopted (Wickramasinghe et al. 2009). Concurrently, however, we are seeing the development and diffusion of Web 2.0 technologies and more interestingly the incorporation of these technologies and applications (such as Facebook and Twitter, wikis, blogs and podcasts) into various healthcare contexts to enhance patient communications, support and information sources in an attempt to

N. Wickramasinghe (✉) · B. Davey
Epworth Chair Health Information Management,
School of Business Information Technology and Logistics,
RMIT University, GPO Box 2476, Melbourne VIC 3001, Australia
e-mail: nilmini.wickramasinghe@rmit.edu.au

B. Davey
e-mail: bill.davey@rmit.edu.au

A. Tatnall
Victoria University, 8001 Melbourne VIC, Australia

R. K. Bali et al. (eds.), *Pervasive Health Knowledge Management*, Healthcare Delivery in the Information Age,
DOI 10.1007/978-1-4614-4514-2_23,

provide improved healthcare and patient services (Barsky and Purdon 2006; Boulos et al. 2006). The purpose of this chapter is to present a review of research into the use of social media and Web 2.0 to facilitate an appreciation and understanding of the possible applications of Web 2.0 for effecting superior healthcare delivery; since, arguably, Web 2.0 has the potential of offering the most pervasive technology solutions for various aspect of healthcare delivery. This synthesis has been taken from a review of the literature as well as the presentation of a specific case study solution in a bariatric setting. Taken together, it clearly shows the myriad of possibilities for Web 2.0 in the healthcare space, or Medicine 2.0 as some have called this latest development of e-health (Eseynbach 2008), and the potential benefits as well as the dangers and the possibilities to facilitate the attainment of superior healthcare delivery.

23.2 Background to Web 2.0 Development

The World Wide Web (WWW) concept was invented in 1989 by Tim Berners-Lee, a software consultant at the European Laboratory for Particle Physics (CERN) in Switzerland (Berners-Lee 1989). Berners-Lee wanted to find a means by which the physicists at CERN could easily share information about their research and the software was developed to improve information sharing and document handling. The WWW allowed pages containing hypertext links to be stored in a way that allowed other computers access to these pages. The main underlying technology for the WWW is hypertext, which provides a dynamic means of organising and accessing information where pages of information are connected together by hyperlinks (or hypertext links). These allow a user to move to the page where the information designated by that link is to be found simply by clicking on the hyperlink.

The second generation of the Web (Web 2.0) has been called the 'Social Web' because, in contrast to Web 1.0, its content can be more easily generated and published by users, and the collective intelligence of users encourages more democratic use. Originally, the WWW was intended to be used to share ideas and promote discussion within a scientific community (Boulos and Wheeler 2007; Berners-Lee 1989). Web 2.0 heralds a return to these original uses and prompts significant changes in the ways the World Wide Web is being used in healthcare and education. Web 2.0 technologies represent a quite revolutionary way of managing and repurposing/remixing online information, in comparison with the traditional Web 1.0 model (Boulos and Wheeler 2007).

It is interesting to note that Berners-Lee is concerned that applications such as Facebook, in creating 'walled sites' with 'closed silos of content', may lead to fragmentation of the Web, which would go against its founding principles (Halliday 2010). Whether or not this happens, time will tell.

On the back of the exponential growth of Web 1.0, Web 2.0 software emerged to facilitate new online activities, many of which could not have been previously achieved. Online social interaction has been enriched through the use of wikis, blogs and podcasts (Beldarrain 2006). Web 2.0 encourages a more human approach to interactivity on the Web, better supports group interaction (Sharp 2006) and fosters a greater sense of community in a potentially 'cold' social environment (Wallace 1999). As Abram (2005) has claimed, the social Web '... is about conversations, interpersonal networking, personalisation and individualism'. It is the 'People-centric' Web (Robinson 2005). This potentially makes it suitable for incorporation into healthcare delivery contexts.

Although Web 2.0 has not supplanted Web 1.0, it has undeniably changed and challenged the perceptions and expectations of those who use it. This study will in part investigate the ability of Web 2.0 software to open up new possibilities for collaborative networked learning in health and healthcare. A useful starting point is to compare earlier Web-based applications with emerging features of the social Web:

- *Flexibility in Web 2.0*: Greater levels of participation, agency and democracy are possible in the social Web, where users act simultaneously as readers and writers. This has been very much helped by the significant growth of computer ownership and Internet use over the past decade (O'Reilly 2005; Parakh 2006).
- *An 'architecture of participation'*: Web 2.0 emphasises the pre-eminence of content creation over content consumption. Information is liberated from corporative control (traditional content owners or their intermediaries), allowing anyone to create, assemble, organise (tag), locate and share content to meet their own needs or the needs of clients—Web 2.0 is structured around open programming interfaces that allow widespread participation (Bolous and Wheeler 2007). The open programming affords users the added advantage of reducing the technical skill required to use the Web 2.0 features, by allowing users to focus on the information and collaborative tasks themselves with few delivery obstacles. Such technology is known as 'transparent technology' (Wheeler et al. 2005).
- *Interactivity in Web 2.0*: Web 2.0 also encourages significantly more interaction between users, a feature that most theorists argue is vital in e-learning. Interaction encourages deeper and more active learning engagement, builds communities of learning (Wenger 2000) and enables *communication* between participants (Fahey 2003). Web 2.0 interactivity creates a feeling of belonging to a community as well as a sense of empowerment and ownership (Barsky and Purdon 2006).

Thus, what is apparent is that Web 2.0 has transformed the Web into an environment that provides richer user experiences by allowing for the combination of disparate information in a variety of data formats, the facilitation of interaction between multiple parties and the collaboration and sharing of information (Cheung et al. 2008).

Given that data, information and knowledge are essential in all healthcare operations (Wickramasinghe et al. 2009), it is only logical to conclude that the technologies and applications of Web 2.0 should be able to be utilised in healthcare contexts to facilitate superior healthcare delivery.

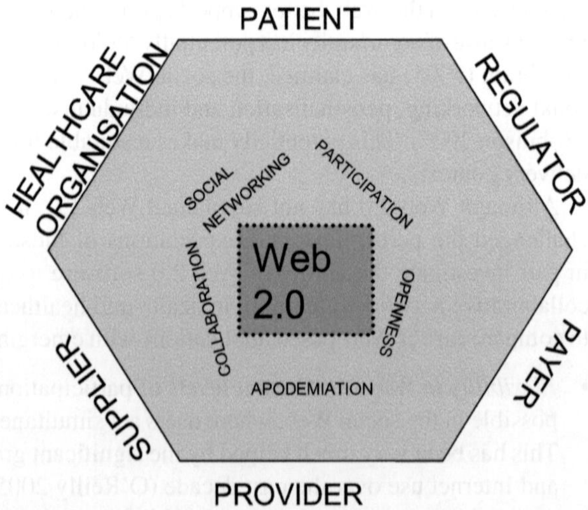

Fig. 23.1 Web 2.0 for health. (Adapted from Eseynbach 2008)

23.3 Web 2.0 in Healthcare

At a time when e-health is still developing and yet to be completely embraced by healthcare systems through out the world, Web 2.0 now begins to offer a broad range of technologies and approaches, such as the personal health application platform or the personally controlled health record (Eseynbach 2008). This wave of innovation has prompted Eseynbach and colleagues to coin the term Medicine 2.0 to describe Web 2.0 for healthcare (ibid).

In trying to understand the benefits of Web 2.0 for healthcare, it is important to try to understand how and/or what Web 2.0 impacts with regard to healthcare delivery. To do this, it is first important to realise that healthcare operations are conducted in a space where a Web of players consisting of healthcare providers, healthcare organisations, regulator, payer(s), suppliers and most importantly patients interact (Wickramasinghe et al. 2009; Fig. 23.1). When the tools, technologies and capabilities of Web 2.0 are introduced into this healthcare operational space, five emerging and key themes become apparent (Eseynbach 2008; Fig. 23.1). Specifically, the five themes are: (1) social networking—which enables and facilitates the development of groups including family, friends, co-workers, etc. with like healthcare problems to develop support groups, (2) participation—which enables users and patients to become more empowered and take an active role in their healthcare, e.g. with chronic disease management, (3) apomediation—which enables data and information to be filtered and rated so consumers have confidence in the validity of the material they are reviewing, (4) collaboration—which enables groups to connect to other groups who would not have been able to connect before and (5) openness—which enables healthcare transactions and treatments to be visible and transparent (ibid). Figure 23.1 serves to depict these key themes together with the Web of healthcare players.

In all three aspects of healthcare, i.e. preventions, diagnosis and treatment, the process is now seen as more than the application of scientific principles: None of these aspects can be effected if the community is not engaged and those involved are not supported. The five themes, presented in Fig. 23.1, enabled by Web 2.0, then can play a key role in regard to the management and support for the patient. Moreover, the various applications now available for health consumers to monitor and manage their health problems by combining the power of mobile computing with social interaction to alter behavior (Spallek et al. 2010) would not be readily available without the advances of Web 2.0.

Research into the means of changing behaviours indicates that the social network may be an important factor (Christakis and Fowler 2008). The transmissive effect of attitudes within social networks also indicates the potential for the network to be valuable or dangerous for any given group (Fowler and Christakis 2011) although there is some question regarding the sense of outcomes from studying self-selecting communities (Cohen-Cole and Fletcher 2008).

Engagement and support, however, should not be limited to just the patient and Web 2.0 facilitates support for healthcare professionals as easily as it does for patients as the following comment serves to highlight:

> Consulting with colleagues is an accepted, expected and essential component of providing comprehensive healthcare to patients. It becomes increasingly critical as technology allows an unprecedented barrage of new scientific information for the healthcare provider to absorb. This can present challenges for a new physician, who may not have established the contacts or credentials to easily find support, or who feels isolated in the midst of experienced clinicians and academicians; it can just as easily be a challenge for the experienced physician who is physically isolated from his peers. (Spallek et al. 2010, p. 96)

In addition, Web 2.0 and the five key themes identified in Fig. 23.1 also provide opportunities for research as well as providing a support for training medical professionals in new knowledge, the use of Web 2.0 includes creating this new knowledge by creating communities of researchers and for allowing researchers to study communities.

The five key themes identified in Fig. 23.1 also have significant and far-reaching impact in the area of teaching and learning in the healthcare context as discussed in the next section.

23.3.1 *Web 2.0 as a Learning Tool in Health*

Web 2.0 applications, particularly wikis, blogs and podcasts, have been increasingly adopted by many online health-related professional and educational services. Because of their ease of use and rapidity of deployment, they offer the opportunity for powerful information sharing and ease of collaboration (Boulos and Wheeler 2007). Wikis are Web sites that can be edited by anyone who has access to them. The word 'blog' is a contraction of 'Web log'—an online Web journal that can offer a resource-rich multimedia environment. Podcasts are repositories of audio and video materials that can be 'pushed' to subscribers, even without user intervention.

Medical and health-related wiki examples include the Flu Wiki (UK), which is intended to help local public health communities prepare for, and perhaps cope, with a possible influenza epidemic (http://www.marshallk.blogspot.com/2005/07/flu-wiki-serious-application-of-new.html, http://www.fluwikie.com/) and Ganfyd, an online collaborative medical reference that is edited by medical professions and invited non-medical experts (http://ganfyd.org).

Medical examples of the use of blogs include Clinical Cases and Images (http://clinicalcases.blogspot.com) and the blog of the Dermatology Interest Group at the University of Texas Medical Branch (DIG@UTMB). Podcast examples in health-related uses include New York University Ophthalmology Continuing Medical Education Program (http://www.asseenfromhere.com), the New England Journal of Medicine podcasts (http://content.nejm.org/misc/podcast.shtml) and McGraw Hill's AccessMedicine podcasts (http://books.mcgraw-hill.com/podcast/acm).

The use of such Web 2.0 technologies (wikis, blogs and podcasts) to encourage learners' deeper engagement with learning materials, and the affordance of shared working spaces to improve collaboration between learners are desirable outcomes. It is generally held by many educators that students of all ages learn best when immersed within a culturally and socially rich environment in which scaffolding of learning can be achieved (Bruner 1990). Furthermore, where learners and peers are committed to achieving the same goals, they tend to regulate each other's performances (Jonassen et al. 1999), a positive outcome that can be facilitated through the use of shared, digital learning environments. The combination of wikis, blogs and podcasting technologies, then, has the potential to both liberate and tie learners together (Jonassen et al. 1999), creating dynamic learning communities.

However, as research has already shown, technology is neutral until it delivers content (Clark 1994) and will lose its effectiveness if it is not applied in a planned and systematic manner (Laurillard 2002). It may also be necessary to re-educate learners regarding their participation within such a dynamic learning environment, for as Jonassen and his colleagues (1999) suggest, old models of education have left their legacy. Many learners have been so busy memorising what teachers tell them that they may need some support when they first attempt to communicate with others using collaborative technologies (Jonassen et al. 1999).

Wheeler et al. (2005) have argued that deeper engagement with learning objects and online discussion groups yields significant benefits for the development of professional practice. Jonassen et al. (1999) suggest that even though the potential impact of wiki, blogs and podcast technologies on higher education is immense, it is perhaps the combined use of the three applications as 'mind tools' that may yield the most powerful learning experiences. According to Jonassen et al. (1999), 'mind tools' act as cognitive reflection and amplification tools, aiding the construction of meaning, through the act of self-design of knowledge databases. The frequency of use and effectiveness of the use of the 'mind tools' approach of Jonassen et al. (1999) in healthcare learning and teaching will be investigated during the course of our study.

As can be seen in the preceding, all five themes of social networking, collaboration, participation, openness and apomediation are not only possible but necessary for such interactions to take place. However, it should also be noted that just having such interaction occurring does not in and of itself lead to superior healthcare delivery. It is essential, for example, that content is correct and updated. In addition, it is necessary that users can find quickly the correct information they require. This means it is also necessary for the tools and techniques of the knowledge economy to be incorporated into the design of such dynamic learning communities; i.e. optimal benefit of such pervasive solutions occurs when coupled with the principles of knowledge management. In this way, it will be more likely that the latest and best possible data information and/or knowledge is transferred.

To provide an illustration of how powerful the incorporation of Web 2.0 capabilities are in a healthcare context, the next section presents the case of ProNex[1] solution for bariatric clinical practice called My ProConnect. The material for this case study vignette was gathered through a combination and synthesis of multi-spectral data including onsite visits where the system is being utilised, the conducting of structured and semi-structured interviews with various key players and examination of documents provided by the vendor. Techniques pertaining to the conducting of high-quality qualitative case study analysis as described and recommended by Yin (1994), Kavale (1996) and Boyatzis (1998) were at all times utilised in the collection and subsequent analysis of the data.

23.3.2 Case Example of MyProConnect

Succinctly stated, MyProConenct is a unique smart portal designed and developed by ProNEx for the Bariatrics environment in the United States. Key advances in Bariatrics require database management and patient tracking as well as better techniques for surgery. Moreover, to be eligible and also qualify for reimbursement for such bariatric surgery in the United States, patients must post-surgery comply with required reporting for at least 5 years, while Bariatric Clinics, if they are to be classified and maintain the status of a centre of excellence must also provide longitudinal reporting and monitoring.

Recognising the futility of trying to do this via traditional paper-based systems, ProNex Inc. investigated possibilities for harnessing the potential of the latest technology advances including Web 2.0 in order to design and then develop My ProConnect—a smart portal that provides the necessary management and longitudinal monitoring of data with support for action in a seamless and intelligent solution for providers and patients alike. Figure 23.2 provides a schematic of the My ProConenct Solution.

The solution consists of three critical aspects as follows:

1. My ProConnect^{TM} offers Bariatric healthcare professionals, as well as their patients, the ability to record and access patient information at the snap of a finger anytime, anywhere and to track outcomes related to patients and procedures.

---

[1] The authors are most appreciative of the CEO Mr. Fred Pira for giving them time and access to all relevant information.

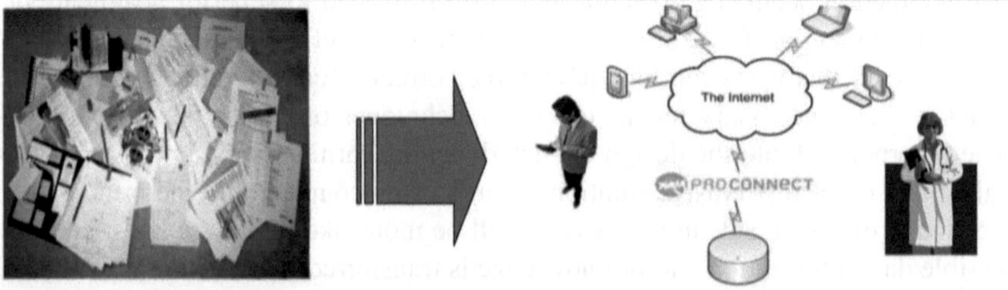

Fig. 23.2 Schematic of the My ProConnect Solution. (Reproduced with the permission of ProNex Inc.)

2. My ProConnect™ provides intake and registration, evaluation, pre-surgery, post-surgery and ongoing monitoring for the Bariatric Center and their patients. The Web-based software's flexibility enables tailoring of the application to include additional elements unique to a particular program and/or practice.
3. My ProConnect™ supports Centers of Excellence requirements such as the Bariatric Outcomes Longitudinal Database (BOLD) interface and is Health Information Portability and Accountability Act (HIPAA)-compliant. This is especially important in the US healthcare system as it significantly impacts costs, billing and reimbursement.

In terms of the five themes presented in Fig. 23.1, the system supports all these themes concurrently. Specifically: (1) apomediation since all information has appropriate references and ranking to show its validity, (2) collaboration because it enables providers and patients to work together to manage their healthcare issue as well as supporting collaboration within the provider network, (3) participation since it supports and enables the patient and key participant in his/her healthcare treatment regimen to become empowered, (4) social networking as it enables patients to develop social networks to support them during their treatment time and beyond and (5) openness since all aspects of the care path are visible and transparent to the patient.

The confluence of these features and capabilities makes MyProConnect a superior tool in the Bariatric space. An essential element here is how the capabilities of Web 2.0 enable the support of multiple needs of the various groups involved. In particular, clinicians and patients are fully supported through this interactive system in a real-time fashion.

Figure 23.3 provides a schematic of the logical design and high-level structure. This unique conceptualisation of healthcare dynamics in the Bariatric context in turn enables users to tailor the application to include additional elements unique to their program and/or practice. To date, MyProConnect is one of few software solutions to be fully utilised in healthcare settings that incorporatesand leverages the full potential of Web 2.0 capabilities to provide superior healthcare delivery.

In the Bariatric setting, especially in the United States, critical to success is: (a) the pre-screening of patients and (b) the post-surgery maintenance. My ProConnect offers simple yet targeted solutions for both these key areas. My ProConnect enables

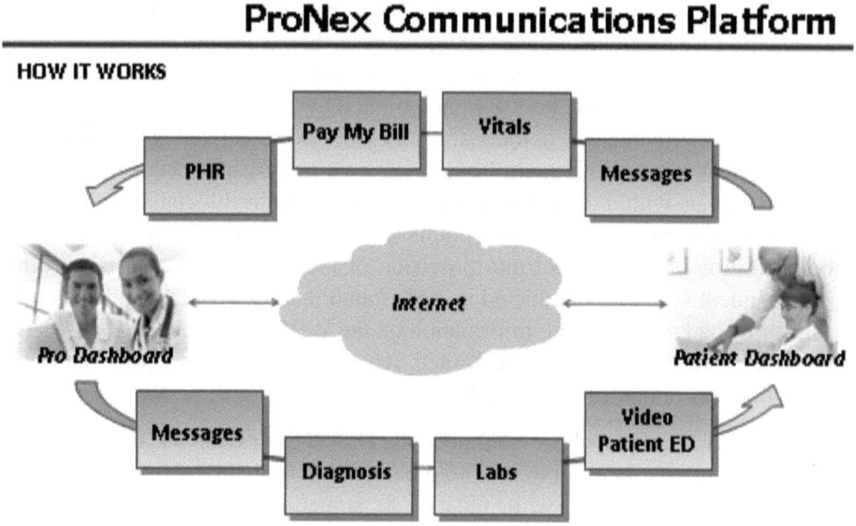

Fig. 23.3 Schematic of Pro and Patient Dashboard Structure. (Reproduced with the permission of ProNex Inc.)

the Bariatric Physicians and their staff to have the best understanding of the patient upon intake and registration, evaluation, pre-surgery and post-surgery. This ensures success not only immediately after surgery but on an ongoing basis.

The client's Dashboard enables the patient to have autonomy and control of their own wellness program. By taking ownership and having a simple yet robust technology tool to support them, the patients can easily stay on track and enjoy the success of their Bariatric procedure for the rest of their life. It is important to note, however, that Web 2.0 is not a panacea for healthcare.

23.4 The Paradox of Social Portals and Healthcare

An individual or group can create a Web page or Web portal with very little funds and no need or approval from any authority. This produces an interesting paradoxical impact on the social fabric: a portal can be used to overcome tyranny, or lend power to a fanatical mob. A portal can also be used to provide instant free medical advice or to cater to the hypochondria latent in all of us (Davey and Tatnall 2007).

Medical portals abound on the Internet. Almost every major disease is represented by at least a support group portal. These portals offer everything from emotional support to possible treatment advice, to contacts within the medical community. Major diseases such as breast cancer and asthma are represented by patient groups, charities and medical groups. Less common problems such as Crohn's disease are also represented by portal sites. Every alternative treatment is also represented by portals.

This can vary from actual vendor portals right across to portals warning of the dangers of alternative medicine. Lewis (2006) suggests that, while the medical literature has a rather pessimistic take on issues like online health consumption debates over cyberchondria and cyberquackery are underpinned by a recognition that doctors are no longer necessarily the sole holders of health knowledge and that many consumers are now increasingly taking control over their own healthcare management. Thus, the quality debate within the medical literature on online health consumption is underpinned by anxieties over what gets counted as legitimate health knowledge today. The penetration of the Internet into provision of medical information is startling. An independent US study conducted in 1999 found that 31 % of respondents under the age of 60 had sought health information on the Web (Brodie et al. 2000). Harris Interactive conducted a study in the United States in 2002 (Taylor 2002) that found that key findings of this survey include:

- The 80 % of all adults who are online in the United States (i.e. 53 % of all adults) sometimes use the Internet to look for healthcare information. However, only 18 % say they do this 'often', while most do so 'sometimes' (35 %), or 'hardly ever' (27 %).
- The 80 % of all those online amounts to 110 million cyberchondriacs nationwide in the United States. This compares with 54 million in 1998, 69 million in 1999 and 97 million last year.
- On average, those who look for healthcare information online do so three times every month.

This is the study that first called health consumers who use the Web 'cyberchondriacs', although the researchers claim they didn't mean to use the term pejoratively but meant it merely as a descriptor.

Another US survey in December 2005 found that one in five (20 %) online Americans said the Internet has greatly improved the way they get information about healthcare (Madden and Fox 2006) and in Europe a survey by the market research company, Datamonitor, of over 4,500 adults in France, Germany, Italy, Spain, the United Kingdom and the United States, found that 57 % of respondents had consulted Internet sources when looking for health information (BBC 2002).

There are two reported problems with all this health information available through the various Web portals: social alienation and problems with the quality of health information available. Shields (1996) finds that one of the dominant popular discourses around Web use is that it produces or worsens processes of social alienation. The argument is that it is possible for interaction through computers to replace person to person contact. Theodosiou and Green (2003) identify five important problems with patients using medical portals to satisfy their needs:

1. Potentially dangerous drugs and other substances may be bought by individuals for themselves or their children.
2. Individuals can spend a lot of money on products or diagnostic procedures that have no scientific backing and no benefit.
3. The information may be more negative than the reality of the situation.

4. Individuals may abandon treatment programmes of proven efficacy to pursue less-mainstream approaches.
5. Users' sites (e.g. for families affected by autism) may contain advice or opinions of questionable ethics (e.g. non-mainstream treatments that are intrusive or punitive).

Several researchers (Craan and Oleske o. J.; D'Alessandro and Dosa 2001) have found indicators that the availability of an independent source of information allows patients to take a more informed position when discussing their medical condition with their medical practitioner (Davey and Tatnall 2007).

Another issue arises from the communities created under Web 2.0. There is a need for professionals to share information if knowledge is to grow and be disseminated. Studies of medical graduates show that new doctors are fluent in Web2.0 tools and are usually associated with several communities (Black et al. 2010). The dilemma of these communities is how confidential patient information can be protected while encouraging professionals to take advantage of the group knowledge within their online community (Thompson et al. 2008).

23.5 Discussion and Implications for Healthcare Delivery

As can be seen from the ProNex Case Study, Web 2.0 is enabling patient empowerment and the better transfer of pertinent information and germane knowledge with the potential end result being superior healthcare delivery. The pervasive nature of Web 2.0 technologies means that this is a benefit that most if not all people can enjoy. In many ways, Web 2.0 has the potential to revolutionise current healthcare delivery practices and/or roles as has been noted throughout this chapter. Moreover, this is not limited just to interactions only between patient and provider. We believe therefore, that in order to fully leverage from the opportunities offered by Web 2.0 technologies, it is important to re-evaluate many current healthcare practices and see where and/or how these might be re-engineered so that it is possible to truly realise the full power and promise that Web 2.0 can provide. In light of the current challenges facing healthcare delivery including exponentially increasing costs and pressures to deliver high-quality outcomes and enable better access, this would appear to be a prudent and necessary step.

23.6 Conclusions

This chapter set out to present a discussion on Web 2.0 and its suitability to alleviate healthcare of its current and most pressing maladies. The World Wide Web was originally a platform where static html information became instantly available globally. Together with search engines, this gave people everywhere access to medical information. These consumers of information might be patients looking for information or medical professionals accessing work in their field from anywhere in the world. The advances provided by Web 2.0 tools allowed this one directional flow of information to become the far richer environment of social networking. A social network might allow professionals to interact with each other, for patients to form communities of interest or for telemedicine to become a truer image of the interaction between a doctor and the geographically local community.

The one way Web allowed global and instant release of important validated outcomes from medical research but also the dissemination of misleading and harmful misinformation. Similarly, the use of Web 2.0 allows both positive and negative forms of community to be formed.

Thus, we have tried to highlight how Web 2.0 can be assimilated into healthcare practice and facilitate not only the design and development of superior e-health solutions but also superior patient-centric healthcare delivery. In closing, we call for further research and warn that Web 2.0 is not a panacea and attention to the key aspects of people, process and technology are essential if we are to realise a healthcare value proposition of excellence in access, quality and value.

References

Abram, S. (2005). Web 2.0—huh? Library 2.0, librarian 2.0. *Information Outlook, 9,* 44–45.

Barsky, E., & Purdon, M. (2006). Introducing Web 2.0: Social networking and social bookmarking for health librarians. *Journal of the Canadian Health Librarians Association, 27,* 65–67.

BBC. (2002). Health websites gaining popularity. http://news.bbc.co.uk/2/hi/health/2249606.stm. Accessed Nov 2011.

Beldarrain, Y. (2006). Distance education trends: Integrating new technologies to foster student interaction and collaboration. *Distance Education, 27,* 139–153.

Berners-Lee, T. (1989). Information management: A proposal. http://www.w3.org/History/1989/proposal.html. Accessed Feb 2010.

Berners-Lee, T. (2006). IBM developerWorks pod cast. http://www-128.ibm.com/developerworks/podcast/dwi/cm-int082206.txt. Accessed Nov 2011.

Black, E., Thompson, L., Dawson, K., Saliba, H., & Black, N. (2010). Revisiting social network utilization by physicians-in-training. *Journal of Graduate Medical Education,* 2(2), 289–293.

Boulos, M. N. K., & Wheeler, S. (2007). The emerging Web 2.0 social software: An enabling suite of sociable technologies in health and healthcare education. *Health Information and Libraries Journal, 23,* 2–23.

Boulos, M. N. K., Maramba, I., & Wheeler, S. (2006). Wikis, blogs and podcasts: A new generation of Web-based tools for virtual collaborative clinical practice and education. *BMC Medical Education, 6*(41), 1–8.

Boyatzis, R. (1998). *Transforming qualitative information thematic analysis and code development.* Thousand Oaks: Sage.

Brodie, M., Flournoy, R. E., et al. (2000). Health information, the Internet, and the digital divide. *Health Affairs, 19*(6), 255–266.

Bruner, J. S. (1990). *Acts of meaning.* Cambridge: Harvard University Press.

Cheung, K.-H., Yip, K. Y., Townsend, J. P., & Scotch, M. (2008). HCLS 2.0/3.0: Health care and life sciences data mashup using Web 2.0/3.0. *Journal of Biomedical Informatics, 41,* 694–705.

Christakis, N., & Fowler, J. (2008). The collective dynamics of smoking in a large social network. *The New England Journal of Medicine, 358,* 2249–2258.

Clark, R. E. (1994). Media will never influence learning. *Education Technology Research and Development, 37*(1), 57–66.

Cohen-Cole, E., & Fletcher, J. (2008). Detecting implausible social network effects in acne, height, and headaches: Longitudinal analysis. *British Medical Journal, 337,* 2533.
Craan, F., & Oleske, D. M. (o. J.). Oleske medical information and the internet: Do you know what you are getting? *Journal of Medical Systems, 26,* 511–518.
D'Alessandro, D. M., & Dosa, N. P. (2001). Empowering children and families with information technology. *Arch Ped Adol Med, 155,* 1131–1136.
Davey, W., & Tatnall, A. (2007). The paradox of social portals. Encyclopaedia of portal technology and applications. A. Tatnall. Hershey, PA. *Information Science Reference, 2,* 689–693.
Eseynbach, G. (2008). Medicine 2.0. *J Med Internet Res, 10*(3), 1–10. http://www.jmir.org/2008/3/e22/.
Fahey, P. J. (2003). Indicators of support in online interaction. *International Review of Research in Open and Distance Learning, 4.* http://www.irrodl.org/index.php/irrodl/article/view/129/600. Accessed 29 Sept 2010.
Fowler, J., & Christakis, N. (2011). Dynamic spread of happiness in a large social network: Longitudinal analysis over 20 years in the Framingham Heart Study. *British Medical Journal, 337,* 1–9.
Halliday, J. (2010). *Facebook a threat, says web founder.* The Age (reprinted from the Gardian). Melbourne, *The Age,* 16.
Jonassen, D. H., Peck, K. L., & Wilson, B. G. (1999). *Learning with technology: A constructivist perspective.* Columbus: Merrill Prentice Hall.
Kavale, S. (1996). *Interviews, an introduction to qualitative research.* London: Sage.
Laurillard, D. (2002). *Rethinking university teaching.* London: Routledge Falmer.
Lewis, T. (2006). Seeking health information on the Internet: Lifestyle choice or bad attack of cyberchondria? *Media, Culture & Society, 28*(4), 521–539.
Madden, M., & Fox, S. (2006). Finding answers online in sickness and in health. Pew Internet & American Life Project Report. http://www.pewinternet.org/Reports/2006/Finding-Answers-Online-in-Sickness-and-in-Health.aspx. Accessed Nov 2011.
O'Reilly, T. (2005). What is Web 2.0? Design patterns and business models for the next generation of software. http://www.oreillynet.com/1pt/a/6228. Accessed 29 Sept 2010.
Parakh, P. (2006). Web 2.0: Catch the Wave, Video clip, 6 October 2006. http://www.youtube.com/. Accessed Nov 2011.
Robinson, K. (2005). Web 2.0? Why should we care? http://www.publish.com/article2/0,1759,1860653,00.asp. Accessed 29 Sept 2010.
Sharp, D. (2006). Smart Internet 2010—Social Networks. http://www.smartinternet.com.au/ArticleDocuments/121/Social-Networks-2010.pdf.aspx. Accessed 29 Sept 2010.
Shields, R. E. (1996). *Cultures of internet: Virtual spaces, real histories, living bodies.* London: Sage.
Spallek, H., O'Donnell, J., Clayton, M., Anderson, P., & Kruger, A. (2010). Paradigm shift or annoying distraction: Emerging implications of Web 2.0 for clinical practice. *Applied Clinical Informatics, 1,* 96–115.
Taylor, H. (2002). The Harris Poll #21: Cyberchondriacs update. http://www.harrisinteractive.com/NewsRoom/HarrisPolls/tabid/447/mid/1508/articleId/448/ctl/ReadCustom%20Default/Default.aspx. Accessed Nov 2011.
Theodosiou, L., & Green, J. (2003). Emerging challenges in using health information from the internet. *Advances in Psychiatric Treatment, 9,* 387–396.
Thompson, L., Dawson, K., Ferdig, R., Black, E., Boyer, J., Coutts, J., & Black, N. (2008). The intersection of online social networking with medical professionalism. *Journal of General Internal Medicine, 23*(7), 954–957.
Wallace, P. (1999). *The psychology of the internet.* Cambridge: Cambridge University Press.
Wenger, E. (2000). Communities of practice social learning systems. *Organisation, 7,* 225–256.
Wheeler, S., Kelly, P., & Gale, K. (2005). The influence of online problem-based learning on teachers' professional practice and identity. *Association for Learning Technology Journal, 13*(2), 125–137.

Wickramasinghe, N., Bali, R., Lehaney, B., Gibbons, C., & Schaffer, J. (2009). *Healthcare knowledge management primer*. London: Routledge.
Wickramasinghe, N., Bali, R., Kirin, S., & Sumoi, R. (2011). *Critical Issues in e-health forthcoming*. New York: Springer.
Yin, R. (1994). *Case study research: Design and methods* (2nd ed.). Newbury Park: Sage.

Chapter 24
E-Health Readiness Assessment Methodology (EHRAM)

JunHua Li and Pradeep Ray

Abstract E-Health is an application of information and communication technologies to promote healthcare services support, delivery and education. However, the implementation of E-Health represents a potentially disruptive change in the healthcare context. Consequently, resistance to change can occur at the individual level as well as at the organisational level. Prior to E-Health implementation, assessment of organisational readiness can reduce the risk of its failure after introduction. The success of an E-Health system is very much dependent on the success of the Electronic Health Records (EHR) system, as EHR forms the core of any E-Health system. This chapter (based on design science research methodology) presents an E-Health Readiness Assessment Methodology (EHRAM) from EHR perspective, which deals with the factors that need to be addressed in the planning of E-Health programmes and assists decision makers in the healthcare organisation to take action to address deficient areas of the readiness. EHRAM encompasses: (1) an E-Health Readiness Assessment Framework (EHRAF), (2) an assessment process, (3) data mining techniques for analysing the assessment data to arrive at a readiness score and (4) an automated tool for the implementation of EHRAM.

Keywords Design science · E-Health · Evaluation · Methodology · Readiness · EHR

24.1 Introduction

Healthcare service is a fundamental right of all citizens and should be efficiently provided and made fully accessible to all (Li et al. 2008a). Many countries (especially developing countries), nonetheless, are plagued with critical healthcare issues such as chronic, infectious and/or pandemic diseases, a lack of basic healthcare programmes and facilities and a shortage of skilled healthcare workers (WHO 2006; Watts and Ibegbulam 2005). Poor healthcare obstructs prosperity and business profitability, and

J. Li (✉) · P. Ray
Asia Pacific u-Health Research Centre (APuHC),
School of Information Systems, Technology and Management,
The University of New South Wales, 2052 Sydney, Australia
e-mail: junhua.li@student.unsw.edu.au

P. Ray
e-mail: p.ray@unsw.edu.au

R. K. Bali et al. (eds.), *Pervasive Health Knowledge Management*,
Healthcare Delivery in the Information Age,
DOI 10.1007/978-1-4614-4514-2_24,

does not help reduce poverty (Li et al. 2008a). More importantly, it directly affects the mortality levels of the people living in these countries.

E-Health refers to health services and information delivered or enhanced through the Internet and related Information and Communication Technologies (ICT; Eysenbach 2001). E-Health applications are the use of digital data transmitted, sorted and retrieved electronically—in support of health services, both at the local site and at a distance (WHO 2005). The success of an E-Health system is very much dependent on the success of Electronic Health Records (EHR) systems, as EHR is a repository of information regarding health information of a subject of care (i.e. patients) in a computer-processable form and forms the core of any E-Health system (ISO Technical Report). A typical EHR system consists of three components (Dickinson et al. 2004):

1. Direct-care EHR functions.
2. Supportive EHR requirements.
3. EHR information infrastructure.

Although EHR systems can typically address some of the problems in paper-based healthcare, e.g. limited access and sharing of patient records, inefficient documentation, breached patient privacy and incomplete and inaccurate health records (Li et al. 2008a), their implementation is still a problem as evidenced by the low (rate of) adoption (e.g. Menachemi et al. 2006). As part of the effort to enhance EHR adoption, a readiness assessment for the innovation becomes an essential requirement for the implementation and use of EHR (and hence E-Health). This is because readiness assessment is a way of identifying the potential causes of failure to innovate (Demiris et al. 2004).

The focus of this chapter is on the development of an assessment methodology at the pre-implementation stage of EHR systems so as to assess the status of E-Health readiness. This chapter has benefited from an ongoing WHO eHCD project involving six countries, which was launched in 2006.

The main objectives for this chapter are to:

- Identify key components for an E-Health readiness assessment and develop an E-Health readiness assessment framework using these components.
- Develop a process to support E-Health readiness assessment.
- Develop a tool facilitating the assessment process.
- Evaluate the methodology with comparative case studies.

The layout of the chapter is as follows. Section 24.2 reviews current E-Health readiness frameworks and identifies research gaps. Section 24.3 develops an E-Health readiness assessment methodology (EHRAM) based on design science research methodology, including an E-Health readiness assessment model, a method to assess E-Health readiness and an E-Health readiness assessment instantiation for the assessment data analysis. Section 24.4 conducts case studies with assessment data collected in two healthcare centres in Vietnam. We summarise the contributions of this chapter in Sect. 24.5, also including some limitations and future work.

24.2 Literature Review

Most EHR evaluation studies have been conducted after its implementation (e.g. EHR benefits and adoption issues) whereas few studies have been done before the implementation, especially in developing countries. Major issues in these countries, such as costs, available information technology, lack of technical expertise and computer skills of staff and lack of data processing facilities need to be addressed before implementation is possible (Watson 2006). Evaluation of these issues before EHR implementation becomes indispensable for the future success.

In order to investigate multiple healthcare providers' view (e.g. physicians, nurses and administrative personnel) for the readiness evaluation of E-Health applications, Campbell et al. (2001) developed a readiness framework by conducting semi-structured interviews (regarding both the video and computer components of a telemedicine system), followed by thematic analysis. Results of thematic analysis reveal six themes (Campbell et al. 2001):

1. *Turf*: A threat to healthcare providers' livelihood or professional autonomy or both.
2. *Efficacy*: Desire to know that E-Health applications will fill a functional need in healthcare providers' practice before they invest time and money in making such a big change.
3. *Practice context*: Barriers to adopting E-Health applications.
4. *Apprehension*: As a human aversion to change.
5. *Time to learn*: Hesitancy among the providers to take the time to learn a new technology and to persuade patients of its worth.
6. *Ownership*: Participants who were professionally and emotionally invested in the technology—stakeholders who acknowledged its benefits, adapted it to their needs, and tried to help others learn.

These six themes comprise the framework to understand three categorised organisational settings, i.e. "fertile soil, somewhat fertile soil, and barren soil" (Campbell et al. 2001). Change strategies are also suggested in every readiness setting. Campbell et al. provided a mechanism for determining and then dealing with three different levels of readiness for implementing E-Health applications. Nevertheless, the mechanism does not involve organisational, public or patient readiness for E-Health (only from healthcare providers' view). Furthermore, Campbell et al.'s framework has not been tested.

Another readiness evaluation study followed the philosophy of existing readiness scales [e.g. the Organisational Information Technology/Systems Innovation Readiness Scale (OITIRS)]; the evaluation is also from healthcare providers' viewpoint. This framework involves staff profiles, staff exposure to technology and institutional resources (Demiris et al. 2004). Using previously validated instruments, it captures organisational readiness for E-Health. Demiris et al.'s (2004) framework, however, focuses solely on assessing practitioners' readiness instead of organisational readiness, as their instruments primarily include staff profiles and staff exposure to technology.

By contrast, the readiness framework from Jennett et al. (2003, 2004, 2005) is relatively more comprehensive in terms of the evaluation scope. Sixteen semi-structured telephone interviews were conducted on four sets of stakeholders (patient, practitioner, organisation and public) to examine complex social, political, organisational and infrastructure factors. As a result, four types of readiness were found: core, engagement, structural readiness and concerns of non-readiness. Six common factors (e.g. projection of benefits) were identified within each type of the readiness. Jennett et al.'s framework suggests a method to determine overall readiness categorisation. It stresses the importance of end-users' ownership of innovation adoption by assessing organisational, health provider, public and patient readiness for E-Health. However, tool reliability has not been assessed and that study provides little information regarding demographics or current technological practices.

Another proposed framework by Wickramasinghe et al. (2005) is concerned with three domains relevant to E-Health readiness—practitioner, organisation and public; it highlights the key elements that are required for successful E-Health initiatives. Wickramasinghe et al.'s framework provides a tool that allows analysis beyond the quantifiable data into a systematic synthesis of the major four impacts and four prerequisites, and the implications of these pre-requisites and impacts on the goals of E-Health, such as efficiency, evidence-based and preventive medicine. Wickramasinghe et al.'s framework contains four main prerequisites:

1. *ICT architecture/infrastructure*: A sound technical infrastructure (phone lines, fibre trunks and submarine cables, telecommunications, electricity, access to computers, etc.) is an essential ingredient to the undertaking of E-Health initiatives by any nation.
2. *Standardisation policies, protocols and procedures*: E-Health by definition spans many parties and geographical dimensions. To enable such far-reaching coverage, a significant amount of document exchange and information flow must be accommodated. Standardisation is the key to this, using widely and universally accepted protocols such as TCP/IP and http.
3. *User access and accessibility policies and infrastructure*: Access to e-commerce is defined by the World Trade Organisation (WTO) as consisting of two critical components: access to Internet services and access to e-services. The former deals with the user infrastructure whereas the latter pertains to specific commitments to electronically accessible services.
4. *Governmental regulation and control*: The key challenges regarding E-Health use include: cost effectiveness; i.e. less costly than traditional healthcare delivery and functionality and ease of use; i.e. they should enable and facilitate many uses for physicians and other healthcare users by combining various types and forms of data as well as being easy and secure to use.

Four impacts of E-Health are embedded in Wickramasinghe et al.'s framework:

1. *Impact of IT education*: An educated population boosts the E-Health initiative.
2. *Impact of world economic standing*: Awareness of importance and critical role of Internet in a country's economy.

Table 24.1 Different perspectives of e-health readiness framework

First author	Patient	Provider	Organisational	Public
Campbell	–	√	–	–
Demiris	–	√	–	–
Jennett	√	√	√	√
Wickramasinghe	–	√	√	√
Khoja	–	√	√	–

3. *Impact of morbidity rate*: Education/awareness and overall health standing of a country.
4. *Impact of cultural/social dimensions*: Culture, traditions and the like.

Wickramasinghe et al.'s (2005) framework based on multiple perspectives, including organisational (e.g. ICT infrastructure), practitioner (e.g. user access) and public (e.g. governmental regulation), can be used to assess the potential of a country and its readiness for E-Health as well as its ability to maximise the goals of E-Health.

A recent study by Khoja et al. (2007) aimed to test the reliability of E-Health readiness evaluation tools for both Managers and healthcare providers with four categories of measurements in developing countries. Separate scores (Cronbach's alpha) were measured for each of the four categories in both the tools. Scores of core-readiness, learning readiness/technological readiness, societal readiness and policy readiness for both tools were all observed to be higher than 0.80 and showed high reliability. Each of the items within the respective four categories for managers or healthcare providers showed Pearson's correlation coefficient greater than 0.35 ($p < 0.05$), so all the items in these categories relate appropriately with other items in the same category (Khoja et al. 2007). Although Khoja et al.'s framework can guide users to take appropriate measures and may also be used to quantitatively assess and improve E-Health readiness, the idea of E-Health is relatively new to healthcare centres in developing countries and thus it would be hard to adopt all the suggested measures to assess all levels of service.

Evaluators—and decision makers—must accept that E-Health evaluation may serve different purposes for different stakeholders (Gagnon and Scott 2005). Existing frameworks for E-Health readiness assessment (Campbell et al. 2001; Jennett et al. 2003, 2004, 2005; Demiris et al. 2004; Wickramasinghe et al. 2005; Khoja et al. 2007), for example, were derived from different perspectives (Table 24.1). Most studied components within the frameworks reflect healthcare providers' and organisational perspectives, however, these components are different more or less from one framework to another. In terms of the components from organisational perspective, ICT architecture/infrastructure was highlighted but core readiness, identified from Jennett et al.'s framework (2005), was neglected in Wickramasinghe et al.'s (2005). This is why E-Health evaluation is often criticised for the lack of common outcome indicators and the absence of an agreed theory (Gagnon and Scott 2005). Furthermore, most of these readiness frameworks have not been tested.

This study aims at developing a methodology for assessing E-Health readiness from an EHR perspective. We need to:

1. Develop an EHR readiness assessment framework from healthcare organisational and providers' perspectives by integrating components of the existing frameworks (see Sect. 24.3.1).
2. Develop a procedure to assess the readiness (see Sect. 24.3.2).
3. Develop a tool to automatically process assessment data to reveal E-Health readiness (see Sect. 24.3.3).
4. Operationalise and evaluate the methodology using case studies in developing countries (see Sect. 24.4).

24.3 Development of EHRAM

Two paradigms (i.e. behavioral science and design science) characterise much of the research in the IS discipline (March and Smith 1995). The behavioral science paradigm develops and verifies theories that explain or predict human or organisational behavior whereas the design science paradigm extends the boundaries of human and organisational capabilities by creating new and innovative artefacts (Hevner et al. 2004). The artefacts, implemented in an organisational context, are often the object of study in IS behavioral-science research (Hevner et al. 2004). The theories seek to predict or explain phenomena with respect to the artefact's use (intention to use), perceived usefulness and impact on individuals and organisations depending on system, service and information quality (DeLone and McLean 1992, 2003; Seddon 1997).

March and Smith (1995) identified two design processes and four design artefacts produced by design science research in IS. The two processes involve building and evaluating the artefacts—constructs, models, methods and instantiations. *Constructs* provide the language in which problems and solutions are defined and communicated (Schön 1983). *Models* use constructs to represent a real-world situation—the design problem and its solution space (Simon 1996). *Models* aid problem and solution understanding. *Methods* define processes. They provide guidance on how to solve problems, that is how to search the solution space. *Instantiations* show that constructs, models or methods can be implemented in a working system. These are concrete prescriptions that enable IS researchers and practitioners to understand and address the problems inherent in developing and successfully implementing information systems within organisations (March and Smith 1995; Nunamaker et al. 1991).

This work builds constructs (Sect. 24.3.1), a model (Fig. 24.2 in Sect. 24.3.2), methods (Fig. 24.1 in Sect. 24.3.2) and an instantiation (Sect. 24.3.3) for E-Health readiness assessment, and then evaluates the artefacts using comparative case studies (in Sect. 24.4). Hence, the output of the research is designed artefacts and the methodology used is design science research.

Table 24.2 Core readiness component of EHRAF

Assessment	High readiness	Medium readiness	Low readiness
R(Core)	V(ED)=0, V(PP)=0, V(CA)=0, V(SR)=0	Other cases, such as V(ED)=1, V(PP)=0, V(CA)=0, V(SR)=0	V(ED)=1, V(PP)=1, V(CA)=1, V(SR)=1

24.3.1 Integrated E-Health Readiness Assessment Framework

Readiness assessment can be conducted for different types of E-Health systems (e.g. EHR, telemedicine and e-referral systems). Our E-Health Readiness Assessment Framework (EHRAF) makes an assumption that a typical EHR system (Dickinson et al. 2004) will be fully implemented. The framework has four dimensions:

1. *Core readiness* refers to evaluators' realisation of problems in the documentation of clinical information and healthcare providers' dissatisfaction with paper health records.
2. *Engagement readiness* is healthcare providers' exposure to EHR systems (e.g. perceived benefits) and willingness to accept EHR training.
3. *Technological readiness* is the ability of existing hardware, software, network and IT support for troubleshooting in a healthcare organisation to support clinical IT/S innovation and healthcare providers' IT skills.
4. *Societal readiness* assesses communication links and partnerships within and between organisations. Societal readiness deals with an organisation's socio-cultural issues related to EHR implementation.

Each component can be assessed as one of three different levels: high, medium and low. Evaluators can directly use this framework for organisations that plan to or will implement EHR systems. It is important to mention here that due to the space constraint, only core construct is used to illustrate the framework.

Core Readiness Provision of care requires the documentation of clinical information as an intrinsic aspect of routine clinical activity and is essential from both professional and legal standpoints (Allan and Englebright 2000). Accordingly, core readiness assessment is concerned about patient records generation, storage and retrieval with paper-based health record systems. In particular, it involves documentation efficiency of patient records, patient privacy, degree of physicians' satisfaction with completeness and accuracy of patient records and sharing of patient records (Li et al. 2008a). The more serious problems are realised to be, and higher dissatisfaction that is expressed, the more ready healthcare organisations and providers are to adopt new practices (EHR) to create change (Jennett et al. 2002, 2005); and vice versa.

Core readiness assessment result (R(Core)) (high, medium or low) is determined by the variables (V), i.e. efficient documentation of patient records (V(ED)), protected patient privacy (V(PP)), satisfaction of completeness and accuracy (V(CA)) as well as of sharing patient records (V(SR)). For each variable, the value is either 1 ("True") or 0 ("False"). According to the definition of core readiness above, R(Core) can be scored in Table 24.2. It is important to mention here that core readiness is only

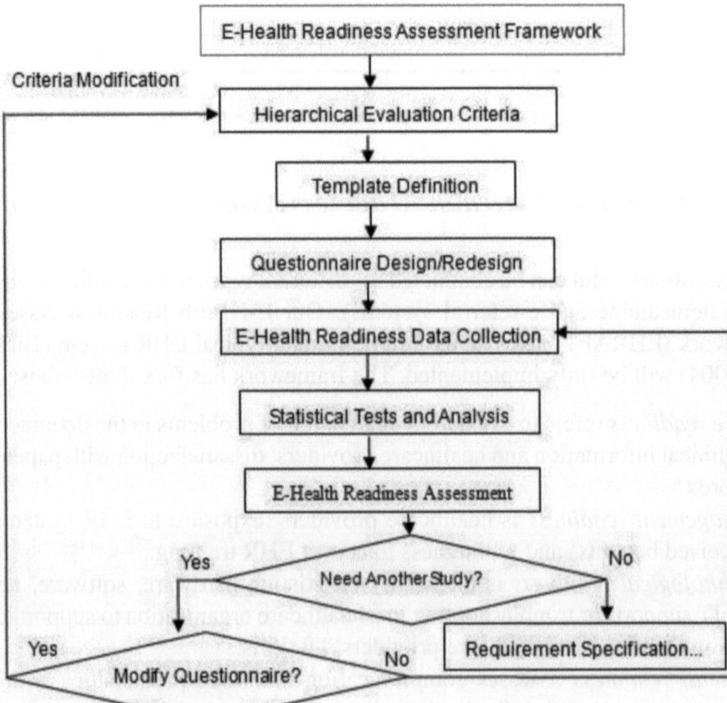

Fig. 24.1 E-health readiness assessment method

assessed as one of three different levels (discretely defined). In real life, the levels can be more fuzzy in nature, i.e. continuous scales.

24.3.2 E-Health Readiness Assessment Method

The Generic Evaluation Approach for the E-Health systems (GEA4EH) proposes an approach for the assessment and requirement specification of E-Health systems (Li et al. 2008b). The assessment process has been modified as shown in Fig. 24.1, so as to highlight the reiteration of assessing E-Health readiness, i.e. once the readiness assessment is done and the organisation takes action to improve the deficiencies, the second readiness assessment can be conducted.

Hierarchical Evaluation Criteria E-business systems do not have any commonly agreed evaluation parameters (Dean 2000). In particular, E-Health, as an emerging E-business application, does not have a set of well-defined evaluation criteria. A part of the chapter aims to mitigate the difficulties with the establishment of parameters for E-Health readiness assessment by modifying CoMENS hierarchical evaluation criteria (Ray 2003), rather than developing the parameters from scratch. The

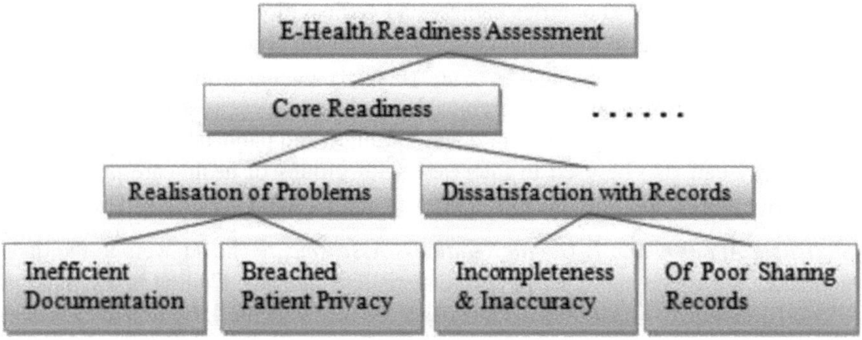

Fig. 24.2 Part of hierarchical e-health readiness assessment criteria

Table 24.3 Definition of evaluation templates

Name	Categorised As	Defined As	Type	Value
Example:				
Incompleteness and inaccuracy	Dissatisfaction with records	Healthcare providers' dissatisfaction with completeness and accuracy of patient records	Interval	Graded user opinion (scale 1–5), 5 stands for quite satisfied. Subjective judgment between 1 and 5

hierarchical model has been modified by incorporating the E-Health readiness assessment framework.

For instance, core readiness is determined by evaluators' realisation of problems and healthcare providers' dissatisfaction with paper health records systems, which are reflected by four variables, such as inefficient documentation. So, part of the hierarchical E-Health readiness assessment criteria are shown in Fig. 24.2. For each attribute at the bottom, there is at least one corresponding question to measure it.

Template Definition The evaluation parameters in the criteria are defined as quantitative items (Ray 2003). These items are specified by evaluators. Efforts are required to achieve maximum consistency of definition across different parameters by defining generic parameters (Dean 2000). The definition of each evaluation template within the hierarchical criteria involves "Name", "Categorised As", "Defined As", "Type" and "Value" (Table 24.3). "Categorised As" is the name of directly linked template at the upper level; "Defined As" gives the definition of the template; "Type" covers the data type—nominal, ordinal, interval, ratio (statistic terms) and narrative and "Value" provides the actual data. Such a proposed template in the CoMENS can be used for the reporting and analysis of information for the evaluation of E-Health systems (Ray 2003).

Questionnaire Design and E-Health Readiness Data Collection The WHO eHCD project has collected data with a questionnaire to understand healthcare status quo in a number of developing countries in the Asia Pacific region (e.g. Vietnam and India), where there are plans to implement different E-Health systems (e.g. EHR and Tele-consultation). However, the data were not yet analysed and synthesised to reveal the readiness status. Based on the hierarchical E-Health readiness assessment criteria and template definition, the questionnaire was modified and published online (Li 2008). The survey can also be used to interview with groups of healthcare practitioners (including physicians, administration officers and IT staff).

Statistical Analysis and E-Health Readiness Assessment The answers to the questionnaires are coded and cleaned before statistical analysis. Coding is necessary to convert qualitative to quantitative units in accordance with the definition of each evaluation template so as to standardise analysis. For example, when the answer from an interviewed physician is "yes, very much" to the question "In your view does the current system of recording patient medical history and information provide complete and accurate patient records?", the value 5 is filled in on a scale where 1 stands for "not satisfied at all" and 5 stands for "very satisfied". The raw qualitative data can also be used to substantiate quantitative results. Care was taken to ensure consistency in coding through consultations and multiple iterations. Then, data cleaning (deletion of un-meaningful or redundant responses) is also necessary to reduce noise in the data. Due to the exploratory nature of the study and the limited data types, the aim was not to undertake causal analysis to establish relationships between variables (e.g. for core readiness). Rather, the study was to identify potential significant interactions between variables by conducting exhaustive cross-tabulations between pairs of parameters. Cross-tabulation test results are usually presented as a contingency table, which is used to record and analyse the relationship between two or more variables simultaneously in a matrix format (Manning and Munro 2006). Each cell shows the number of respondents that gives a specific combination of responses. Cross-tabulation therefore helps to search for patterns of interaction. If certain cells contain disproportionately large (or small) numbers of cases, then this suggests that there might be a pattern of interaction. Then, homing in on those parameters, which give rise to statistically significant correlations ($p < 0.05$), helps explain the status of paper health records in healthcare centres. Descriptive statistics have also been used to address problems in the documentation of clinical information.

If there is a need to conduct another readiness study, the assessment process will re-start from the development of hierarchical evaluation criteria or E-Health readiness study, which is dependent upon whether the questionnaire needs to be modified. The assessment outcomes feed into the requirement specification of E-Health system implementation.

24.3.3 E-Health Readiness Assessment Instantiation/Tool (EHRAT)

Database tables, Forms, Queries and Macros of Microsoft Access were used to develop EHRAT. All the online survey or interview data from different healthcare

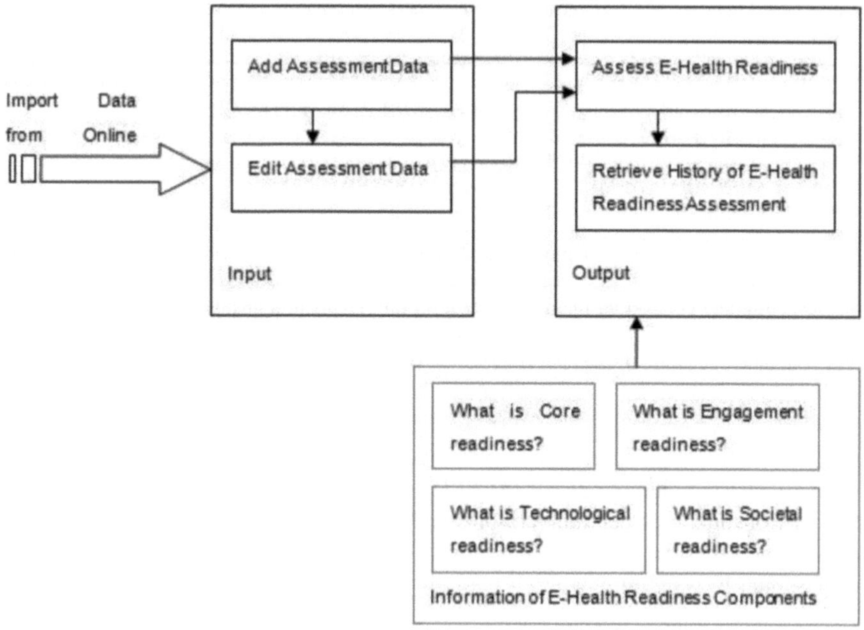

Fig. 24.3 Functions of EHRAT

providers can be imported into EHRAT without any change. Importantly, EHRAT automates the main function of processing the assessment data to reveal E-Health readiness status in terms of core, engagement, technological and societal readiness.

Functions The EHRAT provides functions not only for adding and editing the assessment data from the online surveys but also for processing the data to reveal organisational E-Health readiness, and subsequently retrieving history of the readiness assessment (Fig. 24.3). With the EHRAT, data can be added with two interfaces, respectively, for healthcare administrators and IT staff, and physicians. The edit function is provided to update and delete the added data. The output of EHRAT is used to assess E-Health readiness and to retrieve the assessment result when needed in the future. In addition, the definition of the four readiness components and how to, respectively, position them into high, medium or low readiness level are embedded into the output.

Rules of EHRAT Refer to those which were used to manipulate the input data to reveal E-Health readiness. As shown in Table 24.2, core readiness component, which is dependent upon four variables (i.e. V(ED), V(PP), V(CA), V(SR)), can take three possible values—high, medium or low level. With a view to the WHO data, seven items (questions) were used to measure these variables. They are, respectively, Average number of patient visit each year (Measure(ANP)), Number of physicians (M(NP)), Average time for generating records (M(ATGR)), Average time for storing and retrieving records (M(ATSR)), Accessibility/Confidentiality of

Table 24.4 Measures and variables for core readiness assessment

Variables	Measures	Formulation
V(ED)[a]	M(ANP), M(NP), M(ATGR), M(ATSR)	V(ED) = ((60 × 8 × (5/7) × 365 × M(NP) > (ç(avg(M(ATGR))) + ç(avg(M(ATSR)))) × M(ANP))?1:0)
V(PP)	M(ACR)	V(PP) = (ç(avg(M(ACR))) < 0.5?1:0)
V(CA)	M(DCAR)	V(CA) = (ç(avg(M(DCAR))) > 3?1:0)
V(SR)	M(SSR)	V(SR) = (ç(avg(M(SSR))) > 3?1:0)

[a]The routine core activities for physicians do not merely involve patient visits but also involve other responsibilities such as education concerning prevailing health problems and the methods of preventing and controlling them. Assumed, all physicians in a healthcare organisation spend 60 min × 8 h/day and 5 days/week on healthcare and half of this time on patient visits only. The organisational maximum throughput is 60 × 8 × (5/7) × 365 × M(NP).

records (M(ACR)), Degree of complete and accurate records (M(DCAR)) and Satisfactory sharing patient records (M(SSR)). Accordingly, there is a need to indicate the relationships between the variables and measures for the core readiness assessment, which are summarised in Table 24.4. Relational-Algebra Operations and Logic Conditional IF were employed.

Implementation Three Microsoft Access Database tables are designed for EHRAT. The Forms with different purposes are used to implement functions presented in Fig. 24.3. In total, 48 Macros and 63 Queries of Microsoft Access are developed and embedded into the 16 Forms.

EHRAT Validation The data collected by the WHO eHCD project in 20 healthcare centres of the Philippines were input and processed with EHRAT. Then, the readiness assessment results have been approved by two E-Health experts involved in this project.

24.4 Evaluation of EHRAM

As a research strategy, the case study, used in many situations to contribute to our knowledge of individual, group, organisational, social, political and related phenomena, allows investigators to retain the holistic and meaningful characteristics of real-life events (Yin 2003). The case study has a distinctive place in evaluation research (Cronbach et al. 1980; Guba and Lincoln 1981; Patton 1990; US General Accounting Office, Program Evaluation and Methodology Division 1990). There are various applications. For example, case studies can illustrate certain topics within an evaluation in a descriptive mode (Yin 2003).

Two cases were deliberately selected to operationalise and evaluate the EHRAM (i.e. following the process of the EHRAM to reveal E-Health readiness status in two district healthcare centres in Vietnam) because they offered contrasting situations, and a direct replication was not being sought. These two centres (Gialoc and Hoaiduc,

Table 24.5 Basic statistics of healthcare centres

Healthcare centres	Hoaiduc	Gialoc
General physicians	13	12
Specialist physicians	16	10
Nurses	28	34
Technical officers	9	8
Population served	174,114	15,500
Average No. of patient visits per annum	120,000	75,000

each about 120–140 km to Hanoi, the nearest big city) were identified by the Vietnam Ministry of Health as potential locations for E-Health implementation. The data were collect by the WHO eHCD project. In this design, if the subsequent findings support the hypothesised contrast, the results represent a strong start towards theoretical replication—vastly strengthening the external validity of the findings compared to that from a single case alone (Yin 2003). In the meantime, the data from these centres were input and processed with EHRAT. EHRAT, consequently, has been tested by comparing the readiness assessment results from the case studies and the output of EHRAT.

Table 24.5 shows the basic statistics of these centres. The population of Hoaiduc is 11 times as that of Gialoc. Although Hoaiduc has more access to specialist physicians, a similar number of general physicians serve each centre. Furthermore, the number of patient visits per general physician per annum is substantially high (9,230.8 vs. 6,250, in Hoaiduc and Gialoc, respectively); Hoaiduc's general physicians have a workload (using patient visit data) of about 48 % higher than those in Gialoc. These statistical data demonstrate a much greater shortage of general physicians in Hoaiduc. Moreover, Gialoc is better served in terms of the ratio of nurses and technical officers, per population.

The readiness assessment is conducted manually in Part A, i.e. without assistance of EHRAT. Part B processes the same set of WHO data with EHRAT and then makes a comparison of the readiness assessment results.

24.4.1 Data Analysis

Due to space constraint, this part only gives examples of data analysis for core readiness assessment.

Result Summary (Examples) Incomplete and inaccurate patient records: 50 % of physicians interviewed in Gialoc are not satisfied with it at all (Table 24.6) whereas 70 % in Hoaiduc have medium or even lower satisfaction (Table 24.7). Generally speaking, physicians are not content with the completeness and accuracy of patient records.

Issues in Paper Health Records with Cross-Tabulation Tests (Examples) Inefficiency in Generating Patient Health Records:

Table 24.6 Degree of completeness and accuracy of records in Gialoc

	Frequency	Percent	Valid percent	Cumulative percent
Not satisfied at all	5	50.0	50.0	50.0
Not satisfied	4	40.0	40.0	90.0
Medium	1	10.0	10.0	100.0
Quite satisfied	0	–	–	–
Satisfied	0	–	–	–
Total	*10*	*100.0*	*100.0*	–

Table 24.7 Degree of completeness and accuracy of records in Hoaiduc

	Frequency	Percent	Valid percent	Cumulative percent
Not satisfied at all	1	10.0	10.0	10.0
Not satisfied	1	10.0	10.0	20.0
Medium	5	50.0	50.0	70.0
Quite satisfied	3	30.0	30.0	100.0
Satisfied	0	–	–	–
Total	*10*	*100.0*	*100.0*	–

Table 24.8 Cross-tabulation between "healthcare centres" and "time for generating patient records"

Healthcare centres		Gialoc	Hoaiduc	Total
Time for generating patient records (minutes)	12	0	1 (10 %)	1
	15	2 (20 %)	6 (60 %)	8 (95 %)
	20	1 (10 %)	0	1
	25	2 (20 %)	0	2
	30	0	3 (30 %)	3
	35	3 (30 %)	0	3
	40	2 (20 %)	0	2
Total	–	*10 (100 %)*	*10 (100 %)*	*20*

Table 24.8 shows that in Gialoc it takes at least 15 min to generate all patient health records, the median time being 35 min. In Hoaiduc, 90 % of all patient health records take at least 15 min to be generated, the median time is 15 min. Therefore, the healthcare centre in Hoaiduc is substantially more efficient than Gialoc. When combined, the overall data also show inefficiency in generating patient health records: 95 % of patient health records take at least 15 min to be generated.

Storage and retrieval of patient records consumes 15 min or even longer for a significant majority of the physicians in both centres. So, the time spent by a physician on each patient visit (only considering the record generation, storage and retrieval) will be at least 30 min. Hypothetically, if all 13 general physicians and 16 specialist physicians in Hoaiduc spend 8 h/day and 5 days/week on patient visits only, the throughput will be a maximum of 120,971 patient visits per annum. The routine core activities for physicians, however, do not merely involve patient visits but also involve other responsibilities, such as education concerning prevailing health problems, and the methods of preventing and controlling them. By contrast with the reported number (average annual number of patient visits in Hoaiduc is 120,000), time efficiency apparently becomes a problem with inefficient patient record generation, storage and retrieval.

Core Readiness Assessment While two participating health centres were different in key areas such as the number of staff and population served, they are also similar in many other aspects. Patient health records in these centres were all paper-based only. Unsurprisingly, some issues were identified related to patient records generation, storage and retrieval:

- Inefficiency in generating and retrieving patient health records.
- Incomplete and inaccurate patient records and more dissatisfaction when only physicians generated patient records.
- Lack of access and confidentiality to patient records when generated by multiple staff (physicians and their assistants).
- Dissatisfaction of sharing patient records.

The empirical evidence represents the realisation of problems in documentation of clinical information, which can typically be addressed by EHR systems. Also, it demonstrates physicians' dissatisfaction with present paper health records in terms of completeness and accuracy of patient records, and sharing patient records. Accordingly, the core readiness is high (see Table 24.9). These results have been approved by E-Health experts in Vietnam.

With the understanding of the status of paper health records, some broad requirements of EHR systems that should be incorporated are to:

- Ensure patients' records can be generated by multiple workers when needed.
- Ensure patient records can be generated efficiently.
- Ensure healthcare workers can access patient records efficiently when needed, and security and privacy issues are ensured especially in cases of multiple access; (further exploration is required for who the sharers are, and how and what type of information needs to be shared).
- Explore options to improve the completeness and accuracy of patient health records, as well as exploring ways to improve the human–computer interactional design of the EHR systems to suit end-users (e.g. use of well-designed forms for generating records, possibly with automated data validation checks or even introduction of patient portals).

These broad requirements generated from the above analysis are the start for the consideration and development of more detailed requirements for EHR systems.

24.4.2 Readiness Assessment Results with EHRAT

The same set of data was also processed with EHRAT and the core readiness assessment results are shows in Table 24.10.

Table 24.9 Assessment results

Healthcare centres	R(Core)	Variables
Gialoc	High	V(ED) = 0, V(PP) = 0, V(CA) = 0, V(SR) = 0
Hoaiduc	High	V(ED) = 0, V(PP) = 0, V(CA) = 0, V(SR) = 0

Table 24.10 Assessment results with EHRAT

Healthcare centres	R(Core)	Variables
Gialoc	High	V(ED) = 0, V(PP) = 0, V(CA) = 0, V(SR) = 0
Hoaiduc	Medium	V(ED) = 0, V(PP) = 0, V(CA) = 1, V(SR) = 0

It is observed that the core readiness assessment results in Hoaiduc are not identical between Tables 24.9 and 24.10 because of different values of V(CA). The value of V(CA), according to Table 24.4, is determined by whether the value of ç(avg(M(DCAR))) is greater than 3. The value of M(DCAR) was filled on a scale where 1 stands for "not satisfied at all" with completeness and accuracy of patient records and 5 stands for "very satisfied". Although Table 24.7 shows that in Hoaiduc 20 % of respondents reported dissatisfaction and 80 % reported moderate or higher levels of satisfaction, the value of V(CA) was still filled with 0 because it was suggested that more room for improvement was required on this parameter.

24.5 Conclusions

This chapter has contributed to the development of the EHRAM using design science research methodology. EHRAM involves:

- An EHRAF.
- A process for the readiness assessment.
- A tool for the readiness assessment (EHRAT).

EHRAM deals with the factors that need to be addressed in the planning of E-Health programmes and therefore helps planners evaluate their status and also provides decision makers with a conceptual assessment framework to guide their decision-making processes.

There are some limitations for this chapter:

- The amount of data available was insufficient for the full validation of EHRAM. The sample size for each studied healthcare centre was small.
- Current framework (EHRAF) has limited capability in predicting the success of E-Health in the context of measures such as physicians' acceptance. More measures are needed to predict physicians' acceptance of EHR systems, but the available archive data did not capture these measures.

- Each readiness component in EHRAF was assessed as one of three different levels: high, medium and low (discretely defined). Real-life levels are more fuzzy in nature, i.e. continuous scales may be more realistic.

Further investigation is needed in this area:

- There is need for more sophisticated EHRAF (perhaps incorporating fuzzy levels) in order to get more realistic assessment results.
- More studies are required to validate EHRAM. For example, similar case studies can be conducted to assess E-Health readiness in other developing countries.
- E-Health readiness assessment in this chapter was conducted from EHR perspective and in the future it can be studied from the perspective of holistic E-Health systems (e.g. telemedicine and e-referral systems). The future study is supposed to start with the modification of the readiness components but focus on the coverage of the core readiness, as other E-Health systems using the same platform (e.g. ICT infrastructure, communication links, healthcare providers) that EHR uses provide different types of service.
- The current EHRAF was only concerned with healthcare providers' and organisational readiness. A more comprehensive framework needs to incorporate components from patients' and public perspectives according to future evaluation needs.

Acknowledgments This study sincerely acknowledges the direct/indirect contributions of members of the WHO eHCD project.

References

Allan, J., & Englebright, J. (2000). Patient-centered documentation: An effective and efficient use of clinical information systems. *Journal of Nursing Administration, 30,* 90–95.

Campbell, J. D., Harris, K. D., & Hodge, R. (2001). Introducing telemedicine technology to rural physicians and settings. *The Journal of Family Practice, 50,* 419–424.

Cronbach, L. J., et al. (1980). *Toward reform of program evaluation: Aims, methods, and institutional arrangements.* San Francisco: Jossey-Bass.

Dean, J. (2000). *An evaluation method for COTS software products.* Proceeding of the 12th Annual Software Technology Conference (STC), May, Saltake City, Utah, USA.

DeLone, W. H., & McLean, E. R. (1992). Information systems success: The quest for the dependent variable. *Information Systems Research, 3*(1), 60–95.

DeLone, W. H., & McLean, E. R. (2003). The DeLone and McLean model of information systems success: A ten-year update. *Journal of Management Information Systems, 19*(4), 9–30.

Demiris, G., Oliver, D. R. P., Porock, D., & Courtney, K. (2004). Home telehealth: The Missouri telehospice project: Background and next steps. *Home Health Care Technology Report, 1,* 49, 55–57.

Dickinson, G., Fischetti, L., & Heard, S. (2004). HL EHR system functional model: Draft standard for trial use. http://www.hl7.org/ehr/downloads/index_2004.asp. Accessed 12 Sept 2008.

Eysenbach, G. (2001). What is e-health? (editorial). *Journal of Medical Internet Research, 1*(2), e20.

Gagnon, M. P., & Scott, R. E. (2005). Striving for evidence in e-health evaluation: Lessons from health technology assessment. *Journal of Telemedicine and Telecare, 11*(Suppl. 2), 34–36.

Guba, E. G., & Lincoln, Y. S. (1981). *Effective evaluation.* San Francisco: Jossey-Bass.

Hevner, A. R., March, S. T., Park, J., & Ram, S. (2004). Design science in information systems research. *MIS Quarterly, 28,* 75–106.

ISO Technical Report (ISO-TR20514) Health Informatics, Electronic Health Record, Definition, Scope, and Context. Clause 4.4.

Jennett, P., Jackson, A., Healy, T., Kazanjian, A., Woollard, R., Haydt, S., & Bates, J. (2002). Alliance for building capacity—framework for remote and rural readiness in telehealth. Final Report for CANARIE. http://www.fp.ucalgary.ca/telehealth/Projects-Canarie-Final%20Report,%20Appendix%20A.htm. Accessed 04 Nov 2008.

Jennett, P., Jackson, A., Healy, T., Ho, K., Kazanjian, A., Woollard, R., et al. (2003). A study of a rural community's readiness for telehealth. *Journal of Telemedicine and Telecare, 9,* 259–263.

Jennett, P., Yeo, M., Pauls, M., & Graham, J. (2004). Organizational readiness for telemedicine: Implications for success and failure. *Journal of Telemedicine and Telecare, 9*(Suppl. 2), S27–S30.

Jennett, P., Jackson, A., Ho, K., Healy, T., Kazanjian, A., Woollard, R., et al. (2005). The essence of telehealth readiness in rural communities: An organizational perspective. *Journal of Telemedicine and e-Health, 11,* 137–145.

Khoja, S., Scott, R., Ishaq, A., & Mohsin, M. (2007). eHealth international journal. Testing reliability of eHealth readiness assessment tools for developing countries. *e-Health International Journal, 3*(1), 25–40.

Li, J. (2008). Online surveys for e-Health readiness assessment. http://www.surveymonkey.com/s.aspx?sm=rx6KOh2_2fqh_2fU1rNmfsdh_2fQ_3d_3d, http://www.surveymonkey.com/s.aspx?sm=3hryMFDJzc5eRrF75e4Tjw_3d_3d. Accessed Dec 2011.

Li, J., Land, L., & Ray, P. (2008a). Humanitarian Technology Challenge (HTC)—electronic health records perspective. A Report of Joint Project of IEEE and United Nations Foundation.

Li, J., Land, L., Chattopadhyay, S., & Ray, P. (2008b). *An approach for e-health system assessment & specification.* IEEE 10th International Conference on e-Health Networking, Application & Services, 7–9 July 2008, Singapore.

Manning, M. L., & Munro, D. (2006). *The Survey researcher's SPSS Cookbook.* Australia: Pearson Education.

March, S. T., & Smith, G. (1995). Design and natural science research on information technology. *Decision Support Systems, 15*(4), 251–266.

Menachemi, N., Lee, S. C., Shepherd, J. E., & Brooks, R. G. (2006). Proliferation of electronic health records among obstetrician-gynecologists. *Quality Management in Health Care (Qual Manage Health Care), 15*(3), 150–156.

Nunamaker, J., Chen, M., & Purdin, T. D. M. (1991). Systems development in information systems research. *Journal of Management Information Systems, 7*(3), 89–106.

Patton, M. Q. (1990). *Qualitative evaluation and research methods* (2nd ed.). Thousand Oaks: Sage.

Ray, P. K. (2003). *Integrated management from e-business perspective, concepts, architectures and methodologies.* New York: Kluwer, Plenum.

Schön, D. A. (1983). *The reflective practitioner: How professionals think in action.* New York: Basic Books.

Seddon, P. B. (1997). A respecification and extension of the DeLone and McLean model of IS success. *Information Systems Research, 8*(3), 240–253.

Simon, H. A. (1996). *The sciences of the artificial* (3rd ed.). Cambridge: MIT Press.

US General Accounting Office, Program Evaluation and Methodology Division. (1990). *Case study evaluations.* Washington: Government Printing Office.

Watson, P. J. (2006). Electronic health records—manual for developing countries. http://64.233.179.104/scholar?hl=zh-CN&lr=&q=cache:RlrElvVm-VEJ, http://www.wpro.who.int/NR/rdonlyres/5753F8CF-8A78-4639-BEFC-F0EE9B3CBA0A/0/EHRmanual.pdf + EHR + adoption + developing + countries. Accessed 28 Feb 2008.

Watts, C., & Ibegbulam, I. (2005). Access to electronic healthcare information resources in developing countries: Experiences from the Medical Library, College of Medicine, University of Nigeria. http://72.14.253.104/search?q=cache:wT53fzH_TXEJ, http://www.ifla.org/IV/ifla71/papers/164e-Watts_Ibegbulam.pdf+%22ICT+infrastructure%22+healthcare+%22developing+countries%22&hl=en&ct=clnk&cd=1&gl=au. Accessed 19 Sept 2007.

WHO. (2005). e-Health Report by Secretariat. 58th World Health Assembly A58/21, April.

WHO. (2006). The global shortage of health workers and its impact. http://www.who.int/mediacentre/factsheets/fs302/en/index.html. Accessed 06 Oct 2009.

Wickramasinghe, N. S., Fadlalla, A. M. A., Geisler, E., & Schaffer, J. L. (2005). A framework for assessing e-health preparedness. *International Journal of Electronic Healthcare, 1*(3), 62–81.

Yin, K. R. (2003). *Case study research, design and methods* (3rd ed.). Thousand Oaks: Sage.

Chapter 25
Identifying the Taiwanese Electronic Health Record Systems Evaluation Framework and Instrument by Implementing the Modified Delphi Method

Yung-Yu Su, Khin Than Win and Tieh-Chi Chung

Abstract The aim of this research is to design an appropriate conceptual evaluation framework with a draft instrument to validate the structure of the Taiwanese EHR systems evaluation framework. The modified Delphi method was applied to refine the proposed instrument for practicality in real medical environment. The degree of consensus between and within questions in the proposed instrument by calculating both content validity index for items (I-CVI) and content validity index for scales (S-CVI) were presented in this chapter. An appropriate instrument for achieving its research purpose was achieved in this research.

Keywords Electronic health records system · Delphi method · EHR success · EHR implementation · EHR evaluation · Sociotechnical

25.1 Introduction

Electronic Health Record systems (EHRs) play an important role in modern clinical service based on the development of information technology; while regarding the national goal of promoting EHRs in Taiwan, awareness of EHRs' success is important, as that would assist in providing suitable EHRs for satisfying the requirements of clinical service. It is because EHRs not only help the management of administration and finances for improving working efficiency in clinical services, but also help to reduce human errors in patient care. Based on the issue of user-centeredness for the application of EHRs in healthcare, it is essential to: (1) understanding end-user's opinion for identifying whether EHRs' success would help to recognize the strengths and weaknesses of such systems; (2) providing useful suggestions to

Y.-Y. Su (✉) · T.-C. Chung
Graduate Institute of Health Care, Meiho University 23, Ping Kuang Rd.,
91202 Pingtung County, Taiwan
e-mail: yungyu@meiho.edu.tw

K. T. Win
School of Information Systems and Technology, University of Wollongong,
Northfields Avenue, 2522 Wollongong, Australia
e-mail: win@uow.edu.au

R. K. Bali et al. (eds.), *Pervasive Health Knowledge Management*,
Healthcare Delivery in the Information Age,
DOI 10.1007/978-1-4614-4514-2_25,

improve the functions of EHRs for patient care; and (3) realizing the impact of using such systems in clinical service. Moreover, with proper success assessment, it offers evidence-based information for healthcare executives and EHRs' developers concerning the importance of providing a suitable user-centered EHR system for patient care, so that it will lead safer and acceptable EHRs. As a result, it needs an appropriate evaluation instrument to assess above aims.

The Declaration of Innsbruck suggested that Evaluation studies should be grounded on scientific theory and rigorous approaches (Ammenwerth et al. 2004). Accordingly, this research applies the issue of "Socio-Technical theory" (Bostrom and Heinen 1977) and "User-centered perspective" (Hesse and Shneiderman 2007) to establish a conceptual evaluation framework and design an appropriate instrument for evaluating Taiwanese EHRs. In order to recognize the most appropriate factor/attributes in evaluating EHRs by way of applying the strategy of "Triangulation research method" in health information systems research (Ammenwerth et al. 2003b), especially in the triangulation of investigator and method, this chapter identifies the most appropriate evaluation framework applicable for EHRs by applying the strategy of modified Delphi method (Snyder-Halpern 2001), which could be regarded as a reference for supporting investment decisions in healthcare. In addition, it also presented the results of content valid (Polit and Beck 2006) by calculating content validity index (CVI) for items (I-CVI; Polit and Beck 2006) and content validity index for scales (S-CVI; Hubley and Palepu 2007) to validate the proposed evaluation framework and construct an appropriate questionnaire for the evaluation of Taiwanese EHRs.

25.2 Background and Conceptual Evaluation Framework

A comprehensive framework for evaluating Taiwanese EHRs' success needs to consider the features of the Taiwanese healthcare delivery system (a centralized medical system) and related regulations, such as the Medical Act, the National Health Insurance (NHI), and the Taiwanese Hospital Accreditation Program. In other words, the operational strategies of healthcare administration are affected by the outer healthcare environment in Taiwan, such as health policies and NHI. Secondly, a user-centered evaluation framework needs to cover various aspects, therefore, with regard to the knowledge of Evidence-Based Healthcare Management (Wan 2002), the issue of Social–technical theory (Bostrom and Heinen 1977), the issue of Structure-Process-Outcome (S-P-O) model (Donabedian 2003), and the meaning of Health Information System (HIS) evaluation (Ammenwerth et al. 2003a), it needs to understand the relationships between the technology itself and its users for implementing EHRs based on end-users' opinion of using such systems.

In order to satisfy above requirements and combining the knowledge of aforementioned issues, this study proposed that structure covers aspects of organization and technology; process equates to human aspects; and outcomes are related to net benefits. In addition, the DeLone and McLean IS success model (DeLone and McLean 1992) had been combined with the S-P-O model, however, it still needs empirical research to identify whether the updated D&M IS success model could be combined

Table 25.1 Definitions of the conceptual user-centered evaluation framework

Aspects	Elements	Operational definitions
Organizational	HE	Realizing end-users' impression of national health policies of EHRs
	OB	Recognizing end-users' impressions of the reasons and motivation to implement EHRs within a hospital
Technology	Sys_Q	Identifying end-users' opinions of the performance distinctiveness of the EHRs' processing it provides
	MDQ	Identifying end-users' opinions of the output information produced by the EHRs
	Ser_Q	Considering how to provide accessible help to the stakeholders of the EHRs by the technological vender based on identifying end-users' judgment
	Safe_Q	Identifying end-users' opinions of risk management within EHRs
Human	UU	Measuring the use of the EHR based on end-users' judgment
	US	Measuring the users' responses by using the output information of EHRs
Net benefits	ONB	Realizing the impact and goodness of implementing EHRs in patient care performance based on identifying end-users' judgment

with the S-P-O model and a Social–technical approach in EHR systems evaluation. Moreover, a patient is regarded as an outer customer and a healthcare professional as an inner customer within the issue of organizational behavior. In order to improve the quality of patient care for outer customers, it is essential for healthcare executives to firstly improve the work satisfaction of its inner customers. Accordingly, Organizational aspects need to concern about Healthcare environment (External organization) and Organizational Behaviors (Internal organization). In addition, EHRs include patients' health information, any error or inaccuracy can have impact on patient care; regarding clinical data of EHR and the development of both intranet and Internet in hospitals, therefore, clinical data quality (D'Onofrio and Gendron 2001) and safety quality (Su et al. 2006; Win 2004) are also important for the EHRs. Furthermore, realizing an end-user's attitude of using such systems will provide sufficient information for healthcare executives to access end-users' opinion and to recognize that whether the net benefits of implementing EHR will affect the strategies of hospital management. In short, this study considers that the aspects of Environment cover the dimensions of Healthcare Environment (HE) and Organization Behaviors (OB); the aspects of Technology cover the dimensions of System Quality (Sys_Q), Medical Data Quality (MDQ), Service Quality (Ser_Q), and Safety Quality (Safe_Q); the aspects of Human cover the dimensions of User Usage (UU) and User Satisfaction (US); and the aspects of Net Benefits cover the dimensions of Organization Net Benefits (ONB; Table 25.1 and Fig. 25.1).

25.3 Research Method and Material

According to the features of the modified Delphi method, the process of such a technique is commonly being applied in identifying the content validity of an instrument (Takemura et al. 2006; Rushton and Lindsay 2008), in order to design a suitable evaluation instrument by applying the knowledge of triangulation research method.

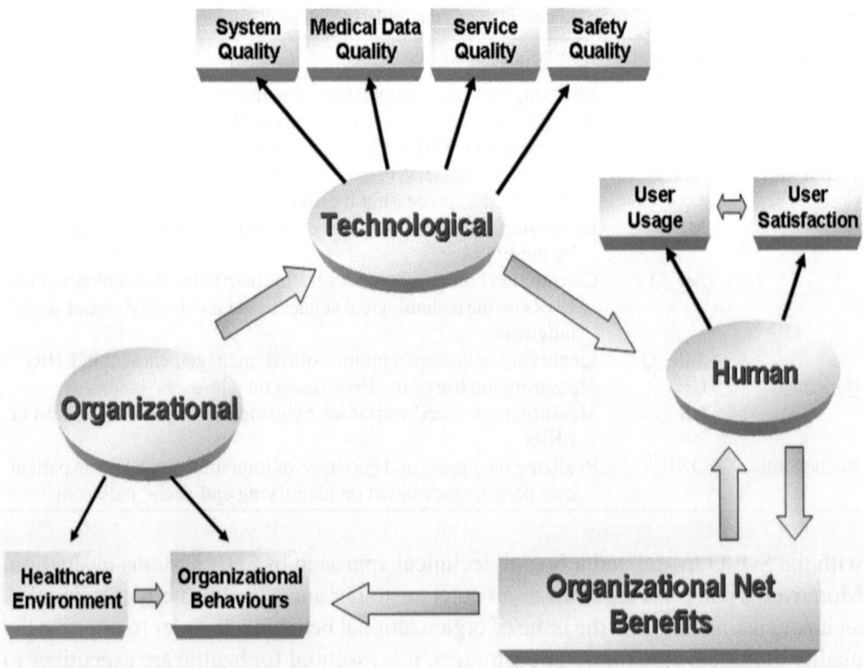

Fig. 25.1 Taiwanese electronic health record systems evaluation framework (TEHR evaluation framework)

1. For method triangulation:
   (a) A quantitative approach indicates the degree of consensus between and within questions by calculating I-CVI and S-CVI to determinate which questions need to be removed from the instrument.
   (b) A qualitative approach provides a reference to modify wording and/or syntaxes of those questions, which could be kept from results of I-CVI and S-CVI.
2. For investigator triangulation, 30 participants (including medical doctors, nurses, medical technicians, high-level healthcare administrators, and the director of the department of information management) were recruited in this Delphi group. Experts within the Delphi group were requested to answer each question in the three main components (Importance, Feasibility, and Confidence).

In this study, the function of the Delphi group is to determinate whether or not each question within the prepared evaluation instrument is appropriate for measuring an end-user's opinion of using EHR systems based on experts' working experience and academic opinions. In order to confirm the content validity or face validity, the prepared evaluation instrument (Table 25.5) consists of three main components:

1. *Importance*: The significance of each evaluation question in its evaluation element.
2. *Feasibility*: The practicality of each evaluation question in a real medical environment.
3. *Confidence*: To measure experts' opinions of whether or not they trust that the results of each question could be used to evaluate end-user's opinion of using EHRs.

This study adopted a 5-point Likeret scale as the answer format (1 = strongly disagree; 2 = disagree; 3 = somewhat disagree; 4 = agree; 5 = strongly agree; Lynn 1986).

Content validity: "*concerns the degree to which a sample of items, taken together, constitutes an adequate operational definition of a construct*" (Polit and Beck 2006). Therefore, a quantitative approach of the Delphi method could be used to identify the content validity by calculating I-CVI (the value of the I-CVI is the summation of agreement [4: agree and 5: highly agree] divided by the total number of experts) to determine which question need to be removed from the proposed instrument, and the content validity index for S-CVI (adopting the average proportion of items, which were approved by the experts and calculating this as the average of the I-CVI values) to recognize the proportion of agreement within the instrument. The determinate criterion (cut-off point) of I-CVI is 0.78 (78 %; Polit and Beck 2006) and 0.90 (90 %) for the S-CVI/Ave.

The special intention of each round is:

1. Round 1 focuses on ranking the aforementioned three main components in each question, and requesting experts to provide their viewpoint of each question if possible.
2. Round 2 not only repeats the same process of round 1 for experts to reconsider their response to each question, but also requests experts to modify the wording and syntax of each question to refine this prepared instrument. If the degree of consensus is stable among experts in round 2, this will complete the process of performing the Delphi method; otherwise, it will be repeated until all inappropriate questions are removed by calculating each I-CVI and the overall S-CVI of the proposed evaluation instrument.

25.4 Results

It took around 9 weeks (from 9 October to 11 December 2006) to collect data from the Delphi Group twice, due to the degree of consensus stability among experts in round 2. In *round 1*, 23 of 30 experts (76.67 %) responded to the questionnaire: 10 were medical doctors, 6 were executive nursing staff, 5 were executive healthcare administrators, and 2 were executive managers of information management. In other words, the ratio of participants (clinical vs. nonclinical) was close to 2.3:1; 16 were health professionals and the others were executive managers. In *round 2*, 19 of 23 experts (82.60 %) responded: 8 were medical doctors, 5 were executive nursing staff, 4 were executive healthcare administrators, and 2 were executive managers of information management. In other words, the ratio of participants (clinical vs. nonclinical) was close to 2.1:1; 13 were health professionals and the others were executive managers.

Based on the results of the two-interactive Delphi methods, the results of I-CVI (Table 25.2) suggest that the following seven questions: HE2, OB2, OB4, UU4, UU5, US2, and US4-1 need to be removed from the proposed instrument:

1. The original content of HE2 is "Do you know that all the hospitals around your hospital are implementing EHRs in their patient service," in other words, several experts of the Delphi group suggested that such a question is not relevant (rated 1 or 2 and 3) to the underlying construct (Healthcare Environment).
2. The original content of OB2 is "Implementing EHR is a kind of management strategy to perform the issue of patient safety and obey the regulation of hospital accreditation in your hospital," and OB7 is "Please display your opinion to explain the reasons that your hospital is going to implement EHR." For this question, experts suggested that the meaning of both questions overlap due to OB7 being a stem, which covers three questions and which could be used to replace OB2.
3. For OB4, the content of the question is "You agreed with the leadership and administration of top managers for adopting EHR within your hospital?" Experts suggested that such a question is inappropriate in this study due to its being a sensitive issue of organizational culture and end-users would not tell the truth.
4. For UU4 and UU5 within the element of User Usage, the original content of UU4 is "What is the average frequency for you to use computer in your daily work?" and "How much time do you use this EHR in your daily work?" in UU5. In round 1, several experts suggested that the EHR system is a multimedia electronic dataset for storing a patient's medical records and providing up-to-date information for patient care and related services. In other words, it is a paperless working environment for health professionals to use an EHR system and operating such a system becomes a part of their daily work. Therefore, both questions are not suitable for measuring the usage of EHR systems.
5. The content of *US*2 is "This EHR needs advance skills of computer operation to use it." Experts commented that such a question neither clearly describes "advanced skills," nor stresses how to use the output information of such system.
6. The content of US4-1 is "This EHR provides you new cure methods for patient care." For the same reason as US2, experts commented that such a question neither clearly describes "new cure methods" nor stresses measuring expectation of the potential benefits of using an EHR system. As a result, those could be used to explain why the values of I-CVI in such questions are lower than 78 % in those three components (Importance, Feasibility, and Confidence).

In addition, five questions (HE3, HE4, UU2, UU3, and US3) need to be modified to be more relevant to their proposed evaluation element. For example:

1. The original content of HE3 was "Implementing EHR helps your hospital to improve the capacity of clinical service within its location." However, experts suggested that such a question needs to be modified as follows:

Table 25.2 Results of I-CVI within the Delphi method

	First round ($n=23$)							Second round ($n=19$)							
	A	B		C		D		A		B		C		D	
	%	N	%	N	%	Mean	%	N	%	N	%	N	%	Mean	%
Important															
HE1	4.35	0	0.00	22	95.65	4.39	87.80	0	0.00	0	0.00	19	100.00	4.37	87.37
HE2	13.04	6	26.09	14	60.87	3.61	72.20	1	5.26	4	21.05	14	73.68	3.89	77.89
HE3	0.00	1	4.35	22	95.65	4.35	87.00	0	0.00	1	5.26	18	94.74	4.42	88.42
HE4	0.00	2	8.70	21	91.30	4.30	86.00	0	0.00	1	5.26	18	94.74	4.32	86.32
OB1	4.35	2	8.70	20	86.96	4.13	82.60	0	0.00	1	5.26	18	94.74	4.16	83.16
OB2	8.70	1	4.35	20	86.96	4.13	82.60	2	10.53	4	21.05	13	68.42	3.79	75.79
OB3	8.70	4	17.39	17	73.91	3.78	75.60	0	0.00	2	10.53	17	89.47	4.32	86.32
OB4	17.39	4	17.39	15	65.22	3.74	74.80	15	78.95	1	5.26	3	15.79	1.95	38.95
OB5	4.35	2	8.70	20	86.96	4.43	88.60	0	0.00	1	5.26	18	94.74	4.42	88.42
OB6	4.35	3	13.04	19	82.61	4.26	85.20	0	0.00	0	0.00	19	100.00	4.53	90.53
OB7-1	4.35	2	8.70	20	86.96	4.22	84.40	0	0.00	1	5.26	18	94.74	4.42	88.42
OB7-2	4.35	1	4.35	21	91.30	4.22	84.40	0	0.00	1	5.26	18	94.74	4.47	89.47
OB7-3	0.00	1	4.35	22	95.65	4.35	87.00	0	0.00	1	5.26	18	94.74	4.37	87.37
OB8	4.35	0	0.00	22	95.65	4.30	86.00	0	0.00	0	0.00	19	100.00	4.63	92.63
Sys_Q1	8.70	1	4.35	20	86.96	4.13	82.60	0	0.00	1	5.26	18	94.74	4.32	86.32
Sys_Q2	4.35	2	8.70	20	86.96	4.13	82.60	0	0.00	1	5.26	18	94.74	4.47	89.47
Sys_Q3	0.00	1	4.35	22	95.65	3.78	75.60	0	0.00	1	5.26	18	94.74	4.37	87.37
Sys_Q4	4.35	5	21.74	17	73.91	3.74	74.80	0	0.00	1	5.26	18	94.74	4.47	89.47
Sys_Q5	0.00	0	0.00	23	100.00	4.43	88.60	0	0.00	1	5.26	18	94.74	4.58	91.58
Sys_Q6	0.00	4	17.39	19	82.61	4.26	85.20	0	0.00	1	5.26	18	94.74	4.53	90.53
Sys_Q7	0.00	0	0.00	23	100.00	4.22	84.40	0	0.00	1	5.26	18	94.74	4.47	89.47
Sys_Q8	4.35	0	0.00	22	95.65	4.22	84.40	0	0.00	0	0.00	19	100.00	4.63	92.63
Sys_Q9	0.00	0	0.00	23	100.00	4.35	87.00	0	0.00	1	5.26	18	94.74	4.47	89.47
MDQ1	4.35	1	4.35	21	91.30	4.48	89.60	1	5.26	0	0.00	18	94.74	4.47	89.47
MDQ2	0.00	0	0.00	23	100.00	4.57	91.40	0	0.00	0	0.00	19	100.00	4.58	91.58
MDQ3	0.00	1	4.35	22	95.65	4.57	91.40	0	0.00	1	5.26	18	94.74	4.47	89.47
MDQ4	0.00	2	8.70	21	91.30	4.57	91.40	0	0.00	0	0.00	19	100.00	4.47	89.47

Table 25.2 (continued)

	First round ($n=23$)							Second round ($n=19$)							
	A	B		C		D		A		B		C		D	
	%	N	%	N	%	Mean	%	N	%	N	%	N	%	Mean	%
Important															
MDQ5	0.00	1	4.35	22	95.65	4.43	88.60	0	0.00	0	0.00	19	100.00	4.42	88.42
MDQ6	0.00	1	4.35	22	95.65	4.43	88.60	0	0.00	0	0.00	19	100.00	4.47	89.47
MDQ7	4.35	1	4.35	21	91.30	4.30	86.00	0	0.00	0	0.00	19	100.00	4.47	89.47
MDQ8	0.00	1	4.35	22	95.65	4.57	91.40	0	0.00	1	5.26	18	94.74	4.47	89.47
MDQ9	0.00	0	0.00	23	100.00	4.48	89.60	0	0.00	1	5.26	18	94.74	4.63	92.63
MDQ10	4.35	0	0.00	22	95.65	4.57	91.40	0	0.00	0	0.00	19	100.00	4.58	91.58
Ser_Q1	0.00	2	8.70	21	91.30	4.43	88.60	0	0.00	1	5.26	18	94.74	4.47	89.47
Ser_Q2	0.00	1	4.35	22	95.65	4.43	88.60	0	0.00	1	5.26	18	94.74	4.53	90.53
Ser_Q3	13.04	0	0.00	20	86.96	4.13	82.60	0	0.00	1	5.26	18	94.74	4.37	87.37
Ser_Q4	4.35	2	8.70	20	86.96	4.35	87.00	0	0.00	1	5.26	18	94.74	4.47	89.47
Ser_Q5	0.00	1	4.35	22	95.65	4.35	87.00	0	0.00	1	5.26	18	94.74	4.53	90.53
Ser_Q6	0.00	3	13.04	20	86.96	4.35	87.00	0	0.00	1	5.26	18	94.74	4.42	88.42
Ser_Q7	4.35	1	4.35	21	91.30	4.52	90.40	0	0.00	1	5.26	18	94.74	4.63	92.63
Safe_Q1	0.00	1	4.35	22	95.65	4.7	94.00	0	0.00	1	5.26	18	94.74	4.63	92.63
Safe_Q2	8.70	1	4.35	20	86.96	4.43	88.60	0	0.00	1	5.26	18	94.74	4.53	90.53
Safe_Q3	0.00	0	0.00	23	100.00	4.78	95.60	0	0.00	0	0.00	19	100.00	4.79	95.79
Safe_Q4	4.35	2	8.70	20	86.96	4.52	90.40	0	0.00	1	5.26	18	94.74	4.68	93.68
Safe_Q5	0.00	0	0.00	23	100.00	4.61	92.20	0	0.00	1	5.26	18	94.74	4.68	93.68
Safe_Q6	4.35	0	0.00	22	95.65	4.61	92.20	0	0.00	1	5.26	18	94.74	4.74	94.74
Safe_Q7	0.00	1	4.35	22	95.65	4.57	91.40	0	0.00	1	5.26	18	94.74	4.58	91.58
Safe_Q8	0.00	2	8.70	21	91.30	4.48	89.60	0	0.00	0	0.00	19	100.00	4.74	94.74
Safe_Q9	4.35	0	0.00	22	95.65	4.35	87.00	0	0.00	1	5.26	18	94.74	4.42	88.42
Safe_Q10	0.00	1	4.35	22	95.65	4.48	89.60	0	0.00	1	5.26	18	94.74	4.79	95.79
Safe_Q11	4.35	2	8.70	20	86.96	4.17	83.40	0	0.00	1	5.26	18	94.74	4.68	93.68
UU1-1	8.70	1	4.35	20	86.96	4.13	82.60	0	0.00	1	5.26	18	94.74	4.68	93.68
UU1-2	8.70	2	8.70	19	82.61	4.26	85.20	0	0.00	0	0.00	19	100.00	4.53	90.53
UU1-3	4.35	2	8.70	20	86.96	4.26	85.20	0	0.00	0	0.00	19	100.00	4.53	90.53
UU1-4	13.04	1	4.35	19	82.61	3.96	79.20	0	0.00	0	0.00	19	100.00	4.37	87.37

Table 25.2 (continued)

	First round ($n = 23$)							Second round ($n = 19$)							
	A	B		C		D		A		B		C		D	
	%	N	%	N	%	Mean	%	N	%	N	%	N	%	Mean	%
Important															
UU2	8.70	4	17.39	17	73.91	3.96	79.20	0	0.00	2	10.53	17	89.47	4.37	87.37
UU3	4.35	0	0.00	22	95.65	4.30	86.00	0	0.00	2	10.53	17	89.47	4.26	85.26
UU4	13.04	1	4.35	19	82.61	4.13	82.60	3	15.79	3	15.79	13	68.42	3.89	77.89
UU5	17.39	0	0.00	19	82.61	3.74	74.80	4	21.05	1	5.26	14	73.68	3.79	75.79
US1	4.35	1	4.35	21	91.30	4.26	85.20	0	0.00	1	5.26	18	94.74	4.37	87.37
US2	17.39	2	8.70	17	73.91	3.83	76.60	4	21.05	1	5.26	14	73.68	3.89	77.89
US3	4.35	1	4.35	21	91.30	4.30	86.00	0	0.00	0	0.00	19	100.00	4.42	88.42
US4-1	17.39	4	17.39	15	65.22	3.52	70.40	8	42.11	1	5.26	10	52.63	3.11	62.11
US4-2	4.35	3	13.04	19	82.61	4.17	83.40	0	0.00	1	5.26	18	94.74	4.37	87.37
US4-3	0.00	1	4.35	22	95.65	4.43	88.60	0	0.00	0	0.00	19	100.00	4.42	88.42
US4-4	4.35	1	4.35	21	91.30	4.35	87.00	0	0.00	1	5.26	18	94.74	4.21	84.21
US5-1	0.00	0	0.00	23	100.00	4.39	87.80	0	0.00	1	5.26	18	94.74	4.37	87.37
US5-2	8.70	2	8.70	19	82.61	4.17	83.40	0	0.00	1	5.26	18	94.74	4.37	87.37
US5-3	4.35	0	0.00	22	95.65	4.26	85.20	0	0.00	1	5.26	18	94.74	4.42	88.42
ONB1	0.00	2	8.70	21	91.30	4.48	89.60	0	0.00	1	5.26	18	94.74	4.47	89.47
ONB2	0.00	1	4.35	22	95.65	4.43	88.60	0	0.00	1	5.26	18	94.74	4.32	86.32
ONB3	4.35	2	8.70	20	86.96	4.13	82.60	0	0.00	1	5.26	18	94.74	4.47	89.47
ONB4	0.00	2	8.70	21	91.30	4.30	86.00	0	0.00	0	0.00	19	100.00	4.47	89.47
ONB5	4.35	2	8.70	20	86.96	4.13	82.60	0	0.00	1	5.26	18	94.74	4.32	86.32
ONB6	0.00	1	4.35	22	95.65	4.48	89.60	0	0.00	1	5.26	18	94.74	4.47	89.47
ONB7	8.70	2	8.70	19	82.61	4.09	81.80	0	0.00	1	5.26	18	94.74	4.42	88.42
Feasibility															
HE1	4.35	2	8.70	20	86.96	3.91	78.20	0	0.00	1	5.26	18	94.74	4.26	85.26
HE2	13.04	4	17.39	16	69.57	3.74	74.80	1	5.26	4	21.05	14	73.68	3.89	77.89
HE3	0.00	1	4.35	22	95.65	4.30	86.00	0	0.00	1	5.26	18	94.74	4.26	85.26
HE4	4.35	4	17.39	18	78.26	3.96	79.20	0	0.00	1	5.26	18	94.74	4.32	86.32

Table 25.2 (continued)

	First round ($n = 23$)							Second round ($n = 19$)							
	A	B		C		D		A		B		C		D	
	%	N	%	N	%	Mean	%	N	%	N	%	N	%	Mean	%
Feasibility															
OB1	4.35	1	4.35	21	91.30	4.04	80.80	0	0.00	1	5.26	18	94.74	4.26	85.26
OB2	13.04	1	4.35	19	82.61	4.25	85.00	3	15.79	2	10.53	14	73.68	3.79	75.79
OB3	17.39	3	13.04	16	69.57	3.65	73.00	0	0.00	2	10.53	17	89.47	4.21	84.21
OB4	26.09	4	17.39	13	56.52	3.43	68.60	15	78.95	1	5.26	3	15.79	2.00	40.00
OB5	0.00	1	4.35	22	95.65	4.35	87.00	0	0.00	1	5.26	18	94.74	4.37	87.37
OB6	8.70	5	21.74	16	69.57	3.96	79.20	0	0.00	0	0.00	19	100.00	4.37	87.37
OB7-1	4.35	1	4.35	21	91.30	4.26	85.20	0	0.00	1	5.26	18	94.74	4.47	89.47
OB7-2	8.70	0	0.00	21	91.30	4.22	84.40	1	5.26	3	15.79	15	78.95	4.16	83.16
OB7-3	13.04	0	0.00	20	86.96	3.96	79.20	0	0.00	1	5.26	18	94.74	4.42	88.42
OB8	0.00	2	8.70	21	91.30	4.04	80.80	0	0.00	0	0.00	19	100.00	4.53	90.53
Sys_Q1	8.70	2	8.70	19	82.61	4.04	80.80	0	0.00	1	5.26	18	94.74	4.26	85.26
Sys_Q2	4.35	5	21.74	17	73.91	4.00	80.00	0	0.00	0	0.00	19	100.00	4.37	87.37
Sys_Q3	0.00	1	4.35	22	95.65	4.22	84.40	0	0.00	1	5.26	18	94.74	4.32	86.32
Sys_Q4	4.35	3	13.04	19	82.61	4.04	80.80	0	0.00	1	5.26	18	94.74	4.37	87.37
Sys_Q5	4.35	1	4.35	21	91.03	4.39	87.80	0	0.00	1	5.26	18	94.74	4.53	90.53
Sys_Q6	0.00	3	13.04	20	86.96	4.35	87.00	0	0.00	1	5.26	18	94.74	4.37	87.37
Sys_Q7	0.00	1	4.35	22	95.65	4.39	87.80	0	0.00	1	5.26	18	94.74	4.37	87.37
Sys_Q8	0.00	1	4.35	22	95.65	4.35	87.00	0	0.00	0	0.00	19	100.00	4.47	89.47
Sys_Q9	0.00	0	0.00	23	100.00	4.39	87.80	0	0.00	1	5.26	18	94.74	4.42	88.42
MDQ1	4.35	0	0.00	22	95.65	4.52	90.40	1	5.26	0	0.00	18	94.74	4.47	89.47
MDQ2	0.00	1	4.35	22	95.65	4.52	90.40	0	0.00	1	5.26	18	94.74	4.47	89.47
MDQ3	0.00	1	4.35	22	95.65	4.52	90.40	0	0.00	1	5.26	18	94.74	4.53	90.53
MDQ4	0.00	1	4.35	22	95.65	4.65	93.00	0	0.00	0	0.00	19	100.00	4.47	89.47
MDQ5	0.00	2	8.70	21	91.30	4.26	85.20	0	0.00	0	0.00	19	100.00	4.47	89.47
MDQ6	0.00	1	4.35	22	95.65	4.43	88.60	0	0.00	1	5.26	18	94.74	4.42	88.42
MDQ7	0.00	1	4.35	22	95.65	4.30	86.00	0	0.00	0	0.00	19	100.00	4.47	89.47
MDQ8	0.00	1	4.35	22	95.65	4.43	88.60	0	0.00	1	5.26	18	94.74	4.53	90.53

Table 25.2 (continued)

	First round ($n=23$)							Second round ($n=19$)							
	A	B		C		D		A		B		C		D	
	%	N	%	N	%	Mean	%	N	%	N	%	N	%	Mean	%
Feasibility															
MDQ9	0.00	0	0.00	23	100.00	4.57	91.40	0	0.00	0	0.00	19	100.00	4.58	91.58
MDQ10	0.00	1	4.35	22	95.65	4.43	88.60	0	0.00	0	0.00	19	100.00	4.47	89.47
Ser_Q1	13.04	2	8.70	18	78.26	3.96	79.20	0	0.00	1	5.26	18	94.74	4.32	86.32
Ser_Q2	17.39	1	4.35	18	78.26	3.91	78.20	0	0.00	1	5.26	18	94.74	4.32	86.32
Ser_Q3	8.70	2	8.70	19	82.61	4.17	83.40	1	5.26	0	0.00	18	94.74	4.21	84.21
Ser_Q4	4.35	2	8.70	20	86.96	4.13	82.60	0	0.00	0	0.00	19	100.00	4.37	87.37
Ser_Q5	4.35	3	13.04	19	82.61	4.00	80.00	0	0.00	1	5.26	18	94.74	4.47	89.47
Ser_Q6	4.35	0	0.00	22	95.65	4.30	86.00	0	0.00	0	0.00	19	100.00	4.47	89.47
Ser_Q7	13.04	2	8.70	18	78.26	3.96	79.20	0	0.00	0	0.00	19	100.00	4.53	90.53
Safe_Q1	0.00	2	8.70	21	91.30	4.61	92.20	0	0.00	1	5.26	18	94.74	4.58	91.58
Safe_Q2	8.70	1	4.35	20	86.96	4.35	87.00	0	0.00	1	5.26	18	94.74	4.42	88.42
Safe_Q3	0.00	0	0.00	23	100.00	4.70	94.00	0	0.00	1	5.26	18	94.74	4.63	92.63
Safe_Q4	4.35	1	4.35	21	91.30	4.43	88.60	0	0.00	0	0.00	19	100.00	4.47	89.47
Safe_Q5	0.00	0	0.00	23	100.00	4.65	93.00	0	0.00	1	5.26	18	94.74	4.58	91.58
Safe_Q6	4.35	0	0.00	22	95.65	4.52	90.40	0	0.00	1	5.26	18	94.74	4.53	90.53
Safe_Q7	0.00	2	8.70	21	91.30	4.43	88.60	0	0.00	1	5.26	18	94.74	4.53	90.53
Safe_Q8	0.00	1	4.35	22	95.65	4.52	90.40	0	0.00	1	5.26	18	94.74	4.53	90.53
Safe_Q9	4.35	1	4.35	21	91.30	4.30	86.00	0	0.00	0	0.00	19	100.00	4.37	87.37
Safe_Q10	0.00	0	0.00	23	100.00	4.48	89.60	0	0.00	0	0.00	19	100.00	4.63	92.63
Safe_Q11	4.35	1	4.35	21	91.30	4.22	84.40	0	0.00	0	0.00	19	100.00	4.79	95.79
UU1-1	4.35	1	4.35	21	91.30	4.09	81.80	0	0.00	1	5.26	18	94.74	4.37	87.37
UU1-2	4.35	2	8.70	20	86.96	4.22	84.40	0	0.00	0	0.00	19	100.00	4.37	87.37
UU1-3	0.00	2	8.70	21	91.30	4.26	85.20	0	0.00	0	0.00	19	100.00	4.32	86.32
UU1-4	8.70	1	4.35	20	86.96	4.04	80.80	0	0.00	0	0.00	19	100.00	4.37	87.37
UU2	4.35	1	4.35	21	91.30	4.13	82.60	0	0.00	2	10.53	17	89.47	4.32	86.32
UU3	0.00	1	4.35	22	95.65	4.43	88.60	0	0.00	2	10.53	17	89.47	4.21	84.21
UU4	17.39	0	0.00	19	82.61	3.91	78.20	4	21.05	1	5.26	14	73.68	3.74	74.74
UU5	8.70	0	0.00	21	91.30	4.00	80.00	4	21.05	1	5.26	14	73.68	3.74	74.74

Table 25.2 (continued)

	First round ($n = 23$)							Second round ($n = 19$)							
	A	B		C		D		A		B		C		D	
	%	N	%	N	%	Mean	%	N	%	N	%	N	%	Mean	%
Feasibility															
US1	4.35	0	0.00	22	95.65	4.22	84.40	0	0.00	0	0.00	19	100.00	4.58	91.58
US2	17.39	2	8.70	17	73.91	3.83	76.60	3	15.79	2	10.53	14	73.68	3.84	76.84
US3	4.35	0	0.00	22	0.96	4.35	87.00	0	0.00	1	5.26	18	94.74	4.42	88.42
US4-1	13.04	4	17.39	16	69.57	3.61	72.20	11	57.89	1	5.26	7	36.84	2.68	53.68
US4-2	4.35	3	13.04	19	82.61	4.17	83.40	1	5.26	1	5.26	17	89.47	4.16	83.16
US4-3	0.00	1	4.35	22	95.65	4.35	87.00	0	0.00	1	5.26	18	94.74	4.37	87.37
US4-4	4.35	2	8.70	20	86.96	4.26	85.20	0	0.00	1	5.26	18	94.74	4.21	84.21
US5-1	0.00	1	4.35	22	95.65	4.35	87.00	0	0.00	1	5.26	18	94.74	4.47	89.47
US5-2	8.70	1	4.35	20	86.96	4.26	85.20	0	0.00	1	5.26	18	94.74	4.37	87.37
US5-3	4.35	0	0	22	95.65	4.35	87.00	0	0.00	0	0.00	19	100.0	4.58	91.58
ONB1	8.70	2	8.70	19	82.61	3.96	79.20	0	0.00	3	15.79	16	84.21	4.26	85.20
ONB2	0.00	1	4.35	22	95.65	4.30	86.00	0	0.00	0	0.00	19	100.00	4.47	89.40
ONB3	4.35	2	8.70	20	86.96	4.09	81.80	0	0.00	0	0.00	19	100.00	4.53	90.60
ONB4	0.00	3	13.04	20	86.96	4.22	84.40	0	0.00	1	5.26	18	94.74	4.32	86.40
ONB5	8.70	0	0.00	21	91.30	3.96	79.20	0	0.00	3	15.79	16	84.21	4.26	85.20
ONB6	4.35	0	0.00	22	95.65	4.30	86.00	0	0.00	1	5.26	18	94.74	4.47	89.40
ONB7	8.70	1	4.35	20	86.96	4.17	83.40	0	0.00	2	10.53	17	89.47	4.37	87.40
Confidence															
HE1	4.35	4	17.39	18	78.26	3.87	77.40	0	0.00	1	5.26	18	94.74	4.16	83.16
HE2	21.74	5	21.74	13	56.52	3.39	67.80	1	5.26	5	26.32	13	68.42	3.84	76.84
HE3	0.00	2	0.09	21	91.30	4.17	83.40	0	0.00	1	5.26	18	94.74	4.26	85.26
HE4	4.35	3	13.04	19	82.61	3.91	78.20	0	0.00	1	5.26	18	94.74	4.37	87.37
OB1	8.70	2	8.70	19	82.61	3.91	78.20	0	0.00	2	10.53	17	89.47	4.21	84.21
OB2	8.70	3	13.04	18	78.26	4.13	82.60	2	10.53	3	15.79	14	73.68	3.84	76.84
OB3	13.04	6	26.09	14	60.87	3.61	72.20	0	0.00	3	15.79	16	84.21	4.11	82.11
OB4	30.43	4	17.39	12	52.17	3.26	65.20	12	63.16	1	5.26	6	31.58	2.42	48.42
OB5	4.35	2	8.70	20	86.96	4.13	82.60	0	0.00	2	10.53	17	89.47	4.21	84.21

Table 25.2 (continued)

	First round ($n=23$)							Second round ($n=19$)							
	A	B		C		D		A		B		C		D	
	%	N	%	N	%	Mean	%	N	%	N	%	N	%	Mean	%
Confidence															
OB6	8.70	5	21.74	16	69.57	3.87	77.40	0	0.00	1	5.26	18	94.74	4.32	86.32
OB7-1	4.35	0	0.00	22	95.65	4.22	84.40	0	0.00	2	10.53	17	89.47	4.26	85.26
OB7-2	8.70	12	52.17	9	39.13	4.3	86.00	0	0.00	1	5.26	18	94.74	4.42	88.42
OB7-3	4.35	3	13.04	19	82.61	3.87	77.40	0	0.00	1	5.26	18	94.74	4.42	88.42
OB8	4.35	3	13.04	19	82.61	4.04	80.80	0	0.00	0	0.00	19	100.00	4.47	89.47
Sys_Q1	13.04	2	8.70	18	78.26	3.78	75.60	0	0.00	1	5.26	18	94.74	4.26	85.26
Sys_Q2	4.35	5	21.74	17	73.91	3.91	78.20	0	0.00	1	5.26	18	94.74	4.37	87.37
Sys_Q3	4.35	2	8.70	20	86.96	4.00	80.00	0	0.00	1	5.26	18	94.74	4.21	84.21
Sys_Q4	4.35	3	13.04	19	82.61	3.96	79.20	0	0.00	1	5.26	18	94.74	4.26	85.26
Sys_Q5	4.35	3	13.04	19	82.61	4.22	84.40	0	0.00	1	5.26	18	94.74	4.47	89.47
Sys_Q6	0.00	5	21.74	18	78.26	4.22	84.40	0	0.00	2	10.53	17	89.47	4.26	85.26
Sys_Q7	0.00	3	13.04	20	86.96	4.13	82.60	0	0.00	1	5.26	18	94.74	4.32	86.32
Sys_Q8	4.35	2	8.70	20	86.96	4.26	85.20	0	0.00	0	0.00	19	100.00	4.37	87.37
Sys_Q9	0.00	4	17.39	19	82.61	4.00	80.00	0	0.00	1	5.26	18	94.74	4.26	85.26
MDQ1	0.00	1	4.35	22	95.65	4.43	88.60	0	0.00	1	5.26	18	94.74	4.37	87.37
MDQ2	0.00	2	8.70	21	91.30	4.39	87.80	0	0.00	1	5.26	18	94.74	4.37	87.37
MDQ3	0.00	1	4.35	22	95.65	4.39	87.80	0	0.00	1	5.26	18	94.74	4.47	89.47
MDQ4	4.35	3	13.04	19	82.61	4.13	82.60	0	0.00	0	0.00	19	100.00	4.37	87.37
MDQ5	0.00	3	13.04	20	86.96	4.13	82.60	0	0.00	1	5.26	18	94.74	4.32	86.32
MDQ6	0.00	2	8.70	21	91.30	4.17	83.40	0	0.00	1	5.26	18	94.74	4.32	86.32
MDQ7	8.70	1	4.35	20	86.96	4.04	80.80	0	0.00	1	5.26	18	94.74	4.37	87.37
MDQ8	0.00		0.00	23	100.00	4.39	87.80	0	0.00	1	5.26	18	94.74	4.53	90.53
MDQ9	0.00		0.00	23	100.00	4.48	89.60	0	0.00	0	0.00	19	100.00	4.47	89.47
MDQ10	0.00	1	4.35	22	95.65	4.52	90.40	0	0.00	0	0.00	19	100.00	4.53	90.53
Ser_Q1	4.35	4	17.39	18	78.26	4.04	80.80	0	0.00	1	5.26	18	94.74	4.32	86.32
Ser_Q2	4.35	4	17.39	18	78.26	4.04	80.80	0	0.00	1	5.26	18	94.74	4.26	85.26
Ser_Q3	13.04	4	17.39	16	69.57	3.70	74.00	1	5.26%	0	0.00	18	94.74	4.16	83.16
Ser_Q4	4.35	3	13.04	19	82.61	4.09	81.80	0	0.00	1	5.26	18	94.74	4.32	86.32

Table 25.2 (continued)

	First round ($n=23$)							Second round ($n=19$)							
	A	B		C		D		A		B		C		D	
	%	N	%	N	%	Mean	%	N	%	N	%	N	%	Mean	%
Confidence															
Ser_Q5	0.00	1	4.35	22	95.65	4.22	84.40	0	0.00	1	5.26	18	94.74	4.53	90.53
Ser_Q6	0.00	5	21.74	18	78.26	4.17	83.40	0	0.00	1	5.26	18	94.74	4.42	88.42
Ser_Q7	4.35	3	13.04	19	82.61	4.09	81.80	0	0.00	1	5.26	18	94.74	4.37	87.37
Safe_Q1	0.00	2	8.70	21	91.30	4.43	88.60	0	0.00	1	5.26	18	94.74	4.53	90.53
Safe_Q2	4.35	2	8.70	20	86.96	4.35	87.00	0	0.00	1	5.26	18	94.74	4.37	87.37
Safe_Q3	0.00	1	4.35	22	95.65	4.61	92.20	0	0.00	0	0.00	19	100.00	4.53	90.53
Safe_Q4	0.00	1	4.35	22	95.65	4.43	88.60	0	0.00	1	5.26	18	94.74	4.47	89.47
Safe_Q5	0.00	1	4.35	22	95.65	4.43	88.60	0	0.00	1	5.26	18	94.74	4.58	91.58
Safe_Q6	0.00	1	4.35	22	95.65	4.48	89.60	0	0.00	1	5.26	18	94.74	4.58	91.58
Safe_Q7	4.35	2	8.70	20	86.96	4.26	85.20	0	0.00	1	5.26	18	94.74	4.42	88.42
Safe_Q8	4.35	1	4.35	21	91.30	4.22	84.40	0	0.00	1	5.26	18	94.74	4.53	90.53
Safe_Q9	4.35	3	13.04	19	82.61	4.13	82.60	0	0.00	1	5.26	18	94.74	4.26	85.26
Safe_Q10	0.00		0.00	23	100.00	4.43	88.60	0	0.00	1	5.26	18	94.74	4.53	90.53
Safe_Q11	0.00	1	4.35	22	95.65	4.26	85.20	0	0.00	0	0.00	19	100.00	4.63	92.63
UU1-1	8.70	2	8.70	19	82.61	3.87	79.20	0	0.00	1	5.26	18	94.74	4.37	87.37
UU1-2	4.35	2	8.70	20	86.96	4.09	81.80	0	0.00	1	5.26	18	94.74	4.21	84.21
UU1-3	4.35	3	13.04	19	82.61	4.04	80.80	0	0.00	1	5.26	18	94.74	4.21	84.21
UU1-4	4.35	1	4.35	21	91.30	4.22	84.40	0	0.00	1	5.26	18	94.74	4.26	85.26
UU2	0.00	3	13.04	20	86.96	4.13	82.60	0	0.00	3	15.79	16	84.21	4.05	81.05
UU3	4.35	1	4.35	21	91.30	4.13	82.60	0	0.00	2	10.53	17	89.47	4.26	85.26
UU4	4.35	1	4.35	21	91.30	4.22	84.40	3	15.79	2	10.53	14	73.68	3.89	77.89
UU5	8.70	2	8.70	19	82.61	3.87	77.40	2	10.53	3	15.79	14	73.68	3.84	76.84
US1	4.35	1	4.35	21	91.30	4.17	83.40	2	10.53	1	5.26	16	84.21	4.00	80.00
US2	13.04	2	8.70	18	78.26	3.83	76.60	0	0.00	6	31.58	13	68.42	4.00	80.00
US3	0.00	1	4.35	22	95.65	4.39	87.80	1	5.26	2	10.53	16	84.21	4.05	81.05
US4-1	4.35	5	21.74	17	73.91	3.83	76.60	11	57.89	1	5.26	7	36.84	2.68	53.68
US4-2	4.35	3	13.04	19	82.61	4.09	81.80	0	0.00	0	0.00	19	100.00	4.53	90.53
US4-3	0.00	2	8.70	21	91.30	4.30	86.00	1	5.26	2	10.53	16	84.21	4.11	82.11

Table 25.2 (continued)

	First round ($n=23$)							Second round ($n=19$)							
	A	B		C		D		A		B		C		D	
	%	N	%	N	%	Mean	%	N	%	N	%	N	%	Mean	%
Confidence															
US4-4	4.35	3	13.04	19	82.61	4.09	81.80	0	0.00	1	5.26	18	94.74	4.32	86.32
US5-1	0.00	2	8.70	21	91.30	4.17	83.40	0	0.00	1	5.26	18	94.74	4.26	85.26
US5-2	0.00	2	8.70	21	91.30	4.17	83.40	0	0.00	1	5.26	18	94.74	4.47	89.47
US5-3	4.35	2	8.70	20	86.96	4.04	80.80	0	0.00	0	0.00	19	100.00	4.53	90.53
ONB1	4.35	2	8.70	20	86.96	4.04	80.80	1	5.26	0	0.00	18	94.74	4.37	87.37
ONB2	0.00		0.00	23	100	4.26	85.20	0	0.00	0	0.00	19	100.00	4.47	89.47
ONB3	0.00	3	13.04	20	86.96	4.13	82.60	0	0.00	0	0.00	19	100.00	4.53	90.53
ONB4	4.35	3	13.04	19	82.61	3.96	79.20	0	0.00	1	5.26	18	94.74	4.32	86.32
ONB5	13.04	1	4.35	19	82.61	3.78	75.60	0	0.00	1	5.26	18	94.74	4.47	89.47
ONB6	4.35	3	13.04	19	82.61	4.13	82.60	0	0.00	1	5.26	18	94.74	4.47	89.47
ONB7	4.35	3	13.04	19	82.61	4.09	81.80	0	0.00	1	5.26	18	94.74	4.42	88.42

A: items rated 1 or 2; *B*: items rated 3; *C*: items rated 4 or 5; *D*: mean of items rated by all experts

(a) Implementing EHR helps your hospital to improve the competition of clinical service within its location.
(b) Implementing EHR helps your hospital to enhance the capacity of patient care within its location.

2. The original content of HE4 was "Implementing EHR helps your hospital to establish a patient-centered medical environment based on the issue of patient safety and increase the chance to cooperate with other Taiwanese hospitals"; such a question needs to be modified as:

   (a) Implementing EHR helps your hospital to establish a patient-centered medical environment based on the issue of patient safety.
   (b) Implementing EHR helps your hospital to cooperate with other hospitals.

3. The original content of UU2 was "The locations and the numbers of computers where they stand are adequate enough and convenient for users to operate this EHR"; such a question needs to be modified as:

   (a) You agreed that the numbers of PC are enough for end-users to key-in patients' record into this EHR.
   (b) You satisfied with the location of PC for key-in patients' record into this EHR.

4. The original content of UU3 was "The interface of this EHR needs users to type/key-in numerous patient data and it is convenient to use it"; such a question needs to be modified as:

   (a) You satisfied with the interface of this EHR.
   (b) You satisfied with the operation method of this EHR.

5. For US3, it was "The presentation style of patient information and the interface in this EHR help you to make an exact diagnosis"; it needs to be modified as:

   (a) You agreed that the interface of this EHR is user-friendly.
   (b) You agreed that the presentation of patients' information in this EHR could help you to operate it.

Accordingly, this study recalculated the values of S-CVI/Ave in the element of HE, OB, UU, and US after those seven questions are removed from the evaluation element in round 2.

According to the results of S-CVI in Table 25.3, some questions of the original elements of HE, OB, UU, and US needed to be removed from the proposed instrument. Therefore, after those inappropriate questions were removed from the instrument, the values of S-CVI/Ave are greater than 90 % (cut-off point); in other words, the elements of HE, OB, UU, and US achieve high content validity and such instrument could be used to evaluate end-users' opinion of using EHRs.

Table 25.3 Results of S-CVI within Delphi method

		HE			*OB*			*Sys_Q*		
		A	B	C	A	B	C	A	B	C
First round	*N* %	79	76	71	96	190	168	189	185	170
($n=23$)		85.87	82.61	77.17	85.22	82.61	73.04	91.3	89.37	82.13
Second round	*N* %	69	68	67	161	159	160	163	164	162
($n=19$)		90.79	89.47	88.16	84.74	83.68	84.21	95.32	95.91	94.74
Revised		96.49	94.74	94.74	95.40	94.01	92.11			
		MDQ			*Ser_Q*			*Safe_Q*		
		A	B	C	A	B	C	A	B	C
First round	*N* %	219	220	213	146	136	130	237	238	234
($n=23$)		95.22	95.65	92.61	90.68	84.47	80.75	93.68	94.07	92.49
Second round	*N* %	186	185	183	126	129	126	200	202	200
($n=19$)		97.89	97.37	96.32	96.74	96.99	96.74	95.69	96.65	95.69
Revised										
		UU			*US*			*ONB*		
		A	B	C	A	B	C	A	B	C
First round	*N* %	155	165	160	200	202	199	145	144	139
($n=23$)		84.24	89.67	86.96	86.96	87.83	86.52	90.06	89.44	86.34
Second round	*N* %	136	138	133	170	166	160	127	123	128
($n=19$)		89.47	90.79	87.5	89.47	87.37	84.21	95.49	92.48	96.24
Revised		95.61	95.61	92.11	96.06	95.40	92.11			

A: important; *B*: feasibility; *C*: confidence.

25.5 Discussion and Conclusion

As there are four features of the Delphi method : *anonymity* (nameless), *iteration* (at least twice), *controlled feedback* (removed inappropriate questions), and *aggregation of group answers* (converting individual viewpoint into group consensus). The modified Delphi method enables this study to provide a prepared questionnaire for Delphi group to reflect on the specific aim of the instrument, and to anonymously write their comments on each question. By the way of two-interactive Delphi method, accordingly, the overall process of both I-CVI and S-CVI helped to ensure the content validity of each question and element. Each question and element in this instrument contains high content validity. Consequently, the number of questions was reduced from 76 to 74, with a free text added to measure end-users' opinion of using EHRs in Taiwan.

Table 25.3 indicates that questions in the aspect of Technological and Net Benefits were not changed; however, there is a minor modification in the Organizational and Human aspects. Significantly, all experts in the Delphi group were executive managers in hospitals. The results of using the two-interactive Delphi method indicate that questions in System Quality, Medical Data Quality, Service Quality, Safety quality, and Organizational Net Benefits are appropriate for supporting decision-making;

Table 25.4 The development of instrument in each version (unit: questions)

Evaluation elements	Original	Delphi method		
		Revised	Removed	Modified
Organizational aspect				
Healthcare environment*	4	5	HE2	HE3, HE4
Organization behaviors*	10	8	OB2, OB4	
Technological aspect				
System quality	9	9	–	–
Medical data quality	10	10	–	–
Service quality	7	7	–	–
Safety quality	11	11	–	–
Human aspect				
User usage*	8	8	UU4, UU5	UU2, UU3
User satisfaction*	10	9	US2, US4-1	US3
Net benefits aspect				
Organizational net benefits	7	7	–	–
Total	76	74		

*Questions have be removed or revised.
–There is no change.

questions that needed to be removed were not relevant to the underlying construct. These responses from a panel of experts enabled the conversion of individual subjective viewpoints into a group objective consensus. This result indicates that the selections of experts as the participants of the Delphi group are important, because they are related to the specific research theme of this study.

Previous research has recommended the Delphi as being an appropriate method in identifying the content validity of an instrument (Takemura et al. 2006; Rushton and Lindsay 2008). Accordingly, a modified Delphi method and the method of both investigators and data were used in this study to develop a suitable instrument for measuring Taiwanese EHRs' success. In order to clarify the main function of *modified Delphi method* and to explain the method of computing I-CVI/S-CVI for confirming the content validity of the proposed instrument, this study also explained its three main elements: (1) function and intention of the Delphi group; (2) selecting appropriate participants as the Delphi group; and (3) methods of identifying content validity index (CVI): the cut-off point of I-CVI being 78 % (90 % for S-CVI).

Results of using the two-interactive Delphi method were discussed based on both quantitative and qualitative research approaches. A total of 23 of 30 experts (76.67 %) responded to round 1, and 19 of 23 (82.60 %) responded to round 2, the degree of consensus being stable among experts in round 2. The overall results of the two-iterative Delphi method indicate that seven questions (HE2, OB2, OB4, UU4, UU5, US2, and US4-1) need to be removed from the proposed instrument, and that five questions (HE3, HE4, UU2, UU3, and US3) need to be modified to be more relevant to the proposed evaluation element. Finally, the number of questions was reduced from 76 to 74, with a free text added to measure end-users' opinion of using EHR system in Taiwan (Table 25.4).

Table 25.5 Questionnaire for the modified Delphi method

Part A : Healthcare Environment

1. The Department of Health (DOH) is willing to assist hospitals to establish EHRs in Taiwan.
2. Do you know that all the hospitals around your hospital are implementing EHRs in their patient service?
3. Implementing EHRs helps your hospital to improve the capacity of clinical service within its location.
4. Implementing EHRs not only helps your hospital to establish a patient-centred medical environment based on the issue of patient safety, but also increase the chance to cooperate with other hospitals

Part B : Organizational Behaviour

1. Healthcare professionals are willing to adopt and accept new medical technology products in your hospital for patient care and clinical service.
2. Implementing EHRs is a kind of operational strategy to perform the issue of patient safety and obey the regulation of hospital accreditation in your hospital.
3. Implementing EHRs is a kind of executive policy to perform the issue of patient safety.
4. You are agreed with the leadership and administration of top managers to adopt EHRs within your hospital.
5. Implementing EHRs are decided and supported by top managers in your hospitals.
6. Healthcare professionals are willing to support the implementation of EHRs within your hospital.
7. Please select an appropriate item to present your opinion about the reason that your hospital is willing to adopt EHRs.
   (1) Obeying related regulations, laws, and national goal to perform EHRs which were executed by the DOH of central government.
   (2) Satisfying the requirements of the program of Hospital Accreditation in Taiwan.
   (3) Performing the issue of patient safety of health care in clinical service.
8. Implementing EHRs needs to satisfy the specific requirements of different departments by providing unique features and functions in your hospital.

Part C: System Quality

1. The EHRs have the capability to permit an end-user importing/exporting data from other applications.
2. The application of the EHRs is correctness and responds to your commands consistently.
3. The application of the EHRs is ease to get access to operate such system and helps you to provide better patient service.
4. Unauthorized users can not use the EHRs based on the issue of operating regulations, (without personal unique passwords).
5. The hardware of the EHRs is easy for new members to use such system without reading user guideline.
6. The application of the EHRs will be able to understand the operation of such system easily by its interfaces.
7. The application of the EHRs is confident of the capability to perform your transactions of patient care.
8. You are satisfied with the response time due to the EHRs response to your commands quickly.
9. The EHRs provide unique features and functions to meet the specific requirements of your department, such as hand-drafting to describe the location of disease.

Part D : Medical Data Quality

1. The EHRs provide error free information.
2. The EHRs present accessibility information of patient care on demand.
3. The EHRs provide useful information includes clinical examine data that you need in clinical diagnosing and decision making.
4. The EHRs offer reliable information of patient care on demand.
5. The EHRs provide constructive and up-to-date information of patient care for different clinical departments.
6. The EHRs supply exactitude information of patient care to support and enhance your clinical decision making.
7. The EHRs provide suitable information that relevant to patient status when you have to making an exact diagnosis.
8. The EHRs offer appropriate information timely to enhance your diagnosis and decision making.
9. The EHRs help you to record and collect patient data on demand for an exact diagnosis.
10. The EHRs assist you to record and organize your specific notes in patient care, such as HIV patients, phthisis patients.

Part E : Service Quality

1. The Department of Information Management (DIM) staffs provide and possess sufficient knowledge to answer your questions about operating the EHRs
2. The DIM staffs always complete user's request for new applications and /or functions, design, expansion, and executions of the EHRs during a reasonable and acceptable time.
3. The DIM staffs always try their best (good manners, flexible methods, and timely of required time) to respond to your request for changing the functions and/or services of the EHRs.
4. The DIM staffs provide efficient knowledge to help users realize and deal with operational problems of the EHRs.
5. The DIM staffs are courteous and willingness to solve your problem of operating the EHRs and make you to feel comfortable with their attitude..
6. The DIM staffs provide essential education and training programs to help you to operate the EHRs.
7. The DIM staffs always provide sufficient support and technology skills to maintain the hardware and software of the EHRs.

Part F : Safety Quality

1. The EHRs display a patient's name in each screen to help you recognize patients' identification.
2. Using unique password to limit and control the access to the EHRs can protect patients' privacy.
3. Using each unique password limits your authority to protect patients' secrecy of disease history.
4. The functions of security in the EHRs are sufficient to defend attack from virus and unauthorized users.
5. Using unique password to manage the access to the EHRs is one of the best ways to perform the issue of consent of patient medical records.
6. The EHRs provide easily understandable procedures for disaster malfunction recovery.
7. The EHRs save your working file automatically while you are recording patient data.
8. The EHRs perform a usual and routine backup.
9. The EHRs help you to double check the dose of drug and for enhancing patient safety.
10. The function of drag interaction alerts helps you to reduce medical errors.
11. This EHR systematically check and identify typing error while you are recording patient data.

Part G : User Use

1. Comparing The EHRs with the traditional paper (hand-writing) medical records that you used, please present your opinion of this EHR depending on your daily work
   (1) The EHRs help you to complete medical record easier than the traditional ones.
   (2) The EHRs help you to search for a patient's previous data easier than the traditional ones.
   (3) The EHRs help you to confirm a patient's medical history and discover potential disease than the traditional ones.
   (4) The EHRs provide you a comprehensive medical record than the traditional ones.

2-1 The locations and numbers of computers where they stand are appropriate for users to operate The EHRs.

2-2 The interfaces of this EHR are convenient for you to operate this EHRs in key-in patient record.

3-1 What is the average frequency for you to use computer in your daily work?
   (1) None. (2)One time per month. (3)Several times per month.
   (4) Several times per week. (5)Several times per day.

3-2 How much time do you use the EHRs in your daily work?
   (1) None. (2)Less than half an hour. (3)More than half an hour and less than one hour. (4) More than one hour and less than three hours.
   (5) More than three hours.

Part H : User Satisfaction

1. The EHRs are very easy to use and you are happy to use it.
2. The EHRs need advance skills of computer operation to use it.
3. The presentation style of patient information and the interface in the EHRs help you to make an exact diagnosis.
4. Please select an appropriate item to present your personal expectation of the potential benefits by using the EHRs that support your daily work within your hospitals.
   (1) The EHRs provide you new cure methods for patient care.
   (2) The EHRs assist within your hospitals to advance the procedures of clinical service. The EHRs assist within your hospitals to improve the procedures of medical records management.
   (3) The EHRs assist within your hospitals to enhance the procedures of healthcare administration.
5. Please select an appropriate item to present your overall satisfaction at the EHRs.
   (1) The EHRs indeed help you to write correct patient records.
   (2) The EHRs indeed help you to save your time in writing patient records.
   (3) The EHRs indeed help you to save your time in waiting for patient records delivery when comparing with the traditional paper records.

Part I : Organization Net Benefits

1. The EHRs help your hospital to enhance the quality of patient service based on the issue of patient safety.
2. The EHRs help your hospital to enhance the quality of medical records writing based on the issue of patient safety.
3. The EHRs help health professionals doing things right in patient care based on the issue of patient safety.
4. The EHRs help health professionals doing right things in clinical service based on the issue of patient safety.
5. The EHRs help health professionals to reduce medical error in writing medical records.
6. The EHRs help health professionals to communicate transmits patient information of consultations between different departments..
7. The EHRs help your hospital to reduce operating cost when compares with traditional paper medical records.

A "good" research instrument needs to demonstrate *construct validity* and *reliability* with larger samples for ensuring both "reliability" and "validity" (Ammenwerth et al. 2003c). However, the first phase for providing a good instrument is to confirm its content validity. The result of this study identifies that the modified Delphi method is indeed a useful technique to combine both quantitative (can be processed statistically) and qualitative (anonymous written explanations in conjunction with controlled feedback) research approaches in designing a suitable instrument. Especially, a qualitative approach provided a reference to modify the wording and/or syntax of questions for implementing such instrument in real medical environment. In short, based on results of this study, an appropriate instrument was provided to measure end-users' opinions of using EHR systems in Taiwan. Table 25.5

References

Ammenwerth, E., Graber, S., Herrmann, G., Burkle, T., & Konig, J. (2003a). Evaluation of health information systems—problems and challenges. *International Journal of Medical Informatics, 71*(2–3), 125.

Ammenwerth, E., Iller, C., & Mansmann, U. (2003b). Can evaluation studies benefit from triangulation? A case study. *International Journal of Medical Informatics, 70*(2–3), 237–248.

Ammenwerth, E., Kaiser, F., Wilhelmy, I., & Hofer, S. (2003c). *Evaluation of user acceptance of information systems in health care—the value of questionnaires. In: Medical Informatics Europe* (MIE 2003) (pp. 643–648). Malo: IOS Press.

Ammenwerth, E., Brender, J., Nykanen, P., Prokosch, H. U., Rigby, M., & Talmon, J. (2004). Visions and strategies to improve evaluation of health information systems: Reflections and lessons based on the his-eval workshop in Innsbruck. *International Journal of Medical Informatics, 73*(6), 479–471.

Bostrom, R. P., & Heinen, J. S. (1977). MIS problems and failures: A socio-technical perspective. Part I. *The causes MIS Quarterly, 1*(3), 17–32.

D'Onofrio, M., & Gendron, M. (2001). Data quality in the healthcare industry. *Data Quality, 7*(1), 14.

DeLone, W. H., & McLean, E. R. (1992). Information systems success: The quest for the dependent variable. *Information System Research, 3*(1), 60–95.

Donabedian, A. (2003). *An introduction to quality assurance in health care/avedis donabedian.* New York: Oxford University Press.

Hesse, B. W., & Shneiderman, B. (2007). Ehealth research from the user's perspective. *American Journal of Preventive Medicine, 32*(5, Suppl. 1), S97–S103.

Hubley, A., & Palepu, A. (2007). Injection drug user quality of life scale (iduqol): Findings from a content validation study. *Health and Quality of Life Outcomes, 5*(1), 46.

Lynn, M. R. (1986). Determination and quantification of content validity. *Nursing Research, 35*(6), 382–385.

Polit, D. F., & Beck, C. T. (2006). The content validity index: Are you sure you know what's being reported? Critique and recommendations. *Research in Nursing & Health, 29,* 489–497.

Rushton, A., & Lindsay, G. (2008). Defining the construct of masters level clinical practice in healthcare based on the UK experience. *Medical Teacher, 30*(4), 100–107.

Snyder-Halpern, R. (2001). Indicators of organizational readiness for clinical information technology/systems innovation: A Delphi study. *International Journal of Medical Informatics, 63*(3), 179–204.

Su, Y. Y., Win, K. T., & Fulcher, J. (2006). *Electronic health record system evaluation based on patient safety*. Asia Pacific Medical Information Association Conference 2006, Taipei, Taiwan, 27–29 2006. Taiwan Medical Information Association, 154.

Takemura, Y., Liu, J., Atsumi, R., & Tsuda, T. (2006). Development of a questionnaire to evaluate patient satisfaction with medical encounters. *Tohoku Journal of Experimental Medicine, 210*(4), 373–381.

Wan, T. T. H. (2002). *Evidence-based health care management: Multivariate modeling approaches*. Boston: Kluwer.

Win, K. T. (2004). *Identifying the risk assessment method applicable to the electronic health record systems*. HIC2004, Brisbane, July 2004. Health Informatics Society of Australia (HISA).

Epilogue

The need for improvement in the delivery of healthcare is paramount. Today, much of the literature pertaining to healthcare continually discusses the many severe challenges such as exponentially increasing costs, pressures to provide appropriate quality and access as well as the need to incorporate best practice and recent new findings at the point of care. Government agencies and the private sector are alarmed with rising costs and the decline in quality, access, and availability of care. In addition, we are now witnessing the increased role of chronic diseases as a major contributor to the cause of death and morbidity, replacing communicable diseases, and draining the resources of an already-strained healthcare delivery system.

Without a doubt then, there is a clear need for solutions to this current crisis in the delivery of care. Till date, the search for a solution has led to the growing focus on technology, especially telemedicine and remote care, as a useful alternative to the prevailing models of inpatient care. The utilization of information and communication technologies (ICT) seems particularly attractive given its possible support of- and enablement of a cost-effective model of care to ensue.

Against this context, we set out to write a book that focuses on a specific subset of possible technology solutions; namely pervasive technology solutions and how they might facilitate superior care. We did this in four sections by first presenting the case for pervasive technology in healthcare, then discussing the benefit of incorporating leading management principles; namely knowledge management (KM) and how and why it can support superior healthcare delivery, then we moved on to discuss in detail a specific pervasive technology solution and how it can facilitate superior healthcare delivery in the context of individuals suffering from diabetes, and then finally we widened the discussion to present various possibilities for pervasive technology as well as some of the future directions we are likely to experience in the fullness of time.

Pervasive technologies are generally still in their infancy and their application into the healthcare domain is truly embryonic at this point. The possibilities are vast and hold the allure of facilitating high-quality cost-effective healthcare delivery for all. We hope that our book has served to introduce you to this important topic that we know will dominate much of the dialogue on how to deliver superior healthcare for at least several decades. We believe that the solutions, technologies, theories, tactics,

R. K. Bali et al. (eds.), *Pervasive Health Knowledge Management*,
Healthcare Delivery in the Information Age,
DOI 10.1007/978-1-4614-4514-2, © Springer Science+Business Media New York 2013

and recommendations as well as benefits and facilitators presented throughout the preceding chapters will provide equal benefit to policy makers, government officials, healthcare providers, practitioners, consultants, scholars, students, and the general community as they try to grapple with the conundrum of how to deliver superior healthcare.

Healthcare is an area that touches us all and we should all be actively engaged in the developments regarding healthcare delivery. A first necessary, yet no sufficient, step is to be informed and have a full understanding of all the possibilities; their relative merits and implications. We trust that even in some small way our book helps you to be prepared and ready to embrace the challenges of delivering superior healthcare.

The Editors

Rajeev Bali, Indrit Troshani,
Steve Goldberg and Nilmini Wickramasinghe

Index

R. K. Bali et al. (eds.), *Pervasive Health Knowledge Management*, Healthcare Delivery in the Information Age,
DOI 10.1007/978-1-4614-4514-2, © Springer Science+Business Media New York 2013

MIX
Papier aus verantwortungsvollen Quellen
Paper from responsible sources
FSC® C105338

If you have any concerns about our products,
you can contact us on
ProductSafety@springernature.com

In case Publisher is established outside the EU,
the EU authorized representative is:
Springer Nature Customer Service Center GmbH
Europaplatz 3, 69115 Heidelberg, Germany

Printed by Libri Plureos GmbH
in Hamburg, Germany